Fast Food NATION

what the all-american meal is doing to the world

ERIC SCHLOSSER

PENGUIN BOOKS

PENGUIN BOOKS

Published by the Penguin Group
Penguin Books Ltd, 80 Strand, London WC2R 0RL, England
Penguin Group (USA) Inc., 375 Hudson Street, New York, New York 10014, USA
Penguin Group (Canada), 90 Eglinton Avenue East, Suite 700, Toronto, Ontario, Canada M4P 2Y3
(a division of Pearson Penguin Canada Inc.)
Penguin Ireland, 25 St Stephen's Green, Dublin 2, Ireland
(a division of Penguin Books Ltd)
Penguin Group (Australia), 250 Camberwell Road, Camberwell, Victoria 3124, Australia
(a division of Pearson Australia Group Pty Ltd)
Penguin Books India Pvt Ltd, 11 Community Centre, Panchsheel Park, New Delhi – 110 017, India
Penguin Group (NZ), 67 Apollo Drive, Rosedale, North Shore 0632, New Zealand
(a division of Pearson New Zealand Ltd)
Penguin Books (South Africa) (Pty) Ltd, 24 Sturdee Avenue, Rosebank, Johannesburg 2196, South Africa

Penguin Books Ltd, Registered Offices: 80 Strand, London WC2R 0RL, England

www.penguin.com

First published in the USA by Houghton Mifflin Company 2001
First published in Great Britain by Allen Lane 2001
Published with a new afterword in Penguin Books 2002
Reissued in this edition 2007
1

ISBN: 978–0–141–03531–4

for Red

contents

Introduction   *1*

I. The American Way

1. The Founding Fathers   *13*
2. Your Trusted Friends   *31*
3. Behind the Counter   *59*
4. Success   *91*

II. Meat and Potatoes

5. Why the Fries Taste Good   *111*
6. On the Range   *133*
7. Cogs in the Great Machine   *149*
8. The Most Dangerous Job   *169*
9. What's in the Meat   *193*
10. Global Realization   *225*

Epilogue: Have It Your Way   *255*
Afterword: The Meaning of
    Mad Cow   *271*

Photo Credits   *293*
Notes   *294*
Bibliography   *359*
Acknowledgments   *365*
Index   *369*

A savage servility
slides by on grease.

— ROBERT LOWELL

Fast Food
NATION

introduction

CHEYENNE MOUNTAIN SITS on the eastern slope of Colorado's Front Range, rising steeply from the prairie and overlooking the city of Colorado Springs. From a distance, the mountain appears beautiful and serene, dotted with rocky outcroppings, scrub oak, and ponderosa pine. It looks like the backdrop of an old Hollywood western, just another gorgeous Rocky Mountain vista. And yet Cheyenne Mountain is hardly pristine. One of the nation's most important military installations lies deep within it, housing units of the North American Aerospace Command, the Air Force Space Command, and the United States Space Command. During the mid-1950s, high-level officials at the Pentagon worried that America's air defenses had become vulnerable to sabotage and attack. Cheyenne Mountain was chosen as the site for a top-secret, underground combat operations center. The mountain was hollowed out, and fifteen buildings, most of them three stories high, were erected amid a maze of tunnels and passageways extending for miles. The four-and-a-half-acre underground complex was designed to survive a direct hit by an atomic bomb. Now officially called the Cheyenne Mountain Air Force Station, the facility is entered through steel blast doors that are three feet thick and weigh twenty-five tons each; they automatically swing shut in less than twenty seconds. The base is closed to the public, and a heavily armed quick response team guards against intruders. Pressurized air within the complex prevents contamination by radioactive fallout and biological weapons. The buildings are mounted on gigantic steel springs to ride out an earthquake or the blast wave of a thermonuclear strike. The hallways and staircases are painted slate gray, the ceilings are low, and there are combination locks on many of the doors. A narrow escape tunnel, entered through a metal hatch, twists and turns its way out of the mountain through solid rock. The place feels like the set of an early James Bond movie, with men in jumpsuits driving little electric vans from one brightly lit cavern to another.

Fifteen hundred people work inside the mountain, maintaining the facility and collecting information from a worldwide network of radars, spy satellites, ground-based sensors, airplanes, and blimps. The Cheyenne Mountain Operations Center tracks every manmade object that enters North American airspace or that orbits the earth. It is the heart of the nation's early warning system. It can detect the firing of a long-range missile, anywhere in the world, before that missile has left the launch pad.

This futuristic military base inside a mountain has the capability to be self-sustaining for at least one month. Its generators can produce enough electricity to power a city the size of Tampa, Florida. Its underground reservoirs hold millions of gallons of water; workers sometimes traverse them in rowboats. The complex has its own underground fitness center, a medical clinic, a dentist's office, a barbershop, a chapel, and a cafeteria. When the men and women stationed at Cheyenne Mountain get tired of the food in the cafeteria, they often send somebody over to the Burger King at Fort Carson, a nearby army base. Or they call Domino's.

Almost every night, a Domino's deliveryman winds his way up the lonely Cheyenne Mountain Road, past the ominous DEADLY FORCE AUTHORIZED signs, past the security checkpoint at the entrance of the base, driving toward the heavily guarded North Portal, tucked behind chain link and barbed wire. Near the spot where the road heads straight into the mountainside, the delivery man drops off his pizzas and collects his tip. And should Armageddon come, should a foreign enemy someday shower the United States with nuclear warheads, laying waste to the whole continent, entombed within Cheyenne Mountain, along with the high-tech marvels, the pale blue jumpsuits, comic books, and Bibles, future archeologists may find other clues to the nature of our civilization — Big King wrappers, hardened crusts of Cheesy Bread, Barbeque Wing bones, and the red, white, and blue of a Domino's pizza box.

what we eat

OVER THE LAST THREE DECADES, fast food has infiltrated every nook and cranny of American society. An industry that began with a handful of modest hot dog and hamburger stands in southern California has spread to every corner of the nation, selling a broad range of foods wherever paying customers may be found. Fast food is now served at restaurants and drive-throughs, at stadiums, airports, zoos, high schools, elementary schools, and universities, on cruise ships, trains, and airplanes, at K-Marts, Wal-Marts, gas stations, and even at hospital cafeterias. In 1970, Americans spent about $6 billion on fast food; in 2001, they spent more than $110 billion. Americans now spend more money on fast food than on higher education, personal computers, computer software, or new cars. They spend more on fast food than on movies, books, magazines, newspapers, videos, and recorded music — combined.

Pull open the glass door, feel the rush of cool air, walk in, get on line, study the backlit color photographs above the counter, place your order, hand over a few dollars, watch teenagers in uniforms pushing various buttons, and moments later take hold of a plastic tray full of food wrapped in colored paper and cardboard. The whole experience of buying fast food has become so routine, so thoroughly unexceptional and mundane, that it is now taken for granted, like brushing your teeth or stopping for a red light. It has become a social custom as American as a small, rectangular, hand-held, frozen, and reheated apple pie.

This is a book about fast food, the values it embodies, and the world it has made. Fast food has proven to be a revolutionary force in American life; I am interested in it both as a commodity and as a metaphor. What people eat (or don't eat) has always been determined by a complex interplay of social, economic, and technological forces. The early Roman Republic was fed by its citizen-farmers; the Roman Empire, by its slaves. A nation's diet can be more revealing than its art or literature. On any given day in the United States about one-quarter of the adult population visits a fast food restaurant. During a relatively brief period of time, the fast food industry has helped to transform not only the American diet, but also our landscape, economy, workforce, and popular culture. Fast food and its consequences have become inescapable, regardless of whether you eat it twice a day, try to avoid it, or have never taken a single bite.

The extraordinary growth of the fast food industry has been driven by fundamental changes in American society. Adjusted for inflation, the hourly wage of the average U.S. worker peaked in 1973 and then steadily declined for the next twenty-five years. During that period, women entered the workforce in record numbers, often motivated less by a feminist perspective than by a need to pay the bills. In 1975, about one-third of American mothers with young children worked outside the home; today almost two-thirds of such mothers are employed. As the sociologists Cameron Lynne Macdonald and Carmen Sirianni have noted, the entry of so many women into the workforce has greatly increased demand for the types of services that housewives traditionally perform: cooking, cleaning, and child care. A generation ago, three-quarters of the money used to buy food in the United States was spent to prepare meals at home. Today about half of the money used to buy food is spent at restaurants — mainly at fast food restaurants.

The McDonald's Corporation has become a powerful symbol of America's service economy, which is now responsible for 90 percent of the country's new jobs. In 1968, McDonald's operated about one thousand restaurants. Today it has about thirty thousand restaurants worldwide and opens almost two thousand new ones each year. An estimated one out of every eight workers in the United States has at some point been employed by McDonald's. The company annually hires about one million people, more than any other American organization, public or private. McDonald's is the nation's largest purchaser of beef, pork, and potatoes — and the second largest purchaser of chicken. The McDonald's Corporation is the largest owner of retail property in the world. Indeed, the company earns the majority of its profits not from selling food but from collecting rent. McDonald's spends more money on advertising and marketing than any other brand. As a result it has replaced Coca-Cola as the world's most famous brand. McDonald's operates more playgrounds than any other private entity in the United States. It is one of the nation's largest distributors of toys. A survey of American schoolchildren found that 96 percent could identify Ronald McDonald. The only fictional character with a higher degree of recognition was Santa Claus. The impact of McDonald's on the way we live today is hard to overstate. The Golden Arches are now more widely recognized than the Christian cross.

In the early 1970s, the farm activist Jim Hightower warned of "the McDonaldization of America." He viewed the emerging fast food industry as a threat to independent businesses, as a step toward a food economy dominated by giant corporations, and as a homogenizing influence on American life. In *Eat Your Heart Out* (1975), he argued that "bigger is *not* better." Much of what Hightower feared has come to pass. The centralized purchasing decisions of the large restaurant chains and their demand for standardized products have given a handful of corporations an unprecedented degree of power over the nation's food supply. Moreover, the tremendous success of the fast food industry has encouraged other industries to adopt similar business methods. The basic thinking behind fast food has become the operating system of today's retail economy, wiping out small businesses, obliterating regional differences, and spreading identical stores throughout the country like a self-replicating code.

America's main streets and malls now boast the same Pizza Huts and Taco Bells, Gaps and Banana Republics, Starbucks and Jiffy-Lubes, Foot Lockers, Snip N' Clips, Sunglass Huts, and Hobbytown USAs. Almost every facet of American life has now been franchised or chained. From the maternity ward at a Columbia/HCA hospital to an embalming room owned by Service Corporation International — "the world's largest provider of death care services," based in Houston, Texas, which since 1968 has grown to include 3,823 funeral homes, 523 cemeteries, and 198 crematoriums, and which today handles the final remains of one out of every nine Americans — a person can now go from the cradle to the grave without spending a nickel at an independently owned business.

The key to a successful franchise, according to many texts on the subject, can be expressed in one word: "uniformity." Franchises and chain stores strive to offer exactly the same product or service at numerous locations. Customers are drawn to familiar brands by an instinct to avoid the unknown. A brand offers a feeling of reassurance when its products are always and everywhere the same. "We have found out . . . that we cannot trust some people who are nonconformists," declared Ray Kroc, one of the founders of McDonald's, angered by some of his franchisees. "We will make conformists out of them in a hurry . . . The organization cannot trust the individual; the individual must trust the organization."

One of the ironies of America's fast food industry is that a business so dedicated to conformity was founded by iconoclasts and self-made men, by entrepreneurs willing to defy conventional opinion. Few of the people who built fast food empires ever attended college, let alone business school. They worked hard, took risks, and followed their own paths. In many respects, the fast food industry embodies the best and the worst of American capitalism at the start of the twenty-first century — its constant stream of new products and innovations, its widening gulf between rich and poor. The industrialization of the restaurant kitchen has enabled the fast food chains to rely upon a low-paid and unskilled workforce. While a handful of workers manage to rise up the corporate ladder, the vast majority lack full-time employment, receive no benefits, learn few skills, exercise little control over their workplace, quit after a few months, and float from job to job. The restaurant industry is now America's largest private employer, and it pays some of the lowest wages. During the economic boom of the 1990s, when many American workers enjoyed their first pay raises in a generation, the real value of wages in the restaurant industry continued to fall. The roughly 3.5 million fast food workers are by far the largest group of minimum wage earners in the United States. The only Americans who consistently earn a lower hourly wage are migrant farm workers.

A hamburger and french fries became the quintessential American meal in the 1950s, thanks to the promotional efforts of the fast food chains. The typical American now consumes approximately three hamburgers and four orders of french fries every week. But the steady barrage of fast food ads, full of thick juicy burgers and long golden fries, rarely mentions where these foods come from nowadays or what ingredients they contain. The birth of the fast food industry coincided with Eisenhower-era glorifications of technology, with optimistic slogans like "Better Living through Chemistry" and "Our Friend the Atom." The sort of technological wizardry that Walt Disney promoted on television and at Disneyland eventually reached its fulfillment in the kitchens of fast food restaurants. Indeed, the corporate culture of McDonald's seems inextricably linked to that of the Disney empire, sharing a reverence for sleek machinery, electronics, and automation. The leading fast food chains still embrace a boundless faith in science — and as a result have changed not just what Americans eat, but also how their food is made.

The current methods for preparing fast food are less likely to be found in cookbooks than in trade journals such as *Food Technologist* and *Food Engineering*. Aside from the salad greens and tomatoes, most fast food is delivered to the restaurant already frozen, canned, dehy-drated, or freeze-dried. A fast food kitchen is merely the final stage in a vast and highly complex system of mass production. Foods that may look familiar have in fact been completely reformulated. What we eat has changed more in the last forty years than in the previous forty thousand. Like Cheyenne Mountain, today's fast food conceals re-markable technological advances behind an ordinary-looking façade. Much of the taste and aroma of American fast food, for example, is now manufactured at a series of large chemical plants off the New Jer-sey Turnpike.

In the fast food restaurants of Colorado Springs, behind the coun-ters, amid the plastic seats, in the changing landscape outside the win-dow, you can see all the virtues and destructiveness of our fast food nation. I chose Colorado Springs as a focal point for this book because the changes that have recently swept through the city are emblematic of those that fast food — and the fast food mentality — have encour-aged throughout the United States. Countless other suburban com-munities, in every part of the country, could have been used to illus-trate the same points. The extraordinary growth of Colorado Springs neatly parallels that of the fast food industry: during the last few decades, the city's population has more than doubled. Subdivisions, shopping malls, and chain restaurants are appearing in the foothills of Cheyenne Mountain and the plains rolling to the east. The Rocky Mountain region as a whole has the fastest-growing economy in the United States, mixing high-tech and service industries in a way that may define America's workforce for years to come. And new restau-rants are opening there at a faster pace than anywhere else in the na-tion.

Fast food is now so commonplace that it has acquired an air of in-evitability, as though it were somehow unavoidable, a fact of modern life. And yet the dominance of the fast food giants was no more preor-dained than the march of colonial split-levels, golf courses, and man-made lakes across the deserts of the American West. The political phi-losophy that now prevails in so much of the West — with its demand for lower taxes, smaller government, an unbridled free market — stands in total contradiction to the region's true economic underpin-nings. No other region of the United States has been so dependent on government subsidies for so long, from the nineteenth-century con-struction of its railroads to the twentieth-century financing of its mili-tary bases and dams. One historian has described the federal government's 1950s highway-building binge as a case study in "interstate socialism" — a phrase that aptly describes how the West was really won. The fast food industry took root alongside that interstate highway system, as a new form of restaurant sprang up beside the new off-ramps. Moreover, the extraordinary growth of this industry over the past quarter-century did not occur in a political vacuum. It took place during a period when the inflation-adjusted value of the minimum wage declined by about 40 percent, when sophisticated mass marketing techniques were for the first time directed at small children, and when federal agencies created to protect workers and consumers too often behaved like branch offices of the companies that were supposed to be regulated. Ever since the administration of President Richard Nixon, the fast food industry has worked closely with its allies in Congress and the White House to oppose new worker safety, food safety, and minimum wage laws. While publicly espousing support for the free market, the fast food chains have quietly pursued and greatly benefited from a wide variety of government subsidies. Far from being inevitable, America's fast food industry in its present form is the logical outcome of certain political and economic choices.

In the potato fields and processing plants of Idaho, in the ranchlands east of Colorado Springs, in the feedlots and slaughterhouses of the High Plains, you can see the effects of fast food on the nation's rural life, its environment, its workers, and its health. The fast food chains now stand atop a huge food-industrial complex that has gained control of American agriculture. During the 1980s, large multinationals — such as Cargill, ConAgra, and IBP — were allowed to dominate one commodity market after another. Farmers and cattle ranchers are losing their independence, essentially becoming hired hands for the agribusiness giants or being forced off the land. Family farms are now being replaced by gigantic corporate farms with absentee owners. Rural communities are losing their middle class and becoming socially stratified, divided between a small, wealthy elite and large numbers of the working poor. Small towns that seemingly belong in a Norman Rockwell painting are being turned into rural ghettos. The hardy, independent farmers whom Thomas Jefferson considered the bedrock of American democracy are a truly vanishing breed. The United States now has more prison inmates than full-time farmers.

The fast food chains' vast purchasing power and their demand for a uniform product have encouraged fundamental changes in how cattle are raised, slaughtered, and processed into ground beef. These changes have made meatpacking — once a highly skilled, highly paid occupation — into the most dangerous job in the United States, performed by armies of poor, transient immigrants whose injuries often go unrecorded and uncompensated. And the same meat industry practices that endanger these workers have facilitated the introduction of deadly pathogens, such as *E. coli* 0157:H7, into America's hamburger meat, a food aggressively marketed to children. Again and again, efforts to prevent the sale of tainted ground beef have been thwarted by meat industry lobbyists and their allies in Congress. The federal government has the legal authority to recall a defective toaster oven or stuffed animal — but still lacks the power to recall tons of contaminated, potentially lethal meat.

I do not mean to suggest that fast food is solely responsible for every social problem now haunting the United States. In some cases (such as the malling and sprawling of the West) the fast food industry has been a catalyst and a symptom of larger economic trends. In other cases (such as the rise of franchising and the spread of obesity) fast food has played a more central role. By tracing the diverse influences of fast food I hope to shed light not only on the workings of an important industry, but also on a distinctively American way of viewing the world.

Elitists have always looked down at fast food, criticizing how it tastes and regarding it as another tacky manifestation of American popular culture. The aesthetics of fast food are of much less concern to me than its impact upon the lives of ordinary Americans, both as workers and consumers. Most of all, I am concerned about its impact on the nation's children. Fast food is heavily marketed to children and prepared by people who are barely older than children. This is an industry that both feeds and feeds off the young. During the two years spent researching this book, I ate an enormous amount of fast food. Most of it tasted pretty good. That is one of the main reasons people buy fast food; it has been carefully designed to taste good. It's also inexpensive and convenient. But the value meals, two-for-one deals, and free refills of soda give a distorted sense of how much fast food actually costs. The real price never appears on the menu.

The sociologist George Ritzer has attacked the fast food industry for celebrating a narrow measure of efficiency over every other human value, calling the triumph of McDonald's "the irrationality of rationality." Others consider the fast food industry proof of the nation's great economic vitality, a beloved American institution that appeals overseas to millions who admire our way of life. Indeed, the values, the culture, and the industrial arrangements of our fast food nation are now being exported to the rest of the world. Fast food has joined Hollywood movies, blue jeans, and pop music as one of America's most prominent cultural exports. Unlike other commodities, however, fast food isn't viewed, read, played, or worn. It enters the body and becomes part of the consumer. No other industry offers, both literally and figuratively, so much insight into the nature of mass consumption.

Hundreds of millions of people buy fast food every day without giving it much thought, unaware of the subtle and not so subtle ramifications of their purchases. They rarely consider where this food came from, how it was made, what it is doing to the community around them. They just grab their tray off the counter, find a table, take a seat, unwrap the paper, and dig in. The whole experience is transitory and soon forgotten. I've written this book out of a belief that people should know what lies behind the shiny, happy surface of every fast food transaction. They should know what really lurks between those sesame-seed buns. As the old saying goes: You are what you eat.

I / the american way

1 / the founding fathers

CARL N. KARCHER is one of the fast food industry's pioneers. His career extends from the industry's modest origins to its current hamburger hegemony. His life seems at once to be a tale by Horatio Alger, a fulfillment of the American dream, and a warning about unintended consequences. It is a fast food parable about how the industry started and where it can lead. At the heart of the story is southern California, whose cities became prototypes for the rest of the nation, whose love of the automobile changed what America looks like and what Americans eat.

Carl was born in 1917 on a farm near Upper Sandusky, Ohio. His father was a sharecropper who moved the family to new land every few years. The Karchers were German-American, industrious, and devoutly Catholic. Carl had six brothers and a sister. "The harder you work," their father always told them, "the luckier you become." Carl dropped out of school after the eighth grade and worked twelve to fourteen hours a day on the farm, harvesting with a team of horses, baling hay, milking and feeding the cows. In 1937, Ben Karcher, one of Carl's uncles, offered him a job in Anaheim, California. After thinking long and hard and consulting with his parents, Carl decided to go west. He was twenty years old and six-foot-four, a big strong farm boy. He had never set foot outside of northern Ohio. The decision to leave home felt momentous, and the drive to California took a week. When he arrived in Anaheim — and saw the palm trees and orange groves, and smelled the citrus in the air — Carl said to himself, "This is heaven."

Anaheim was a small town in those days, surrounded by ranches and farms. It was located in the heart of southern California's citrus belt, an area that produced almost all of the state's oranges, lemons, and tangerines. Orange County and neighboring Los Angeles County were the leading agricultural counties in the United States, growing fruits, nuts, vegetables, and flowers on land that only a generation earlier had been a desert covered in sagebrush and cactus. Massive irrigation projects, built with public money to improve private land, brought water from hundreds of miles away. The Anaheim area alone boasted about 70,000 acres of Valencia oranges, as well as lemon groves and walnut groves. Small ranches and dairy farms dotted the land, and sunflowers lined the back roads. Anaheim had been settled in the late nineteenth century by German immigrants hoping to create a local wine industry and by a group of Polish expatriates trying to establish a back-to-the-land artistic community. The wineries flourished for three decades; the art colony collapsed within a few months. After World War I, the heavily German character of Anaheim gave way to the influence of newer arrivals from the Midwest, who tended to be Protestant and conservative and evangelical about their faith. Reverend Leon L. Myers — pastor of the Anaheim Christian Church and founder of the local Men's Bible Club — turned the Ku Klux Klan into one of the most powerful organizations in town. During the early 1920s, the Klan ran Anaheim's leading daily newspaper, controlled the city government for a year, and posted signs on the outskirts of the city greeting newcomers with the acronym "KIGY" (Klansmen I Greet You).

Carl's uncle Ben owned Karcher's Feed and Seed Store, right in the middle of downtown Anaheim. Carl worked there seventy-six hours a week, selling goods to local farmers for their chickens, cattle, and hogs. During Sunday services at St. Boniface Catholic Church, Carl spotted an attractive young woman named Margaret Heinz sitting in a nearby pew. He later asked her out for ice cream, and the two began dating. Carl became a frequent visitor to the Heinz farm on North Palm Street. It had ten acres of orange trees and a Spanish-style house where Margaret, her parents, her seven brothers, and her seven sisters lived. The place seemed magical. In the social hierarchy of California's farmers, orange growers stood at the very top; their homes were set amid fragrant evergreen trees that produced a lucrative income. As a young boy in Ohio, Carl had been thrilled on Christmas mornings to receive a single orange as a gift from Santa. Now oranges seemed to be everywhere.

Margaret worked as a secretary at a law firm downtown. From her office window on the fourth floor, she could watch Carl grinding feed outside his uncle's store. After briefly returning to Ohio, Carl went to work for the Armstrong Bakery in Los Angeles. The job soon paid $24 a week, $6 more than he'd earned at the feed store — and enough to start a family. Carl and Margaret were married in 1939 and had their first child within a year.

Carl drove a truck for the bakery, delivering bread to restaurants and markets in west L.A. He was amazed by the number of hot dog stands that were opening and by the number of buns they went through every week. When Carl heard that a hot dog cart was for sale — on Florence Avenue across from the Goodyear factory — he decided to buy it. Margaret strongly opposed the idea, wondering where he'd find the money. He borrowed $311 from the Bank of America, using his car as collateral for the loan, and persuaded his wife to give him $15 in cash from her purse. "I'm in business for myself now," Carl thought, after buying the cart, "I'm on my way." He kept his job at the bakery and hired two young men to work the cart during the hours he was delivering bread. They sold hot dogs, chili dogs, and tamales for a dime each, soda for a nickel. Five months after Carl bought the cart, the United States entered World War II, and the Goodyear plant became very busy. Soon he had enough money to buy a second hot dog cart, which Margaret often ran by herself, selling food and counting change while their daughter slept nearby in the car.

Southern California had recently given birth to an entirely new lifestyle — and a new way of eating. Both revolved around cars. The cities back East had been built in the railway era, with central business districts linked to outlying suburbs by commuter train and trolley. But the tremendous growth of Los Angeles occurred at a time when automobiles were finally affordable. Between 1920 and 1940, the population of southern California nearly tripled, as about 2 million people arrived from across the United States. While cities in the East expanded through immigration and became more diverse, Los Angeles became more homogenous and white. The city was inundated with middle-class arrivals from the Midwest, especially in the years leading up to the Great Depression. Invalids, retirees, and small businessmen were drawn to southern California by real estate ads promising a warm climate and a good life. It was the first large-scale migration conducted mainly by car. Los Angeles soon became unlike any other city the world had ever seen, sprawling and horizontal, a thoroughly suburban metropolis of detached homes — a glimpse of the future, molded by the automobile. About 80 percent of the population had been born elsewhere; about half had rolled into town during the previous five years. Restlessness, impermanence, and speed were embedded in the culture that soon emerged there, along with an openness to anything new. Other cities were being transformed by car ownership, but none was so profoundly altered. By 1940, there were about a million cars in Los Angeles, more cars than in forty-one states.

The automobile offered drivers a feeling of independence and control. Daily travel was freed from the hassles of rail schedules, the needs of other passengers, and the location of trolley stops. More importantly, driving seemed to cost much less than using public transport — an illusion created by the fact that the price of a new car did not include the price of building new roads. Lobbyists from the oil, tire, and automobile industries, among others, had persuaded state and federal agencies to assume that fundamental expense. Had the big auto companies been required to pay for the roads — in the same way that trolley companies had to lay and maintain track — the landscape of the American West would look quite different today.

The automobile industry, however, was not content simply to reap the benefits of government-subsidized road construction. It was determined to wipe out railway competition by whatever means necessary. In the late 1920s, General Motors secretly began to purchase trolley systems throughout the United States, using a number of front corporations. Trolley systems in Tulsa, Oklahoma, and Montgomery, Alabama, in Cedar Rapids, Iowa, and El Paso, Texas, in Baltimore, Chicago, New York City, and Los Angeles — more than one hundred trolley systems in all — were purchased by GM and then completely dismantled, their tracks ripped up, their overhead wires torn down. The trolley companies were turned into bus lines, and the new buses were manufactured by GM.

General Motors eventually persuaded other companies that benefited from road building to help pay for the costly takeover of America's trolleys. In 1947, GM and a number of its allies in the scheme were indicted on federal antitrust charges. Two years later, the workings of the conspiracy, and its underlying intentions, were exposed during a trial in Chicago. GM, Mack Truck, Firestone, and Standard Oil of California were all found guilty on one of the two counts by the federal jury. The investigative journalist Jonathan Kwitny later argued that the case was "a fine example of what can happen when important matters of public policy are abandoned by government to the self-in-

terest of corporations." Judge William J. Campbell was not so outraged. As punishment, he ordered GM and the other companies to pay
a fine of $5,000 each. The executives who had secretly plotted and car-
ried out the destruction of America's light rail network were fined $1
each. And the postwar reign of the automobile proceeded without
much further challenge.

The nation's car culture reached its height in southern California,
inspiring innovations such as the world's first motel and the first
drive-in bank. A new form of eating place emerged. "People with cars
are so lazy they don't want to get out of them to eat!" said Jesse G.
Kirby, the founder of an early drive-in restaurant chain. Kirby's first
"Pig Stand" was in Texas, but the chain soon thrived in Los Angeles,
alongside countless other food stands offering "curb service." In the
rest of the United States, drive-ins were usually a seasonal phenome-
non, closing at the end of every summer. In southern California, it felt
like summer all year long, the drive-ins never closed, and a whole new
industry was born.

The southern California drive-in restaurants of the early 1940s
tended to be gaudy and round, topped with pylons, towers, and flashing signs. They were "circular meccas of neon," in the words of drive-
in historian Michael Witzel, designed to be easily spotted from the
road. The triumph of the automobile encouraged not only a geographic separation between buildings, but also a manmade landscape
that was loud and bold. Architecture could no longer afford to be subtle; it had to catch the eye of motorists traveling at high speed. The
new drive-ins competed for attention, using all kinds of visual lures,
decorating their buildings in bright colors and dressing their waitresses in various costumes. Known as "carhops," the waitresses — who
carried trays of food to patrons in parked cars — often wore short
skirts and dressed up like cowgirls, majorettes, Scottish lasses in kilts.
They were likely to be attractive, often received no hourly wages, and
earned their money through tips and a small commission on every
item they sold. The carhops had a strong economic incentive to be
friendly to their customers, and drive-in restaurants quickly became
popular hangouts for teenage boys. The drive-ins fit perfectly with the
youth culture of Los Angeles. They were something genuinely new
and different, they offered a combination of girls and cars and late-
night food, and before long they beckoned from intersections all
over town.

speedee service

BY THE END OF 1944, Carl Karcher owned four hot dog carts in Los Angeles. In addition to running the carts, he still worked full-time for the Armstrong Bakery. When a restaurant across the street from the Heinz farm went on sale, Carl decided to buy it. He quit the bakery, bought the restaurant, fixed it up, and spent a few weeks learning how to cook. On January 16, 1945, his twenty-eighth birthday, Carl's Drive-In Barbeque opened its doors. The restaurant was small, rectangular, and unexceptional, with red tiles on the roof. Its only hint of flamboyance was a five-pointed star atop the neon sign in the parking lot. During business hours, Carl did the cooking, Margaret worked behind the cash register, and carhops served most of the food. After closing time, Carl stayed late into the night, cleaning the bathrooms and mopping the floors. Once a week, he prepared the "special sauce" for his hamburgers, making it in huge kettles on the back porch of his house, stirring it with a stick and then pouring it into one-gallon jugs.

After World War II, business soared at Carl's Drive-In Barbeque, along with the economy of southern California. The oil business and the film business had thrived in Los Angeles during the 1920s and 1930s. But it was World War II that transformed southern California into the most important economic region in the West. The war's effect on the state, in the words of historian Carey McWilliams, was a "fabulous boom." Between 1940 and 1945, the federal government spent nearly $20 billion in California, mainly in and around Los Angeles, building airplane factories and steel mills, military bases and port facilities. During those six years, federal spending was responsible for nearly half of the personal income in southern California. By the end of World War II, Los Angeles was the second-largest manufacturing center in America, with an industrial output surpassed only by that of Detroit. While Hollywood garnered most of the headlines, defense spending remained the focus of the local economy for the next two decades, providing about one-third of its jobs.

The new prosperity enabled Carl and Margaret to buy a house five blocks away from their restaurant. They added more rooms as the family grew to include twelve children: nine girls and three boys. In the early 1950s Anaheim began to feel much less rural and remote. Walt Disney bought 160 acres of orange groves just a few miles from Carl's Drive-In Barbeque, chopped down the trees, and started to build Disneyland. In the neighboring town of Garden Grove, the Reverend Robert Schuller founded the nation's first Drive-in Church, preaching on Sunday mornings at a drive-in movie theater, spreading the Gospel through the little speakers at each parking space, attracting large crowds with the slogan "Worship as you are . . . in the family car." The city of Anaheim started to recruit defense contractors, eventually persuading Northrop, Boeing, and North American Aviation to build factories there. Anaheim soon became the fastest-growing city in the nation's fastest-growing state. Carl's Drive-In Barbeque thrived, and Carl thought its future was secure. And then he heard about a restaurant in the "Inland Empire," sixty miles east of Los Angeles, that was selling high-quality hamburgers for 15 cents each — 20 cents less than what Carl charged. He drove to E Street in San Bernardino and saw the shape of things to come. Dozens of people were standing in line to buy bags of "McDonald's Famous Hamburgers."

Richard and Maurice McDonald had left New Hampshire for southern California at the start of the Depression, hoping to find jobs in Hollywood. They worked as set builders on the Columbia Film Studios back lot, saved their money, and bought a movie theater in Glendale. The theater was not a success. In 1937 they opened a drive-in restaurant in Pasadena, trying to cash in on the new craze, hiring three carhops and selling mainly hot dogs. A few years later they moved to a larger building on E Street in San Bernardino and opened the McDonald Brothers Burger Bar Drive-In. The new restaurant was located near a high school, employed twenty carhops, and promptly made the brothers rich. Richard and "Mac" McDonald bought one of the largest houses in San Bernardino, a hillside mansion with a tennis court and a pool.

By the end of the 1940s the McDonald brothers had grown dissatisfied with the drive-in business. They were tired of constantly looking for new carhops and short-order cooks — who were in great demand — as the old ones left for higher-paying jobs elsewhere. They were tired of replacing the dishes, glassware, and silverware their teenage customers constantly broke or ripped off. And they were tired of their teenage customers. The brothers thought about selling the restaurant. Instead, they tried something new.

The McDonalds fired all their carhops in 1948, closed their restaurant, installed larger grills, and reopened three months later with a radically new method of preparing food. It was designed to increase the speed, lower prices, and raise the volume of sales. The brothers eliminated almost two-thirds of the items on their old menu. They got rid of everything that had to be eaten with a knife, spoon, or fork. The only sandwiches now sold were hamburgers or cheeseburgers. The brothers got rid of their dishes and glassware, replacing them with paper cups, paper bags, and paper plates. They divided the food preparation into separate tasks performed by different workers. To fill a typical order, one person grilled the hamburger; another "dressed" and wrapped it; another prepared the milk shake; another made the fries; and another worked the counter. For the first time, the guiding principles of a factory assembly line were applied to a commercial kitchen. The new division of labor meant that a worker only had to be taught how to perform one task. Skilled and expensive short-order cooks were no longer necessary. All of the burgers were sold with the same condiments: ketchup, onions, mustard, and two pickles. No substitutions were allowed. The McDonald brothers' Speedee Service System revolutionized the restaurant business. An ad of theirs seeking franchisees later spelled out the benefits of the system: "Imagine — No Carhops — No Waitresses — No Dishwashers — No Bus Boys — The McDonald's System is Self-Service!"

Richard McDonald designed a new building for the restaurant, hoping to make it easy to spot from the road. Though untrained as an architect, he came up with a design that was simple, memorable, and archetypal. On two sides of the roof he put golden arches, lit by neon at night, that from a distance formed the letter *M*. The building effortlessly fused advertising with architecture and spawned one of the most famous corporate logos in the world.

The Speedee Service System, however, got off to a rocky start. Customers pulled up to the restaurant and honked their horns, wondering what had happened to the carhops, still expecting to be served. People were not yet accustomed to waiting in line and getting their own food. Within a few weeks, however, the new system gained acceptance, as word spread about the low prices and good hamburgers. The McDonald brothers now aimed for a much broader clientele. They employed only young men, convinced that female workers would attract teenage boys to the restaurant and drive away other customers. Families soon lined up to eat at McDonald's. Company historian John F. Love explained the lasting significance of McDonald's new self-service system: "Working-class families could finally afford to feed their kids restaurant food."

San Bernardino at the time was an ideal setting for all sorts of cultural experimentation. The town was an odd melting-pot of agriculture and industry located on the periphery of the southern California boom, a place that felt out on the edge. Nicknamed "San Berdoo," it was full of citrus groves, but sat next door to the smokestacks and steel mills of Fontana. San Bernardino had just sixty thousand inhabitants, but millions of people passed through there every year. It was the last stop on Route 66, end of the line for truckers, tourists, and migrants from the East. Its main street was jammed with drive-ins and cheap motels. The same year the McDonald brothers opened their new self-service restaurant, a group of World War II veterans in San Berdoo, alienated by the dullness of civilian life, formed a local motorcycle club, borrowing the nickname of the U.S. Army's Eleventh Airborne Division: "Hell's Angels." The same town that gave the world the golden arches also gave it a biker gang that stood for a totally antithetical set of values. The Hell's Angels flaunted their dirtiness, celebrated disorder, terrified families and small children instead of trying to sell them burgers, took drugs, sold drugs, and injected into American pop culture an anger and a darkness and a fashion statement — T-shirts and torn jeans, black leather jackets and boots, long hair, facial hair, swastikas, silver skull rings and other satanic trinkets, earrings, nose rings, body piercings, and tattoos — that would influence a long line of rebels from Marlon Brando to Marilyn Manson. The Hell's Angels were the anti-McDonald's, the opposite of clean and cheery. They didn't care if you had a nice day, and yet were as deeply American in their own way as any purveyors of Speedee Service. San Bernardino in 1948 supplied the nation with a new yin and yang, new models of conformity and rebellion. "They get angry when they read about how filthy they are," Hunter Thompson later wrote of the Hell's Angels, "but instead of shoplifting some deodorant, they strive to become even filthier."

burgerville usa

AFTER VISITING SAN BERNARDINO and seeing the long lines at McDonald's, Carl Karcher went home to Anaheim and decided to open his own self-service restaurant. Carl instinctively grasped that the new car culture would forever change America. He saw what was coming, and his timing was perfect. The first Carl's Jr. restaurant opened in 1956 — the same year that America got its first shopping mall and that Congress passed the Interstate Highway Act. President Dwight D. Eisenhower had pushed hard for such a bill; during World War II, he'd been enormously impressed by Adolf Hitler's Reichsautobahn, the world's first superhighway system. The Interstate Highway Act brought autobahns to the United States and became the largest public works project in the nation's history, building 46,000 miles of road with more than $130 billion of federal money. The new highways spurred car sales, truck sales, and the construction of new suburban homes. Carl's first self-service restaurant was a success, and he soon opened others near California's new freeway off-ramps. The star atop his drive-in sign became the mascot of his fast food chain. It was a smiling star in little booties, holding a burger and a shake.

Entrepreneurs from all over the country went to San Bernardino, visited the new McDonald's, and built imitations of the restaurant in their hometowns. "Our food was exactly the same as McDonald's," the founder of a rival chain later admitted. "If I had looked at McDonald's and saw someone flipping hamburgers while he was hanging by his feet, I would have copied it." America's fast food chains were not launched by large corporations relying upon focus groups and market research. They were started by door-to-door salesmen, short-order cooks, orphans, and dropouts, by eternal optimists looking for a piece of the next big thing. The start-up costs of a fast food restaurant were low, the profit margins promised to be high, and a wide assortment of ambitious people were soon buying grills and putting up signs.

William Rosenberg dropped out of school at the age of fourteen, delivered telegrams for Western Union, drove an ice cream truck, worked as a door-to-door salesman, sold sandwiches and coffee to factory workers in Boston, and then opened a small doughnut shop in 1948, later calling it Dunkin' Donuts. Glen W. Bell, Jr., was a World War II veteran, a resident of San Bernardino who ate at the new McDonald's and decided to copy it, using the assembly-line system to make Mexican food and founding a restaurant chain later known as Taco Bell. Keith G. Cramer, the owner of Keith's Drive-In Restaurant in Daytona Beach, Florida, heard about the McDonald brothers' new restaurant, flew to southern California, ate at McDonald's, returned to Florida, and with his father-in-law, Matthew Burns, opened the first Insta-Burger-King in 1953. Dave Thomas started working in a restaurant at the age of twelve, left his adoptive father, took a room at the YMCA, dropped out of school at fifteen, served as a busboy and a cook, and eventually opened his own place in Columbus, Ohio, calling it Wendy's Old-Fashioned Hamburgers restaurant. Thomas S. Monaghan spent much of his childhood in a Catholic orphanage and a series of foster homes, worked as a soda jerk, barely graduated from high school, joined the Marines, and bought a pizzeria in Ypsilanti, Michigan, with his brother, securing the deal through a down payment of $75. Eight months later Monaghan's brother decided to quit and accepted a used Volkswagen Beetle for his share of a business later known as Domino's.

The story of Harland Sanders is perhaps the most remarkable. Sanders left school at the age of twelve, worked as a farm hand, a mule tender, and a railway fireman. At various times he worked as a lawyer without having a law degree, delivered babies as a part-time obstetrician without having a medical degree, sold insurance door to door, sold Michelin tires, and operated a gas station in Corbin, Kentucky. He served home-cooked food at a small dining-room table in the back, later opened a popular restaurant and motel, sold them to pay off debts, and at the age of sixty-five became a traveling salesman once again, offering restaurant owners the "secret recipe" for his fried chicken. The first Kentucky Fried Chicken restaurant opened in 1952, near Salt Lake City, Utah. Lacking money to promote the new chain, Sanders dressed up like a Kentucky colonel, sporting a white suit and a black string tie. By the early 1960s, Kentucky Fried Chicken was the largest restaurant chain in the United States, and Colonel Sanders was a household name. In his autobiography, *Life As I Have Known It Has Been "Finger-lickin' Good,"* Sanders described his ups and downs, his decision at the age of seventy-four to be rebaptized and born again, his lifelong struggle to stop cursing. Despite his best efforts and a devout faith in Christ, Harland Sanders admitted that it was still awfully hard "not to call a no-good, lazy, incompetent, dishonest s.o.b. by anything else but his rightful name."

For every fast food idea that swept the nation, there were countless others that flourished briefly — or never had a prayer. There were chains with homey names, like Sandy's, Carrol's, Henry's, Winky's, and Mr. Fifteen's. There were chains with futuristic names, like the Satellite Hamburger System and Kelly's Jet System. Most of all, there were chains named after their main dish: Burger Chefs, Burger Queens, Burgerville USAs, Yumy Burgers, Twitty Burgers, Whataburgers, Dundee Burgers, Biff-Burgers, O.K. Big Burgers, and Burger Boy Food-O-Ramas.

Many of the new restaurants advertised an array of technological wonders. Carhops were rendered obsolete by various remote-control ordering systems, like the Fone-A-Chef, the Teletray, and the Electro-Hop. The Motormat was an elaborate rail system that transported food and beverages from the kitchen to parked cars. At the Biff-Burger chain, Biff-Burgers were "roto-broiled" beneath glowing quartz tubes that worked just like a space heater. Insta-Burger-King restaurants featured a pair of "Miracle Insta Machines," one to make milk shakes, the other to cook burgers. "Both machines have been *thoroughly perfected*," the company assured prospective franchisees, "are of foolproof design — can be easily operated even by a moron." The Insta-Burger Stove was an elaborate contraption. Twelve hamburger patties entered it in individual wire baskets, circled two electric heating elements, got cooked on both sides, and then slid down a chute into a pan of sauce, while hamburger buns toasted in a nearby slot. This Miracle Insta Machine proved overly complex, frequently malfunctioned, and was eventually abandoned by the Burger King chain.

The fast food wars in southern California — the birthplace of Jack in the Box, as well as McDonald's, Taco Bell, and Carl's Jr. — were especially fierce. One by one, most of the old drive-ins closed, unable to compete against the less expensive, self-service burger joints. But Carl kept at it, opening new restaurants up and down the state, following the new freeways. Four of these freeways — the Riverside, the Santa Ana, the Costa Mesa, and the Orange — soon passed through Anaheim. Although Carl's Jr. was a great success, a few of Carl's other ideas should have remained on the drawing board. Carl's Whistle Stops featured employees dressed as railway workers, "Hobo Burgers," and toy electric trains that took orders to the kitchen. Three were built in 1966 and then converted to Carl's Jr. restaurants a few years later. A coffee shop chain with a Scottish theme also never found its niche. The waitresses at "Scot's" wore plaid skirts, and the dishes had unfortunate names, such as "The Clansman."

The leading fast food chains spread nationwide; between 1960 and 1973, the number of McDonald's restaurants grew from roughly 250 to 3,000. The Arab oil embargo of 1973 gave the fast food industry a bad scare, as long lines at gas stations led many to believe that America's car culture was endangered. Amid gasoline shortages, the value of McDonald's stock fell. When the crisis passed, fast food stock prices recovered, and McDonald's intensified its efforts to open urban, as well as suburban, restaurants. Wall Street invested heavily in the fast food chains, and corporate managers replaced many of the early pioneers. What had begun as a series of small, regional businesses became a fast food industry, a major component of the American economy.

progress

IN 1976, THE NEW HEADQUARTERS of Carl Karcher Enterprises, Inc. (CKE) was built on the same land in Anaheim where the Heinz farm had once stood. The opening-night celebration was one of the high points of Carl's life. More than a thousand people gathered for a black-tie party at a tent set up in the parking lot. There was dinner and dancing on a beautiful, moonlit night. Thirty-five years after buying his first hot dog cart, Carl Karcher now controlled one of the largest privately owned fast food chains in the United States. He owned hundreds of restaurants. He considered many notable Americans to be his friends, including Governor Ronald Reagan, former president Richard Nixon, Gene Autry, Art Linkletter, Lawrence Welk, and Pat Boone. Carl's nickname was "Mr. Orange County." He was a benefactor of Catholic charities, a Knight of Malta, a strong supporter of right-to-life causes. He attended private masses at the Vatican with the Pope. And then, despite all the hard work, Carl's luck began to change.

During the 1980s CKE went public, opened Carl's Jr. restaurants in Texas, added higher-priced dinners to the menu, and for the first time began to expand by selling franchises. The new menu items and the restaurants in Texas fared poorly. The value of CKE's stock fell. In 1988, Carl and half a dozen members of his family were accused of insider trading by the Securities and Exchange Commission (SEC). They had sold large amounts of CKE stock right before its price tumbled. Carl vehemently denied the charges and felt humiliated by the publicity surrounding the case. Nevertheless, Carl agreed to a settlement with the SEC — to avoid a long and expensive legal battle, he said — and paid more than half a million dollars in fines.

During the early 1990s, a number of Carl's real estate investments proved unwise. When new subdivisions in Anaheim and the Inland Empire went bankrupt, Carl was saddled with many of their debts. He had allowed real estate developers to use his CKE stock as collateral for their bank loans. He became embroiled in more than two dozen lawsuits. He suddenly owed more than $70 million to various banks. The falling price of CKE stock hampered his ability to repay the loans. In May of 1992, his brother Don — a trusted adviser and the president of

CKE — died. The new president tried to increase sales at Carl's Jr. restaurants by purchasing food of a lower quality and cutting prices. The strategy began to drive customers away.

As the chairman of CKE, Carl searched for ways to save his company and pay off his debts. He proposed selling Mexican food at Carl's Jr. restaurants as part of a joint venture with a chain called Green Burrito. But some executives at CKE opposed the plan, arguing that it would benefit Carl much more than the company. Carl had a financial stake in the deal; upon its acceptance by the board of CKE, he would receive a $6 million personal loan from Green Burrito. Carl was outraged that his motives were being questioned and that his business was being run into the ground. CKE now felt like a much different company than the one he'd founded. The new management team had ended the longtime practice of starting every executive meeting with the prayer of St. Francis of Assisi and the pledge of allegiance to the flag. Carl insisted that the Green Burrito plan would work and demanded that the board of directors vote on it. When the board rejected the plan, Carl tried to oust its members. Instead, they ousted him. On March 1, 1993, CKE's board voted five to two to fire Carl N. Karcher. Only Carl and his son Carl Leo opposed the dismissal. Carl felt deeply betrayed. He had known many of the board members for years; they were old friends; he had made them rich. In a statement released after the firing, Carl described the CKE board as "a bunch of turncoats" and called it "one of the saddest days" of his life. At the age of seventy-six, more than five decades after starting the business, Carl N. Karcher was prevented from entering his own office, and new locks were put on the doors.

The headquarters of CKE is still located on the property where the Heinz family once grew oranges. Today there's no smell of citrus in the air, no orange groves in sight. In a town that once had endless rows of orange and lemon trees, stretching far as the eye could see, there's not an acre of them left, not a single acre devoted to commercial citrus growing. Anaheim's population is now about three hundred thousand, roughly thirty times what it was when Carl first arrived. On the corner where Carl's Drive-In Barbeque once stood, there's a strip mall. Near the CKE headquarters on Harbor Boulevard, there's an Exxon station, a discount mattress store, a Shoe City, a Las Vegas Auto Sales store, and an off-ramp of the Riverside Freeway. The CKE building has a modern, Spanish design, with white columns, red brick arches, and dark plate-glass windows. When I visited recently, it was cool and quiet inside. After passing a life-size wooden statue of St. Francis of Assisi on a stairway landing, I was greeted at the top of the stairs by Carl N. Karcher.

Carl looked like a stylish figure from the big-band era, wearing a brown checked jacket, a white shirt, a brown tie, and jaunty two-tone shoes. He was tall and strong, and seemed in remarkably good shape. The walls of his office were covered with plaques and mementos, with photographs of Carl beside presidents, famous ballplayers, former employees, grandchildren, priests, cardinals, Mikhail Gorbachev, the Pope. Carl proudly removed a framed object from the wall and handed it to me. It was the original receipt for $326, confirming the purchase of his first hot dog cart.

Eight weeks after being locked out of his office in 1993, Carl engineered a takeover of the company. Through a complex series of transactions, a partnership headed by financier William P. Foley II assumed some of Carl's debts, received much of his stock in return, and took control of CKE. Foley became the new chairman of the board. Carl was named chairman emeritus and got his old office back. Almost all of the executives and directors who had opposed him subsequently left the company. The Green Burrito plan was adopted and proved a success. The new management at CKE seemed to have turned the company around, raising the value of its stock. In July of 1997, CKE purchased Hardee's for $327 million, thereby becoming the fourth-largest hamburger chain in the United States, joining McDonald's, Burger King, and Wendy's at the top. And signs bearing the Carl's Jr. smiling little star started going up across the United States.

Carl seemed amazed by his own life story as he told it. He'd been married to Margaret for sixty years. He'd lived in the same Anaheim house for almost fifty years. He had twenty granddaughters and twenty grandsons. For a man of eighty, he had an impressive memory, quickly rattling off names, dates, and addresses from half a century ago. He exuded the genial optimism and good humor of his old friend Ronald Reagan. "My whole philosophy is — never give up," Carl told me. "The word 'can't' should not exist . . . Have a great attitude . . . Watch the pennies and the dollars will take care of themselves . . . Life is beautiful, life is fantastic, and that is how I feel about every day of my life." Despite CKE's expansion, Carl remained millions of dollars in debt. He'd secured new loans to pay off the old ones. During the worst of his financial troubles, advisers pleaded with him to declare bankruptcy. Carl refused; he'd borrowed more than $8 million from family members and friends, and he would not walk away from his obligations. Every weekday he was attending Mass at six o'clock in the morning and getting to the office by seven. "My goal in the next two years," he said, "is to pay off all my debts."

I looked out the window and asked how he felt driving through Anaheim today, with its fast food restaurants, subdivisions, and strip malls. "Well, to be frank about it," he said, "I couldn't be happier." Thinking that he'd misunderstood the question, I rephrased it, asking if he ever missed the old Anaheim, the ranches and citrus groves.

"No," he answered. "I believe in Progress."

Carl grew up on a farm without running water or electricity. He'd escaped a hard rural life. The view outside his office window was not disturbing to him, I realized. It was a mark of success.

"When I first met my wife," Carl said, "this road here was gravel . . . and now it's blacktop."

2/ your trusted friends

EFORE ENTERING the Ray A. Kroc Museum, you have to walk through McStore. Both sit on the ground floor of McDonald's corporate headquarters, located at One McDonald's Plaza in Oak Brook, Illinois. The headquarters building has oval windows and a gray concrete façade — a look that must have seemed space-age when the building opened three decades ago. Now it seems stolid and drab, an architectural relic of the Nixon era. It resembles the American embassy compounds that always used to attract antiwar protesters, student demonstrators, flag burners. The eighty-acre campus of Hamburger University, McDonald's managerial training center, is a short drive from headquarters. Shuttle buses constantly go back and forth between the campus and McDonald's Plaza, ferrying clean-cut young men and women in khakis who've come to study for their "Degree in Hamburgerology." The course lasts two weeks and trains a few thousand managers, executives, and franchisees each year. Students from out of town stay at the Hyatt on the McDonald's campus. Most of the classes are devoted to personnel issues, teaching lessons in teamwork and employee motivation, promoting "a common McDonald's language" and "a common McDonald's culture." Three flagpoles stand in front of McDonald's Plaza, the heart of the hamburger empire. One flies the Stars and Stripes, another flies the Illinois state flag, and the third flies a bright red flag with golden arches.

You can buy bean-bag McBurglar dolls at McStore, telephones shaped like french fries, ties, clocks, key chains, golf bags and duffel bags, jewelry, baby clothes, lunch boxes, mouse pads, leather jackets, postcards, toy trucks, and much more, all of it bearing the stamp of McDonald's. You can buy T-shirts decorated with a new version of the

American flag. The fifty white stars have been replaced by a pair of golden arches.

At the back of McStore, past the footsteps of Ronald McDonald stenciled on the floor, past the shelves of dishes and glassware, a bronze bust of Ray Kroc marks the entrance to his museum. Kroc was the founder of the McDonald's Corporation, and his philosophy of QSC and V — Quality, Service, Cleanliness, and Value — still guide it. The man immortalized in bronze is balding and middle-aged, with smooth cheeks and an intense look in his eyes. A glass display case nearby holds plaques, awards, and letters of praise. "One of the highlights of my sixty-first birthday celebration," President Richard Nixon wrote in 1974, "was when Tricia suggested we needed a 'break' on our drive to Palm Springs, and we turned in at McDonald's. I had heard for years from our girls that the 'Big Mac' was really something special, and while I've often credited Mrs. Nixon with making the best hamburgers in the world, we are both convinced that McDonald's runs a close second . . . The next time the cook has a night off we will know where to go for fast service, cheerful hospitality — and probably one of the best food buys in America." Other glass cases contain artifacts of Kroc's life, mementos of his long years of struggle and his twilight as a billionaire. The museum is small and dimly lit, displaying each object with reverence. The day I visited, the place was empty and still. It didn't feel like a traditional museum, where objects are coolly numbered, catalogued, and described. It felt more like a shrine.

Many of the exhibits at the Ray A. Kroc Museum incorporate neat technological tricks. Dioramas appear and then disappear when certain buttons are pushed. The voices of Kroc's friends and coworkers — one of them identified as a McDonald's "vice president of individuality" — boom from speakers at the appropriate cue. Darkened glass cases are suddenly illuminated from within, revealing their contents. An artwork on the wall, when viewed from the left, displays an image of Ray Kroc. Viewed from the right, it shows the letters QSC and V. The museum does not have a life-size, Audio-Animatronic version of McDonald's founder telling jokes and anecdotes. But one wouldn't be out of place. An interactive exhibit called "Talk to Ray" shows video clips of Kroc appearing on the *Phil Donahue Show,* being interviewed by Tom Snyder, and chatting with Reverend Robert Schuller at the altar of Orange County's Crystal Cathedral. "Talk to Ray" permits the viewer to ask Kroc as many as thirty-six predetermined questions about various subjects; old videos of Kroc supply the answers.

The exhibit wasn't working properly the day of my visit. Ray wouldn't take my questions, and so I just listened to him repeating the same speeches.

The Disneyesque tone of the museum reflects, among other things, many of the similarities between the McDonald's Corporation and the Walt Disney Company. It also reflects the similar paths of the two men who founded these corporate giants. Ray Kroc and Walt Disney were both from Illinois; they were born a year apart, Disney in 1901, Kroc in 1902; they knew each other as young men, serving together in the same World War I ambulance corps; and they both fled the Midwest and settled in southern California, where they played central roles in the creation of new American industries. The film critic Richard Schickel has described Disney's powerful inner need "to order, control, and keep clean any environment he inhabited." The same could easily be said about Ray Kroc, whose obsession with cleanliness and control became one of the hallmarks of his restaurant chain. Kroc cleaned the holes in his mop wringer with a toothbrush.

Kroc and Disney both dropped out of high school and later added the trappings of formal education to their companies. The training school for Disney's theme-park employees was named Disneyland University. More importantly, the two men shared the same vision of America, the same optimistic faith in technology, the same conservative political views. They were charismatic figures who provided an overall corporate vision and grasped the public mood, relying on others to handle the creative and financial details. Walt Disney neither wrote, nor drew the animated classics that bore his name. Ray Kroc's attempts to add new dishes to McDonald's menu — such as Kolacky, a Bohemian pastry, and the Hulaburger, a sandwich featuring grilled pineapple and cheese — were unsuccessful. Both men, however, knew how to find and motivate the right talent. While Disney was much more famous and achieved success sooner, Kroc may have been more influential. His company inspired more imitators, wielded more power over the American economy — and spawned a mascot even more famous than Mickey Mouse.

Despite all their success as businessmen and entrepreneurs, as cultural figures and advocates for a particular brand of Americanism, perhaps the most significant achievement of these two men lay elsewhere. Walt Disney and Ray Kroc were masterful salesmen. They perfected the art of selling things to children. And their success led many others to aim marketing efforts at kids, turning America's youngest consumers into a demographic group that is now avidly studied, analyzed, and targeted by the world's largest corporations.

walt and ray

RAY KROC TOOK THE McDonald brothers' Speedee Service System and spread it nationwide, creating a fast food empire. Although he founded a company that came to symbolize corporate America, Kroc was never a buttoned-down corporate type. He was a former jazz musician who'd played at speakeasies — and at a bordello, on at least one occasion — during Prohibition. He was a charming, funny, and indefatigable traveling salesman who endured many years of disappointment, a Willy Loman who finally managed to hit it big in his early sixties. Kroc grew up in Oak Park, Illinois, not far from Chicago. His father worked for Western Union. As a high school freshman, Ray Kroc discovered the joys of selling while employed at his uncle's soda fountain. "That was where I learned you could influence people with a smile and enthusiasm," Kroc recalled in his autobiography, *Grinding It Out*, "and sell them a sundae when what they'd come for was a cup of coffee."

Over the years, Kroc sold coffee beans, sheet music, paper cups, Florida real estate, powdered instant beverages called "Malt-a-Plenty" and "Shake-a-Plenty," a gadget that could dispense whipped cream or shaving lather, square ice cream scoops, and a collapsible table-and-bench combination called "Fold-a-Nook" that retreated into the wall like a Murphy bed. The main problem with square scoops of ice cream, he found, was that they slid off the plate when you tried to eat them. Kroc used the same basic technique to sell all these things: he tailored his pitch to fit the buyer's tastes. Despite one setback after another, he kept at it, always convinced that success was just around the corner. "If you believe in it, and you believe in it hard," Kroc later told audiences, "it's impossible to fail. I don't care what it is — you can get it!"

Ray Kroc was selling milk-shake mixers in 1954 when he first visited the new McDonald's Self-Service Restaurant in San Bernardino. The McDonald brothers were two of his best customers. The Multimixer unit that Kroc sold could make five milk shakes at once. He wondered why the McDonald brothers needed eight of the machines. Kroc had visited a lot of restaurant kitchens, out on the road, demonstrating the Multimixer — and had never seen anything like the Mc-Donald's Speedee Service System. "When I saw it," he later wrote, "I felt like some latter-day Newton who'd just had an Idaho potato caromed off his skull." He looked at the restaurant "through the eyes of a salesman" and envisioned putting a McDonald's at busy intersections all across the land.

Richard and "Mac" McDonald were less ambitious. They were clearing $100,000 a year in profits from the restaurant, a huge sum in those days. They already owned a big house and three Cadillacs. They didn't like to travel. They'd recently refused an offer from the Carnation Milk Company, which thought that opening more McDonald's would increase the sales of milk shakes. Nevertheless, Kroc convinced the brothers to sell him the right to franchise McDonald's nationwide. The two could stay at home, while Kroc traveled the country, making them even richer. A deal was signed. Years later Richard McDonald described his first memory of Kroc, a moment that would soon lead to the birth of the world's biggest restaurant chain: "This little fellow comes in, with a high voice, and says, 'hi.'"

After finalizing the agreement with the McDonald brothers, Kroc sent a letter to Walt Disney. In 1917 the two men had both lied about their ages to join the Red Cross and see battle in Europe. A long time had clearly passed since their last conversation. "Dear Walt," the letter said. "I feel somewhat presumptuous addressing you in this way yet I feel sure you would not want me to address you any other way. My name is Ray A. Kroc . . . I look over the Company A picture we had taken at Sound Beach, Conn., many times and recall a lot of pleasant memories." After the warm-up came the pitch: "I have very recently taken over the national franchise of the McDonald's system. I would like to inquire if there may be an opportunity for a McDonald's in your Disneyland Development."

Walt Disney sent Kroc a cordial reply and forwarded his proposal to an executive in charge of the theme park's concessions. Disneyland was still under construction, its opening was eagerly awaited by millions of American children, and Kroc may have had high hopes. According to one account, Disney's company asked Kroc to raise the price of McDonald's french fries from ten cents to fifteen cents; Disney would keep the extra nickel as payment for granting the concession; and the story ends with Ray Kroc refusing to gouge his loyal customers. The account seems highly unlikely, a belated effort by someone at McDonald's to put the best spin on a sales pitch that went nowhere. When Disneyland opened in July of 1955 — an event that Ronald Reagan cohosted for ABC — it had food stands run by Welch's, Stouffer's, and Aunt Jemima's, but no McDonald's. Kroc was not yet in their league. His recollection of Walt Disney as a young man, briefly mentioned in *Grinding It Out*, is not entirely flattering. "He was regarded as a strange duck," Kroc wrote of Disney, "because whenever we had time off and went out on the town to chase girls, he stayed in camp drawing pictures."

Whatever feelings existed between the two men, Walt Disney proved in many respects to be a role model for Ray Kroc. Disney's success had come much more quickly. At the age of twenty-one he'd left the Midwest and opened his own movie studio in Los Angeles. He was famous before turning thirty. In *The Magic Kingdom* (1997) Steven Watts describes Walt Disney's efforts to apply the techniques of mass production to Hollywood moviemaking. He greatly admired Henry Ford and introduced an assembly line and a rigorous division of labor at the Disney Studio, which was soon depicted as a "fun factory." Instead of drawing entire scenes, artists were given narrowly defined tasks, meticulously sketching and inking Disney characters while supervisors watched them and timed how long it took them to complete each cel. During the 1930s the production system at the studio was organized to function like that of an automobile plant. "Hundreds of young people were being trained and fitted," Disney explained, "into a machine for the manufacture of entertainment."

The working conditions at Disney's factory, however, were not always fun. In 1941 hundreds of Disney animators went on strike, expressing support for the Screen Cartoonists Guild. The other major cartoon studios in Hollywood had already signed agreements with the union. Disney's father was an ardent socialist, and Disney's films had long expressed a populist celebration of the common man. But Walt's response to the strike betrayed a different political sensibility. He fired employees who were sympathetic to the union, allowed private guards to rough up workers on the picket line, tried to impose a phony company union, brought in an organized crime figure from Chicago to rig a settlement, and placed a full-page ad in *Variety* that accused leaders of the Screen Cartoonists Guild of being Communists. The strike finally ended when Disney acceded to the union's demands. The experience left him feeling embittered. Convinced that Communist agents had been responsible for his troubles, Disney subsequently appeared as a friendly witness before the House Un-American Activities Committee, served as a secret informer for the FBI, and strongly supported the Hollywood blacklist. During the height of labor tension at his studio, Disney had made a speech to a group of employees, arguing that the solution to their problems rested not with a labor union, but with *a good day's work.* "Don't forget this," Disney told them, "it's the law of the universe that the strong shall survive and the weak must fall by the way, and I don't give a damn what idealistic plan is cooked up, nothing can change that."

Decades later, Ray Kroc used similar language to outline his own political philosophy. Kroc's years on the road as a traveling salesman — carrying his own order forms and sample books, knocking on doors, facing each new customer alone, and having countless doors slammed in his face — no doubt influenced his view of humanity. "Look, it is ridiculous to call this an industry," Kroc told a reporter in 1972, dismissing any high-minded analysis of the fast food business. "This is not. This is rat eat rat, dog eat dog. I'll kill 'em, and I'm going to kill 'em before they kill me. You're talking about the American way of survival of the fittest."

While Disney backed right-wing groups and produced campaign ads for the Republican Party, Kroc remained aloof from electoral politics — with one notable exception. In 1972, Kroc gave $250,000 to President Nixon's reelection campaign, breaking the gift into smaller donations, funneling the money through various state and local Republican committees. Nixon had every reason to like McDonald's, long before tasting one of its hamburgers. Kroc had never met the president; the gift did not stem from any personal friendship or fondness. That year the fast food industry was lobbying Congress and the White House to pass new legislation — known as the "McDonald's bill" — that would allow employers to pay sixteen- and seventeen-year-old kids wages 20 percent lower than the minimum wage. Around the time of Kroc's $250,000 donation, McDonald's crew members earned about $1.60 an hour. The subminimum wage proposal would reduce some wages to $1.28 an hour.

The Nixon administration supported the McDonald's bill and permitted McDonald's to raise the price of its Quarter Pounders, despite the mandatory wage and price controls restricting other fast food chains. The size and the timing of Kroc's political contribution sparked Democratic accusations of influence peddling. Outraged by the charges, Kroc later called his critics "sons of bitches." The uproar left him wary of backing political candidates. Nevertheless, Kroc retained a soft spot for Calvin Coolidge, whose thoughts on hard work and self-reliance were prominently displayed at McDonald's corporate headquarters.

better living

DESPITE A PASSIONATE OPPOSITION to socialism and to any government meddling with free enterprise, Walt Disney relied on federal funds in the 1940s to keep his business afloat. The animators' strike had left the Disney Studio in a precarious financial condition. Disney began to seek government contracts — and those contracts were soon responsible for 90 percent of his studio's output. During World War II, Walt Disney produced scores of military training and propaganda films, including *Food Will Win the War, High-Level Precision Bombing,* and *A Few Quick Facts About Venereal Disease.* After the war, Disney continued to work closely with top military officials and military contractors, becoming America's most popular exponent of Cold War science. For audiences living in fear of nuclear annihilation, Walt Disney became a source of reassurance, making the latest technical advances seem marvelous and exciting. His faith in the goodness of American technology was succinctly expressed by the title of a film that the Disney Studio produced for Westinghouse Electric: *The Dawn of Better Living.*

Disney's passion for science found expression in "Tomorrowland," the name given to a section of his theme park and to segments of his weekly television show. Tomorrowland encompassed everything from space travel to the household appliances of the future, depicting progress as a relentless march toward greater convenience for consumers. And yet, from the very beginning, there was a dark side to this Tomorrowland. It celebrated technology without moral qualms. Some of the science it espoused later proved to be not so benign — and some of the scientists it promoted were unusual role models for the nation's children.

In the mid-1950s Wernher von Braun cohosted and helped produce a series of Disney television shows on space exploration. "Man in Space" and the other Tomorrowland episodes on the topic were enormously popular and fueled public support for an American space program. At the time, von Braun was the U.S. Army's leading rocket scientist. He had served in the same capacity for the German army during World War II. He had been an early and enthusiastic member of the Nazi party, as well as a major in the SS. At least 20,000 slave laborers, many of them Allied prisoners of war, died at Dora-Nordhausen, the factory where von Braun's rockets were built. Less than ten years after the liberation of Dora-Nordhausen, von Braun was giving orders to Disney animators and designing a ride at Disneyland called Rocket to the Moon. Heinz Haber, another key Tomorrowland adviser — and eventually the chief scientific consultant to Walt Disney Productions — spent much of World War II conducting research on high-speed, high-altitude flight for the Luftwaffe Institute for Aviation Medicine. In order to assess the risks faced by German air force pilots, the institute performed experiments on hundreds of inmates at the Dachau concentration camp near Munich. The inmates who survived these experiments were usually killed and then dissected. Haber left Germany after the war and shared his knowledge of aviation medicine with the U.S. Army Air Force. He later cohosted Disney's "Man in Space" with von Braun. When the Eisenhower administration asked Walt Disney to produce a show championing the civilian use of nuclear power, Heinz Haber was given the assignment. He hosted the Disney broadcast called "Our Friend the Atom" and wrote a popular children's book with the same title, both of which made nuclear fission seem fun, instead of terrifying. "Our Friend the Atom" was sponsored by General Dynamics, a manufacturer of nuclear reactors. The company also financed the atomic submarine ride at Disneyland's Tomorrowland.

The future heralded at Disneyland was one in which every aspect of American life had a corporate sponsor. Walt Disney was the most beloved children's entertainer in the country. He had unrivaled access to impressionable young minds — and other corporations, with other agendas to sell, were eager to come along for the ride. Monsanto built Disneyland's House of the Future, which was made of plastic. General Electric backed the Carousel of Progress, which featured an Audio-Animatronic housewife, standing in her futuristic kitchen, singing about "a great big beautiful tomorrow." Richfield Oil offered utopian fantasies about cars and a ride aptly named Autopia. "Here you leave Today," said the plaque at the entrance to Disneyland, "and enter the world of Yesterday, Tomorrow, and Fantasy."

At first, Disneyland offered visitors an extraordinary feeling of escape; people had never seen anything like it. The great irony, of course, is that Disney's suburban, corporate world of Tomorrow would soon become the Anaheim of Today. Within a decade of its opening, Disneyland was no longer set amid a rural idyll of orange groves, it was stuck in the middle of cheap motels, traffic jams on the Santa Ana freeway, fast food joints, and industrial parks. Walt Disney frequently slept at his small apartment above the firehouse in Disneyland's Main Street, USA. By the early 1960s, the hard realities of Today were more and more difficult to ignore, and Disney began dreaming of bigger things, of Disney World, a place even farther removed from the forces he'd helped to unleash, a fantasy that could be even more thoroughly controlled.

Among other cultural innovations, Walt Disney pioneered the marketing strategy now known as "synergy." During the 1930s, he signed licensing agreements with dozens of firms, granting them the right to use Mickey Mouse on their products and in their ads. In 1938 *Snow White* proved a turning point in film marketing: Disney had signed seventy licensing deals prior to the film's release. Snow White toys, books, clothes, snacks, and records were already for sale when the film opened. Disney later used television to achieve a degree of synergy beyond anything that anyone had previously dared. His first television broadcast, *One Hour in Wonderland* (1950), culminated in a promotion for the upcoming Disney film *Alice in Wonderland*. His first television series, *Disneyland* (1954), provided weekly updates on the construction work at his theme park. ABC, which broadcast the show, owned a large financial stake in the Anaheim venture. Disneyland's other major investor, Western Printing and Lithography, printed Disney books such as *The Walt Disney Story of Our Friend the Atom*. In the guise of televised entertainment, episodes of *Disneyland* were often thinly disguised infomercials, promoting films, books, toys, an amusement park — and, most of all, Disney himself, the living, breathing incarnation of a brand, the man who neatly tied all the other commodities together into one cheerful, friendly, patriotic idea.

Ray Kroc could only dream, during McDonald's tough early years, of having such marketing tools at his disposal. He was forced to rely instead on his wits, his charisma, and his instinct for promotion. Kroc believed completely in whatever he sold and pitched McDonald's franchises with an almost religious fervor. He also knew a few things about publicity, having auditioned talent for a Chicago radio station in the 1920s and performed in nightclubs for years. Kroc hired a publicity firm led by a gag writer and a former MGM road manager to get McDonald's into the news. Children would be the new restaurant chain's target customers. The McDonald brothers had aimed for a family crowd, and now Kroc improved and refined their marketing strategy. He'd picked the right moment. America was in the middle of a baby boom; the number of children had soared in the decade after World War II. Kroc wanted to create a safe, clean, all-American place for kids. The McDonald's franchise agreement required every new restaurant to fly the Stars and Stripes. Kroc understood that how he sold food was just as important as how the food tasted. He liked to tell people that he was really in show business, not the restaurant business. Promoting McDonald's to children was a clever, pragmatic decision. "A child who loves our TV commercials," Kroc explained, "and brings her grandparents to a McDonald's gives us two more customers."

The McDonald's Corporation's first mascot was Speedee, a winking little chef with a hamburger for a head. The character was later renamed Archie McDonald. Speedy was the name of Alka-Seltzer's mascot, and it seemed unwise to imply any connection between the two brands. In 1960, Oscar Goldstein, a McDonald's franchisee in Washington, D.C., decided to sponsor *Bozo's Circus,* a local children's television show. Bozo's appearance at a McDonald's restaurant drew large crowds. When the local NBC station canceled *Bozo's Circus* in 1963, Goldstein hired its star — Willard Scott, later the weatherman on NBC's *Today* show — to invent a new clown who could make restaurant appearances. An ad agency designed the outfit, Scott came up with the name Ronald McDonald, and a star was born. Two years later the McDonald's Corporation introduced Ronald McDonald to the rest of the United States through a major ad campaign. But Willard Scott no longer played the part. He was deemed too overweight; McDonald's wanted someone thinner to sell its burgers, shakes, and fries.

The late-1960s expansion of the McDonald's restaurant chain coincided with declining fortunes at the Walt Disney Company. Disney was no longer alive, and his vision of America embodied just about everything that kids of the sixties were rebelling against. Although McDonald's was hardly a promoter of whole foods and psychedelia, it had the great advantage of seeming new — and there was something trippy about Ronald McDonald, his clothes, and his friends. As McDonald's mascot began to rival Mickey Mouse in name recognition, Kroc made plans to create his own Disneyland. He was a highly competitive man who liked, whenever possible, to settle the score. "If they were drowning to death," Kroc once said about his business rivals, "I would put a hose in their mouth." He planned to buy 1,500 acres of land northeast of Los Angeles and build a new amusement park there. The park, tentatively called Western World, would have a cowboy theme. Other McDonald's executives opposed the idea, worried that Western World would divert funds from the restaurant business and lose millions. Kroc offered to option the land with his own money, but finally listened to his close advisers and scrapped the plan. The McDonald's Corporation later considered buying Astro World in Houston. Instead of investing in a large theme park, the company pursued a more decentralized approach. It built small Playlands and McDonaldlands all over the United States.

The fantasy world of McDonaldland borrowed a good deal from Walt Disney's Magic Kingdom. Don Ament, who gave McDonaldland its distinctive look, was a former Disney set designer. Richard and Robert Sherman — who had written and composed, among other things, all the songs in Disney's *Mary Poppins,* Disneyland's "It's a Great, Big, Beautiful Tomorrow" and "It's a Small World, After All" — were enlisted for the first McDonaldland commercials. Ronald McDonald, Mayor McCheese, and the other characters in the ads made McDonald's seem like more than just another place to eat. McDonaldland — with its hamburger patch, apple pie trees, and Filet-O-Fish fountain — had one crucial thing in common with Disneyland. Almost everything in it was for sale. McDonald's soon loomed large in the imagination of toddlers, the intended audience for the ads. The restaurant chain evoked a series of pleasing images in a youngster's mind: bright colors, a playground, a toy, a clown, a drink with a straw, little pieces of food wrapped up like a present. Kroc had succeeded, like his old Red Cross comrade, at selling something intangible to children, along with their fries.

kid kustomers

TWENTY-FIVE YEARS AGO, only a handful of American companies directed their marketing at children — Disney, McDonald's, candy makers, toy makers, manufacturers of breakfast cereal. Today children are being targeted by phone companies, oil companies, and automobile companies, as well as clothing stores and restaurant chains. The explosion in children's advertising occurred during the 1980s. Many working parents, feeling guilty about spending less time with their kids, started spending more money on them. One marketing expert has called the 1980s "the decade of the child consumer." After largely ignoring children for years, Madison Avenue began to scrutinize and pursue them. Major ad agencies now have children's divisions, and a variety of marketing firms focus solely on kids. These groups tend to have sweet-sounding names: Small Talk, Kid Connection, Kid2Kid, the Gepetto Group, Just Kids, Inc. At least three industry publications — *Youth Market Alert, Selling to Kids,* and *Marketing to Kids Report* — cover the latest ad campaigns and market research. The growth in children's advertising has been driven by efforts to increase not just current, but also future, consumption. Hoping that nostalgic childhood memories of a brand will lead to a lifetime of purchases, companies now plan "cradle-to-grave" advertising strategies. They have come to believe what Ray Kroc and Walt Disney realized long ago — a person's "brand loyalty" may begin as early as the age of two. Indeed, market research has found that children often recognize a brand logo before they can recognize their own name.

The discontinued Joe Camel ad campaign, which used a hip cartoon character to sell cigarettes, showed how easily children can be influenced by the right corporate mascot. A 1991 study published in the *Journal of the American Medical Association* found that nearly all of America's six-year-olds could identify Joe Camel, who was just as familiar to them as Mickey Mouse. Another study found that one-third of the cigarettes illegally sold to minors were Camels. More recently, a marketing firm conducted a survey in shopping malls across the country, asking children to describe their favorite TV ads. According to the CME KidCom Ad Traction Study II, released at the 1999 Kids' Marketing Conference in San Antonio, Texas, the Taco Bell commercials featuring a talking chihuahua were the most popular fast food ads. The kids in the survey also liked Pepsi and Nike commercials, but their favorite television ad was for Budweiser.

The bulk of the advertising directed at children today has an immediate goal. "It's not just getting kids to whine," one marketer explained in *Selling to Kids,* "it's giving them a specific reason to ask for the product." Years ago sociologist Vance Packard described children as "surrogate salesmen" who had to persuade other people, usually their parents, to buy what they wanted. Marketers now use different terms to explain the intended response to their ads — such as "leverage," "the nudge factor," "pester power." The aim of most children's advertising is straightforward: get kids to nag their parents and nag them well.

James U. McNeal, a professor of marketing at Texas A&M University, is considered America's leading authority on marketing to children. In his book *Kids As Customers* (1992), McNeal provides marketers with a thorough analysis of "children's requesting styles and appeals." He classifies juvenile nagging tactics into seven major categories. A *pleading* nag is one accompanied by repetitions of words like "please" or "mom, mom, mom." A *persistent* nag involves constant requests for the coveted product and may include the phrase "I'm gonna ask just one more time." *Forceful* nags are extremely pushy and may include subtle threats, like "Well, then, I'll go and ask Dad." *Demonstrative* nags are the most high-risk, often characterized by full-blown tantrums in public places, breath-holding, tears, a refusal to leave the store. *Sugar-coated* nags promise affection in return for a purchase and may rely on seemingly heartfelt declarations like "You're the best dad in the world." *Threatening* nags are youthful forms of blackmail, vows of eternal hatred and of running away if something isn't bought. *Pity* nags claim the child will be heartbroken, teased, or socially stunted if the parent refuses to buy a certain item. "All of these appeals and styles may be used in combination," McNeal's research has discovered, "but kids tend to stick to one or two of each that prove most effective . . . for their own parents."

McNeal never advocates turning children into screaming, breath-holding monsters. He has been studying "Kid Kustomers" for more than thirty years and believes in a more traditional marketing approach. "The key is getting children to see a firm . . . in much the same way as [they see] mom or dad, grandma or grandpa," McNeal argues. "Likewise, if a company can ally itself with universal values such as patriotism, national defense, and good health, it is likely to nurture belief in it among children."

Before trying to affect children's behavior, advertisers have to learn about their tastes. Today's market researchers not only conduct surveys of children in shopping malls, they also organize focus groups for kids as young as two or three. They analyze children's artwork, hire children to run focus groups, stage slumber parties and then question children into the night. They send cultural anthropologists into homes, stores, fast food restaurants, and other places where kids like to gather, quietly and surreptitiously observing the behavior of prospective customers. They study the academic literature on child development, seeking insights from the work of theorists such as Erik Erikson and Jean Piaget. They study the fantasy lives of young children, then apply the findings in advertisements and product designs.

Dan S. Acuff — the president of Youth Market System Consulting and the author of *What Kids Buy and Why* (1997) — stresses the importance of dream research. Studies suggest that until the age of six, roughly 80 percent of children's dreams are about animals. Rounded, soft creatures like Barney, Disney's animated characters, and the Teletubbies therefore have an obvious appeal to young children. The Character Lab, a division of Youth Market System Consulting, uses a proprietary technique called Character Appeal Quadrant Analysis to help companies develop new mascots. The technique purports to create imaginary characters who perfectly fit the targeted age group's level of cognitive and neurological development.

Children's clubs have for years been considered an effective means of targeting ads and collecting demographic information; the clubs appeal to a child's fundamental need for status and belonging. Disney's Mickey Mouse Club, formed in 1930, was one of the trailblazers. During the 1980s and 1990s, children's clubs proliferated, as corporations used them to solicit the names, addresses, zip codes, and personal comments of young customers. "Marketing messages sent through a club not only can be personalized," James McNeal advises, "they can be tailored for a certain age or geographical group." A well-designed and well-run children's club can be extremely good for business. According to one Burger King executive, the creation of a Burger King Kids Club in 1991 increased the sales of children's meals as much as 300 percent.

The Internet has become another powerful tool for assembling data about children. In 1998 a federal investigation of Web sites aimed at children found that 89 percent requested personal information from kids; only 1 percent required that children obtain parental approval before supplying the information. A character on the McDonald's Web site told children that Ronald McDonald was "the ultimate authority in everything." The site encouraged kids to send Ronald an e-mail revealing their favorite menu item at McDonald's, their favorite book, their favorite sports team — and their name. Fast food Web sites no longer ask children to provide personal information without first gaining parental approval; to do so is now a violation of federal law, thanks to the Children's Online Privacy Protection Act, which took effect in April of 2000.

Despite the growing importance of the Internet, television remains the primary medium for children's advertising. The effects of these TV ads have long been a subject of controversy. In 1978, the Federal Trade

Commission (FTC) tried to ban all television ads directed at children seven years old or younger. Many studies had found that young children often could not tell the difference between television programming and television advertising. They also could not comprehend the real purpose of commercials and trusted that advertising claims were true. Michael Pertschuk, the head of the FTC, argued that children need to be shielded from advertising that preys upon their immaturity. "They cannot protect themselves," he said, "against adults who exploit their present-mindedness."

The FTC's proposed ban was supported by the American Academy of Pediatrics, the National Congress of Parents and Teachers, the Consumers Union, and the Child Welfare League, among others. But it was attacked by the National Association of Broadcasters, the Toy Manufacturers of America, and the Association of National Advertisers. The industry groups lobbied Congress to prevent any restrictions on children's ads and sued in federal court to block Pertschuk from participating in future FTC meetings on the subject. In April of 1981, three months after the inauguration of President Ronald Reagan, an FTC staff report argued that a ban on ads aimed at children would be impractical, effectively killing the proposal. "We are delighted by the FTC's reasonable recommendation," said the head of the National Association of Broadcasters.

The Saturday-morning children's ads that caused angry debates twenty years ago now seem almost quaint. Far from being banned, TV advertising aimed at kids is now broadcast twenty-four hours a day, closed-captioned and in stereo. Nickelodeon, the Disney Channel, the Cartoon Network, and the other children's cable networks are now responsible for about 80 percent of all television viewing by kids. None of these networks existed before 1979. The typical American child now spends about twenty-one hours a week watching television — roughly one and a half months of TV every year. That does not include the time children spend in front of a screen watching videos, playing video games, or using the computer. Outside of school, the typical American child spends more time watching television than doing any other activity except sleeping. During the course of a year, he or she watches more than thirty thousand TV commercials. Even the nation's youngest children are watching a great deal of television. About one-quarter of American children between the ages of two and five have a TV in their room.

perfect synergy

ALTHOUGH THE FAST FOOD chains annually spend about $3 billion on television advertising, their marketing efforts directed at children extend far beyond such conventional ads. The McDonald's Corporation now operates more than eight thousand playgrounds at its restaurants in the United States. Burger King has more than two thousand. A manufacturer of "playlands" explains why fast food operators build these largely plastic structures: "Playlands bring in children, who bring in parents, who bring in money." As American cities and towns spend less money on children's recreation, fast food restaurants have become gathering spaces for families with young children. Every month about 90 percent of American children between the ages of three and nine visit a McDonald's. The seesaws, slides, and pits full of plastic balls have proven to be an effective lure. "But when it gets down to brass tacks," a *Brandweek* article on fast food notes, "the key to attracting kids is toys, toys, toys."

The fast food industry has forged promotional links with the nation's leading toy manufacturers, giving away simple toys with children's meals and selling more elaborate ones at a discount. The major toy crazes of recent years — including Pokémon cards, Cabbage Patch Kids, and Tamogotchis — have been abetted by fast food promotions. A successful promotion easily doubles or triples the weekly sales volume of children's meals. The chains often distribute numerous versions of a toy, encouraging repeat visits by small children and adult collectors who hope to obtain complete sets. In 1999 McDonald's distributed eighty different types of Furby. According to a publication called *Tomart's Price Guide to McDonald's Happy Meal Collectibles,* some fast food giveaways are now worth hundreds of dollars.

Rod Taylor, a *Brandweek* columnist, called McDonald's 1997 Teenie Beanie Baby giveaway one of the most successful promotions in the history of American advertising. At the time McDonald's sold about 10 million Happy Meals in a typical week. Over the course of ten days in April of 1997, by including a Teenie Beanie Baby with each purchase, McDonald's sold about 100 million Happy Meals. Rarely has a marketing effort achieved such an extraordinary rate of sales among its intended consumers. Happy Meals are marketed to children between the ages of three and nine; within ten days about four Teenie

Beanie Baby Happy Meals were sold for every American child in that age group. Not all of those Happy Meals were purchased for children. Many adult collectors bought Teenie Beanie Baby Happy Meals, kept the dolls, and threw away the food.

The competition for young customers has led the fast food chains to form marketing alliances not just with toy companies, but with sports leagues and Hollywood studios. McDonald's has staged promotions with the National Basketball Association and the Olympics. Pizza Hut, Taco Bell, and KFC signed a three-year deal with the NCAA. Wendy's has linked with the National Hockey League. Burger King and Nickelodeon, Denny's and Major League Baseball, McDonald's and the Fox Kids Network have all formed partnerships that mix advertisements for fast food with children's entertainment. Burger King has sold chicken nuggets shaped like Teletubbies. McDonald's now has its own line of children's videos starring Ronald McDonald. *The Wacky Adventures of Ronald McDonald* is being produced by Klasky-Csupo, the company that makes *Rugrats* and *The Simpsons*. The videos feature the McDonaldland characters and sell for $3.49. "We see this as a great opportunity," a McDonald's executive said in a press release, "to create a more meaningful relationship between Ronald and kids."

All of these cross-promotions have strengthened the ties between Hollywood and the fast food industry. In the past few years, the major studios have started to recruit fast food executives. Susan Frank, a former director of national marketing for McDonald's, later became a marketing executive at the Fox Kids Network. She now runs a new family-oriented cable network jointly owned by Hallmark Entertainment and the Jim Henson Company, creator of the Muppets. Ken Snelgrove, who for many years worked as a marketer for Burger King and McDonald's, now works at MGM. Brad Ball, a former senior vice president of marketing at McDonald's, is now the head of marketing for Warner Brothers. Not long after being hired, Ball told the *Hollywood Reporter* that there was little difference between selling films and selling hamburgers. John Cywinski, the former head of marketing at Burger King, became the head of marketing for Walt Disney's film division in 1996, then left the job to work for McDonald's. Forty years after Bozo's first promotional appearance at a McDonald's, amid all the marketing deals, giveaways, and executive swaps, America's fast food culture has become indistinguishable from the popular culture of its children.

In May of 1996, the Walt Disney Company signed a ten-year global marketing agreement with the McDonald's Corporation. By linking with a fast food company, a Hollywood studio typically gains anywhere from $25 million to $45 million in additional advertising for a film, often doubling its ad budget. These licensing deals are usually negotiated on a per-film basis; the 1996 agreement with Disney gave McDonald's exclusive rights to that studio's output of films and videos. Some industry observers thought Disney benefited more from the deal, gaining a steady source of marketing funds. According to the terms of the agreement, Disney characters could never be depicted sitting in a McDonald's restaurant or eating any of the chain's food. In the early 1980s, the McDonald's Corporation had turned away offers to buy Disney; a decade later, McDonald's executives sounded a bit defensive about having given Disney greater control over how their joint promotions would be run. "A lot of people can't get used to the fact that two big global brands with this kind of credibility can forge this kind of working relationship," a McDonald's executive told a reporter. "It's about their theme parks, their next movie, their characters, their videos . . . It's bigger than a hamburger. It's about the integration of our two brands, long-term."

The life's work of Walt Disney and Ray Kroc had come full-circle, uniting in perfect synergy. McDonald's began to sell its hamburgers and french fries at Disney's theme parks. The ethos of McDonaldland and of Disneyland, never far apart, have finally become one. Now you can buy a Happy Meal at the Happiest Place on Earth.

the brand essence

THE BEST INSIGHT INTO the thinking of fast food marketers comes from their own words. Confidential documents from a recent McDonald's advertising campaign give a clear sense of how the restaurant chain views its customers. The McDonald's Corporation was facing a long list of problems. "Sales are decreasing," one memo noted. "People are telling us Burger King and Wendy's are doing a better job of giving . . . better food at the best price," another warned. Consumer research indicated that future sales in some key areas were at risk. "More customers are telling us," an executive wrote, "that McDonald's is a big company that just wants to sell . . . sell as much as it can." An emotional connection to McDonald's that customers had formed "as toddlers" was now eroding. The new radio and television advertising had to make people feel that McDonald's still cared about them. It had to link the McDonald's of today to the one people loved in the past. "The challenge of the campaign," wrote Ray Bergold, the chain's top marketing executive, "is to make customers believe that McDonald's is their 'Trusted Friend.'"

According to these documents, the marketing alliances with other brands were intended to create positive feelings about McDonald's, making consumers associate one thing they liked with another. Ads would link the company's french fries "to the excitement and fanaticism people feel about the NBA." The feelings of pride inspired by the Olympics would be used in ads to help launch a new hamburger with more meat than the Big Mac. The link with the Walt Disney Company was considered by far the most important, designed to "enhance perceptions of Brand McDonald's." A memo sought to explain the underlying psychology behind many visits to McDonald's: parents took their children to McDonald's because they "want the kids to love them . . . it makes them feel like a good parent." Purchasing something from Disney was the "*ultimate*" way to make kids happy, but it was too expensive to do every day. The advertising needed to capitalize on these feelings, letting parents know that "ONLY MCDONALD'S MAKES IT EASY TO GET A BIT OF DISNEY MAGIC." The ads aimed at "minivan parents" would carry an unspoken message about taking your children to McDonald's: "It's an easy way to feel like a good parent."

The fundamental goal of the "My McDonald's" campaign that stemmed from these proposals was to make a customer feel that McDonald's "cares about me" and "knows about me." A corporate memo introducing the campaign explained: "The essence McDonald's is embracing is 'Trusted Friend' . . . 'Trusted Friend' captures all the goodwill and the unique emotional connection customers have with the McDonald's experience . . . [Our goal is to make] customers believe McDonald's is their 'Trusted Friend.' Note: this should be done without using the words 'Trusted Friend' . . . Every commercial [should be] honest . . . Every message will be in good taste and feel like it comes from a trusted friend." The words "trusted friend" were never to be mentioned in the ads because doing so might prematurely "wear out a brand essence" that could prove valuable in the future for use among different national, ethnic, and age groups. Despite McDonald's faith in its trusted friends, the opening page of this memo said in bold red letters: "ANY UNAUTHORIZED USE OR COPYING OF THIS MATERIAL MAY LEAD TO CIVIL OR CRIMINAL PROSECUTION."

mcteachers and coke dudes

NOT SATISFIED WITH MARKETING to children through play-grounds, toys, cartoons, movies, videos, charities, and amusement parks, through contests, sweepstakes, games, and clubs, via television, radio, magazines, and the Internet, fast food chains are now gaining access to the last advertising-free outposts of American life. In 1993 District 11 in Colorado Springs started a nationwide trend, becoming the first public school district in the United States to place ads for Burger King in its hallways and on the sides of its school buses. Like other school systems in Colorado, District 11 faced revenue shortfalls, thanks to growing enrollments and voter hostility to tax increases for education. The initial Burger King and King Sooper ad contracts were a disappointment for the district, gaining it just $37,500 a year — little more than $1 per student. In 1996, school administrators decided to seek negotiating help from a professional, hiring Dan DeRose, president of DD Marketing, Inc., of Pueblo, Colorado. DeRose assembled special advertising packages for corporate sponsors. For $12,000, a company got five school-bus ads, hallway ads in all fifty-two of the district's schools, ads in their school newspapers, a stadium banner, ads over the stadium's public-address system during games, and free tickets to high school sporting events.

Within a year, DeRose had nearly tripled District 11's ad revenues. But his greatest success was still to come. In August of 1997, DeRose brokered a ten-year deal that made Coca-Cola the district's exclusive beverage supplier, bringing the schools up to $11 million during the life of the contract (minus DD Marketing's fee). The deal also provided free use of a 1998 Chevy Cavalier to a District 11 high school senior, chosen by lottery, who had good grades and a perfect attendance record.

District 11's marketing efforts were soon imitated by other school districts in Colorado, by districts in Pueblo, Fort Collins, Denver, and Cherry Creek. Administrators in Colorado Springs did not come up with the idea of using corporate sponsorship to cover shortfalls in a school district's budget. But they took it to a whole new level, packaging it, systematizing it, leading the way. Hundreds of public school districts across the United States are now adopting or considering similar arrangements. Children spend about seven hours a day, one hundred and fifty days a year, in school. Those hours have in the past been largely free of advertising, promotion, and market research — a source of frustration to many companies. Today the nation's fast food chains are marketing their products in public schools through conventional ad campaigns, classroom teaching materials, and lunchroom franchises, as well as a number of unorthodox means.

The proponents of advertising in the schools argue that it is necessary to prevent further cutbacks; opponents contend that schoolchildren are becoming a captive audience for marketers, compelled by law to attend school and then forced to look at ads as a means of paying for their own education. America's schools now loom as a potential gold mine for companies in search of young customers. "Discover your own river of revenue at the schoolhouse gates," urged a brochure at the 1997 Kids Power Marketing Conference. "Whether it's first-graders learning to read or teenagers shopping for their first car, we can guarantee an introduction of your product and your company to these students in the traditional setting of the classroom."

DD Marketing, with offices in Colorado Springs and Pueblo, has emerged as perhaps the nation's foremost negotiator of ad contracts for schools. Dan DeRose began his career as the founder of the Minor League Football System, serving in the late 1980s as both a team owner and a player. In 1991, he became athletic director at the University of Southern Colorado in Pueblo. During his first year, he raised $250,000 from corporate sponsors for the school's teams. Before long he was raising millions of dollars to build campus sports facilities. He was good at getting money out of big corporations, and formed DD Marketing to use this skill on behalf of schools and nonprofits. Beverage companies and athletic shoe companies had long supported college sports programs, and during the 1980s began to put up the money for new high school scoreboards. Dan DeRose saw marketing opportunities that were still untapped. After negotiating his first Colorado Springs package deal in 1996, he went to work for the Grapevine-Colleyville School District in Texas. The district would never have sought advertising, its deputy superintendent told the *Houston Chronicle*, "if it weren't for the acute need for funds." DeRose started to solicit ads not only for the district's hallways, stadiums, and buses, but also for its rooftops — so that passengers flying in or out of the nearby

Dallas–Forth Worth airport could see them — and for its voice-mail systems. "You've reached Grapevine-Colleyville school district, proud partner of Dr Pepper," was a message that DeRose proposed. Although some people in the district were skeptical about the wild ideas of this marketer from Colorado, DeRose negotiated a $3.4 million dollar exclusive deal between the Grapevine-Colleyville School District and Dr Pepper in June of 1997. And Dr Pepper ads soon appeared on school rooftops.

Dan DeRose tells reporters that his work brings money to school districts that badly need it. By pitting one beverage company against another in bidding wars for exclusive deals, he's raised the prices being offered to schools. "In Kansas City they were getting 67 cents a kid before," he told one reporter, "and now they're getting $27." The major beverage companies do not like DeRose and prefer not to deal with him. He views their hostility as a mark of success. He doesn't think that advertising in the schools will corrupt the nation's children and has little tolerance for critics of the trend. "There are critics to penicillin," he told the *Fresno Bee*. In the three years following his groundbreaking contract for School District 11 in Colorado Springs, Dan DeRose negotiated agreements for seventeen universities and sixty public school systems across the United States, everywhere from Greenville, North Carolina, to Newark, New Jersey. His 1997 deal with a school district in Derby, Kansas, included the commitment to open a Pepsi GeneratioNext Resource Center at an elementary school. Thus far, DeRose has been responsible for school and university beverage deals worth more than $200 million. He typically accepts no money up front, then charges schools a commission that takes between 25 and 35 percent of the deal's total revenues.

The nation's three major beverage manufacturers are now spending large sums to increase the amount of soda that American children consume. Coca-Cola, Pepsi, and Cadbury-Schweppes (the maker of Dr Pepper) control 90.3 percent of the U.S. market, but have been hurt by declining sales in Asia. Americans already drink soda at an annual rate of about fifty-six gallons per person — that's nearly six hundred twelve-ounce cans of soda per person. Coca-Cola has set itself the goal of raising consumption of its products in the United States by at least 25 percent a year. The adult market is stagnant; selling more soda to kids has become one of the easiest ways to meet sales projections. "Influencing elementary school students is very important to soft drink marketers," an article in the January 1999 issue of *Beverage*

Industry explained, "because children are still establishing their tastes and habits." Eight-year-olds are considered ideal customers; they have about sixty-five years of purchasing in front of them. "Entering the schools makes perfect sense," the trade journal concluded.

The fast food chains also benefit enormously when children drink more soda. The chicken nuggets, hamburgers, and other main courses sold at fast food restaurants usually have the lowest profit margins. Soda has by far the highest. "We at McDonald's are thankful," a top executive once told the *New York Times*, "that people like drinks with their sandwiches." Today McDonald's sells more Coca-Cola than anyone else in the world. The fast food chains purchase Coca-Cola syrup for about $4.25 a gallon. A medium Coke that sells for $1.29 contains roughly 9 cents' worth of syrup. Buying a large Coke for $1.49 instead, as the cute girl behind the counter always suggests, will add another 3 cents' worth of syrup — and another 17 cents in pure profit for McDonald's.

"Liquid Candy," a 1999 study by the Center for Science in the Public Interest, describes who is not benefiting from the beverage industry's latest marketing efforts: the nation's children. In 1978, the typical teenage boy in the United States drank about seven ounces of soda every day; today he drinks nearly three times that amount, deriving 9 percent of his daily caloric intake from soft drinks. Soda consumption among teenaged girls has doubled within the same period, reaching an average of twelve ounces a day. A significant number of teenage boys are now drinking five or more cans of soda every day. Each can contains the equivalent of about ten teaspoons of sugar. Coke, Pepsi, Mountain Dew, and Dr Pepper also contain caffeine. These sodas provide empty calories and have replaced far more nutritious beverages in the American diet. Excessive soda consumption in childhood can lead to calcium deficiencies and a greater likelihood of bone fractures. Twenty years ago, teenage boys in the United States drank twice as much milk as soda; now they drink twice as much soda as milk. Soft-drink consumption has also become commonplace among American toddlers. About one-fifth of the nation's one- and two-year-olds now drink soda. "In one of the most despicable marketing gambits," Michael Jacobson, the author of "Liquid Candy" reports, "Pepsi, Dr Pepper and Seven-Up encourage feeding soft drinks to babies by licensing their logos to a major maker of baby bottles, Munchkin Bottling, Inc." A 1997 study published in the *Journal of Dentistry for Children* found that many infants were indeed being fed soda in those bottles.

The school marketing efforts of the large soda companies have not gone entirely unopposed. Administrators in San Francisco and Seattle have refused to allow any advertising in their schools. "It's our responsibility to make it clear that schools are here to serve children, not commercial interests," declared a member of the San Francisco Board of Education. Individual protests have occurred as well. In March of 1998, 1,200 students at Greenbrier High School in Evans, Georgia, assembled in the school parking lot, many of them wearing red and white clothing, to spell out the word "Coke." It was Coke in Education Day at the school, and a dozen Coca-Cola executives had come for the occasion. Greenbrier High was hoping for a $500 prize, which had been offered to the local high school that came up with the best marketing plan for Coca-Cola discount cards. As part of the festivities, Coke executives had lectured the students on economics and helped them bake a Coca-Cola cake. A photographer was hoisted above the parking lot by a crane, ready to record the human C-O-K-E for posterity. When the photographer started to take pictures, Mike Cameron — a Greenbrier senior, standing amid the letter *C* — suddenly revealed a T-shirt that said "Pepsi." His act of defiance soon received nationwide publicity, as did the fact that he was immediately suspended from school. The principal said Cameron could have been suspended for a week for the prank, but removed him from classes for just a day. "I don't consider this a prank," Mike Cameron told the *Washington Post*. "I like to be an individual. That's the way I am."

Most school advertising campaigns are more subtle than Greenbrier High's Coke in Education Day. The spiraling cost of textbooks has led thousands of American school districts to use corporate-sponsored teaching materials. A 1998 study of these teaching materials by the Consumers Union found that 80 percent were biased, providing students with incomplete or slanted information that favored the sponsor's products and views. Procter & Gamble's *Decision Earth* program taught that clear-cut logging was actually good for the environment; teaching aids distributed by the Exxon Education Foundation said that fossil fuels created few environmental problems and that alternative sources of energy were too expensive; a study guide sponsored by the American Coal Foundation dismissed fears of a greenhouse effect, claiming that "the earth could benefit rather than be harmed from increased carbon dioxide." The Consumers Union found Pizza Hut's Book It! Program — which awards a free Personal Pan Pizza to children who reach targeted reading levels — to be "highly commercial." About twenty million elementary school students participated in Book It! during the 1999–2000 school year; Pizza Hut recently expanded the program to include a million preschoolers.

Lifetime Learning Systems is the nation's largest marketer and producer of corporate-sponsored teaching aids. The group claims that its publications are used by more than 60 million students every year. "Now you can enter the classroom through custom-made learning materials created with your specific marketing objectives in mind," Lifetime Learning said in one of its pitches to corporate sponsors. "Through these materials, your product or point of view becomes the focus of discussions in the classroom," it said in another, ". . . the centerpiece in a dynamic process that generates long-term awareness and lasting attitudinal change." The tax cuts that are hampering America's schools have proved to be a marketing bonanza for companies like Exxon, Pizza Hut, and McDonald's. The money that these corporations spend on their "educational" materials is fully tax-deductible.

The fast food chains run ads on Channel One, the commercial television network whose programming is now shown in classrooms, almost every school day, to eight million of the nation's middle, junior, and high school students — a teen audience fifty times larger than that of MTV. The fast food chains place ads with Star Broadcasting, a Minnesota company that pipes Top 40 radio into school hallways, lounges, and cafeterias. And the chains now promote their food by selling school lunches, accepting a lower profit margin in order to create brand loyalty. At least twenty school districts in the United States have their own Subway franchises; an additional fifteen hundred districts have Subway delivery contracts; and nine operate Subway sandwich carts. Taco Bell products are sold in about forty-five hundred school cafeterias. Pizza Hut, Domino's, and McDonald's are now selling food in the nation's schools. The American School Food Service Association estimates that about 30 percent of the public high schools in the United States offer branded fast food. Elementary schools in Fort Collins, Colorado, now serve food from Pizza Hut, McDonald's, and Subway on special lunch days. "We try to be more like the fast food places where these kids are hanging out," a Colorado school administrator told the *Denver Post*. "We want kids to think school lunch is a cool thing, the cafeteria a cool place, that we're 'with it,' that we're not institutional . . ."

The new corporate partnerships often put school officials in an awkward position. The Coca-Cola deal that DD Marketing negotiated for Colorado Springs School District 11 was not as lucrative as it first seemed. The contract specified annual sales quotas. School District 11 was obligated to sell at least seventy thousand cases of Coca-Cola products a year, within the first three years of the contract, or it would face reduced payments by Coke. During the 1997–98 school year, the district's elementary, middle, and high schools sold only twenty-one thousand cases of Coca-Cola products. Cara DeGette, the news editor of the *Colorado Springs Independent,* a weekly newspaper, obtained a memorandum sent to school principals by John Bushey, a District 11 administrator. On September 28, 1998, at the start of the new school year, Bushey warned the principals that beverage sales were falling short of projections and that as a result school revenues might be affected. Allow students to bring Coke products into the classrooms, he suggested; move Coke machines to places where they would be accessible to students all day. "Research shows that vendor purchases are closely linked to availability," Bushey wrote. "Location, location, location is the key." If the principals felt uncomfortable allowing kids to drink Coca-Cola during class, he recommended letting them drink the fruit juices, teas, and bottled waters also sold in the Coke machines. At the end of the memo, John Bushey signed his name and then identified himself as "the Coke dude."

Bushey left Colorado Springs in 2000 and moved to Florida. He is now the principal of the high school in Celebration, a planned community run by The Celebration Company, a subsidiary of Disney.

3 / behind the counter

THE VIEW OF COLORADO SPRINGS from Gold Camp Road is
spectacular. The old road takes you from the city limits to Cripple Creek, once a gold mining town with real outlaws, now an
outpost of casino gambling full of one-armed bandits and day-
trippers from Aurora. The tourist buses drive to Cripple Creek
on Highway 67, which is paved. Gold Camp Road is a dirt road
through the foothills of Pikes Peak, a former wagon trail that has narrow hairpin turns, no guardrails, and plenty of sheer drops. For years,
kids from Cheyenne Mountain High School have come up here on
weekend nights, parked at spots with good aerial views, and partied.
On a clear night the stars in the sky and the lights of the city seem
linked, as though one were reflecting the other. The cars and trucks on
Interstate 25, heading north to Denver and south toward Pueblo, are
tiny, slow-moving specks of white. The lights dwindle as the city gives
way to the plains; at the horizon the land looks darker than the sky.
The great beauty of this scene is diminished when the sun rises and
you can clearly see what's happening down below.

Driving through the neighborhoods of Colorado Springs often
seems like passing through layers of sedimentary rock, each one providing a snapshot of a different historical era. Downtown Colorado
Springs still has an old-fashioned, independent spirit. Aside from a
Kinko's, a Bruegger's Bagel Bakery, a Subway, and a couple of Starbucks, there are no chain stores, not a single Gap in sight. An eclectic
mixture of locally owned businesses line Tejon Street, the main drag.
The Chinook Bookshop, toward the north end, is as fiercely independent as they come — the sort of literate and civilized bookstore going
out of business nationwide. Further down Tejon there's an ice cream
parlor named Michelle's that has been in business for almost fifty

years and, around the corner, there's a western wear shop called Lorig's that's outfitted local ranchers since 1932. An old movie palace, nicknamed "the Peak" and renovated with lots of neon, has a funky charm that could never be mass produced. But when you leave downtown and drive northeast, you head toward a whole new world.

The north end of the city near Colorado College is full of old Victorian houses and Mission-style bungalows from the early part of this century. Then come Spanish-style and adobe houses that were popular between the world wars. Then come split-level colonials and ranch-style houses from the *Leave It to Beaver* era, small, modest, cheery homes.

Once you hit Academy Boulevard, you are surrounded by the hard, tangible evidence of what has happened in Colorado during the last twenty years. Immense subdivisions with names like Sagewood, Summerfield, and Fairfax Ridge blanket the land, thousands upon thousands of nearly identical houses — the architectural equivalent of fast food — covering the prairie without the slightest respect for its natural forms, built on hilltops and ridgetops, just begging for a lightning strike, ringed by gates and brick walls and puny, newly planted trees that bend in the wind. The houses seem not to have been constructed by hand but manufactured by some gigantic machine, cast in the same mold and somehow dropped here fully made. You can easily get lost in these new subdivisions, lost for hours passing from Nor'wood, to Briargate, to Stetson Hills, from Antelope Meadows to Chapel Ridge, without ever finding anything of significance to differentiate one block from another — except their numbers. Roads end without warning, and sidewalks run straight into the prairie, blocked by tall, wild grasses that have not yet been turned into lawns.

Academy Boulevard lies at the heart of the new sprawl, serving as its main north–south artery. Every few miles, clusters of fast food joints seem to repeat themselves, Burger Kings, Wendy's, and McDonald's, Subways, Pizza Huts, and Taco Bells, they keep appearing along the road, the same buildings and signage replaying like a tape loop. You can drive for twenty minutes, pass another fast food cluster, and feel like you've gotten nowhere. In the bumper-to-bumper traffic of the evening rush hour, when the cars and the pavement and the strip malls are bathed in twilight, when the mountains in the distance are momentarily obscured, Academy Boulevard looks just like Harbor Boulevard in Anaheim, except newer. It looks like countless other retail strips in Orange County — and the resemblance is hardly coincidental.

space mountain

THE NEW HOUSING DEVELOPMENTS in Colorado Springs not only resemble those of southern California, they are inhabited by thousands of people who've recently left California. An entire way of life, along with its economic underpinnings, has been transposed from the West Coast to the Rockies. Since the early 1990s Colorado Springs has been one of the fastest-growing cities in the nation. The mountains, clear air, wide-open spaces, and unusually mild climate have drawn people tired of the traffic, crime, and pollution elsewhere. About a third of the city's inhabitants have lived there less than five years. In many ways Colorado Springs today is what Los Angeles was fifty years ago — a mecca for the disenchanted middle class, a harbinger of cultural trends, a glimpse of the future. Since 1970 the population of the Colorado Springs metropolitan area has more than doubled, reaching about half a million. The city is now an exemplar of low-density sprawl. Denver's population is about four times larger, and yet Colorado Springs covers more land.

Much like Los Angeles, Colorado Springs was a sleepy tourist town in the early part of the twentieth century, an enclave of wealthy invalids and retirees, surrounded by ranchland. Nicknamed "Little London," the city was a playground for the offspring of eastern financiers, penniless aristocrats, and miners who'd struck it rich in Cripple Creek. The town's leading attractions were the Broadmoor Hotel and the Garden of the Gods, an assortment of large rock formations. During the Great Depression, tourism plummeted, people moved away, and about one-fifth of the city's housing sat vacant. The outbreak of World War II provided a great economic opportunity. Like Los Angeles, Colorado Springs soon became dependent on military spending. The opening of Camp Carson and Peterson Army Air Base brought thousands of troops to the area, along with a direct capital investment of $30 million and an annual payroll of twice that amount. After the war, Colorado Springs gained a series of new military bases, thanks to its strategic location (midcontinent, beyond the range of Soviet bombers), its fine weather, and the friendships formed between local busi-

nessmen and air force officers at the Broadmoor. In 1951, the Air Defense Command moved to the city, eventually becoming the North
American Aerospace Command, with its outpost deep within Cheyenne Mountain. Three years later, 18,000 acres north of town were
chosen as the site of the new Air Force Academy. The number of army
and air force personnel stationed in Colorado Springs subsequently
grew to be larger than the city's entire population before World
War II.

Although the local economy is far more diversified today, nearly
half the jobs in Colorado Springs still depend upon military spending.
During the 1990s, while major bases were being shut down across the
country, new facilities kept opening in Colorado Springs. Much of the
Star Wars antimissile defense system is being designed and tested at
Schriever Air Force Base, a dozen miles east of the city. And Peterson
Air Force Base now houses one of America's newest and most high-
tech units — the Space Command. It launches, operates, and defends
America's military satellites. It tests, maintains, and upgrades the nation's ballistic missiles. And it guides research on exotic space-based
weaponry to attack enemy satellites, aircraft, and even targets on the
ground. Officers at the Space Command believe that before long the
United States will fight its first war in space. Should that day ever
come, Colorado Springs will be at the center of the action. The motto
of a local air force unit promises a new kind of American firepower:
"In Your Face from Outer Space."

The presence of these high-tech military installations attracted
defense contractors to Colorado Springs, mainly from California.
Kaman Services arrived in 1957. Hewlett Packard followed in 1962.
TRW, a southern California firm, opened its first Colorado Springs
branch in 1968. Litton Data Systems moved one of its divisions from
Van Nuys, California, to Colorado Springs in 1976. Not long afterward
Ford Aerospace sold ten acres of land in Orange County and used the
money to buy three hundred acres in Colorado Springs. Today a long
list of defense contractors does business in the city. The advanced
communications networks installed to serve those companies and the
military have drawn computer chip manufacturers, telemarketers, and
software companies to Colorado Springs. The quality of life is a big
selling point, along with the well-educated workforce and the local
attitudes toward labor. A publication distributed by the Colorado
Springs Chamber of Commerce notes that in the city's private industry, the rate of union membership stands at 0.0 percent. Colorado

Springs now views itself as a place on the cutting edge, the high-tech capital of the Rockies. Business leaders promote the town with nicknames like "Silicon Mountain," "Space Mountain," and "The Space Capital of the Free World."

The new businesses and residents from southern California brought a new set of attitudes. In 1946, R. C. Hoiles, the owner of the *Orange County Register* and later the founder of the Freedom Newspaper chain, purchased the largest daily newspaper in Colorado Springs, the *Gazette-Telegraph*. Hoiles was politically conservative, a champion of competition and free enterprise; his editorials had attacked Herbert Hoover for being too left-wing. In the 1980s the Freedom Newspaper chain purchased the *Gazette*'s only rival in town, the *Colorado Springs Sun*, a struggling paper with a more liberal outlook. After buying the *Sun*, Freedom Newspapers fired all its employees and shut it down. In 1990, James Dobson decided to move Focus on the Family, a religious organization, from the Los Angeles suburb of Pomona to Colorado Springs. Dobson is a child psychologist and radio personality as well as the author of a best-selling guide for parents, *Dare to Discipline* (1970). He blames weak parents for the excesses of the sixties youth counterculture, advocates spanking disobedient children with a "neutral object," and says that parents must convey to preschoolers two fundamental messages: "(1) I love you, little one, more than you can possibly understand . . . (2) Because I love you so much, I must teach you to obey me." Although less well known than Jerry Falwell's Moral Majority and Pat Robertson's Christian Coalition, Dobson's Focus on the Family generates much larger annual revenues.

The arrival of Focus on the Family helped turn Colorado Springs into a magnet for evangelical Christian groups. The city had always been more conservative than Denver, but that conservatism was usually expressed in the sort of live-and-let-live attitude common in the American West. During the early 1990s, religious groups in Colorado Springs became outspoken opponents of feminism, homosexuality, and Darwin's theory of evolution. The city became the headquarters for roughly sixty religious organizations, some of them large, some of them painfully obscure. Members and supporters of the International Bible Society, the Christian Booksellers Association, the World Radio Missionary Fellowship, Young Life, the Fellowship of Christian Cowboys, and World Christian Incorporated, among others, settled in Colorado Springs.

Today there is not a single elected official in Colorado Springs — or

in El Paso County, the surrounding jurisdiction — who's a registered
Democrat. Indeed, the Democratic Party did not even run a candidate for Congress there in 2000. The political changes that have lately
swept through the city have also taken place, in a less extreme form,
throughout the Rocky Mountain West. A generation ago, the region
was one of the most liberal in the country. In 1972, all of the governors in the eight mountain states — Arizona, Colorado, Montana,
Nevada, New Mexico, Wyoming, even Idaho and Utah — were Democrats. By 1998, all of the governors in these states were Republicans, as
were three-quarters of the U.S. senators. The region is now more
staunchly Republican than the American South.

As in Colorado Springs, the huge influx of white, middle-class voters from southern California has played a decisive role in the Rocky
Mountain West's shift to the right. During the early 1990s, for the first
time in California history, more people moved out of the state than
into it. Between 1990 and 1995, approximately one million people left
southern California, many of them heading to the mountain states.
William H. Frey, a former professor of demography at the University
of Michigan, has called this migration "the new white flight." In 1998,
the white population of California fell below 50 percent for the first
time since the Gold Rush. The exodus of whites has changed California's political equation as well, turning the birthplace of the Reagan
Revolution into one of the nation's most solidly Democratic states.

Many of the problems that caused white, middle-class families to
leave southern California are now appearing in the Rocky Mountain
states. During the early 1990s, about 100,000 people moved to Colorado every year. But spending on government services did not increase
at a corresponding rate — because Colorado voters enacted a Taxpayers Bill of Rights in 1992 that placed strict limits on new government spending. The initiative was modeled after California's Proposition 13 and championed by Douglas Bruce, a Colorado Springs
landlord who'd recently arrived from Los Angeles. By the late 1990s,
Colorado's spending on education ranked forty-ninth in the nation;
fire departments throughout the state were understaffed; and parts of
Interstate 25 in Colorado Springs were clogged with three times the
number of cars that the highway was designed to hold. Meanwhile, the
state government had an annual surplus of about $700 million that by
law could not be used to solve any of these problems. The development along Colorado's Front Range is not yet as all-encompassing as
the sprawl of Los Angeles — where one-third of the surface area is

now covered by freeways, roads, and parking lots — but someday it may be.

Colorado Springs now has the feel of a city whose identity is not yet fixed. Many longtime residents strongly oppose the extremism of the newcomers, sporting bumper stickers that say, "Don't Californicate Colorado." The city is now torn between opposing visions of what America should be. Colorado Springs has twenty-eight Charismatic Christian churches and almost twice as many pawnbrokers, a Lord's Vineyard Bookstore and a First Amendment Adult Bookstore, a Christian Medical and Dental Society and a Holey Rollers Tattoo Parlor. It has a Christian summer camp whose founder, David Noebel, outlined the dangers of rock 'n' roll· in his pamphlet *Communism, Hypnotism, and the Beatles*. It has a gay entertainment complex called The Hide & Seek, where the Gay Rodeo Association meets. It has a public school principal who recently disciplined a group of sixth-grade girls for reading a book on witchcraft and allegedly casting spells. The loopiness once associated with Los Angeles has come full-blown to Colorado Springs — the strange, creative energy that crops up where the future's consciously being made, where people walk the fine line separating a visionary from a total nutcase. At the start of a new century, all sorts of things seem possible there. The cultural and the physical landscapes of Colorado Springs are up for grabs.

Despite all the talk in Colorado about aerospace, biotech, computer software, telecommunications, and other industries of the future, the largest private employer in the state today is the restaurant industry. In Colorado Springs, the restaurant industry has grown much faster than the population. Over the last three decades the number of restaurants has increased fivefold. The number of chain restaurants has increased tenfold. In 1967, Colorado Springs had a total of twenty chain restaurants. Now it has twenty-one McDonald's.

The fast food chains feed off the sprawl of Colorado Springs, accelerate it, and help set its visual tone. They build large signs to attract motorists and look at cars the way predators view herds of prey. The chains thrive on traffic, lots of it, and put new restaurants at intersections where traffic is likely to increase, where development is heading but real estate prices are still low. Fast food restaurants often serve as the shock troops of sprawl, landing early and pointing the way. Some chains prefer to play follow the leader: when a new McDonald's opens, other fast food restaurants soon open nearby on the assumption that it must be a good location.

Regardless of the billions spent on marketing and promotion, all the ads on radio and TV, all the efforts to create brand loyalty, the major chains must live with the unsettling fact that more than 70 percent of fast food visits are "impulsive." The decision to stop for fast food is made on the spur of the moment, without much thought. The vast majority of customers do not set out to eat at a Burger King, a Wendy's, or a McDonald's. Often, they're not even planning to stop for food — until they see a sign, a familiar building, a set of golden arches. Fast food, like the tabloids at a supermarket checkout, is an impulse buy. In order to succeed, fast food restaurants must be seen.

The McDonald's Corporation has perfected the art of restaurant site selection. In the early days Ray Kroc flew in a Cessna to find schools, aiming to put new restaurants nearby. McDonald's later used helicopters to assess regional growth patterns, looking for cheap land along highways and roads that would lie at the heart of future suburbs. In the 1980s, the chain become one of the world's leading purchasers of commercial satellite photography, using it to predict sprawl from outer space. McDonald's later developed a computer software program called Quintillion that automated its site-selection process, combining satellite imagery with detailed maps, demographic information, CAD drawings, and sales information from existing stores. "Geographic information systems" like Quintillion are now routinely used as site-selection tools by fast food chains and other retailers. As one marketing publication observed, the software developed by McDonald's permits businessmen to "spy on their customers with the same equipment once used to fight the cold war."

The McDonald's Corporation has used Colorado Springs as a test site for other types of restaurant technology, for software and machines designed to cut labor costs and serve fast food even faster. Steve Bigari, who owns five local McDonald's, showed me the new contraptions at his place on Constitution Avenue. It was a rounded, postmodern McDonald's on the eastern edge of the city. The drive-through lanes had automatic sensors buried in the asphalt to monitor the traffic. Robotic drink machines selected the proper cups, filled them with ice, and then filled them with soda. Dispensers powered by compressed carbon dioxide shot out uniform spurts of ketchup and mustard. An elaborate unit emptied frozen french fries from a white plastic bin into wire-mesh baskets for frying, lowered the baskets into hot oil, lifted them a few minutes later and gave them a brief shake, put them back into the oil until the fries were perfectly cooked, and then dumped the fries underneath heat lamps, crisp and ready to be served. Television monitors in the kitchen instantly displayed the customer's order. And advanced computer software essentially ran the kitchen, assigning tasks to various workers for maximum efficiency, predicting future orders on the basis of ongoing customer flow.

Bigari was cordial, good-natured, passionate about his work, proud of the new devices. He told me the new software brought the "just in time" production philosophy of Japanese automobile plants to the fast food business, a philosophy that McDonald's has renamed Made for You. As he demonstrated one contraption after another — including a wireless hand-held menu that uses radio waves to transmit orders — a group of construction workers across the street put the finishing touches on a new subdivision called Constitution Hills. The streets had patriotic names, and the cattle ranch down the road was for sale.

throughput

EVERY SATURDAY ELISA ZAMOT gets up at 5:15 in the morning. It's a struggle, and her head feels groggy as she steps into the shower. Her little sisters, Cookie and Sabrina, are fast asleep in their beds. By 5:30, Elisa's showered, done her hair, and put on her McDonald's uniform. She's sixteen, bright-eyed and olive-skinned, pretty and petite, ready for another day of work. Elisa's mother usually drives her the half-mile or so to the restaurant, but sometimes Elisa walks, leaving home before the sun rises. Her family's modest townhouse sits beside a busy highway on the south side of Colorado Springs, in a largely poor and working-class neighborhood. Throughout the day, sounds of traffic fill the house, the steady whoosh of passing cars. But when Elisa heads for work, the streets are quiet, the sky's still dark, and the lights are out in the small houses and rental apartments along the road.

When Elisa arrives at McDonald's, the manager unlocks the door and lets her in. Sometimes the husband-and-wife cleaning crew are just finishing up. More often, it's just Elisa and the manager in the restaurant, surrounded by an empty parking lot. For the next hour or so, the two of them get everything ready. They turn on the ovens and grills. They go downstairs into the basement and get food and supplies for the morning shift. They get the paper cups, wrappers, cardboard containers, and packets of condiments. They step into the big freezer and get the frozen bacon, the frozen pancakes, and the frozen cinnamon rolls. They get the frozen hash browns, the frozen biscuits, the frozen McMuffins. They get the cartons of scrambled egg mix and orange juice mix. They bring the food upstairs and start preparing it before any customers appear, thawing some things in the microwave and cooking other things on the grill. They put the cooked food in special cabinets to keep it warm.

The restaurant opens for business at seven o'clock, and for the next hour or so, Elisa and the manager hold down the fort, handling all the orders. As the place starts to get busy, other employees arrive. Elisa works behind the counter. She takes orders and hands food to customers from breakfast through lunch. When she finally walks home, after seven hours of standing at a cash register, her feet hurt. She's wiped out. She comes through the front door, flops onto the living room couch, and turns on the TV. And the next morning she gets up at 5:15 again and starts the same routine.

Up and down Academy Boulevard, along South Nevada, Circle Drive, and Woodman Road, teenagers like Elisa run the fast food restaurants of Colorado Springs. Fast food kitchens often seem like a scene from *Bugsy Malone*, a film in which all the actors are children pretending to be adults. No other industry in the United States has a workforce so dominated by adolescents. About two-thirds of the nation's fast food workers are under the age of twenty. Teenagers open the fast food outlets in the morning, close them at night, and keep them going at all hours in between. Even the managers and assistant managers are sometimes in their late teens. Unlike Olympic gymnastics — an activity in which teenagers consistently perform at a higher level than adults — there's nothing about the work in a fast food kitchen that requires young employees. Instead of relying upon a small, stable, well-paid, and well-trained workforce, the fast food industry seeks out part-time, unskilled workers who are willing to accept low pay. Teenagers have been the perfect candidates for these jobs, not only because they are less expensive to hire than adults, but also because their youthful inexperience makes them easier to control.

The labor practices of the fast food industry have their origins in the assembly line systems adopted by American manufacturers in the early twentieth century. Business historian Alfred D. Chandler has argued that a high rate of "throughput" was the most important aspect of these mass production systems. A factory's throughput is the speed and volume of its flow — a much more crucial measurement, according to Chandler, than the number of workers it employs or the value of its machinery. With innovative technology and the proper organization, a small number of workers can produce an enormous amount of goods cheaply. Throughput is all about increasing the speed of assembly, about doing things faster in order to make more.

Although the McDonald brothers had never encountered the term "throughput" or studied "scientific management," they instinctively grasped the underlying principles and applied them in the Speedee Service System. The restaurant operating scheme they developed has been widely adopted and refined over the past half century. The ethos of the assembly line remains at its core. The fast food industry's obsession with throughput has altered the way millions of Americans work, turned commercial kitchens into small factories, and changed familiar foods into commodities that are manufactured.

At Burger King restaurants, frozen hamburger patties are placed on a conveyer belt and emerge from a broiler ninety seconds later fully cooked. The ovens at Pizza Hut and at Domino's also use conveyer belts to ensure standardized cooking times. The ovens at McDonald's look like commercial laundry presses, with big steel hoods that swing down and grill hamburgers on both sides at once. The burgers, chicken, french fries, and buns are all frozen when they arrive at a McDonald's. The shakes and sodas begin as syrup. At Taco Bell restaurants the food is "assembled," not prepared. The guacamole isn't made by workers in the kitchen; it's made at a factory in Michoacán, Mexico, then frozen and shipped north. The chain's taco meat arrives frozen and precooked in vacuum-sealed plastic bags. The beans are dehydrated and look like brownish corn flakes. The cooking process is fairly simple. "Everything's add water," a Taco Bell employee told me. "Just add hot water."

Although Richard and Mac McDonald introduced the division of labor to the restaurant business, it was a McDonald's executive named Fred Turner who created a production system of unusual thoroughness and attention to detail. In 1958, Turner put together an operations and training manual for the company that was seventy-five pages long, specifying how almost everything should be done. Hamburgers were always to be placed on the grill in six neat rows; french fries had to be exactly 0.28 inches thick. The McDonald's operations manual today has ten times the number of pages and weighs about four pounds. Known within the company as "the Bible," it contains precise instructions on how various appliances should be used, how each item on the menu should look, and how employees should greet customers. Operators who disobey these rules can lose their franchises. Cooking instructions are not only printed in the manual, they are often designed into the machines. A McDonald's kitchen is full of buzzers and flashing lights that tell employees what to do.

At the front counter, computerized cash registers issue their own commands. Once an order has been placed, buttons light up and suggest other menu items that can be added. Workers at the counter are told to increase the size of an order by recommending special promotions, pushing dessert, pointing out the financial logic behind the purchase of a larger drink. While doing so, they are instructed to be upbeat and friendly. "Smile with a greeting and make a positive first impression," a Burger King training manual suggests. "Show them you are GLAD TO SEE THEM. Include eye contact with the cheerful greeting."

The strict regimentation at fast food restaurants creates standardized products. It increases the throughput. And it gives fast food companies an enormous amount of power over their employees. "When management determines exactly how every task is to be done . . . and can impose its own rules about pace, output, quality, and technique," the sociologist Robin Leidner has noted, "[it] makes workers increasingly interchangeable." The management no longer depends upon the talents or skills of its workers — those things are built into the operating system and machines. Jobs that have been "de-skilled" can be filled cheaply. The need to retain any individual worker is greatly reduced by the ease with which he or she can be replaced.

Teenagers have long provided the fast food industry with the bulk of its workforce. The industry's rapid growth coincided with the babyboom expansion of that age group. Teenagers were in many ways the ideal candidates for these low-paying jobs. Since most teenagers still lived at home, they could afford to work for wages too low to support an adult, and until recently, their limited skills attracted few other employers. A job at a fast food restaurant became an American rite of passage, a first job soon left behind for better things. The flexible terms of employment in the fast food industry also attracted housewives who needed extra income. As the number of baby-boom teenagers declined, the fast food chains began to hire other marginalized workers: recent immigrants, the elderly, and the handicapped.

English is now the second language of at least one-sixth of the nation's restaurant workers, and about one-third of that group speaks no

English at all. The proportion of fast food workers who cannot speak English is even higher. Many know only the names of the items on the menu; they speak "McDonald's English."

The fast food industry now employs some of the most disadvantaged members of American society. It often teaches basic job skills — such as getting to work on time — to people who can barely read, whose lives have been chaotic or shut off from the mainstream. Many individual franchisees are genuinely concerned about the well-being of their workers. But the stance of the fast food industry on issues involving employee training, the minimum wage, labor unions, and overtime pay strongly suggests that its motives in hiring the young, the poor, and the handicapped are hardly altruistic.

stroking

AT A 1999 conference on foodservice equipment, top American executives from Burger King, McDonald's, and Tricon Global Restaurants, Inc. (the owner of Taco Bell, Pizza Hut, and KFC) appeared together on a panel to discuss labor shortages, employee training, computerization, and the latest kitchen technology. The three corporations now employ about 3.7 million people worldwide, operate about 60,000 restaurants, and open a new fast food restaurant every two hours. Putting aside their intense rivalry for customers, the executives had realized at a gathering the previous evening that when it came to labor issues, they were in complete agreement. "We've come to the conclusion that we're in support of each other," Dave Brewer, the vice president of engineering at KFC, explained. "We are aligned as a team to support this industry." One of the most important goals they held in common was the redesign of kitchen equipment so that less money needed to be spent training workers. "Make the equipment intuitive, make it so that the job is easier to do right than to do wrong," advised Jerry Sus, the leading equipment systems engineer at McDonald's. "The easier it is for him [the worker] to use, the easier it is for us not to have to train him." John Reckert — director of strategic operations and of research and development at Burger King — felt optimistic about the benefits that new technology would bring the industry. "We can develop equipment that only works one way," Reckert said. "There are many different ways today that employees can abuse our product, mess up the flow . . . If the equipment only allows one process, there's very little to train." Instead of giving written instructions to crew members, another panelist suggested, rely as much as possible on photographs of menu items, and "if there are instructions, make them very simple, write them at a fifth-grade level, and write them in Spanish and English." All of the executives agreed that "zero training" was the fast food industry's ideal, though it might not ever be attained.

While quietly spending enormous sums on research and technology to eliminate employee training, the fast food chains have accepted hundreds of millions of dollars in government subsidies for "training" their workers. Through federal programs such as the Targeted Jobs Tax Credit and its successor, the Work Opportunity Tax Credit, the chains have for years claimed tax credits of up to $2,400 for each new low-income worker they hired. In 1996 an investigation by the U.S. Department of Labor concluded that 92 percent of these workers would have been hired by the companies anyway — and that their new jobs were part-time, provided little training, and came with no benefits. These federal subsidy programs were created to reward American companies that gave job training to the poor.

Attempts to end these federal subsidies have been strenuously opposed by the National Council of Chain Restaurants and its allies in Congress. The Work Opportunity Tax Credit program was renewed in 1996. It offered as much as $385 million in subsidies the following year. Fast food restaurants had to employ a worker for only four hundred hours to receive the federal money — and then could get more money as soon as that worker quit and was replaced. American taxpayers have in effect subsidized the industry's high turnover rate, providing company tax breaks for workers who are employed for just a few months and receive no training. The industry front group formed to defend these government subsidies is called the "Committee for Employment Opportunities." Its chief lobbyist, Bill Signer, told the *Houston Chronicle* there was nothing wrong with the use of federal subsidies to create low-paying, low-skilled, short-term jobs for the poor. Trying to justify the minimal amount of training given to these workers, Signer said, "They've got to crawl before they can walk."

The employees whom the fast food industry expects to crawl are by far the biggest group of low-wage workers in the United States today. The nation has about 1 million migrant farm workers and about 3.5 million fast food workers. Although picking strawberries is orders of magnitude more difficult than cooking hamburgers, both jobs are now filled by people who are generally young, unskilled, and willing to work long hours for low pay. Moreover, the turnover rates for both jobs are among the highest in the American economy. The annual turnover rate in the fast food industry is now about 300 to 400 percent. The typical fast food worker quits or is fired every three to four months.

The fast food industry pays the minimum wage to a higher proportion of its workers than any other American industry. Consequently, a low minimum wage has long been a crucial part of the fast food industry's business plan. Between 1968 and 1990, the years when the fast food chains expanded at their fastest rate, the real value of the U.S. minimum wage fell by almost 40 percent. In the late 1990s, the real value of the U.S. minimum wage still remained about 27 percent lower than it was in the late 1960s. Nevertheless, the National Restaurant Association (NRA) has vehemently opposed any rise in the minimum wage at the federal, state, or local level. About sixty large foodservice companies — including Jack in the Box, Wendy's, Chevy's, and Red Lobster — have backed congressional legislation that would essentially eliminate the federal minimum wage by allowing states to disregard it. Pete Meersman, the president of the Colorado Restaurant Association, advocates creating a federal guest worker program to import low-wage foodservice workers from overseas.

While the real value of the wages paid to restaurant workers has declined for the past three decades, the earnings of restaurant company executives have risen considerably. According to a 1997 survey in *Nation's Restaurant News*, the average corporate executive bonus was $131,000, an increase of 20 percent over the previous year. Increasing the federal minimum wage by a dollar would add about two cents to the cost of a fast food hamburger.

In 1938, at the height of the Great Depression, Congress passed legislation to prevent employers from exploiting the nation's most vulnerable workers. The Fair Labor Standards Act established the first federal minimum wage. It also imposed limitations on child labor. And it mandated that employees who work more than forty hours a week be paid overtime wages for each additional hour. The overtime wage was set at a minimum of one and a half times the regular wage.

Today few employees in the fast food industry qualify for overtime — and even fewer are paid it. Roughly 90 percent of the nation's fast food workers are paid an hourly wage, provided no benefits, and scheduled to work only as needed. Crew members are employed "at will." If the restaurant's busy, they're kept longer than usual. If business is slow, they're sent home early. Managers try to make sure that each worker is employed less than forty hours a week, thereby avoiding any overtime payments. A typical McDonald's or Burger King restaurant has about fifty crew members. They work an average of thirty hours a week. By hiring a large number of crew members for each restaurant, sending them home as soon as possible, and employing them for fewer than forty hours a week whenever possible, the chains keep their labor costs to a bare minimum.

A handful of fast food workers are paid regular salaries. A fast food restaurant that employs fifty crew members has four or five managers and assistant managers. They earn about $23,000 a year and usually receive medical benefits, as well as some form of bonus or profit sharing. They have an opportunity to rise up the corporate ladder. But they also work long hours without overtime — fifty, sixty, seventy hours a week. The turnover rate among assistant managers is extremely high. The job offers little opportunity for independent decision-making. Computer programs, training manuals, and the machines in the kitchen determine how just about everything must be done.

Fast food managers do have the power to hire, fire, and schedule workers. Much of their time is spent motivating their crew members. In the absence of good wages and secure employment, the chains try to inculcate "team spirit" in their young crews. Workers who fail to work hard, who arrive late, or who are reluctant to stay extra hours are made to feel that they're making life harder for everyone else, letting their friends and coworkers down. For years the McDonald's Corporation has provided its managers with training in "transactional analysis," a set of psychological techniques popularized in the book *I'm OK — You're OK* (1969). One of these techniques is called "stroking" — a form of positive reinforcement, deliberate praise, and recognition that many teenagers don't get at home. Stroking can make a worker feel that his or her contribution is sincerely valued. And it's much less expensive than raising wages or paying overtime.

The fast food chains often reward managers who keep their labor costs low, a practice that often leads to abuses. In 1997 a jury in Washington State found that Taco Bell had systematically coerced its crew members into working off the clock in order to avoid paying them overtime. The bonuses of Taco Bell restaurant managers were tied to their success at cutting labor costs. The managers had devised a number of creative ways to do so. Workers were forced to wait until things got busy at a restaurant before officially starting their shifts. They were forced to work without pay after their shifts ended. They were forced to clean restaurants on their own time. And they were sometimes compensated with food, not wages. Many of the workers involved were minors and recent immigrants. Before the penalty phase of the Washington lawsuit, the two sides reached a settlement; Taco Bell agreed to pay millions of dollars in back wages, but admitted no wrongdoing. As many as 16,000 current and former employees were owed money by the company. One employee, a high school dropout named Regina Jones, regularly worked seventy to eighty hours a week but was paid for only forty. Lawsuits involving similar charges against Taco Bell are now pending in Oregon and California.

detecting lies

AFTER WORKING AT Burger King restaurants for about a year, the sociologist Ester Reiter concluded that the trait most valued in fast food workers is "obedience." In other mass production industries ruled by the assembly line, labor unions have gained workers higher wages, formal grievance procedures, and a voice in how the work is performed. The high turnover rates at fast food restaurants, the part-time nature of the jobs, and the marginal social status of the crew members have made it difficult to organize their workers. And the fast food chains have fought against unions with the same zeal they've displayed fighting hikes in the minimum wage.

The McDonald's Corporation insists that its franchise operators follow directives on food preparation, purchasing, store design, and countless other minute details. Company specifications cover everything from the size of the pickle slices to the circumference of the paper cups. When it comes to wage rates, however, the company is remarkably silent and laissez-faire. This policy allows operators to set their wages according to local labor markets — and it absolves the McDonald's Corporation of any formal responsibility for roughly three-quarters of the company's workforce. McDonald's decentralized hiring practices have helped thwart efforts to organize the company's workers. But whenever a union gains support at a particular restaurant, the McDonald's Corporation suddenly shows tremendous interest in the emotional and financial well-being of the workers there.

During the late 1960s and early 1970s, McDonald's workers across the country attempted to join unions. In response the company developed sophisticated methods for keeping unions out of its restaurants. A "flying squad" of experienced managers and corporate executives was sent to a restaurant the moment union activity was suspected. Seemingly informal "rap sessions" were held with disgruntled employees. The workers were encouraged to share their feelings. They were flattered and stroked. And more importantly, they were encouraged to share information about the union's plans and the names of union sympathizers. If the rap sessions failed to provide adequate information, the stroking was abandoned for a more direct approach.

In 1973, amid a bitter organizing drive in San Francisco, a group of young McDonald's employees claimed that managers had forced them to take lie detector tests, interrogated them about union activities, and threatened them with dismissal if they refused to answer. Spokesmen for McDonald's admitted that polygraph tests had been administered, but denied that any coercion was involved. Bryan Seale, San Francisco's labor commissioner, closely studied some of McDonald's old job applications and found a revealing paragraph in small print near the bottom. It said that employees who wouldn't submit to lie detector tests could face dismissal. The labor commissioner ordered McDonald's to halt the practice, which was a violation of state law. He also ordered the company to stop accepting tips at its restaurants, since customers were being misled: the tips being left for crew members were actually being kept by the company.

The San Francisco union drive failed, as did every other McDonald's union drive — with one exception. Workers at a McDonald's in Mason City, Iowa, voted to join the United Food and Commercial Workers union in 1971. The union lasted just four years. The McDonald's Corporation no longer asks crew members to take lie detector tests and advises its franchisees to obey local labor laws. Nevertheless, top McDonald's executives still travel from Oak Brook, Illinois, to the site of a suspected union drive, even when the restaurant is overseas. Rap sessions and high-priced attorneys have proved to be effective tools for ending labor disputes. The company's guidance has helped McDonald's franchisees defeat literally hundreds of efforts to unionize.

Despite more than three decades of failure, every now and then another group of teenagers tries to unionize a McDonald's. In February of 1997 workers at a McDonald's restaurant in St. Hubert, a suburb of Montreal, applied to join the Teamsters union. More than three-quarters of the crew members signed union cards, hoping to create the only unionized McDonald's in North America. Tom and Mike Cappelli, the operators of the restaurant, employed fifteen attorneys — roughly one lawyer for every four crew members — and filed a series of legal motions to stall the union certification process. Union leaders argued that any delay would serve McDonald's interests, because turnover in the restaurant's workforce would allow the Cappellis to hire anti-union employees. After a year of litigation, a majority of the McDonald's workers still supported the Teamsters. The Quebec labor commissioner scheduled a final certification hearing for the union on March 10, 1998.

Tom and Mike Cappelli closed the St. Hubert McDonald's on February 12, just weeks before the union was certified. Workers were given notice on a Thursday; the McDonald's shut down for good the following day, Friday the thirteenth. Local union officials were outraged. Clement Godbout, head of the Quebec Federation of Labour, accused the McDonald's Corporation of shutting down the restaurant in order to send an unmistakable warning to its other workers in Canada. Godbout called McDonald's "one of the most anti-union companies on the planet." The McDonald's Corporation denied that it had anything to do with the decision. Tom and Mike Cappelli claimed that the St. Hubert restaurant was a money-loser, though it had operated continuously at the same location for seventeen years.

McDonald's has roughly a thousand restaurants in Canada. The odds against a McDonald's restaurant in Canada going out of business — based on the chain's failure rate since the early 1990s — is about 300 to 1. "Did somebody say McUnion?" a Canadian editorial later asked. "Not if they want to keep their McJob."

This was not the first time that a McDonald's restaurant suddenly closed in the middle of a union drive. During the early 1970s, workers were successfully organizing a McDonald's in Lansing, Michigan. All the crew members were fired, the restaurant was shut down, a new McDonald's was built down the block — and the workers who'd signed union cards were not rehired. Such tactics have proven remarkably successful. As of this writing, none of the workers at the roughly fifteen thousand McDonald's in North America is represented by a union.

protecting youth

ALMOST EVERY FAST FOOD restaurant in Colorado Springs has a banner or sign that says "Now Hiring." The fast food chains have become victims of their own success, as one business after another tries to poach their teenage workers. Teenagers now sit behind the front desk at hotels, make calls for telemarketers, sell running shoes at the mall. The low unemployment rate in Colorado Springs has made the task of finding inexpensive workers even more difficult. Meanwhile, the competition among fast food restaurants has increased. Chains that have competed in the city for years keep opening new outlets, while others are entering the market for the first time. Carl's Jr. has come to Colorado Springs, opening stand-alone restaurants and "co-branded" outlets inside Texaco gas stations. When a fast food restaurant goes out of business, a new one often opens at the same location, like an army that's seized the outpost of a conquered foe. Instead of a new flag being raised, a big new plastic sign goes up.

Local fast food franchisees have little ability to reduce their fixed costs: their lease payments, franchise fees, and purchases from company-approved suppliers. Franchisees do, however, have some control over wage rates and try to keep them as low as possible. The labor structure of the fast food industry demands a steady supply of young and unskilled workers. But the immediate needs of the chains and the long-term needs of teenagers are fundamentally at odds.

At Cheyenne Mountain High School, set in the foothills, with a grand view of the city, few of the students work at fast food restaurants. Most of them are white and upper-middle class. During the summers, the boys often work as golf caddies or swimming pool lifeguards. The girls often work as babysitters at the Broadmoor. When Cheyenne Mountain kids work during the school year, they tend to find jobs at the mall, the girls employed at clothing stores like the Gap or the Limited, the boys at sporting goods stores like the Athlete's Foot. These jobs provide discounts on merchandise and a chance to visit with school friends who are out shopping. The pay of a job is often less important than its social status. Working as a hostess at an upscale chain restaurant like Carriba's, T.G.I. Friday's, or the Outback Steakhouse is considered a desirable job, even if it pays minimum wage. Working at a fast food restaurant is considered bottom of the heap.

Jane Trogdon is head of the guidance department at Harrison High School in Colorado Springs. Harrison has the reputation of being a "rough" school, a "gang" school. The rap is not entirely deserved; it may have stuck because Harrison is where many of the city's poorest teenagers go to school. Harrison is where you will find an abundance of fast food workers. About 60 percent of the students come from low-income families. In a town with a relatively low minority population, only 40 percent of the students at Harrison are white. The school occupies a clean, modern building on the south side of town, right next to I-25. From some of the classroom windows, you can see the cars zooming past. On the other side of the interstate, a new multiplex theater with twenty-four screens beckons students to cut class.

Teachers often don't want to teach at Harrison, and some don't last there for long. Jane Trogdon has worked at the school since the day it opened in 1967. Over the past three decades, Trogdon has observed tremendous changes in the student body. Harrison was always the school on the wrong side of the tracks, but the kids today seem poorer than ever. It used to be, even in many low-income families, that the father worked and the mother stayed home to raise the children. Now it seems that no one's home and that both parents work just to make ends meet, often holding down two or three jobs. Many of the kids at Harrison are on their own from an early age. Parents increasingly turn to the school for help, asking teachers to supply discipline and direction. The teachers do their best, despite a lot of disrespect from students and the occasional threat of violence. Trogdon worries about the number of kids at Harrison who leave school in the afternoon and go straight to work, mainly at fast food restaurants. She also worries about the number of hours they're working.

Although some students at Harrison work at fast food restaurants to help their families, most of the kids take jobs after school in order to have a car. In the suburban sprawl of Colorado Springs, having your own car seems like a necessity. Car payments and insurance easily come to $300 a month. As more and more kids work to get their own wheels, fewer participate in after-school sports and activities. They stay at their jobs late into the night, neglect their homework, and come to school exhausted. In Colorado, kids can drop out of school at the age of sixteen. Dropping out often seems tempting to sophomores who are working in the "real world," earning money, being eagerly recruited by local fast food chains, retail chains, and telemarketers. Thirty years ago, businesses didn't pursue teenage workers so aggressively. Harrison usually has about four hundred students in its freshman class. About half of them eventually graduate; perhaps fifty go to college.

When Trogdon first came to work at Harrison, the Vietnam war was at its peak, and angry battles raged between long-haired students and kids whose fathers were in the military. Today she senses a profound apathy at the school. The turmoil of an earlier era has been replaced by a sad and rootless anomie. "I have lots and lots of kids who are terribly depressed," Trogdon says. "I've never seen so many, so young, feel this way."

Trogdon's insights about teenagers and after-school jobs are supported by *Protecting Youth at Work,* a report on child labor published by the National Academy of Sciences in 1998. It concluded that the long hours many American teenagers now spend on the job pose a great risk to their future educational and financial success. Numerous studies have found that kids who work up to twenty hours a week during the school year generally benefit from the experience, gaining an increased sense of personal responsibility and self-esteem. But kids who work more than that are far more likely to cut classes and drop out of high school. Teenage boys who work longer hours are much more likely to develop substance abuse problems and commit petty crimes. The negative effects of working too many hours are easy to explain: when kids go to work, they are neither at home nor at school. If the job is boring, overly regimented, or meaningless, it can create a lifelong aversion to work. All of these trends are most pronounced among poor and disadvantaged teenagers. While stressing the great benefits of work in moderation, the National Academy of Sciences report warned that short-term considerations are now limiting what millions of American kids can ever hope to achieve.

Elisa Zamot is a junior at Harrison High. In addition to working at McDonald's on the weekends, she also works there two days a week after school. All together, she spends about thirty to thirty-five hours a week at the restaurant. She earns the minimum wage. Her parents, Carlos and Cynthia, are loving but strict. They're Puerto Rican and moved to Colorado Springs from Lakewood, New Jersey. They make sure Elisa does all her homework and impose a midnight curfew. Elisa's usually too tired to stay out late, anyway. Her school bus arrives at six in the morning, and classes start at seven.

Elisa had wanted to work at McDonald's ever since she was a toddler — a feeling shared by many of the McDonald's workers I met in

Colorado Springs. But now she hates the job and is desperate to quit. Working at the counter, she constantly has to deal with rude remarks and complaints. Many of the customers look down on fast food workers and feel entitled to treat them with disrespect. Sweet-faced Elisa is often yelled at by strangers angry that their food's taking too long or that something is wrong with their order. One elderly woman threw a hamburger at her because there was mustard on it. Elisa hopes to find her next job at a Wal-Mart, at a clothing store, anywhere but a fast food restaurant. A good friend of hers works at FutureCall, the largest telemarketer in Colorado Springs and a big recruiter of teenaged labor. Her friend works there about forty hours a week, on top of attending Harrison High. The pay is terrific, but the job sounds miserable. The sort of workplace regimentation that the fast food chains pioneered has been taken to new extremes by America's telemarketers.

"IT'S TIME FOR BRINGING IN THE GREEN!" a FutureCall recruiting ad says: "Lots O' Green!" The advertisement promises wages of $10 to $15 an hour for employees who work more than forty hours a week. Elisa's friend is sixteen. After school, she stays at the FutureCall building on North Academy Boulevard until ten o'clock at night, staring at a computer screen. The computer automatically dials people throughout the United States. When somebody picks up the phone, his or her name flashes on the screen, along with the sales pitch that FutureCall's "teleservice representative" (TSR) is supposed to make on behalf of well-known credit card companies, phone companies, and retailers. TSRs are instructed never to let someone refuse a sales pitch without being challenged. The computer screen offers a variety of potential "rebuttals." TSRs make about fifteen "presentations" an hour, going for a sale, throwing out one rebuttal after another to avoid being shot down. About nine out of ten people decline the offer, but the one person who says yes makes the whole enterprise quite profitable. Supervisors walk up and down the rows, past hundreds of identical cubicles, giving pep talks, eavesdropping on phone calls, suggesting rebuttals, and making sure none of the teenage workers is doing homework on the job. The workplace at FutureCall is even more rigorously controlled than the one at McDonald's.

After graduating from Harrison, Elisa hopes to go to Princeton. She's saving most of her earnings to buy a car. The rest is spent on clothes, shoes, and school lunches. A lot of kids at Harrison don't save any of the money earned at their fast food jobs. They buy beepers, cellular phones, stereos, and designer clothes. Kids are wearing Tommy

Hilfiger and FUBU at Harrison right now; Calvin Klein is out. Hip-hop culture reigns, the West Coast brand, filtered through Compton and L.A.

During my interviews with local high school kids, I heard numerous stories of fifteen-year-olds working twelve-hour shifts at fast food restaurants and sophomores working long past midnight. The Fair Labor Standards Act prohibits the employment of kids under the age of sixteen for more than three hours on a school day, or later than seven o'clock at night. Colorado state law prohibits the employment of kids under the age of eighteen for more than eight hours a day and also prohibits their employment at jobs involving hazardous machinery. According to the workers I met, violations of these state and federal labor laws are now fairly commonplace in the fast food restaurants of Colorado Springs. George, a former Taco Bell employee, told me that he sometimes helped close the restaurant, staying there until two or three in the morning. He was sixteen at the time. Robbie, a sixteen-year-old Burger King employee, said he routinely worked ten-hour shifts. And Tommy, a seventeen-year-old who works at McDonald's, bragged about his skill with the electric tomato dicer, a machine that should have been off-limits. "I'm like an expert at using the damn thing," he said, "'cause I'm the only one that knows how to work it." He also uses the deep fryer, another labor code violation. None of these teenagers had been forced to break the law; on the contrary, they seemed eager to do it.

Most of the high school students I met liked working at fast food restaurants. They complained that the work was boring and monotonous, but enjoyed earning money, getting away from school and parents, hanging out with friends at work, and goofing off as much as possible. Few of the kids liked working the counter or dealing with customers. They much preferred working in the kitchen, where they could talk to friends and fool around. Food fights were popular. At one Taco Bell, new employees, departing employees, and employees who were merely disliked became targets for the sour cream and guacamole guns. "This kid, Leo, he smelled like guacamole for a month," one of the attackers later bragged.

The personality of a fast food restaurant's manager largely determined whether working there would be an enjoyable experience or an unpleasant one. Good managers created a sense of pride in the work and an upbeat atmosphere. They allowed scheduling changes and encouraged kids to do their schoolwork. Others behaved arbitrarily, picked on workers, yelled at workers, and made unreasonable demands. They were personally responsible for high rates of turnover. An assistant manager at a McDonald's in Colorado Springs always brought her five-year-old daughter to the restaurant and expected crew members to baby-sit for her. The assistant manager was a single mother. One crew member whom I met loved to look after the little girl; another resented it; and both found it hard to watch the child playing for hours amid the busy kitchen, the counter staff, the customers at their tables, and the life-size statue of Ronald McDonald.

None of the fast food workers I met in Colorado Springs spoke of organizing a union. The thought has probably never occurred to them. When these kids don't like the working conditions or the manager, they quit. Then they find a job at another restaurant, and the cycle goes on and on.

inside jobs

THE INJURY RATE OF teenage workers in the United States is about twice as high as that of adult workers. Teenagers are far more likely to be untrained, and every year, about 200,000 are injured on the job. The most common workplace injuries at fast food restaurants are slips, falls, strains, and burns. The fast food industry's expansion, however, coincided with a rising incidence of workplace violence in the United States. Roughly four or five fast food workers are now murdered on the job every month, usually during the course of a robbery. Although most fast food robberies end without bloodshed, the level of violent crime in the industry is surprisingly high. In 1998, more restaurant workers were murdered on the job in the United States than police officers.

America's fast food restaurants are now more attractive to armed robbers than convenience stores, gas stations, or banks. Other retail businesses increasingly rely upon credit card transactions, but fast food restaurants still do almost all of their business in cash. While convenience store chains have worked hard to reduce the amount of money in the till (at 7-Eleven stores the average robbery results in a loss of about thirty-seven dollars), fast food restaurants often have thousands of dollars on the premises. Gas stations and banks now routinely shield employees behind bullet-resistant barriers, a security measure that would be impractical at most fast food restaurants. And the same features that make these restaurants so convenient — their location near intersections and highway off-ramps, even their drive-through windows — facilitate a speedy getaway.

A fast food robbery is most likely to occur when only a few crew members are present: early in the morning before customers arrive or late at night near closing time. A couple of sixteen-year-old crew members and a twenty-year-old assistant manager are often the only people locking up a restaurant, long after midnight. When a robbery takes place, the crew members are frequently herded into the basement freezer. The robbers empty the cash registers and the safe, then hit the road.

The same demographic groups widely employed at fast food restaurants — the young and the poor — are also responsible for much of the nation's violent crime. According to industry studies, about two-thirds of the robberies at fast food restaurants involve current or former employees. The combination of low pay, high turnover, and ample cash in the restaurant often leads to crime. A 1999 survey by the National Food Service Security Council, a group funded by the large chains, found that about half of all restaurant workers engaged in some form of cash or property theft — not including the theft of food. The typical employee stole about $218 a year; new employees stole almost $100 more. Studies conducted by Jerald Greenberg, a professor of management at the University of Ohio and an expert on workplace crime, have found that when people are treated with dignity and respect, they're less likely to steal from their employer. "It may be common sense," Greenberg says, "but it's obviously not common practice." The same anger that causes most petty theft, the same desire to strike back at an employer perceived as unfair, can escalate to armed robbery. Restaurant managers are usually, but not always, the victims of fast food crimes. Not long ago, the day manager of a McDonald's in Moorpark, California, recognized the masked gunman emptying the safe. It was the night manager.

The Occupational Safety and Health Administration (OSHA) attempted in the mid-1990s to issue guidelines for preventing violence at restaurants and stores that do business at night. OSHA was prompted, among other things, by the fact that homicide had become the leading cause of workplace fatalities among women. The proposed guidelines were entirely voluntary and seemed innocuous. OSHA recommended, for example, that late-night retailers improve visibility within their stores and make sure their parking lots were well lit. The

National Restaurant Association, along with other industry groups, responded by enlisting more than one hundred congressmen to oppose any OSHA guidelines on retail violence. An investigation by the *Los Angeles Times* found that many of the congressmen had recently accepted donations from the NRA and the National Association of Convenience Stores. "Who would oppose putting out guidelines on saving women's lives in the workplace?" Joseph Dear, a former head of OSHA, said to a *Times* reporter. "The companies that employ those women."

The restaurant industry has continued to fight not only guidelines on workplace violence, but any enforcement of OSHA regulations. At a 1997 restaurant industry "summit" on violence, executives representing the major chains argued that OSHA guidelines could be used by plaintiffs in lawsuits stemming from a crime, that guidelines were completely unnecessary, and that there was no need to supply the government with "potentially damaging" robbery statistics. The group concluded that OSHA should become just an information clearinghouse without the authority to impose fines or compel security measures. For years, one of OSHA's most severe critics in Congress has been Jay Dickey, an Arkansas Republican who once owned two Taco Bells. In January of 1999 the National Council of Chain Restaurants helped to form a new organization to lobby against OSHA regulations. The name of the industry group is the "Alliance for Workplace Safety."

The leading fast food chains have tried to reduce violent crime by spending millions on new security measures — video cameras, panic buttons, drop-safes, burglar alarms, additional lighting. But even the most heavily guarded fast food restaurants remain vulnerable. In April of 2000 a Burger King on the grounds of Offut Air Force Base in Nebraska was robbed by two men in ski masks carrying shotguns. They were wearing purple Burger King shirts and got away with more than $7,000. Joseph A. Kinney, the president of the National Safe Workplace Institute, argues that the fast food industry needs to make fundamental changes in its labor relations. Raising wages and making a real commitment to workers will do more to cut crime than investing in hidden cameras. "No other American industry," Kinney notes, "is robbed so frequently by its own employees."

Few of the young fast food workers I met in Colorado Springs were aware that working early in the morning or late at night placed them in some danger. Jose, on the other hand, had no illusions. He was a nineteen-year-old assistant manager with a sly, mischievous look. Before going to work at McDonald's, Jose had been a drug courier and a drug dealer in another state. He'd witnessed the murder of close friends. Many of his relatives were in prison for drug-related and violent crimes. Jose had left all that behind; his job at McDonald's was part of a new life; and he liked being an assistant manager because the work didn't seem hard. He was not, however, going to rely on McDonald's for his personal safety. He said that video cameras weren't installed at his restaurant until the Teeny Beanie Babies arrived. "Man, people really want to rip those things off," he said. "You've got to keep your eye on them." Jose often counts the money and closes the restaurant late at night. He always brings an illegal handgun to work, and a couple of his employees carry handguns, too. He's not afraid of what might happen if an armed robber walks in the door one night. "Ain't nothing that he could do to me," Jose said, matter-of-factly, "that I couldn't do to him."

The May 2000 murder of five Wendy's employees during a robbery in Queens, New York, received a great deal of media attention. The killings were gruesome, one of the murderers had previously worked at the restaurant, and the case unfolded in the media capital of the nation. But crime and fast food have become so ubiquitous in American society that their frequent combination usually goes unnoticed. Just a few weeks before the Wendy's massacre in Queens, two former Wendy's employees in South Bend, Indiana, received prison terms for murdering a pair of coworkers during a robbery that netted $1,400. Earlier in the year two former Wendy's employees in Anchorage, Alaska, were charged with the murder of their night manager during a robbery. Hundreds of fast food restaurants are robbed every week. The FBI does not compile nationwide statistics on restaurant robberies, and the restaurant industry will not disclose them. Local newspaper accounts, however, give a sense of these crimes.

In recent years: Armed robbers struck nineteen McDonald's and Burger King restaurants along Interstate 85 in Virginia and North Carolina. A former cook at a Shoney's in Nashville, Tennessee, became a fast food serial killer, murdering two workers at a Captain D's, three workers at a McDonald's, and a pair of Baskin Robbins workers whose bodies were later found in a state park. A dean at Texas Southern University was shot and killed during a carjacking in the drive-through lane of a KFC in Houston. The manager of a Wal-Mart McDonald's in Durham, North Carolina, was shot during a robbery by two masked assailants. A nine-year-old girl was killed during a shootout between a robber and an off-duty police officer waiting in line at a McDonald's in Barstow, California. A twenty-year-old manager was killed during an armed robbery at a Sacramento, California, McDonald's; the manager had recognized one of the armed robbers, a former McDonald's employee; it was the manager's first day in the job. A former employee at a McDonald's in Vallejo, California, shot three women who worked at the restaurant after being rejected for a new job; one of the women was killed, and the murderer left the restaurant laughing. And in Colorado Springs, a jury convicted a former employee of first degree murder for the execution-style slayings of three teenage workers and a female manager at a Chuck E. Cheese's restaurant. The killings took place in Aurora, Colorado, at closing time, and police later arrived to find a macabre scene. The bodies lay in an empty restaurant as burglar alarms rang, game lights flashed, a vacuum cleaner ran, and Chuck E. Cheese mechanical animals continued to perform children's songs.

making it fun

AT THE THIRTY-EIGHTH Annual Multi-Unit Foodserver Operators Conference held a few years ago in Los Angeles, the theme was "People: The Single Point of Difference." Most of the fourteen hundred attendees were chain restaurant operators and executives. The ballroom at the Century Plaza Hotel was filled with men and women in expensive suits, a well-to-do group whose members looked as though they hadn't grilled a burger or mopped a floor in a while. The conference workshops had names like "Dual Branding: Case Studies from the Field" and "Segment Marketing: The Right Message for the Right Market" and "In Line and on Target: The Changing Dimensions of Site Selection." Awards were given for the best radio and television ads. Restaurants were inducted into the Fine Dining Hall of Fame. Chains competed to be named Operator of the Year. Foodservice companies filled a nearby exhibition space with their latest products: dips, toppings, condiments, high-tech ovens, the latest in pest control. The leading topic of conversation at the scheduled workshops, in the hallways and hotel bars, was how to find inexpensive workers in an American economy where unemployment had fallen to a twenty-four-year low.

James C. Doherty, the publisher of *Nation's Restaurant News* at the time, gave a speech urging the restaurant industry to move away from relying on a low-wage workforce with high levels of turnover and to promote instead the kind of labor policies that would create long-term careers in foodservice. How can workers look to this industry for a career, he asked, when it pays them the minimum wage and provides them no health benefits? Doherty's suggestions received polite applause.

The keynote speech was given by David Novak, the president of Tricon Global Restaurants. His company operates more restaurants than any other company in the world — 30,000 Pizza Huts, Taco Bells, and KFCs. A former advertising executive with a boyish face and the earnest delivery style of a motivational speaker, Novak charmed the crowd. He talked about the sort of recognition his company tried to give its employees, the pep talks, the prizes, the special awards of plastic chili peppers and rubber chickens. He believed the best way to motivate people is to have fun. "Cynics need to be in some other industry," he said. Employee awards created a sense of pride and esteem, they showed that management was watching, and they did not cost a lot of money. "We want to be a great company for the people who make it great," Novak announced. Other speakers talked about teamwork, empowering workers, and making it "fun."

During the President's Panel, the real sentiments of the assembled restaurant operators and executives became clear. Norman Brinker — a legend in the industry, the founder of Bennigan's and Steak and Ale, the current owner of Chili's, a major donor to the Republican Party — spoke to the conference in language that was simple, direct, and free of platitudes. "I see the possibility of unions," he warned. The thought "chilled" him. He asked everyone in the audience to give more money to the industry's key lobbying groups. "And [Senator] Kennedy's pushing hard on a $7.25 minimum wage," he continued. "That'll be fun, won't it? I love the idea of that. I sure do — strike me dead!" As the crowd laughed and roared and applauded Brinker's call to arms against unions and the government, the talk about teamwork fell into the proper perspective.

4 / success

MATTHEW KABONG glides his '83 Buick LeSabre through the streets of Pueblo, Colorado, at night, looking for a trailer park called Meadowbrook. Two Little Caesars pizzas and a bag of Crazy Bread sit in the back seat. "Welcome to my office," he says, reaching down, turning up the radio, playing some mellow rhythm and blues. Kabong was born in Nigeria and raised in Atlanta, Georgia. He studies electrical engineering at a local college, hopes to own a Radio Shack some day, and delivers pizzas for Little Caesars four or five nights a week. He earns the minimum wage, plus a dollar for each delivery, plus tips. On a good night he makes about fifty bucks. We cruise past block after block of humble little houses, whitewashed and stucco, built decades ago, with pickup trucks in the driveways and children's toys on the lawns. Pueblo is the southernmost city along the Front Range, forty miles from Colorado Springs, but for generations a world apart, largely working class and Latino, a town with steel mills that was never hip like Boulder, bustling like Denver, or aristocratic like Colorado Springs. Nobody ever built a polo field in Pueblo, and snobs up north still call it "the asshole of Colorado."

We turn a corner and find Meadowbrook. All the trailers look the same, slightly ragged around the edges, lined up in neat rows. Kabong parks the car, and when the radio and the headlights shut off, the street suddenly feels empty and dark. Then somewhere a dog barks, the door of a nearby trailer opens, and light spills onto the gravel driveway. A little white girl with blonde hair, about seven years old, smiles at this big Nigerian bringing pizza, hands him fifteen dollars, takes the food, and tells him to keep the change. Behind her there's movement in the trailer, a brief glimpse of someone else's life, a tidy kitchen, the flickering shadows of a TV. The door closes, and Kabong heads back to the Buick, his office, beneath a huge sky full of stars. He has a $1.76 tip in his pocket, the biggest tip so far tonight.

The wide gulf between Colorado Springs and Pueblo — a long-standing social, cultural, political, and economic division — is starting to narrow. As you drive through the streets of Pueblo, you can feel the change coming, something palpable in the air. During the 1980s, the city's unemployment rate hovered at about 12 percent, and not much was built. New things now seem to appear every month, new roads around the Pueblo Mall, new movie theaters, a new Applebee's, an Olive Garden, a Home Depot, a great big Marriott. Subdivisions are creeping south from Colorado Springs along I-25, turning cattle ranches into street after street of ranch-style homes. Pueblo has not boomed yet; it seems ready, right on the verge, about to become more like the rest.

The Little Caesars where Kabong works is in the Belmont section of town, across the street from a Dunkin' Donuts, not far from the University of Southern Colorado campus. The small square building the Little Caesars occupies used to house a Godfather's Pizza and before that, a Dairy Bar. The restaurant has half a dozen brown Formica tables, red brick walls, a gumball machine near the counter, white-and-brown flecked linoleum floors. The place is clean but has not been redecorated for a while. The customers who drop by or call for pizza are college students, ordinary working people, people with large families, and the poor. Little Caesars pizzas are big and inexpensive, often providing enough food for more than one meal.

Five crew members work in the kitchen, putting toppings on pizzas, putting the pizzas in the oven, getting drinks, taking orders over the phone. Julio, a nineteen-year-old kid with two kids of his own, slides a pizza off the old Blodgett oven's conveyer belt. He makes $6.50 an hour. He enjoys making pizza. The ovens have been automated at Little Caesars and at the other pizza chains, but the pizzas are still handmade. They're not just pulled out of a freezer. Scott, another driver, waits for his next delivery. He wears a yellow Little Caesars shirt that says, "Think Big!" He's working here to pay off student loans and the $4,000 debt on his 1988 Jeep. He goes to the University of Southern Colorado and wants to attend law school, then join the FBI. Dave Feamster, the owner of the restaurant, is completely at ease behind the counter, hanging out with his Latino employees and customers — but at the same time seems completely out of place.

Feamster was born and raised in a working-class neighborhood of Detroit. He grew up playing in youth hockey leagues and later attended college in Colorado Springs on an athletic scholarship. He was an All-American during his senior year, a defenseman picked by the Chicago Black Hawks in the college draft. After graduating from Colorado College with a degree in business, Feamster played in the National Hockey League, a childhood dream come true. The Black Hawks reached the playoffs during his first three years on the team, and Feamster got to compete against some of his idols, against Wayne Gretzky and Mark Messier. Feamster was not a big star, but he loved the game, earned a good income, and traveled all over the country; not bad for a blue-collar kid from Detroit.

On March 14, 1984, Feamster was struck from behind by Paul Holmgren during a game with the Minnesota North Stars. Feamster never saw the hit coming and slammed into the boards head first. He felt dazed, but played out the rest of the game. Later, in the shower, his back started to hurt. An x-ray revealed a stress fracture of a bone near the base of his spine. For the next three months Feamster wore a brace that extended from his chest to his waist. The cracked bone didn't heal. At practice sessions the following autumn, he didn't feel right. The Black Hawks wanted him to play, but a physician at the Mayo Clinic examined him and said, "If you were my son, I'd say, find another job; move on." Feamster worked out for hours at the gym every day, trying to strengthen his back. He lived with two other Black Hawk players. Every morning the three of them would eat breakfast together, then his friends would leave for practice, and Feamster would find himself just sitting there at the table.

The Black Hawks never gave him a good-bye handshake or wished him good luck. He wasn't even invited to the team Christmas party. They paid off the remainder of his contract, and that was it. He floundered for a year, feeling lost. He had a business degree, but had spent most of his time in college playing hockey. He didn't know anything about business. He enrolled in a course to become a travel agent. He was the only man in a classroom full of eighteen- and nineteen-year-old women. After three weeks, the teacher asked to see him after class. He went to her office, and she said, "What are you doing here? You seem like a sharp guy. This isn't for you." He dropped out of travel agent school that day, then drove around aimlessly for hours, listening to Bruce Springsteen and wondering what the hell to do.

At a college reunion in Colorado Springs, an old friend suggested that Feamster become a Little Caesars franchisee. Feamster had played on youth hockey teams in Detroit with the sons of the company's founder, Mike Ilitch. He was too embarrassed to call the Ilitch family and ask for help. His friend dialed the phone. Within weeks, Feamster was washing dishes and making pizzas at Little Caesars restaurants in Chicago and Denver. It felt a long, long way from the NHL. Before gaining the chance to own a franchise, he had to spend months learning every aspect of the business. He was trained like any other assistant manager and earned $300 a week. At first he wondered if this was a good idea. The Little Caesars franchise fee was $15,000, almost all the money he had left in the bank.

devotion to a new faith

BECOMING A FRANCHISEE IS an odd combination of starting your own business and going to work for someone else. At the heart of a franchise agreement is the desire by two parties to make money while avoiding risk. The franchisor wants to expand an existing company without spending its own funds. The franchisee wants to start his or her own business without going it alone and risking everything on a new idea. One provides a brand name, a business plan, expertise, access to equipment and supplies. The other puts up the money and does the work. The relationship has its built-in tensions. The franchisor gives up some control by not wholly owning each operation; the franchisee sacrifices a great deal of independence by having to obey the company's rules. Everyone's happy when the profits are rolling in, but when things go wrong the arrangement often degenerates into a mismatched battle for power. The franchisor almost always wins.

Franchising schemes have been around in one form or another since the nineteenth century. In 1898 General Motors lacked the capital to hire salesmen for its new automobiles, so it sold franchises to prospective car dealers, giving them exclusive rights to certain territories. Franchising was an ingenious way to grow a new company in a new industry. "Instead of the company paying the salesmen," Stan Luxenberg, a franchise historian, explained, "the salesmen would pay the company." The automobile, soft drink, oil, and motel industries later relied upon franchising for much of their initial growth. But it was the fast food industry that turned franchising into a business model soon emulated by retail chains throughout the United States.

Franchising enabled the new fast food chains to expand rapidly by raising the hopes and using the money of small investors. Traditional methods of raising capital were not readily available to the founders of these chains, the high school dropouts and drive-in owners who lacked "proper" business credentials. Banks were not eager to invest in this new industry; nor was Wall Street. Dunkin' Donuts and Kentucky Fried Chicken were among the first chains to start selling franchises. But it was McDonald's that perfected new franchising techniques, increasing the chain's size while maintaining strict control of its products.

Ray Kroc's willingness to be patient, among other things, contributed to McDonald's success. Other chains demanded a large fee up front, sold off the rights to entire territories, and earned money by selling supplies directly to their franchises. Kroc wasn't driven by greed; the initial McDonald's franchising fee was only $950. He seemed much more interested in making a sale than in working out financial details, more eager to expand McDonald's than to make a quick buck. Indeed, during the late 1950s, McDonald's franchisees often earned more money than the company's founder.

After selling many of the first franchises to members of his country club, Kroc decided to recruit people who would operate their own restaurants, instead of wealthy businessmen who viewed McDonald's as just another investment. Like other charismatic leaders of new faiths, Kroc asked people to give up their former lives and devote themselves fully to McDonald's. To test the commitment of prospective franchisees, he frequently offered them a restaurant far from their homes and forbade them from engaging in other businesses. New franchisees had to start their lives anew with just one McDonald's restaurant. Those who contradicted or ignored Kroc's directives would never get the chance to obtain a second McDonald's. Although Kroc could be dictatorial, he also listened carefully to his franchisees' ideas and complaints. Ronald McDonald, the Big Mac, the Egg McMuffin, and the Filet-O-Fish sandwich were all developed by local franchisees. Kroc was an inspiring, paternalistic figure who looked for people with "common sense," "guts and staying power," and "a love of hard work." Becoming a successful McDonald's franchisee, he noted, didn't require "any unusual aptitude or intellect." Most of all, Kroc wanted loyalty and utter devotion from his franchisees — and in return, he promised to make them rich.

While Kroc traveled the country, spreading the word about McDonald's, selling new franchises, his business partner, Harry J. Sonneborn, devised an ingenious strategy to ensure the chain's financial success and provide even more control of its franchisees. Instead of earning money by demanding large royalties or selling supplies, the McDonald's Corporation became the landlord for nearly all of its American franchisees. It obtained properties and leased them to franchisees with at least a 40 percent markup. Disobeying the McDonald's Corporation became tantamount to violating the terms of the lease, behavior that could lead to a franchisee's eviction. Additional rental fees were based on a restaurant's annual revenues. The new franchising strategy proved enormously profitable for the McDonald's Corporation. "We are not basically in the food business," Sonneborn once told a group of Wall Street investors, expressing an unsentimental view of McDonald's that Kroc never endorsed. "We are in the real estate business. The only reason we sell fifteen cent hamburgers is because they are the greatest producer of revenue from which our tenants can pay us our rent."

In the 1960s and 1970s McDonald's was much like the Microsoft of the 1990s, creating scores of new millionaires. During a rough period for the McDonald's Corporation, when money was still tight, Kroc paid his secretary with stock. June Martino's 10 percent stake in McDonald's later allowed her to retire and live comfortably at an oceanfront Palm Beach estate. The wealth attained by Kroc's secretary vastly exceeded that of the McDonald brothers, who relinquished their claim to 0.5 percent of the chain's annual revenues in 1961. After taxes, the sale brought Richard and Mac McDonald about $1 million each. Had the brothers held on to their share of the company's revenues, instead of selling it to Ray Kroc, the income from it would have reached more than $180 million a year.

Kroc's relationship with the McDonalds had been stormy from the outset. He deeply resented the pair, claiming that while he was doing the hard work — "grinding it out, grunting and sweating like a galley slave" — they were at home, reaping the rewards. His original agreement with the McDonalds gave them a legal right to block any changes in the chain's operating system. Until 1961 the brothers retained ultimate authority over the restaurants which bore their name, a fact that galled Kroc. He had to borrow $2.7 million to buy out the

McDonalds; Sonneborn secured financing for the deal from a small group of institutional investors headed by Princeton University. As part of the buyout, the McDonald brothers insisted upon keeping their San Bernardino restaurant, birthplace of the chain. "Eventually I opened a McDonald's across the street from that store, which they had renamed The Big M," Kroc proudly noted in his memoir, "and it ran them out of business."

The enormous success of McDonald's spawned imitators not only in the fast food industry, but throughout America's retail economy. Franchising proved to be a profitable means of establishing new companies in everything from the auto parts business (Meineke Discount Mufflers) to the weight control business (Jenny Craig International). Some chains grew through franchised outlets; others through company-owned stores; and McDonald's eventually expanded through both. In the long run, the type of financing used to grow a company proved less crucial than other aspects of the McDonald's business model: the emphasis on simplicity and uniformity, the ability to replicate the same retail environment at many locations. In 1969, Donald and Doris Fisher decided to open a store in San Francisco that would sell blue jeans the way McDonald's, Burger King, and KFC sold food. They aimed at the youth market, choosing a name that would appeal to counterculture teens alienated by the "generation gap." Thirty years later, there were more than seventeen hundred company-owned Gap, GapKids, and babyGap stores in the United States. Among other innovations, Gap Inc. changed how children's clothing is marketed, adapting its adult fashions to fit toddlers and even infants.

As franchises and chain stores opened across the United States, driving along a retail strip became a shopping experience much like strolling down the aisle of a supermarket. Instead of pulling something off the shelf, you pulled into a driveway. The distinctive architecture of each chain became its packaging, as strictly protected by copyright law as the designs on a box of soap. The McDonald's Corporation led the way in the standardization of America's retail environments, rigorously controlling the appearance of its restaurants inside and out. During the late 1960s, McDonald's began to tear down the restaurants originally designed by Richard McDonald, the buildings with golden arches atop their slanted roofs. The new restaurants had brick walls and mansard roofs. Worried about how customers might react to the switch, the McDonald's Corporation hired Louis Cheskin — a prominent design consultant and psychologist —

to help ease the transition. He argued against completely eliminating the golden arches, claiming they had great Freudian importance in the subconscious mind of consumers. According to Cheskin, the golden arches resembled a pair of large breasts: "mother McDonald's breasts." It made little sense to lose the appeal of that universal, and yet somehow all-American, symbolism. The company followed Cheskin's advice and retained the golden arches, using them to form the *M* in McDonald's.

free enterprise with federal loans

TODAY IT COSTS ABOUT $1.5 million to become a franchisee at Burger King or Carl's Jr.; a McDonald's franchisee pays roughly one-third that amount to open a restaurant (since the company owns or holds the lease on the property). Gaining a franchise from a less famous chain — such as Augie's, Buddy's Bar-B-Q, Happy Joe's Pizza & Ice Cream Parlor, the Chicken Shack, Gumby Pizza, Hot Dog on a Stick, or Tippy's Taco House — can cost as little as $50,000. Franchisees often choose a large chain in order to feel secure; others prefer to invest in a smaller, newer outfit, hoping that chains like Buck's Pizza or K-Bob's Steakhouses will become the next McDonald's.

Advocates of franchising have long billed it as the safest way of going into business for yourself. The International Franchise Association (IFA), a trade group backed by the large chains, has for years released studies "proving" that franchisees fare better than independent businessmen. In 1998 an IFA survey claimed that 92 percent of all franchisees said they were "successful." The survey was based on a somewhat limited sample: franchisees who were still in business. Franchisees who'd gone bankrupt were never asked if they felt successful. Timothy Bates, a professor of economics at Wayne State University, believes that the IFA has vastly overstated the benefits of franchising. A study that Bates conducted for a federal loan agency found that within four to five years of opening, 38.1 percent of new franchised businesses had failed. The failure rate of new independent businesses during the same period was 6.2 percent lower. According to another study, three-quarters of the American companies that started selling franchises in 1983 had gone out of business by 1993. "In short," Bates argues, "the franchise route to self-employment is associated with higher business failure rates and lower profits than independent business ownership."

In recent years conflicts between franchisees and franchisors have become much more common. As the American market for fast food grows more saturated, restaurants belonging to the same chain are frequently being put closer to one another. Franchisees call the practice "encroachment" and angrily oppose it. Their sales go down when another outlet of the same chain opens nearby, drawing away customers. Most franchisors, on the other hand, earn the bulk of their profits from royalties based on total sales — and more restaurants usually means more sales. In 1978 Congress passed the first federal legislation to regulate franchising. At the time, a few chains were operated much like pyramid schemes. They misrepresented potential risks, accepted large fees up front, and bilked millions of dollars from small investors. The FTC now requires chains to provide lengthy disclosure statements that spell out their rules for prospective franchisees. The statements are often a hundred pages long, with a lot of small print.

Federal law demands full disclosure prior to a sale, but does not regulate how franchises are run thereafter. Once a contract is signed, franchisees are largely on their own. Although franchisees must obey corporate directives, they are not covered by federal laws that protect employees. Although they must provide the investment capital for their businesses, they are not covered by the laws that protect independent businessmen. And although they must purchase all their own supplies, they are not covered by consumer protection laws. It is perfectly legal under federal law for a fast food chain to take kickbacks (known as "rebates") from its suppliers, to open a new restaurant next door to an existing franchisee, and to evict a franchisee without giving cause or paying any compensation.

According to Susan Kezios, president of the American Franchise Association, the contracts offered by fast food chains often require a franchisee to waive his or her legal right to file complaints under state law; to buy only from approved suppliers, regardless of the price; to sell the restaurant only to a buyer approved by the chain; and to accept termination of the contract, for any cause, at the discretion of the chain. When a contract is terminated, the franchisee can lose his or her entire investment. Franchisees are sometimes afraid to criticize their chains in public, fearing reprisals such as the denial of additional restaurants, the refusal to renew a franchise contract at the end of its twenty-year term, or the immediate termination of an existing contract. Ralston-Purina once terminated the contracts of 642 Jack in the Box franchisees, giving them just thirty days to move out. A group of

McDonald's franchisees, unhappy with the chain's encroachment on their territories, has formed an organization called Consortium Members, Inc. The group issues statements through Richard Adams, a former McDonald's franchisee, because its members are reluctant to disclose their names.

The fast food chains are periodically sued by franchisees who are upset about encroachment, about inflated prices charged by suppliers, about bankruptcies and terminations that seemed unfair. During the 1990s, Subway was involved in more legal disputes with franchisees than any other chain — more than Burger King, KFC, McDonald's, Pizza Hut, Taco Bell, and Wendy's combined. Dean Sager, a former staff economist for the U.S. House of Representatives' Small Business Committee, has called Subway the "worst" franchise in America. "Subway is the biggest problem in franchising," Sager told *Fortune* magazine in 1998, "and emerges as one of the key examples of every [franchise] abuse you can think of."

Subway was founded in 1965 by Frederick DeLuca, who borrowed $1,000 from a family friend to open a sandwich shop in Bridgeport, Connecticut. DeLuca was seventeen at the time. Today Subway has about fifteen thousand restaurants, second only to McDonald's, and opens about a thousand new ones every year. DeLuca is determined to build the world's largest fast food chain. Many of the complaints about Subway arise from its unusual system for recruiting new franchisees. The chain relies on "development agents" to sell new Subway franchises. The development agents are not paid a salary by Subway; they are technically independent contractors, salesmen whose income is largely dependent on the number of Subways that open in their territory. They receive half of the franchise fee paid by new recruits, plus one-third of the annual royalties, plus one-third of the "transfer fee" paid whenever a restaurant is resold. Agents who fail to meet their monthly sales quotas are sometimes forced to pay the company for their shortfall. They are under constant pressure to keep opening new Subways, regardless of how that affects the sales of Subways that are already operating nearby. According to a 1995 investigation by Canada's *Financial Post*, Subway's whole system seems "almost as geared to selling franchises as it is to selling sandwiches."

It costs about $100,000 to open a Subway restaurant, the lowest investment required by any of the major fast food chains. The annual royalty Subway takes from its franchisees — 8 percent of total revenues — is among the highest. A top Subway executive has acknowledged that perhaps 90 percent of the chain's new franchisees sign their contracts without reading them and without looking at the FTC filings. Roughly 30 to 50 percent of Subway's new franchisees are immigrants, many of whom are not fluent in English. In order to earn a decent living, they must often work sixty to seventy hours a week and buy more than one Subway.

In November of 1999, Congressman Howard Coble, a conservative Republican from North Carolina, introduced legislation that would make franchisors obey the same fundamental business principles as other American companies. Coble's bill would for the first time obligate franchise chains to act in "good faith," a basic tenet of the nation's Uniform Commercial Code. The bill would also place limits on encroachment, require "good cause" before a contract can be terminated, permit franchisees to form their own associations, allow them to purchase from a variety of suppliers, and give them the right to sue franchisors in federal court. "We are not seeking to penalize anyone," Coble said, before introducing his plan for franchise reform. "We only seek to bring some order and sanity to a segment of our economy which is growing and may be growing out of control." Iowa adopted similar franchise rules in 1992, without driving Burger King or McDonald's out of the state. Nevertheless, the IFA and the fast food chains strongly oppose Coble's bill. The IFA has hired Allen Coffey, Jr., the former general counsel of the House Judiciary Committee, and Andy Ireland, a former Republican congressman who was the ranking member of the House Small Business Committee, to help thwart greater federal regulation of franchising. While in Congress, Ireland had criticized franchisees who sought legal reforms, calling them "whiny butts" who came running to the government instead of taking responsibility for their own business mistakes.

After congressional hearings were held on Coble's bill in 1999, the IFA claimed in a press release that federal regulation of franchising would interfere with "free enterprise contract negotiations" and seriously harm one of the most vital and dynamic sectors of the American economy. "Small businesses and franchising succeed by relying on marketplace solutions," said Don DeBolt, the president of the IFA. Despite its public opposition to any government interference with the workings of the free market, the IFA has long supported programs that enable fast food chains to expand using government-backed loans.

For more than three decades the fast food industry has used the

Small Business Administration (SBA) to finance new restaurants — thereby turning a federal agency that was created to help independent, small businesses into one that eliminates them. A 1981 study by the General Accounting Office found that the SBA had guaranteed 18,000 franchise loans between 1967 and 1979, subsidizing the launch of new Burger Kings and McDonald's, among others. Ten percent of these franchise loans ended in default. During the same period, only 4 percent of the independent businesses receiving SBA loans defaulted. In New York City, the SBA backed thirteen loans to Burger King franchisees; eleven of them defaulted. The chain was "experimenting," according to a congressional investigation, using government-backed loans to open restaurants in marginal locations. Burger King did not lose money when these restaurants closed. American taxpayers had covered the franchise fees, paid for the buildings, real estate, equipment, and supplies.

According to a recent study by the Heritage Foundation, the SBA is still providing free investment capital to some of the nation's largest corporations. In 1996, the SBA guaranteed almost $1 billion in loans to new franchisees. More of those loans went to the fast food industry than to any other industry. Almost six hundred new fast food restaurants, representing fifty-two different national chains, were launched in 1996 thanks to government-backed loans. The chain that benefited the most from SBA loans was Subway. Of the 755 new Subways opened that year, 109 relied upon the U.S. government for financing.

the world beyond pueblo

THE FRANCHISE AGREEMENT THAT Dave Feamster signed in 1984 gave him the exclusive right to open Little Caesars restaurants in the Pueblo area. In addition to the franchise fee, he had to promise the company 5 percent of his annual revenues and contribute an additional 4 percent to an advertising pool. Most Little Caesars franchisees have to supply the capital for the purchase or construction of their own restaurants. Since Feamster did not have the money, the company gave him a loan. Before selling a single pizza, he was $200,000 in debt.

Although Feamster had spent four years in college at Colorado Springs, less than an hour away, he'd never visited Pueblo. He rented a small house near his new restaurant, on a block full of steelworkers. It was the sort of neighborhood where he'd grown up. Feamster expected to stay there for just a few months, but wound up living there alone for six years, pouring all his energy into his business. He opened the restaurant every morning and closed it at night, made pizzas, delivered pizzas, swept the floors, did whatever needed to be done. His lack of experience in the restaurant business was offset by his skill at getting along with all sorts of different people. When an elderly customer phoned him and complained about the quality of a pizza, Feamster listened patiently and then hired her to handle future customer complaints.

It took Feamster three years to pay off his initial debt. Today he owns five Little Caesars restaurants: four in Pueblo and one in the nearby town of Lamar. His annual revenues are about $2.5 million. He earns a good income, but lives modestly. When I visited a Colorado Springs restaurant operated by a rival pizza chain, the company flew in a publicist from New York City to accompany me at all times. Feamster gave me free rein to interview his employees in private and to poke around his business for as long as I liked. He says there's nothing to hide. His small office behind the Belmont store, however, is in an advanced state of disarray, crammed with stacks of sagging banker's boxes. While his competitors use highly computerized operating systems that instantaneously display a customer's order on TV monitors in the kitchen, Feamster's restaurants remain firmly planted in the era of ballpoint pens and yellow paper receipts.

Feamster has established strong roots in Pueblo. His wife is a schoolteacher, a fifth-generation native of the city. His community work occupies much of his time and doesn't seem driven by publicity needs. He donates money to local charities and gives speeches at local schools. He pays some of the college tuition of his regular employees, so long as they maintain a 3.0 grade average or higher. And he recently helped organize the city's first high school hockey team, which draws players from throughout the district. Feamster paid for uniforms and equipment, and he serves as an assistant coach. The majority of the players are Latino, from the sorts of backgrounds that do not have a long and illustrious tradition on the ice. The team regularly plays against high schools from Colorado Springs, which have well-established hockey programs. The Pueblo hockey team has made it to the playoffs in two of its first three seasons.

Despite all the hard work, the future success of Feamster's business is by no means guaranteed. Little Caesars is the nation's fourth-largest pizza chain, but has been losing market share since 1992. Hundreds of

Little Caesars restaurants have closed. Many of the chain's franchisees, unhappy with the company's management, have formed an independent association. Some franchisees have withheld their contributions to the chain's advertising pool. Feamster feels loyal to the Ilitch family and to the company that gave him a break, but worries about the reduced spending on ads. Even more worrying is the recent arrival of Papa John's in Pueblo. Papa John's is the fastest-growing pizza chain in the United States, adding about thirty new restaurants every month. In the fall of 1998, Papa John's opened its first unit in Pueblo, and the following year, it opened three more.

The fate of Dave Feamster's restaurants now depends on how his employees serve his customers at every meal. Rachel Vasquez, the manager of the Belmont Little Caesars, takes her job seriously and does her best to motivate crew members. She's worked for Feamster since 1988. She was sixteen at the time, and no one else would hire her. The following year she bought a car with her earnings. She now makes about $22,000 a year for a fifty-hour workweek. She also receives health insurance. And Feamster annually contributes a few thousand dollars to her pension fund. Rachel met her husband at this Little Caesars in 1991, when she was a co-manager and he was a trainee. "We made more than pizza," she says, laughing. Her husband's now employed as a clerk for an industrial supply company. They have two small children. A grandmother looks after the kids while Rachel is at work. At the back of the kitchen, inside a small storage closet, Rachel has a makeshift office. There's a black table, a chair, a battered filing cabinet, a list of employee phone numbers taped to a box, and a sign that says "Smile."

Fourteen of Feamster's employees meet at the Belmont store around seven o'clock on a Tuesday morning. Feamster has tickets to an event called "Success" at the McNichols Sports Arena in Denver. It starts at eight-fifteen in the morning, runs until six in the evening, and features a dozen guest speakers, including Henry Kissinger, Barbara Bush, and former British Prime Minister John Major. The event is being sponsored by a group called "Peter Lowe International, the Success Authority." The tickets cost Feamster $90 each. He's rented a van and given these employees the day off. He doesn't know exactly what to expect, but hopes to provide a day to remember. It seems like an opportunity not to be missed. Feamster wants his young workers to see "there's a world out there, a whole world beyond the south side of Pueblo."

The parking lot at the McNichols Arena is jammed. The event has been sold out for days. Men and women leave their cars and walk briskly toward the arena. There's a buzz of anticipation. Public figures of this stature don't appear in Denver every week. The arena is filled with eighteen thousand people, and almost every single one of them is white, clean-cut, and prosperous — though not as prosperous as they'd like. These people want more. They are salespeople, middle managers, franchisees. In the hallways and corridors where you'd normally buy hot dogs and Denver Nuggets hats, *Peter Lowe's Success Yearbook* is being sold for $19.95, "American Sales Leads on CD-Rom" is available for $375, and Zig Ziglar is offering "Secrets of Closing the Sale" (a twelve-tape collection) for $120 and "Everything of Zig's" (fifty-seven tapes, four books, and eleven videos) for the discount price of $995, thanks to "Special Day of Seminar Pricing."

Peter Lowe has been staging these large-scale events since 1991. He's a forty-two-year-old "success authority" based in Tampa, Florida. His parents were Anglican missionaries who gave up the material comforts of their middle-class life in Vancouver to work among the poor. Lowe was born in Pakistan and educated at the Woodstock School in Mussoorie, India, but he chose a different path. In 1984 he quit his job as a computer salesman and organized his first "success seminar." The appearance of Ronald Reagan at one of these events soon encouraged other celebrities to endorse Peter Lowe's work. In return, he pays them between $30,000 and $60,000 for a speech — for about half an hour of work. Among those who've recently joined Peter Lowe onstage are: George Bush, Oliver North, Barbara Walters, William Bennett, Colin Powell, Charlton Heston, Dr. Joyce Brothers, and Mario Cuomo.

Rachel Vasquez can hardly believe that she's sitting among so many people who own their own businesses, among so many executives in suits and ties. The Little Caesars employees have seats just a few yards from the stage. They've never seen anything like this. Though the arena's huge, it seems like these fourteen fast food workers from Pueblo can almost reach out and touch the famous people who appear at the podium.

"You are the elite of America," Brian Tracy, author of *The Psychology of Selling*, tells the crowd. "Say to yourself: I like me! I like me! I like me!" He is followed by Henry Kissinger, who tells some foreign policy anecdotes. And then Peter Lowe's attractive wife, Tamara, leads the audience in a dance contest; the winner gets a free trip to Disneyland. Four contestants climb onstage, dozens of beach balls are tossed into the crowd, the sound system blasts the Beach Boys' "Surfin' USA," and eighteen thousand people start to dance. Barbara Bush is next, arriving to "Fanfare for the Common Man," her smile projected onto two gigantic television screens. She tells a story that begins, "We had the whole gang at Kennebunkport . . ."

When Peter Lowe arrives, fireworks go off and multicolored confetti drops from the ceiling. He is a slender, red-haired man in a gray, double-breasted suit. He advises the audience to be cheerful, to train themselves for courage, to feed themselves with optimism, and never quit. He recommends his tape series, "Success Talk," on sale at the arena, which promises a monthly interview with "one of the most successful people of our time." After a short break, he reveals what is ultimately necessary to achieve success. "Lord Jesus, I need You," Peter Lowe asks the crowd to pray. "I want you to come into my life and forgive me for the things I've done."

Lowe has broken from the Christianity of his parents, a faith that now seems hopelessly out of date. The meek shall no longer inherit the earth; the go-getters will get it and everything that goes with it. The Christ who went among the poor, the sick, the downtrodden, among lepers and prostitutes, clearly had no marketing savvy. He has been transfigured into a latter-day entrepreneur, the greatest superstar salesperson of all time, who built a multinational outfit from scratch. Lowe speaks to the crowd about mercy. But the worship of selling and of celebrity infuses his literature, his guest lists, his radio shows and seminars. "Don't network haphazardly," Peter Lowe preaches in his $19.95 *Peter Lowe's Success Yearbook*. "Set goals to meet key people. Imagine yourself talking to them. Plan in advance what questions to ask them . . . When there is an important individual you want to network with, be prepared to say something insightful to them that shows you're aware of their achievements . . . Everyone loves to receive a present. It's hard to be resistant or standoffish to someone who has just given you a nice gift . . . Adopt the attitude of a superstar . . . Smile. A smile tells people you like them, are interested in them. What an appealing message to send!" These are the teachings of his gospel, the good news that fills arenas and sells cassettes.

As the loudspeakers play the theme song from *Chariots of Fire*, Lowe wheels Christopher Reeve onstage. The crowd wildly applauds. Reeve's handsome face is framed by longish gray hair. A respirator tube extends from the back of his blue sweatshirt to a square box on his wheelchair. Reeve describes how it once felt to lie in a hospital bed at two o'clock in the morning, alone and unable to move and thinking that daylight would never come. His voice is clear and strong, but he needs to pause for breath after every few words. He thanks the crowd for its support and confesses that their warm response is one reason he appears at these events; it helps to keep his spirits up. He donates the speaking fees to groups that conduct spinal cord research.

"I've had to leave the physical world," Reeve says. A stillness falls upon the arena; the place is silent during every pause. "By the time I was twenty-four, I was making millions," he continues. "I was pretty pleased with myself . . . I was selfish and neglected my family . . . Since my accident, I've been realizing . . . that success means something quite different." Members of the audience start to weep. "I see people who achieve these conventional goals," he says in a mild, even tone. "*None of it matters.*"

His words cut through all the snake oil of the last few hours, calmly and with great precision. Everybody in the arena, no matter how greedy or eager for promotion, all eighteen thousand of them, know deep in their hearts that what Reeve has just said is true — too true. Their latest schemes, their plans to market and subdivide and franchise their way up, whatever the cost, the whole spirit now gripping Colorado, vanish in an instant. Men and women up and down the aisles wipe away tears, touched not only by what this famous man has been through but also by a sudden awareness of something hollow about their own lives, something gnawing and unfulfilled.

Moments after Reeve is wheeled off the stage, Jack Groppel, the next speaker, walks up to the microphone and starts his pitch, "Tell me friends, in your lifetime, have you ever been on a diet?"

II / meat and potatoes

5 / why the fries taste good

TO REACH THE J. R. SIMPLOT PLANT in Aberdeen, Idaho, you drive through downtown Aberdeen, population 2,000, and keep heading north, past the half dozen shops on Main Street. Then turn right at the Tiger Hut, an old hamburger stand named after a local high school team, cross the railroad tracks where freight cars are loaded with sugar beets, drive another quarter of a mile, and you're there. It smells like someone's cooking potatoes. The Simplot plant is low and square, clean and neat. The employee parking lot is filled with pickup trucks, and there's a big American flag flying out front. Aberdeen sits in the heart of Bingham County, which grows more potatoes than any other county in Idaho. The Simplot plant runs twenty-four hours a day, three hundred and ten days a year, turning potatoes into french fries. It's a small facility, by industry standards, built in the late 1950s. It processes about a million pounds of potatoes a day.

Inside the building, a maze of red conveyer belts crisscrosses in and out of machines that wash, sort, peel, slice, blanch, blow-dry, fry, and flash-freeze potatoes. Workers in white coats and hard hats keep everything running smoothly, monitoring the controls, checking the fries for imperfections. Streams of sliced potatoes pour from machines. The place has a cheerful, humble, Eisenhower-era feeling, as though someone's dream of technological progress, of better living through frozen food, has been fulfilled. Looming over the whole enterprise is the spirit of one man: John Richard Simplot, America's great potato baron, whose seemingly inexhaustible energy and willingness to take risks built an empire based on french fries. By far the most important figure in one of the nation's most conservative states, Simplot displays the contradictory traits that have guided the economic development of the American West, the odd mixture of rugged individualism and a dependence upon public land and resources. In a portrait that hangs above the reception desk at the Aberdeen plant, J. R. Simplot has the sly grin of a gambler who's scored big.

Simplot was born in 1909. His family left Dubuque, Iowa, the following year and eventually settled in Idaho. The Snake River Reclamation Project was offering cheap water for irrigation, funded by the U.S. government, that would convert the desert of southern Idaho into lush farmland. Simplot's father became a homesteader, obtaining land for free and clearing it with a steel rail dragged between two teams of horses. Simplot grew up working hard on the farm. He rebelled against his domineering father, dropped out of school at the age of fifteen, and left home. He found work at a potato warehouse in the small town of Declo, Idaho. He sorted potatoes with a "shaker sorter," a hand-held device, nine to ten hours a day for 30 cents an hour. At the boarding house where he rented a room, Simplot met a group of schoolteachers who were being paid not in cash but in interest-bearing scrip. Simplot bought the scrip from the teachers for 50 cents on the dollar — and then sold the scrip to a local bank for 90 cents on the dollar. With his earnings, Simplot bought a rifle, an old truck, and 600 hogs for $1 a head. He built a cooker in the desert, stoked it with sagebrush, shot wild horses, skinned them, sold their hides for $2 each, cooked their meat, and fed the horse meat to his hogs through the winter. That spring, J. R. Simplot sold the hogs for $12.50 a head and, at the age of sixteen, became a potato farmer.

The Idaho potato industry was just getting started in the 1920s. The state's altitude, warm days, cool nights, light volcanic soil, and abundance of irrigation water made it an ideal setting for growing Russet Burbank potatoes. Simplot leased 160 acres, then bought farm equipment and a team of horses. He learned how to grow potatoes from his landlord, Lindsay Maggart, who raised yields by planting fresh seed every year. In 1928, Simplot and Maggart purchased an electric potato sorter; it seemed a remarkable invention. Simplot began sorting potatoes for his friends and neighbors, but Maggart did not want to share the new device with anyone else. The two men fought over the potato sorter and then agreed to settle who owned it with the flip of a coin. J. R. Simplot won the coin toss, got the sorter, sold all his farm equipment, and started his own business in a potato cellar in Declo. He traveled the Idaho countryside, plugging the rudimentary machine into the nearest available light socket and sorting potatoes for farmers.

Soon he was buying and selling potatoes, opening warehouses, forming relationships with commodities brokers nationwide. When J. R.
Simplot needed timber for a new warehouse, he and his men would
just head down to Yellowstone and chop down some trees. Within a
decade, Simplot was the largest shipper of potatoes in the West, operating thirty-three warehouses in Oregon and Idaho.

Simplot also shipped onions. In 1941, he started to wonder why
the Burbank Corporation, an outfit in California, was ordering so
many of his onions. Simplot went to California and followed one of
the company's trucks to a prune orchard in Vacaville, where the Burbank Corporation was using prune dryers to make dehydrated onions.
Simplot immediately bought a six-tunnel prune dryer and set up his
own dehydration plant in Caldwell, Idaho. The plant opened on October 8, 1941. Two months later, the United States entered World War II,
and Simplot began selling dehydrated onions to the U.S. Army. It was
a profitable arrangement. The dehydrated onion powder, he later recalled, was like "gold dust."

The J. R. Simplot Dehydrating Company soon perfected a new
method for drying potatoes and became one of the principal suppliers
of food to the American military during World War II. In 1942, the
company had a hundred workers at the Caldwell plant; by 1944, it had
about twelve hundred. The Caldwell facility became the largest dehydrating plant in the world. J. R. Simplot used the profits earned as a
military contractor to buy potato farms and cattle ranches, to build
fertilizer plants and lumber mills, to stake mining claims and open a
huge phosphate mine on the Fort Hall Indian Reservation. By the end
of World War II, Simplot was growing his own potatoes, fertilizing
them with his own phosphate, processing them at his factories, shipping them in boxes from his lumber yards, and feeding the leftover
potato scraps to his cattle. He was thirty-six years old.

After the war, Simplot invested heavily in frozen food technology,
betting that it would provide the meals of the future. Clarence Birdseye had patented a number of techniques for flash-freezing in the
1920s. But sales of Birdseye's new products were hampered, among
other things, by the fact that few American grocery stores, and even
fewer households, owned a freezer. The sales of refrigerators, freezers,
and other kitchen appliances soared after World War II. The 1950s
soon became "the Golden Age of Food Processing," in the words of
historian Harvey Levenstein, a decade in which one marvelous innovation after another promised to simplify the lives of American house-

wives: frozen orange juice, frozen TV dinners, the Chicken-of-Tomorrow, "Potato salad from a package!", Cheese Whiz, Jell-O salads, Jet-Puffed Marshmallows, Miracle Whip. Depression-era scarcity gave way to a cornucopia of new foods on the shelves of new suburban supermarkets. Ad campaigns made processed foods seem better than fresh ones, more space-age and up to date. According to Levenstein, many restaurants proudly displayed their canned soups, and a chain called Tad's 30 Varieties of Meals featured frozen dinners on its menu. Customers at Tad's cooked the frozen meals at tableside microwave ovens.

Postwar refrigerators came with freezer compartments, and J. R. Simplot thought about the foods that housewives might want to put in them. He assembled a team of chemists, led by Ray Dunlap, to develop a product that seemed to have enormous potential: the frozen french fry. Americans were eating more fries than ever before, and the Russet Burbank, with its large size and high starch content, was the perfect potato for frying. Simplot wanted to create an inexpensive frozen fry that tasted just as good as a fresh one. Although Thomas Jefferson had brought the Parisian recipe for *pommes frites* to the United States in 1802, french fries did not become well known in this country until the 1920s. Americans traditionally ate their potatoes boiled, mashed, or baked. French fries were popularized in the United States by World War I veterans who'd enjoyed them in Europe and by the drive-in restaurants that subsequently arose in the 1930s and 1940s. Fries could be served without a fork or a knife, and they were easy to eat behind the wheel. But they were extremely time-consuming to prepare. Simplot's chemists experimented with various methods for the mass production of french fries, enduring a number of setbacks, learning the hard way that fries will sink to the bottom of a potato chip fryer and then burn. One day Dunlap walked into J. R. Simplot's office with some frozen fries that had just been reheated. Simplot tasted them, realized the manufacturing problems had been solved, and said, "That's a helluva thing."

J. R. Simplot started selling frozen french fries in 1953. Sales were initially disappointing. Although the frozen fries were precooked and could be baked in an oven, they tasted best when heated in hot oil, limiting their appeal to busy homemakers. Simplot needed to find institutional customers, restaurant owners who'd recognize the tremendous labor-saving benefits of his frozen fries.

"The french fry [was] . . . almost sacrosanct for me," Ray Kroc wrote in his memoir, "its preparation a ritual to be followed religiously." The success of Richard and Mac McDonald's hamburger stand had been based as much on the quality of their fries as on the taste of their burgers. The McDonald brothers had devised an elaborate system for making crisp french fries, one that was later improved by the restaurant chain. McDonald's cooked thinly sliced Russet Burbanks in special fryers to keep the oil temperature above 325 degrees. As the chain expanded, it became more difficult — and yet all the more important — to maintain the consistency and quality of the fries. J. R. Simplot met with Ray Kroc in 1965. The idea of switching to frozen french fries appealed to Kroc, as a means of ensuring uniformity and cutting labor costs. McDonald's obtained its fresh potatoes from about 175 different local suppliers, and crew members spent a great deal of time peeling and slicing potatoes. Simplot offered to build a new factory solely for the manufacture of McDonald's french fries. Kroc agreed to try Simplot's fries, but made no long-term commitment. The deal was sealed with a handshake.

McDonald's began to sell J. R. Simplot's frozen french fries the following year. Customers didn't notice any difference in taste. And the reduced cost of using a frozen product made french fries one of the most profitable items on the menu — far more profitable than hamburgers. Simplot quickly became the main supplier of french fries to McDonald's. At the time, McDonald's had about 725 restaurants in the United States. Within a decade, it had more than 3,000. Simplot sold his frozen fries to other restaurant chains, accelerating the growth of the fast food industry and changing the nation's eating habits. Americans have long consumed more potatoes than any other food except dairy products and wheat flour. In 1960, the typical American ate eighty-one pounds of fresh potatoes and about four pounds of frozen french fries. Today the typical American eats about forty-nine pounds of fresh potatoes every year — and more than thirty pounds of frozen french fries. Ninety percent of those fries are purchased at fast food restaurants. Indeed, french fries have become the most widely sold foodservice item in the United States.

J. R. Simplot, an eighth-grade dropout, is now one of the richest men in the United States. His privately held company grows and processes corn, peas, broccoli, avocados, and carrots, as well as potatoes; feeds and processes cattle; manufactures and distributes fertilizer; mines phosphate and silica; produces oil, ethanol, and natural gas. In 1980, Simplot provided $1 million in start-up funds to a couple of engineers working in the basement of a dentist's office in Boise, Idaho. Twenty years later, his investment in Micron Technology — a manufacturer of computer memory chips and the largest private employer in Idaho — was worth about $1.5 billion. Simplot is also one of the nation's biggest landowners. "I've been a land hog all my life," Simplot told me, laughing. While still in his teens, he bought 18,000 acres along the Snake River, paying 50 cents an acre for it with borrowed money. His company now has 85,000 acres of irrigated farmland, and Simplot personally owns more than twice that amount of ranchland. He owns much of downtown Boise and a big hillside home overlooking the city. At home he flies a gigantic American flag on a pole that's ten stories high. In addition to what he owns, Simplot leases more than 2 million acres of land from the federal government. His ZX Ranch in southern Oregon is the largest cattle ranch in the United States, measuring 65 miles wide and 163 miles long. Altogether, Simplot controls a bloc of North American land that's bigger than the state of Delaware.

Despite being a multibillionaire, J. R. Simplot has few pretensions. He wears cowboy boots and blue jeans, eats at McDonald's, and drives his own car, a Lincoln Continental with license plates that say "MR. SPUD." He seems to have little patience for abstractions, viewing religion as a bunch of "hocus-pocus" and describing his potato empire matter-of-factly: "It's big and it's real, it ain't bullshit." Recently Simplot has been slowing down. A bad fall made him give up horseback riding at the age of eighty; in 1999 he turned ninety and quit skiing. He stepped down as the chief executive of his company in 1994, but keeps buying more land and scouting new factories. "Hell, fellow, I'm just an old farmer got some luck," Simplot said, when I asked about the key to his success. "The only thing I did smart, and just remember this — ninety-nine percent of people would have sold out when they got their first twenty-five or thirty million. I didn't sell out. I just hung on."

the mistake of standing alone

THE PRODUCTION OF frozen french fries has become an intensely competitive business. Although the J. R. Simplot Company supplies the majority of the french fries that McDonald's sells in the United States, two other fry companies are now larger: Lamb Weston, the nation's leading producer of fries, and McCain, a Canadian firm that became the number-two fry company after buying Ore-Ida in 1997. Simplot, Lamb Weston, and McCain now control about 80 percent of the American market for frozen french fries, having eliminated or acquired most of their smaller rivals. The three french fry giants compete for valuable contracts to supply the fast food chains. Frozen french fries have become a bulk commodity, manufactured in high volumes at a low profit margin. Price differences of just a few pennies a pound can mean the difference between winning or losing a major contract. All of this has greatly benefited the fast food chains, lowering their wholesale costs and making their retail sales of french fries even more profitable. Burger King's assault on the supremacy of the McDonald's french fry, launched in 1997 with a $70 million advertising campaign, was driven in large part by the huge markups that are possible with fries. The fast food companies purchase frozen fries for about 30 cents a pound, reheat them in oil, then sell them for about $6 a pound.

Idaho's potato output surpassed Maine's in the late 1950s, owing to the rise of the french fry industry and the productivity gains made by Idaho farmers. Since 1980, the tonnage of potatoes grown in Idaho has almost doubled, while the average yield per acre has risen by nearly 30 percent. But the extraordinary profits being made from the sale of french fries have barely trickled down to the farmers. Paul Patterson, an extension professor of agricultural economics at the University of Idaho, describes the current market for potatoes as an "oligopsony" — a market in which a small number of buyers exert power over a large number of sellers. The giant processing companies do their best to drive down the prices offered to potato farmers. The increased productivity of Idaho farmers has lowered prices even further, shifting more of the profits to the processors and the fast food chains. Out of every $1.50 spent on a large order of fries at a fast food restaurant, perhaps 2 cents goes to the farmer who grew the potatoes.

Idaho's potato farmers now face enormous pressure to get bigger — or get out of the business. Adding more acreage increases total revenues and allows more capital investment; but the risks get bigger, too. The latest potato harvesting equipment — bright red, beautiful machines manufactured in Idaho by a company called Spudnik — can set a farmer back hundreds of thousands of dollars. It costs about $1,500 an acre to grow potatoes in Bingham County. The average potato farmer there, who plants about four hundred acres, is more than

half a million dollars in the hole before selling a single potato. In order
to break even, the farmer needs to receive about $5 per hundredweight
of potatoes. During the 1996–97 season, potato prices fell as low as
$1.50 per hundredweight. That year was a disaster for Idaho potato
farmers, perhaps the worst in history. Record harvests nationwide and
a flood of cheap imports from Canada created an enormous glut of
potatoes. For many farmers, letting potatoes rot in the field would
have been more profitable than selling them at such low prices. That
was not a viable option, however; rotting potatoes can damage the
land. Prices have recovered since then, but remain unusually low. An
Idaho potato farmer's annual income is now largely determined by the
weather, the world market, and the whims of the giant processors.
"The only thing I can really control," one farmer told me, "is what
time I get out of bed in the morning."

Over the past twenty-five years, Idaho has lost about half of its potato farmers. During the same period, the amount of land devoted to
potatoes has increased. Family farms are giving way to corporate
farms that stretch for thousands of acres. These immense corporate
farms are divided into smaller holdings for administrative purposes,
and farmers who've been driven off the land are often hired to manage
them. The patterns of land ownership in the American West more and
more resemble those of rural England. "We've come full circle," says
Paul Patterson. "You increasingly find two classes of people in rural
Idaho: the people who run the farms and the people who own them."

The headquarters of the Potato Growers of Idaho (PGI) is a strip-
mall office suite, not far from a potato museum in Blackfoot. The PGI
is a nonprofit organization that supplies market information to farmers and helps them negotiate contracts with processors. Bert Moulton,
a longtime PGI staff member, is a big man with a crew cut who looks
like a Goldwater Republican but sounds like an old-fashioned populist. Moulton thinks forming some sort of co-op, an association to co-
ordinate marketing and production levels, may be the last hope for
Idaho's potato farmers. At the moment, most farmers live in areas
where there are only one or two processors buying potatoes — and
oddly enough, those processors never seem to be bidding for potatoes
on the same day. "Legally, the processors aren't supposed to be talking
to one another," Moulton says. "But you know that they do." Not long
ago, the major french fry companies in Idaho were owned by people
with strong ties to the local community. J. R. Simplot was highly regarded by most Idaho farmers; he always seemed willing to help carry

them through a lean year. Moulton says the fry companies now tend to be run by outsiders, by "MBA's from Harvard who don't know if a potato grows on a tree or underground." The multinational food companies operate french fry plants in a number of different regions, constantly shifting production to take advantage of the lowest potato prices. The economic fortunes of individual farmers or local communities matter little in the grand scheme.

A few years ago, the PGI tried to create a formal alliance with potato farmers in Oregon and Washington, an effort that would have linked producers in the three states that grow most of the nation's potatoes. The alliance was undermined by one of the big processors, which cut lucrative deals with a core group of potato farmers. Moulton believes that Idaho's farmers deserve some of the blame for their own predicament. Long regarded as the aristocrats of rural Idaho, potato farmers remain stubbornly independent and unwilling to join forces. "Some of them are independent to the point of poverty," he says. Today there are roughly 1,100 potato farmers left in Idaho — few enough to fit in a high school auditorium. About half of them belong to the PGI, but the organization needs at least three-quarters of them as members to gain real bargaining power. The "joint ventures" now being offered by processing companies provide farmers with the potato seed and financing for their crop, an arrangement that should dispel any lingering illusions about their independence. "If potato farmers don't band together," Bert Moulton warns, "they'll wind up sharecroppers."

The behavior of Idaho's potato growers often betrays a type of faulty reasoning described in most college-level economics textbooks. "The fallacy of composition" is a logical error — a mistaken belief that what seems good for an individual will still be good when others do the same thing. For example, someone who stands at a crowded concert may get a better view of the stage. But if everyone at the concert stands up, nobody's view is improved. Since the end of World War II, farmers in the United States have been persuaded to adopt one new technology after another, hoping to improve their yields, reduce their costs, and outsell their neighbors. By embracing this industrial model of agriculture — one that focuses narrowly on the level of inputs and outputs, that encourages specialization in just one crop, that relies heavily on chemical fertilizers, pesticides, fungicides, herbicides, advanced harvesting and irrigation equipment — American farmers have become the most productive farmers on earth. Every increase in productivity, however, has driven more American farmers off the land. And it has left those who remain beholden to the companies that supply the inputs and the processors that buy the outputs. William Heffernan, a professor of rural sociology at the University of Missouri, says that America's agricultural economy now resembles an hourglass. At the top there are about 2 million ranchers and farmers; at the bottom there are 275 million consumers; and at the narrow portion in the middle, there are a dozen or so multinational corporations earning a profit from every transaction.

food product design

THE TASTE OF McDonald's french fries has long been praised by customers, competitors, and even food critics. James Beard loved McDonald's fries. Their distinctive taste does not stem from the type of potatoes that McDonald's buys, the technology that processes them, or the restaurant equipment that fries them. Other chains buy their french fries from the same large processing companies, use Russet Burbanks, and have similar fryers in their restaurant kitchens. The taste of a fast food fry is largely determined by the cooking oil. For decades, McDonald's cooked its french fries in a mixture of about 7 percent cottonseed oil and 93 percent beef tallow. The mix gave the fries their unique flavor — and more saturated beef fat per ounce than a McDonald's hamburger.

Amid a barrage of criticism over the amount of cholesterol in their fries, McDonald's switched to pure vegetable oil in 1990. The switch presented the company with an enormous challenge: how to make fries that subtly taste like beef without cooking them in tallow. A look at the ingredients now used in the preparation of McDonald's french fries suggests how the problem was solved. Toward the end of the list is a seemingly innocuous, yet oddly mysterious phrase: "natural flavor". That ingredient helps to explain not only why the fries taste so good, but also why most fast food — indeed, most of the food Americans eat today — tastes the way it does.

Open your refrigerator, your freezer, your kitchen cupboards, and look at the labels on your food. You'll find "natural flavor" or "artificial flavor" in just about every list of ingredients. The similarities between these two broad categories of flavor are far more significant than their differences. Both are man-made additives that give most processed food most of its taste. The initial purchase of a food item may be driven by its packaging or appearance, but subsequent purchases are determined mainly by its taste. About 90 percent of the money that Americans spend on food is used to buy processed food. But the canning, freezing, and dehydrating techniques used to process food destroy most of its flavor. Since the end of World War II, a vast industry has arisen in the United States to make processed food palatable. Without this flavor industry, today's fast food industry could not exist. The names of the leading American fast food chains and the bestselling menu items have become famous worldwide, embedded in our popular culture. Few people, however, can name the companies that manufacture fast food's taste.

The flavor industry is highly secretive. Its leading companies will not divulge the precise formulas of flavor compounds or the identities of clients. The secrecy is deemed essential for protecting the reputation of beloved brands. The fast food chains, understandably, would like the public to believe that the flavors of their food somehow originate in their restaurant kitchens, not in distant factories run by other firms.

The New Jersey Turnpike runs through the heart of the flavor industry, an industrial corridor dotted with refineries and chemical plants. International Flavors & Fragrances (IFF), the world's largest flavor company, has a manufacturing facility off Exit 8A in Dayton, New Jersey; Givaudan, the world's second-largest flavor company, has a plant in East Hanover. Haarmann & Reimer, the largest German flavor company, has a plant in Teterboro, as does Takasago, the largest Japanese flavor company. Flavor Dynamics has a plant in South Plainfield; Frutarom is in North Bergen; Elan Chemical is in Newark. Dozens of companies manufacture flavors in the corridor between Teaneck and South Brunswick. Indeed, the area produces about two-thirds of the flavor additives sold in the United States.

The IFF plant in Dayton is a huge pale blue building with a modern office complex attached to the front. It sits in an industrial park, not far from a BASF plastics factory, a Jolly French Toast factory, and a plant that manufactures Liz Claiborne cosmetics. Dozens of tractor-trailers were parked at the IFF loading dock the afternoon I visited, and a thin cloud of steam floated from the chimney. Before entering the plant, I signed a nondisclosure form, promising not to reveal the brand names of products that contain IFF flavors. The place reminded me of Willy Wonka's chocolate factory. Wonderful smells drifted through the hallways, men and women in neat white lab coats cheerfully went about their work, and hundreds of little glass bottles sat on laboratory tables and shelves. The bottles contained powerful but fragile flavor chemicals, shielded from light by the brown glass and the round plastic caps shut tight. The long chemical names on the little white labels were as mystifying to me as medieval Latin. They were the odd-sounding names of things that would be mixed and poured and turned into new substances, like magic potions.

I was not invited to see the manufacturing areas of the IFF plant, where it was thought I might discover trade secrets. Instead, I toured various laboratories and pilot kitchens, where the flavors of well-established brands are tested or adjusted, and where whole new flavors are created. IFF's snack and savory lab is responsible for the flavor of potato chips, corn chips, breads, crackers, breakfast cereals, and pet food. The confectionery lab devises the flavor for ice cream, cookies, candies, toothpastes, mouthwashes, and antacids. Everywhere I looked, I saw famous, widely advertised products sitting on laboratory desks and tables. The beverage lab is full of brightly colored liquids in clear bottles. It comes up with the flavor for popular soft drinks, sport drinks, bottled teas, and wine coolers, for all-natural juice drinks, organic soy drinks, beers, and malt liquors. In one pilot kitchen I saw a dapper food technologist, a middle-aged man with an elegant tie beneath his lab coat, carefully preparing a batch of cookies with white frosting and pink-and-white sprinkles. In another pilot kitchen I saw a pizza oven, a grill, a milk-shake machine, and a french fryer identical to those I'd seen behind the counter at countless fast food restaurants.

In addition to being the world's largest flavor company, IFF manufactures the smell of six of the ten best-selling fine perfumes in the United States, including Estée Lauder's Beautiful, Clinique's Happy, Lancôme's Trésor, and Calvin Klein's Eternity, It also makes the smell of household products such as deodorant, dishwashing detergent, bath soap, shampoo, furniture polish, and floor wax. All of these aromas are made through the same basic process: the manipulation of volatile chemicals to create a particular smell. The basic science behind the scent of your shaving cream is the same as that governing the flavor of your TV dinner.

The aroma of a food can be responsible for as much as 90 percent of its flavor. Scientists now believe that human beings acquired the sense of taste as a way to avoid being poisoned. Edible plants generally taste sweet; deadly ones, bitter. Taste is supposed to help us differentiate food that's good for us from food that's not. The taste buds on our tongues can detect the presence of half a dozen or so basic tastes, including: sweet, sour, bitter, salty, astringent, and umami (a taste discovered by Japanese researchers, a rich and full sense of deliciousness triggered by amino acids in foods such as shellfish, mushrooms, potatoes, and seaweed). Taste buds offer a relatively limited means of detection, however, compared to the human olfactory system, which can perceive thousands of different chemical aromas. Indeed "flavor" is primarily the smell of gases being released by the chemicals you've just put in your mouth.

The act of drinking, sucking, or chewing a substance releases its volatile gases. They flow out of the mouth and up the nostrils, or up the passageway in the back of the mouth, to a thin layer of nerve cells called the olfactory epithelium, located at the base of the nose, right between the eyes. The brain combines the complex smell signals from the epithelium with the simple taste signals from the tongue, assigns a flavor to what's in your mouth, and decides if it's something you want to eat.

Babies like sweet tastes and reject bitter ones; we know this because scientists have rubbed various flavors inside the mouths of infants and then recorded their facial reactions. A person's food preferences, like his or her personality, are formed during the first few years of life, through a process of socialization. Toddlers can learn to enjoy hot and spicy food, bland health food, or fast food, depending upon what the people around them eat. The human sense of smell is still not fully understood and can be greatly affected by psychological factors and expectations. The mind filters out the overwhelming majority of chemical aromas that surround us, focusing intently on some, ignoring others. People can grow accustomed to bad smells or good smells; they stop noticing what once seemed overpowering. Aroma and memory are somehow inextricably linked. A smell can suddenly evoke a long-forgotten moment. The flavors of childhood foods seem to leave an indelible mark, and adults often return to them, without always knowing why. These "comfort foods" become a source of pleasure and reassurance, a fact that fast food chains work hard to promote. Childhood memories of Happy Meals can translate into frequent adult visits to McDonald's, like those of the chain's "heavy users," the customers who eat there four or five times a week.

The human craving for flavor has been a largely unacknowledged and unexamined force in history. Royal empires have been built, unexplored lands have been traversed, great religions and philosophies have been forever changed by the spice trade. In 1492 Christopher Columbus set sail to find seasoning. Today the influence of flavor in the world marketplace is no less decisive. The rise and fall of corporate empires — of soft drink companies, snack food companies, and fast food chains — is frequently determined by how their products taste.

The flavor industry emerged in the mid-nineteenth century, as processed foods began to be manufactured on a large scale. Recognizing the need for flavor additives, the early food processors turned to perfume companies that had years of experience working with essential oils and volatile aromas. The great perfume houses of England, France, and the Netherlands produced many of the first flavor compounds. In the early part of the twentieth century, Germany's powerful chemical industry assumed the technological lead in flavor production. Legend has it that a German scientist discovered methyl anthranilate, one of the first artificial flavors, by accident while mixing chemicals in his laboratory. Suddenly the lab was filled with the sweet smell of grapes. Methyl anthranilate later became the chief flavoring compound of grape Kool-Aid. After World War II, much of the perfume industry shifted from Europe to the United States, settling in New York City near the garment district and the fashion houses. The flavor industry came with it, subsequently moving to New Jersey to gain more plant capacity. Man-made flavor additives were used mainly in baked goods, candies, and sodas until the 1950s, when sales of processed food began to soar. The invention of gas chromatographs and mass spectrometers — machines capable of detecting volatile gases at low levels — vastly increased the number of flavors that could be synthesized. By the mid-1960s the American flavor industry was churning out compounds to supply the taste of Pop Tarts, Bac-Os, Tab, Tang, Filet-O-Fish sandwiches, and literally thousands of other new foods.

The American flavor industry now has annual revenues of about $1.4 billion. Approximately ten thousand new processed food products are introduced every year in the United States. Almost all of them require flavor additives. And about nine out of every ten of these new food products fail. The latest flavor innovations and corporate realignments are heralded in publications such as *Food Chemical News, Food Engineering, Chemical Market Reporter,* and *Food Product Design.*

The growth of IFF has mirrored that of the flavour industry as a whole. IFF was formed in 1958, through the merger of two small companies. Its annual revenues have grown almost fifteenfold since the early 1970s, and it now has manufacturing facilities in twenty countries.

The quality that people seek most of all in a food, its flavor, is usually present in a quantity too infinitesimal to be measured by any traditional culinary terms such as ounces or teaspoons. Today's sophisticated spectrometers, gas chromatographs, and headspace vapor analyzers provide a detailed map of a food's flavor components, detecting chemical aromas in amounts as low as one part per billion. The human nose, however, is still more sensitive than any machine yet invented. A nose can detect aromas present in quantities of a few parts per trillion — an amount equivalent to 0.000000000003 percent. Complex aromas, like those of coffee or roasted meat, may be composed of volatile gases from nearly a thousand different chemicals. The smell of a strawberry arises from the interaction of at least 350 different chemicals that are present in minute amounts. The chemical that provides the dominant flavor of bell pepper can be tasted in amounts as low as .02 parts per billion; one drop is sufficient to add flavor to five average size swimming pools. The flavor additive usually comes last, or second to last, in a processed food's list of ingredients (chemicals that add color are frequently used in even smaller amounts). As a result, the flavor of a processed food often costs less than its packaging. Soft drinks contain a larger proportion of flavor additives than most products. The flavor in a twelve-ounce can of Coke costs about half a cent.

The Food and Drug Administration does not require flavor companies to disclose the ingredients of their additives, so long as all the chemicals are considered by the agency to be GRAS (Generally Regarded As Safe). This lack of public disclosure enables the companies to maintain the secrecy of their formulas. It also hides the fact that flavor compounds sometimes contain more ingredients than the foods being given their taste. The ubiquitous phrase "artificial strawberry flavor" gives little hint of the chemical wizardry and manufacturing skill that can make a highly processed food taste like a strawberry.

A typical artificial strawberry flavor, like the kind found in a Burger King strawberry milk shake, contains the following ingredients: amyl acetate, amyl butyrate, amyl valerate, anethol, anisyl formate, benzyl acetate, benzyl isobutyrate, butyric acid, cinnamyl isobutyrate, cinnamyl valerate, cognac essential oil, diacetyl, dipropyl ketone, ethyl acetate, ethyl amyl ketone, ethyl butyrate, ethyl cinnamate, ethyl heptanoate, ethyl heptylate, ethyl lactate, ethyl methylphenyl-glycidate, ethyl nitrate, ethyl propionate, ethyl valerate, heliotropin, hydroxyphenyl-2-butanone (10 percent solution in alcohol), α-ionone, isobutyl anthranilate, isobutyl butyrate, lemon essential oil, maltol, 4-methylacetophenone, methyl anthranilate, methyl benzoate, methyl cinnamate, methyl heptine carbonate, methyl naphthyl ketone, methyl salicylate, mint essential oil, neroli essential oil, nerolin, neryl isobutyrate, orris butter, phenethyl alcohol, rose, rum ether, γ-undecalactone, vanillin, and solvent.

Although flavors usually arise from a mixture of many different volatile chemicals, a single compound often supplies the dominant aroma. Smelled alone, that chemical provides an unmistakable sense of the food. Ethyl-2-methyl butyrate, for example, smells just like an apple. Today's highly processed foods offer a blank palette: whatever chemicals you add to them will give them specific tastes. Adding methyl-2-peridylketone makes something taste like popcorn. Adding ethyl-3-hydroxybutanoate makes it taste like marshmallow. The possibilities are now almost limitless. Without affecting the appearance or nutritional value, processed foods could even be made with aroma chemicals such as hexanal (the smell of freshly cut grass) or 3-methyl butanoic acid (the smell of body odor).

The 1960s were the heyday of artificial flavors. The synthetic versions of flavor compounds were not subtle, but they did not need to be, given the nature of most processed food. For the past twenty years food processors have tried hard to use only "natural flavors" in their products. According to the FDA, these must be derived entirely from natural sources — from herbs, spices, fruits, vegetables, beef, chicken, yeast, bark, roots, etc. Consumers prefer to see natural flavors on a label, out of a belief that they are healthier. The distinction between artificial and natural flavors can be somewhat arbitrary and absurd, based more on how the flavor has been made than on what it actually contains. "A natural flavor," says Terry Acree, a professor of food science at Cornell University, "is a flavor that's been derived with an out-of-date technology." Natural flavors and artificial flavors sometimes contain exactly the same chemicals, produced through different methods. Amyl acetate, for example, provides the dominant note of banana flavor. When you distill it from bananas with a solvent, amyl acetate is a natural flavor. When you produce it by mixing vinegar with amyl alcohol, adding sulfuric acid as a catalyst, amyl acetate is an artificial flavor. Either way it smells and tastes the same. The phrase "natural flavor" is now listed among the ingredients of everything from Stonyfield Farm Organic Strawberry Yogurt to Taco Bell Hot Taco Sauce.

A natural flavor is not necessarily healthier or purer than an artificial one. When almond flavor (benzaldehyde) is derived from natural sources, such as peach and apricot pits, it contains traces of hydrogen cyanide, a deadly poison. Benzaldehyde derived through a different process — by mixing oil of clove and the banana flavor, amyl acetate — does not contain any cyanide. Nevertheless, it is legally considered an artificial flavor and sells at a much lower price. Natural and artificial flavors are now manufactured at the same chemical plants, places that few people would associate with Mother Nature. Calling any of these flavors "natural" requires a flexible attitude toward the English language and a fair amount of irony.

The small and elite group of scientists who create most of the flavor in most of the food now consumed in the United States are called "flavorists." They draw upon a number of disciplines in their work: biology, psychology, physiology, and organic chemistry. A flavorist is a chemist with a trained nose and a poetic sensibility. Flavors are created by blending scores of different chemicals in tiny amounts, a process governed by scientific principles but demanding a fair amount of art. In an age when delicate aromas, subtle flavors, and microwave ovens do not easily coexist, the job of the flavorist is to conjure illusions about processed food and, in the words of one flavor company's literature, to ensure "consumer likeability." The flavorists with whom I spoke were charming, cosmopolitan, and ironic. They were also discreet, in keeping with the dictates of their trade. They were the sort of scientist who not only enjoyed fine wine, but could also tell you the chemicals that gave each vintage its unique aroma. One flavorist compared his work to composing music. A well-made flavor compound will have a "top note," followed by a "dry-down," and a "leveling-off," with different chemicals responsible for each stage. The taste of a food can be radically altered by minute changes in the flavoring mix. "A little odor goes a long way," one flavorist said.

In order to give a processed food the proper taste, a flavorist must always consider the food's "mouthfeel" — the unique combination of textures and chemical interactions that affects how the flavor is perceived. The mouthfeel can be adjusted through the use of various fats, gums, starches, emulsifiers, and stabilizers. The aroma chemicals of a food can be precisely analyzed, but mouthfeel is much harder to measure. How does one quantify a french fry's crispness? Food technologists are now conducting basic research in rheology, a branch of physics that examines the flow and deformation of materials. A number of companies sell sophisticated devices that attempt to measure mouthfeel. The TA.XT2i Texture Analyzer, produced by the Texture Technologies Corporation, performs calculations based on data derived from as many as 250 separate probes. It is essentially a mechanical mouth. It gauges the most important rheological properties of a food — the bounce, creep, breaking point, density, crunchiness, chewiness, gumminess, lumpiness, rubberiness, springiness, slipperiness, smoothness, softness, wetness, juiciness, spreadability, springback, and tackiness.

Some of the most important advances in flavor manufacturing are now occurring in the field of biotechnology. Complex flavors are being made through fermentation, enzyme reactions, fungal cultures, and tissue cultures. All of the flavors being created through these methods — including the ones being synthesized by funguses — are considered natural flavors by the FDA. The new enzyme-based processes are responsible for extremely lifelike dairy flavors. One company now offers not just butter flavor, but also fresh creamy butter, cheesy butter, milky butter, savory melted butter, and super-concentrated butter flavor, in liquid or powder form. The development of new fermentation techniques, as well as new techniques for heating mixtures of sugar and amino acids, have led to the creation of much more realistic meat flavors. The McDonald's Corporation will not reveal the exact origin of the natural flavor added to its french fries. In response to inquiries from *Vegetarian Journal,* however, McDonald's did acknowledge that its fries derive some of their characteristic flavor from "animal products."

Other popular fast foods derive their flavor from unexpected sources. Wendy's Grilled Chicken Sandwich, for example, contains beef extracts. Burger King's BK Broiler Chicken Breast Patty contains "natural smoke flavor." A firm called Red Arrow Products Company specializes in smoke flavor, which is added to barbecue sauces and processed meats. Red Arrow manufactures natural smoke flavor by charring sawdust and capturing the aroma chemicals released into the air. The smoke is captured in water and then bottled, so that other companies can sell food which seems to have been cooked over a fire.

In a meeting room at IFF, Brian Grainger let me sample some of the company's flavors. It was an unusual taste test; there wasn't any food to taste. Grainger is a senior flavorist at IFF, a soft-spoken chemist with graying hair, an English accent, and a fondness for understatement. He could easily be mistaken for a British diplomat or the owner of a West End brasserie with two Michelin stars. Like many in the flavor industry, he has an Old World, old-fashioned sensibility which seems out of step with our brand-conscious, egocentric age. When I suggested that IFF should put its own logo on the products that contain its flavors — instead of allowing other brands to enjoy the consumer loyalty and affection inspired by those flavors — Grainger politely disagreed, assuring me such a thing would never be done. In the absence of public credit or acclaim, the small and secretive fraternity of flavor chemists praises one another's work. Grainger can often tell, by analyzing the flavor formula of a product, which of his counterparts at a rival firm devised it. And he enjoys walking down supermarket aisles, looking at the many products that contain his flavors, even if no one else knows it.

Grainger had brought a dozen small glass bottles from the lab. After he opened each bottle, I dipped a fragrance testing filter into it. The filters were long white strips of paper designed to absorb aroma chemicals without producing off-notes. Before placing the strips of paper before my nose, I closed my eyes. Then I inhaled deeply, and one food after another was conjured from the glass bottles. I smelled fresh cherries, black olives, sautéed onions, and shrimp. Grainger's most remarkable creation took me by surprise. After closing my eyes, I suddenly smelled a grilled hamburger. The aroma was uncanny, almost miraculous. It smelled like someone in the room was flipping burgers on a hot grill. But when I opened my eyes, there was just a narrow strip of white paper and a smiling flavorist.

millions and millions of fries

AT THE HEIGHT OF the potato harvest, I visited the Lamb Weston plant in American Falls, Idaho. It's one of the biggest fry factories in the world and makes french fries for McDonald's. It has a production capacity more than three times larger than that of the Simplot plant in

Aberdeen. It is a state-of-the-art processing facility where raw commodities and man-made additives are combined to make America's most popular food.

Lamb Weston was founded in 1950 by F. Gilbert Lamb, the inventor of a crucial piece of french fry–making technology. The Lamb Water Gun Knife uses a high-pressure hose to shoot potatoes at a speed of 117 feet per second through a grid of sharpened steel blades, thereby creating perfectly sliced french fries. After coming up with the idea, Gil Lamb tested the first Water Gun Knife in a company parking lot, shooting potatoes out of a fire hose. Lamb sold his company to ConAgra in 1988. Lamb Weston now manufactures more than 130 different types of french fries, including: Steak House Fries, CrissCut Fries, Hi-Fries, Mor-Fries, Burger Fries, Taterbabies, Taterboy Curley QQQ Fries, and Rus-Ettes Special Dry Fry Shoestrings.

Bud Mandeville, the plant manager, led me up a narrow, wooden staircase inside one of the plant's storage buildings. On the top floor, the staircase led to a catwalk, and beneath my feet I saw a mound of potatoes that was twenty feet deep and a hundred feet wide and almost as long as two football fields. The building was cool and dark, kept year-round at a steady 46 degrees. In the dim light the potatoes looked like grains of sand on a beach. This was one of seven storage buildings on the property.

Outside, tractor-trailers arrived from the fields, carrying potatoes that had just been harvested. The trucks dumped their loads onto spinning rods that brought the larger potatoes into the building and let the small potatoes, dirt, and rocks fall to the ground. The rods led to a rock trap, a tank of water in which the potatoes floated and the rocks sank to the bottom. The plant used water systems to float potatoes gently this way and that way, guiding different sizes out of different holding bays, then flushing them into a three-foot-deep stream that ran beneath the cement floor. The interior of the processing plant was gray, massive, and well-lit, with huge pipes running along the walls, steel catwalks, workers in hardhats, and plenty of loud machinery. If there weren't potatoes bobbing and floating past, you might think the place was an oil refinery.

Conveyer belts took the wet, clean potatoes into a machine that blasted them with steam for twelve seconds, boiled the water under their skins, and exploded their skins off. Then the potatoes were pumped into a preheat tank and shot through a Lamb Water Gun Knife. They emerged as shoestring fries. Four video cameras scrutinized them from different angles, looking for flaws. When a french fry with a blemish was detected, an optical sorting machine time-sequenced a single burst of compressed air that knocked the bad fry off the production line and onto a separate conveyer belt, which carried it to a machine with tiny automated knives that precisely removed the blemish. And then the fry was returned to the main production line.

Sprays of hot water blanched the fries, gusts of hot air dried them, and 25,000 pounds of boiling oil fried them to a slight crisp. Air cooled by compressed ammonia gas quickly froze them, a computerized sorter divided them into six-pound batches, and a device that spun like an out-of-control lazy Susan used centrifugal force to align the french fries so that they all pointed in the same direction. The fries were sealed in brown bags, then the bags were loaded by robots into cardboard boxes, and the boxes were stacked by robots onto wooden pallets. Forklifts driven by human beings took the pallets to a freezer for storage. Inside that freezer I saw 20 million pounds of french fries, most of them destined for McDonald's, the boxes of fries stacked thirty feet high, the stacks extending for roughly forty yards. And the freezer was half empty. Every day about a dozen railroad cars and about two dozen tractor-trailers pulled up to the freezer, loaded up with french fries, and departed for McDonald's restaurants in Boise, Pocatello, Phoenix, Salt Lake City, Denver, Colorado Springs, and points in between.

Near the freezer was a laboratory where women in white coats analyzed french fries day and night, measuring their sugar content, their starch content, their color. During the fall, Lamb Weston added sugar to the fries; in the spring it leached sugar out of them; the goal was to maintain a uniform taste and appearance throughout the year. Every half hour, a new batch of fries was cooked in fryers identical to those used in fast food kitchens. A middle-aged woman in a lab coat handed me a paper plate full of premium extra longs, the type of french fries sold at McDonald's, and a salt shaker, and some ketchup. The fries on the plate looked wildly out of place in this laboratory setting, this surreal food factory with its computer screens, digital readouts, shiny steel platforms, and evacuation plans in case of ammonia gas leaks. The french fries were delicious — crisp and golden brown, made from potatoes that had been in the ground that morning. I finished them and asked for more.

6/on the range

HANK WAS THE FIRST PERSON I met in Colorado Springs. He was a prominent local rancher, and I'd called him to learn how development pressures and the dictates of the fast food industry were affecting the area's cattle business. In July of 1997, he offered to give me a tour of the new subdivisions that were rising on land where cattle once roamed. We met in the lobby of my hotel. Hank was forty-two years old and handsome enough to be a Hollywood cowboy, tall and rugged, wearing blue jeans, old boots, and a big white hat. But the Dodge minivan he drove didn't quite go with that image, and he was too smart to fit any stereotype. Hank proved to be good company from the first handshake. He had strong opinions, but didn't take himself too seriously. We spent hours driving around Colorado Springs, looking at how the New West was burying the Old.

As we drove through neighborhoods like Broadmoor Oaks and Broadmoor Bluffs, amid the foothills of Cheyenne Mountain, Hank pointed out that all these big new houses on small lots sat on land that every few generations burned. The houses were surrounded by lovely pale brown grasses, tumbleweed, and scrub oak — ideal kindling. As in southern California, these hillsides could erupt in flames with the slightest spark, a cigarette tossed from a car window. The homes looked solid and prosperous, gave no hint of their vulnerability, and had wonderful views.

Hank's ranch was about twenty miles south of town. As we headed there, the landscape opened up and began to show glimpses of the true West — the wide-open countryside that draws its beauty from the absence of people, attracts people, and then slowly loses its appeal. Through leadership positions in a variety of local and statewide groups, Hank was trying to bridge the gap between ranchers and environmentalists, to establish some common ground between longtime enemies. He was not a wealthy, New Age type playing at being a cowboy. His income came from the roughly four hundred head of cattle on his ranch. He didn't care what was politically correct and had little patience for urban environmentalists who vilified the cattle industry. In his view, good ranchers did far less damage to the land than city-dwellers. "Nature isn't an abstraction for me," he said. "My family lives with it every day."

When we got to the ranch, Hank's wife, Susan, was leading her horse out of a ring. She was blond and attractive, but no pushover: tall, fit, and strong. Their daughters, Allie and Kris, aged six and eight, ran over to greet us, full of excitement that their dad was home and had brought a visitor. They scrambled into the minivan and joined us for a drive around the property. Hank wanted me to see the difference between his form of ranching and "raping the land." As we took off onto a dirt road, I looked back at his house and thought about how small it looked amid this landscape. On acreage hundreds if not thousands of times larger than the front lawns and back yards surrounding the mansions of Colorado Springs, the family lived in a modest log cabin.

Hank was practicing a form of range management inspired by the grazing patterns of elk and buffalo herds, animals who'd lived for millennia on this short-grass prairie. His ranch was divided into thirty-five separate pastures. His cattle spent ten or eleven days in one pasture, then were moved to the next, allowing the native plants, the blue grama and buffalo grass, time to recover. Hank stopped the minivan to show me a nearby stream. On land that has been overgrazed, the stream banks are usually destroyed first, as cattle gather in the cool shade beside the water, eating everything in sight. Hank's stream was fenced off with barbed wire, and the banks were lush and green. Then he took me to see Fountain Creek, which ran straight through the ranch, and I realized that he'd given other guests the same tour. It had a proper sequence and a point.

Fountain Creek was a long, ugly gash about twenty yards wide and fifteen feet deep. The banks were collapsing from erosion, fallen trees and branches littered the creek bed, and a small trickle of water ran down the middle. "This was done by storm runoff from Colorado Springs," Hank said. The contrast between his impact on the land and the city's impact was hard to miss. The rapid growth of Colorado Springs had occurred without much official planning, zoning, or spending on drainage projects. As more pavement covered land within the city limits, more water flowed straight into Fountain Creek instead of being absorbed into the ground. The runoff from Colorado Springs eroded the land beside the creek, carrying silt and debris downstream all the way to Kansas. Hank literally lost part of his ranch every year. It got washed away by the city's rainwater. A nearby rancher once lost ten acres of land in a single day, thanks to runoff from a fierce storm in Colorado Springs. While Hank stood on the crumbling bank, giving an impassioned speech about the watershed protection group that he'd helped to organize, telling me about holding ponds, landscaped greenways, and the virtues of permeable parking lots covered in gravel, I lost track of his words. And I thought: "This guy's going to be governor of Colorado someday."

Toward sunset we spotted a herd of antelope and roared after them. That damn minivan bounced over the prairie like a horse at full gallop, Hank wild behind the wheel, Allie and Kris squealing in the back seat. We had a Chrysler engine, power steering, and disk brakes, but the antelope had a much superior grace, making sharp and unexpected turns, about two dozen of them, bounding effortlessly, butts held high. After a futile chase, Hank let the herd go on its way, then veered right and guided the minivan up a low hill. There was something else he wanted to show me. The girls looked intently out the window, faces flushed, searching for more wildlife. When we reached the crest of the hill, I looked down and saw an immense oval structure, shiny and brand-new. For an instant, I couldn't figure out what it was. It looked like a structure created by some alien civilization and plopped in the middle of nowhere. "Stock car racing," Hank said matter-of-factly. The grandstands around the track were enormous, and so was the parking lot. Acres of black asphalt and white lines now spread across the prairie, thousands of empty spaces waiting for cars.

The speedway was new, and races were being held there every weekend in the summer. You could hear the engines and the crowd from Hank's house. The races weren't the main problem, though. It was the practice runs that bothered Hank and Susan most. In the middle of the day, in one of America's most beautiful landscapes, they would suddenly hear the drone of stock cars going round and round. For a moment, we sat quietly on top of the hill, staring at the speedway bathed in twilight, at this oval strip of pavement, this unsettling omen. Hank stopped there long enough for me to ponder what it meant, the threat now coming his way, then drove back down the hill. The speed-way was gone again, out of sight, and the girls were still happy in the back seat, chatting away, oblivious, as the sun dropped behind the mountains.

a new trust

RANCHERS AND COWBOYS HAVE long been the central icons of the American West. Traditionalists have revered them as symbols of freedom and self-reliance. Revisionists have condemned them as rac-ists, economic parasites, and despoilers of the land. The powerful feel-ings evoked by cattlemen reflect opposing views of our national iden-tity, attempts to sustain old myths or create new ones. There is one indisputable fact, however, about American ranchers: they are rapidly disappearing. Over the last twenty years, about half a million ranchers sold off their cattle and quit the business. Many of the nation's re-maining eight hundred thousand ranchers are faring poorly. They're taking second jobs. They're selling cattle at break-even prices or at a loss. The ranchers who are faring the worst run three to four hundred head of cattle, manage the ranch themselves, and live solely off the proceeds. The sort of hard-working ranchers long idealized in cowboy myths are the ones most likely to go broke today. Without receiving a fraction of the public attention given to the northwestern spotted owl, America's independent cattlemen have truly become an endangered species.

Ranchers currently face a host of economic problems: rising land prices, stagnant beef prices, oversupplies of cattle, increased ship-ments of live cattle from Canada and Mexico, development pressures, inheritance taxes, health scares about beef. On top of all that, the growth of the fast food chains has encouraged consolidation in the meatpacking industry. McDonald's is the nation's largest purchaser of beef. In 1968, McDonald's bought ground beef from 175 local suppli-ers. A few years later, seeking to achieve greater product uniformity as it expanded, McDonald's reduced the number of beef suppliers to five. Much like the french fry industry, the meatpacking industry has been transformed by mergers and acquisitions over the last twenty years. Many ranchers now argue that a few large corporations have gained a stranglehold on the market, using unfair tactics to drive down the price of cattle. Anger toward the large meatpackers is growing, and a new range war threatens to erupt, one that will determine the social and economic structure of the rural West.

A century ago, American ranchers found themselves in a similar predicament. The leading sectors of the nation's economy were controlled by corporate alliances known as "trusts." There was a Sugar Trust, a Steel Trust, a Tobacco Trust — and a Beef Trust. It set the prices offered for cattle. Ranchers who spoke out against this monopoly power were often blackballed, unable to sell their cattle at any price. In 1917, at the height of the Beef Trust, the five largest meatpacking companies — Armour, Swift, Morris, Wilson, and Cudahy — controlled about 55 percent of the market. The early twentieth century had trusts, but it also had "trustbusters," progressive government officials who believed that concentrated economic power posed a grave threat to American democracy. The Sherman Antitrust Act had been passed in 1890 after a congressional investigation of price fixing in the meatpacking industry, and for the next two decades the federal government tried to break up the Beef Trust, with little success. In 1917 President Woodrow Wilson ordered the Federal Trade Commission to investigate the industry. The FTC inquiry concluded that the five major meatpacking firms had secretly fixed prices for years, had colluded to divide up markets, and had shared livestock information to guarantee that ranchers received the lowest possible price for their cattle. Afraid that an antitrust trial might end with an unfavorable verdict, the five meatpacking companies signed a consent decree in 1920 that forced them to sell off their stockyards, retail meat stores, railway interests, and livestock journals. A year later Congress created the Packers and Stockyards Administration (P&SA), a federal agency with a broad authority to prevent price-fixing and monopolistic behavior in the beef industry.

For the next fifty years, ranchers sold their cattle in a relatively competitive marketplace. The price of cattle was set through open bidding at auctions. The large meatpackers competed with hundreds of small regional firms. In 1970 the top four meatpacking firms slaughtered only 21 percent of the nation's cattle. A decade later, the Reagan administration allowed these firms to merge and combine without fear of antitrust enforcement. The Justice Department and the P&SA's successor, the Grain Inspection, Packers and Stockyards Administration (GIPSA), stood aside as the large meatpackers gained control of one local cattle market after another. Today the top four meatpacking firms — ConAgra, IBP, Excel, and National Beef — slaughter about 84 percent of the nation's cattle. Market concentration in the beef industry is now at the highest level since record-keeping began in the early twentieth century.

Today's unprecedented degree of meatpacking concentration has helped depress the prices that independent ranchers get for their cattle. Over the last twenty years, the rancher's share of every retail dollar spent on beef has fallen from 63 cents to 46 cents. The four major meatpacking companies now control about 20 percent of the live cattle in the United States through "captive supplies" — cattle that are either maintained in company-owned feedlots or purchased in advance through forward contracts. When cattle prices start to rise, the large meatpackers can flood the market with their own captive supplies, driving prices back down. They can also obtain cattle through confidential agreements with wealthy ranchers, never revealing the true price being paid. ConAgra and Excel operate their own gigantic feedlots, while IBP has private arrangements with some of America's biggest ranchers and feeders, including the Bass brothers, Paul Engler, and J. R. Simplot. Independent ranchers and feedlots now have a hard time figuring out what their cattle are actually worth, let alone finding a buyer for them at the right price. On any given day in the nation's regional cattle markets, as much as 80 percent of the cattle being exchanged are captive supplies. The prices being paid for these cattle are never disclosed.

To get a sense of what an independent rancher now faces, imagine how the New York Stock Exchange would function if large investors could keep the terms of all their stock trades secret. Ordinary investors would have no idea what their own stocks were really worth — a fact that wealthy traders could easily exploit. "A free market requires many buyers as well as many sellers, all with equal access to accurate information, all entitled to trade on the same terms, and none with a big enough share of the market to influence price," said a report by Nebraska's Center for Rural Affairs. "Nothing close to these conditions now exists in the cattle market."

The large meatpacking firms have thus far shown little interest in buying their own cattle ranches. "Why would they want the hassle?" Lee Pitts, the editor of *Livestock Market Digest,* told me. "Raising cattle is a business with a high overhead, and most of the capital's tied up in the land." Instead of buying their own ranches, the meatpacking companies have been financing a handful of large feedlot owners who lease ranches and run cattle for them. "It's just another way of control ling prices through captive supply," Pitts explained. "The packers now own some of these big feeders lock, stock, and barrel, and tell them exactly what to do."

the breasts of mr. mcdonald

MANY RANCHERS NOW FEAR that the beef industry is deliberately being restructured along the lines of the poultry industry. They do not want to wind up like chicken growers — who in recent years have become virtually powerless, trapped by debt and by onerous contracts written by the large processors. The poultry industry was also transformed by a wave of mergers in the 1980s. Eight chicken processors now control about two-thirds of the American market. These processors have shifted almost all of their production to the rural South, where the weather tends to be mild, the workforce is poor, unions are weak, and farmers are desperate to find some way of staying on their land. Alabama, Arkansas, Georgia, and Mississippi now produce more than half the chicken raised in the United States. Although many factors helped revolutionize the poultry industry and increase the power of the large processors, one innovation played an especially important role. The Chicken McNugget turned a bird that once had to be carved at a table into something that could easily be eaten behind the wheel of a car. It turned a bulk agricultural commodity into a manufactured, value-added product. And it encouraged a system of production that has turned many chicken farmers into little more than serfs.

"I have an idea," Fred Turner, the chairman of McDonald's, told one of his suppliers in 1979. "I want a chicken finger-food without bones, about the size of your thumb. Can you do it?" The supplier, an executive at Keystone Foods, ordered a group of technicians to get to work in the lab, where they were soon joined by food scientists from McDonald's. Poultry consumption in the United States was growing, a trend with alarming implications for a fast food chain that only sold hamburgers. The nation's chicken meat had traditionally been provided by hens that were too old to lay eggs; after World War II a new poultry industry based in Delaware and Virginia lowered the cost of raising chicken, while medical research touted the health benefits of eating it. Fred Turner wanted McDonald's to sell a chicken dish that wouldn't clash with the chain's sensibility. After six months of intensive research, the Keystone lab developed new technology for the manufacture of McNuggets — small pieces of reconstituted chicken, composed mainly of white meat, that were held together by stabilizers, breaded, fried, frozen, then reheated. The initial test-marketing of McNuggets was so successful that McDonald's enlisted another company, Tyson Foods, to guarantee an adequate supply. Based in Arkansas, Tyson was one of the nation's leading chicken processors, and it soon developed a new breed of chicken to facilitate the production of McNuggets. Dubbed "Mr. McDonald," the new breed had unusually large breasts.

Chicken McNuggets were introduced nationwide in 1983. Within one month of their launch, the McDonald's Corporation had become the second-largest purchaser of chicken in the United States, surpassed only by KFC. McNuggets tasted good, they were easy to chew, and they appeared to be healthier than other items on the menu at McDonald's. After all, they were made out of chicken. But their health benefits were illusory. A chemical analysis of McNuggets by a researcher at Harvard Medical School found that their "fatty acid profile" more closely resembled beef than poultry. They were cooked in beef tallow, like McDonald's fries. The chain soon switched to vegetable oil, adding "beef extract" to McNuggets during the manufacturing process in order to retain their familiar taste. Today Chicken McNuggets are wildly popular among young children — and contain twice as much fat per ounce as a hamburger.

The McNugget helped change not only the American diet but also its system for raising and processing poultry. "The impact of McNuggets was so huge that it changed the industry," the president of ConAgra Poultry, the nation's third-largest chicken processor, later acknowledged. Twenty years ago, most chicken was sold whole; today about 90 percent of the chicken sold in the United States has been cut into pieces, cutlets, or nuggets. In 1992 American consumption of chicken for the first time surpassed the consumption of beef. Gaining the McNugget contract helped turn Tyson Foods into the world's largest chicken processor. Tyson now manufactures about half of the nation's McNuggets and sells chicken to ninety of the one hundred largest restaurant chains. It is a vertically integrated company that breeds, slaughters, and processes chicken. It does not, however, raise the birds. It leaves the capital expenditures and the financial risks of that task to thousands of "independent contractors."

A Tyson chicken grower never owns the birds in his or her poultry houses. Like most of the other leading processors, Tyson supplies its growers with one-day-old chicks. Between the day they are born and the day they are killed, the birds spend their entire lives on the grower's property. But they belong to Tyson. The company supplies the feed, veterinary services, and technical support. It determines feeding schedules, demands equipment upgrades, and employs "flock supervisors" to make sure that corporate directives are being followed. It hires the trucks that drop off the baby chicks and return seven weeks later to pick up full-grown chickens ready for slaughter. At the processing plant, Tyson employees count and weigh the birds. A grower's income is determined by a formula based upon that count, that weight, and the amount of feed used.

The chicken grower provides the land, the labor, the poultry houses, and the fuel. Most growers must borrow money to build the houses, which cost about $150,000 each and hold about 25,000 birds. A 1995 survey by Louisiana Tech University found that the typical grower had been raising chicken for fifteen years, owned three poultry houses, remained deeply in debt, and earned perhaps $12,000 a year. About half of the nation's chicken growers leave the business after just three years, either selling out or losing everything. The back roads of rural Arkansas are now littered with abandoned poultry houses.

Most chicken growers cannot obtain a bank loan without already having a signed contract from a major processor. "We get the check first," a loan officer told the *Arkansas Democrat-Gazette*. A chicken grower who is unhappy with his or her processor has little power to do anything about it. Poultry contracts are short-term. Growers who complain may soon find themselves with empty poultry houses and debts that still need to be paid. Twenty-five years ago, when the United States had dozens of poultry firms, a grower stood a much better chance of finding a new processor and of striking a better deal. Today growers who are labeled "difficult" often have no choice but to find a new line of work. A processor can terminate a contract with a grower whenever it likes. It owns the birds. Short of that punishment, a processor can prolong the interval between the departure of one flock and the arrival of another. Every day that poultry houses sit empty, the grower loses money.

The large processors won't publicly disclose the terms of their contracts. In the past, such contracts have not only required that growers surrender all rights to file a lawsuit against the company, but have also forbidden them from joining any association that might link growers in a strong bargaining unit. The processors do not like the idea of chicken growers joining forces to protect their interests. "Our relationship with our growers is a one-on-one contractual relationship . . . ," a Tyson executive told a reporter in 1998. "We want to see that it remains that way."

captives

THE FOUR LARGE meatpacking firms claim that an oversupply of beef, not any corporate behavior, is responsible for the low prices that American ranchers are paid for their cattle. A number of studies by the U.S. Department of Agriculture (USDA) have reached the same conclusion. Annual beef consumption in the United States peaked in 1976, at about ninety-four pounds per person. Today the typical American eats about sixty-eight pounds of beef every year. Although the nation's population has grown since the 1970s, it has not grown fast enough to compensate for the decline in beef consumption. Ranchers trying to stabilize their incomes fell victim to their own fallacy of composition. They followed the advice of agribusiness firms and gave their cattle growth hormones. As a result, cattle are much bigger today; fewer cattle are sold; and most American beef cannot be exported to the European Union, where the use of bovine growth hormones has been banned.

The meatpacking companies claim that captive supplies and formula pricing systems are means of achieving greater efficiency, not of controlling cattle prices. Their slaughterhouses require a large and steady volume of cattle to operate profitably; captive supplies are one reliable way of sustaining that volume. The large meatpacking companies say that they've become a convenient scapegoat for ranchers, when the real problem is low poultry prices. A pound of chicken costs about half as much as a pound of beef. The long-term deals now being offered to cattlemen are portrayed as innovations that will save, not destroy, the beef industry. Responding in 1998 to a USDA investigation of captive supplies in Kansas, IBP defended such "alternative methods for selling fed cattle." The company argued that these practices were "similar to changes that have already occurred . . . for selling other agricultural commodities," such as poultry.

Many independent ranchers are convinced that captive supplies are used primarily to control the market, not to achieve greater slaughterhouse efficiency. They do not oppose large-scale transactions or long-term contracts; they oppose cattle prices that are kept secret. Most of all, they do not trust the meatpacking giants. The belief that agribusiness executives secretly talk on the phone with their competitors, set prices, and divide up the worldwide market for commodities — a belief widely held among independent ranchers and farmers — may seem like a paranoid fantasy. But that is precisely what executives at Archer Daniels Midland, "supermarket to the world," did for years.

Three of Archer Daniels Midland's top officials, including Michael Andreas, its vice chairman, were sent to federal prison in 1999 for conspiring with foreign rivals to control the international market for lysine (an important feed additive). The Justice Department's investigation of this massive price-fixing scheme focused on the period between August of 1992 and December of 1995. Within that roughly three-and-a-half-year stretch, Archer Daniels Midland and its co-conspirators may have overcharged farmers by as much as $180 million. During the same period, Archer Daniels Midland executives also met with their overseas rivals to set the worldwide price for citric acid (a common food additive). At a meeting with Japanese executives that was secretly recorded, the president of Archer Daniels Midland preached the virtues of collaboration. "We have a saying at this company," he said. "Our competitors are our friends, and our customers are our enemies." Archer Daniels Midland remains the world's largest producer of lysine, as well as the world's largest processor of soybeans and corn. It is also one of the largest shareholders of IBP.

A 1996 USDA investigation of concentration in the beef industry found that many ranchers were afraid to testify against the large meatpacking companies, fearing retaliation and "economic ruin." That year Mike Callicrate, a cattleman from St. Francis, Kansas, decided to speak out against corporate behavior he thought was not just improper but criminal. "I was driving down the road one day," Callicrate told me, "and I kept thinking, when is someone going to do something about this? And I suddenly realized that maybe nobody's going to do it, and I had to give it a try." He claims that after his testimony before the USDA committee, the large meatpackers promptly stopped bidding on his cattle. "I couldn't sell my cattle," he said. "They'd drive right past my feed yard and buy cattle from a guy two hundred miles further away." His business has recovered somewhat; ConAgra and Excel now bid on his cattle. The experience has turned him into an activist. He refuses to "make the transition to slavery quietly." He has spoken at congressional hearings and has joined a dozen other cattlemen in a class-action lawsuit against IBP. The lawsuit claims that IBP has for many years violated the Packers and Stockyards Act through a wide variety of anticompetitive tactics. According to Callicrate, the suit will demonstrate that the company's purported efficiency in production is really "an efficiency in stealing." IBP denies the charges. "It makes no sense for us to do anything to hurt cattle producers," a top IBP executive told a reporter, "when we depend upon them to supply our plants."

the threat of wealthy neighbors

THE COLORADO CATTLEMEN'S ASSOCIATION filed an amicus brief in Mike Callicrate's lawsuit against IBP, demanding a competitive marketplace for cattle and a halt to any illegal buying practices being used by the large meatpacking firms. Ranchers in Colorado today, however, face threats to their livelihood that are unrelated to fluctuations in cattle prices. During the past twenty years, Colorado has lost roughly 1.5 million acres of ranchland to development. Population growth and the booming market for vacation homes have greatly driven up land costs. Some ranchland that sold for less than $200 an acre in the 1960s now sells for hundreds of times that amount. The new land prices make it impossible for ordinary ranchers to expand their operations. Each head of cattle needs about thirty acres of pasture for grazing, and until cattle start producing solid gold nuggets instead of sirloin, it's hard to sustain beef production on such expensive land. Ranching families in Colorado tend to be land-rich and cash-poor. Inheritance taxes can claim more than half of a cattle ranch's land value. Even if a family manages to operate its ranch profitably, handing it down to the next generation may require selling off large chunks of land, thereby diminishing its productive capacity.

Along with the ranches, Colorado is quickly losing its ranching culture. Among the students at Harrison High you see a variety of fashion statements: gangsta wannabes, skaters, stoners, goths, and punks. What you don't see — in the shadow of Pikes Peak, in the heart of the Rocky Mountain West — is anyone dressed even remotely like a cowboy. Nobody's wearing shirts with snaps or Justin boots. In 1959, eight of the nation's top ten TV shows were Westerns. The networks ran thirty-five Westerns in prime time every week, and places like Colorado, where real cowboys lived, were the stuff of youthful daydreams. That America now seems as dead and distant as the England of King Arthur. I saw hundreds of high school students in Colorado Springs, and only one of them wore a cowboy hat. His name was Philly Favorite, he played guitar in a band called the Deadites, and his cowboy hat was made out of fake zebra fur.

The median age of Colorado's ranchers and farmers is about fifty-five, and roughly half of the state's open land will change hands during the next two decades — a potential boon for real estate developers. A number of Colorado land trusts are now working to help ranchers obtain conservation easements. In return for donating future development rights to one of these trusts, a rancher receives an immediate tax break and the prospect of lower inheritance taxes. The land remains private property, but by law can never be turned into golf courses, shopping malls, or subdivisions. In 1995 the Colorado Cattlemen's Association formed the first land trust in the United States that is devoted solely to the preservation of ranchland. It has thus far protected almost 40,000 acres, a significant achievement. But ranchland in Colorado is now vanishing at the rate of about 90,000 acres a year.

Conservation easements are usually of greatest benefit to wealthy gentleman ranchers who earn large incomes from other sources. The doctors, lawyers, and stockbrokers now running cattle on some of Colorado's most beautiful land can own big ranches, preserve open space with easements, and enjoy the big tax deductions. Ranchers whose annual income comes entirely from selling cattle usually don't earn enough to benefit from that sort of tax break. And the value of their land, along with the pressure to sell it, often increases when a wealthy neighbor obtains a conservation easement, since the views in the area are more likely to remain unspoiled.

The Colorado ranchers who now face the greatest economic difficulty are the ones who run a few hundred head of cattle, who work their own land, who don't have any outside income, and who don't stand to gain anything from a big tax write-off. They have to compete with gentleman ranchers whose operations don't have to earn a profit and with part-time ranchers whose operations are kept afloat by second jobs. Indeed, the ranchers most likely to be in financial trouble today are the ones who live the life and embody the values supposedly at the heart of the American West. They are independent and self-sufficient, cherish their freedom, believe in hard work — and as a result are now paying the price.

a broken link

HANK DIED IN 1998. He took his own life the week before Christmas. He was forty-three.

When I heard the news, it made no sense to me, none at all. The man that I knew was full of fire and ready to go, the kind of person who seemed always to be throwing himself into the middle of things. He did not hide away. He got involved in the community, served on countless boards and committees. He had a fine sense of humor. He loved his family. The way he died seemed to contradict everything else about his life.

It would be wrong to say that Hank's death was caused by the consolidating and homogenizing influence of the fast food chains, by monopoly power in the meatpacking industry, by depressed prices in the cattle market, by the economic forces bankrupting independent ranchers, by the tax laws that favor wealthy ranchers, by the unrelenting push of Colorado's real estate developers. But it would not be entirely wrong. Hank was under enormous pressure at the time of his death. He was trying to find a way of gaining conservation easements that would protect his land but not sacrifice the financial security of his family. Cattle prices had fallen to their lowest point in more than a decade. And El Paso County was planning to build a new highway right through the heart of his ranch. The stress of these things and others led to sleepless nights, then to a depression that spiraled downward fast, and before long he was gone.

The suicide rate among ranchers and farmers in the United States is now about three times higher than the national average. The issue briefly received attention during the 1980s farm crisis, but has been pretty much ignored ever since. Meanwhile, across rural America, a slow and steady death toll mounts. As the rancher's traditional way of life is destroyed, so are many of the beliefs that go with it. The code of the rancher could hardly be more out of step with America's current state of mind. In Silicon Valley, entrepreneurs and venture capitalists regard failure as just a first step toward success. After three failed Internet start-ups, there's still a chance that the fourth one will succeed. What's being sold ultimately matters less than how well it sells. In ranching, a failure is much more likely to be final. The land that has been lost is not just a commodity. It has meaning that cannot be measured in dollars and cents. It is a tangible connection with the past, something that was meant to be handed down to children and never sold. As Osha Gray Davidson observes in his book *Broken Heartland* (1996), "To fail several generations of relatives . . . to see yourself as the one weak link in a strong chain . . . is a terrible, and for some, an unbearable burden."

When Hank was eight years old, he was the subject of a children's book. It combined text with photographs and told the story of a boy's first roundup. Young Hank wears blue jeans and a black hat in the book, rides a white horse, tags along with real cowboys, stares down a herd of cattle in a corral. You can see in these pictures why Hank was chosen for the part. His face is lively and expressive; he can ride; he can lasso; and he looks game, willing to jump a fence or chase after a steer ten times his size. The boy in the story starts out afraid of animals on the ranch, but in the end conquers his fear of cattle, snakes, and coyotes. There's a happy ending, and the final image echoes the last scene of a classic Hollywood Western, affirming the spirit of freedom and independence. Accompanied by an older cowhand and surrounded by a herd of cattle, young Hank rides his white horse across a vast, wide-open prairie, heading toward the horizon.

In life he did not get that sort of ending. He was buried at his ranch, in a simple wooden coffin made by friends.

7/cogs in the great machine

YOU CAN SMELL Greeley, Colorado, long before you can see it. The smell is hard to forget but not easy to describe, a combination of live animals, manure, and dead animals being rendered into dog food. The smell is worst during the summer months, blanketing Greeley day and night like an invisible fog. Many people who live there no longer notice the smell; it recedes into the background, present but not present, like the sound of traffic for New Yorkers. Others can't stop thinking about the smell, even after years; it permeates everything, gives them headaches, makes them nauseous, interferes with their sleep. Greeley is a modern-day factory town where cattle are the main units of production, where workers and machines turn large steer into small, vacuum-sealed packages of meat. The billions of fast food hamburgers that Americans now eat every year come from places like Greeley. The industrialization of cattle-raising and meatpacking over the past two decades has completely altered how beef is produced — and the towns that produce it. Responding to the demands of the fast food and supermarket chains, the meatpacking giants have cut costs by cutting wages. They have turned one of the nation's best-paying manufacturing jobs into one of the lowest-paying, created a migrant industrial workforce of poor immigrants, tolerated high injury rates, and spawned rural ghettos in the American heartland. Crime, poverty, drug abuse, and homelessness have lately taken root in towns where you'd least expect to find them. The effects of this new meatpacking regime have become as inescapable as the odors that drift from its feedlots, rendering plants, and pools of slaughterhouse waste.

The ConAgra Beef Company runs the nation's biggest meatpacking complex just a few miles north of downtown Greeley. Weld County, which includes Greeley, earns more money every year from livestock products than any other county in the United States. ConAgra is the largest private employer in Weld County, running a beef slaughterhouse and a sheep slaughterhouse, as well as rendering and processing facilities.

To supply the beef slaughterhouse, ConAgra operates a pair of enormous feedlots. Each of them can hold up to one hundred thousand head of cattle. At times the animals are crowded so closely together it looks like a sea of cattle, a mooing, moving mass of brown and white fur that goes on for acres. These cattle don't eat blue grama and buffalo grass off the prairie. During the three months before slaughter, they eat grain dumped into long concrete troughs that resemble highway dividers. The grain fattens the cattle quickly, aided by the anabolic steroids implanted in their ear. A typical steer will consume more than three thousand pounds of grain during its stay at a feedlot, just to gain four hundred pounds in weight. The process involves a fair amount of waste. Each steer deposits about fifty pounds of urine and manure every day. Unlike human waste, the manure is not sent to a treatment plant. It is dumped into pits, huge pools of excrement that the industry calls "lagoons." The amount of waste left by the cattle that pass through Weld County is staggering. The two Monfort feedlots outside Greeley produce more excrement than the cities of Denver, Boston, Atlanta, and St. Louis — combined.

Before Greeley became a meatpacking town, it was a utopian community of small farmers. It was founded in 1870 by Nathan Meeker, a newspaper editor from New York City who wanted to create a city in the American West dedicated to agriculture, education, mutual aid, and high moral values. Meeker named the idealistic new settlement after his boss at the *New York Tribune,* Horace Greeley, who had given some career advice that proved legendary: "Go west, young man." The town of Greeley, Colorado, eventually thrived, becoming a major producer of beans and sugar beets. But Nathan Meeker did not live long enough to enjoy its success. In 1879, Meeker got into a dispute with a group of Ute Indians, who killed him and then scalped him.

For many years the farmers of Greeley held themselves apart from local ranchers, at one point building a wooden fence around the town to keep cattle out — a fence fifty miles long. During the Depression, when commodity prices hit rock bottom, a Greeley schoolteacher named Warren Monfort started to buy grain from local farmers and feed it to his cattle. At the time, American cattle were mainly grass-fed, not grain-fed. They roamed the range, eating native grasses, or they lived on farms and ate hay. Monfort soon became one of the nation's first large-scale cattle feeders, buying cheap corn, sugar beets, and alfalfa from his neighbors. His feedlot business greatly expanded after World War II. By feeding cattle year-round, Monfort could control the timing of his livestock sales and wait for the best prices at the Chicago stockyards. The meat of grain-fed beef was fatty and tender; unlike grass-fed beef, it did not need to be aged for a few weeks; it could be eaten within days of the slaughter. Feedlots began to open throughout the rural Midwest. American grain surpluses, largely fueled by government price supports, provided inexpensive food for livestock and made cattle-feeding a standard practice in the beef industry. Warren Monfort started his business in the 1930s with eighteen head of cattle. By the late 1950s he was feeding about twenty thousand.

In 1960 Monfort and his son Kenneth opened a small slaughterhouse in Greeley near his feedlots. They signed a generous union contract with the Amalgamated Butcher Workmen, granting benefits like seniority rights and pay bonuses for work on the late shift. Jobs at the Monfort slaughterhouse were among the highest paying in Greeley, and there was a long waiting list of people seeking work at the plant. Greeley became a company town, dominated by the Monfort family and ruled with a compassionate paternalism. Ken Monfort was a familiar presence at the slaughterhouse. Workers felt comfortable approaching him with suggestions and complaints. He had an unusual background for a meatpacking executive. He was a liberal Democrat who had served two terms in the state legislature. He was an outspoken opponent of the Vietnam war, one of the two people from Colorado to earn a place on President Nixon's "enemies list." Appearing on that list, in Monfort's view, was a great honor. After a union vote at the Greeley slaughterhouse in 1970, Ken Monfort sent the newly elected steward a warm personal letter. "If I can ever be of help to you," he wrote, "my door is open." The prosperity and labor peace in Greeley, however, were soon threatened by fundamental changes sweeping through the meatpacking industry — an upheaval that came to be known as "the IBP revolution."

go west

WHEN THE SLAUGHTERHOUSE IN Greeley first opened, its rural location was unusual. Meatpacking plants were much more likely to be found in urban areas. Most large American cities had a meatpacking district with its own stockyards and slaughterhouses. Cattle were shipped there by rail, slaughtered, carved into sides of beef, then sold to local butchers and wholesalers. Omaha and Kansas City were prominent meatpacking towns, and the United Nations building now stands on land once occupied by New York City's stockyards. For more than a century, however, Chicago reigned as the meatpacking capital of the world. The Beef Trust was born there, the major meatpacking firms were headquartered there, and roughly forty thousand people were employed there in a square-mile meat district anchored by the Union Stockyards. Refrigerated sides of beef were shipped from Chicago not only throughout the United States, but also throughout Europe. At the dawn of the twentieth century, Upton Sinclair considered Chicago's Packingtown to be "the greatest aggregation of labor and capital ever gathered in one place." It was in his view the supreme achievement of American capitalism, as well as its greatest disgrace.

The old Chicago slaughterhouses were usually brick buildings, four or five stories high. Cattle were herded up wooden ramps to the top floor, where they were struck on the head with a sledgehammer, slaughtered, then disassembled by skilled workers. The animals eventually left the building on the ground floor, coming out as sides of beef, cans of beef, or boxes of sausage ready to be loaded into railcars.

The working conditions in these meatpacking plants were brutal. In *The Jungle* (1906) Upton Sinclair described a litany of horrors: severe back and shoulder injuries, lacerations, amputations, exposure to dangerous chemicals, and memorably, a workplace accident in which a man fell into a vat and got turned into lard. The plant kept running, and the lard was sold to unsuspecting consumers. Human beings, Sinclair argued, had been made "cogs in the great packing machine," easily replaced and entirely disposable. President Theodore Roosevelt ordered an independent investigation of *The Jungle*'s sensational details. The accuracy of the book was confirmed by federal investigators, who found that Chicago's meatpacking workers labored "under conditions that are entirely unnecessary and unpardonable, and which are a constant menace not only to their own health, but to the health of those who use the food products prepared by them."

The popular outrage inspired by *The Jungle* led Congress to enact food safety legislation in 1906. Little was done, however, to improve the lives of packinghouse workers, whose misfortune had inspired Upton Sinclair to write the book. "I aimed for the public's heart," he later wrote in his autobiography, "and by accident I hit it in the stomach." For the next thirty years, unions battled to gain representation among Chicago's stockyard and slaughterhouse workers, who were mainly eastern European immigrants. The large meatpacking firms used company spies, blacklists, and African-American strikebreakers to thwart organizing efforts. Nevertheless, most of Chicago's packinghouse workers had gained union representation by the end of the Depression. After World War II, their wages greatly improved, soon exceeding the national average for workers in manufacturing. Meatpacking was still a backbreaking, dangerous job, but for many it was also a well-paid and desirable one. It provided a stable, middle-class income. Swift & Company, the largest firm in the industry until the early 1960s, was also the last of the big five meatpackers to remain privately controlled. Much like Ken Monfort, Harold Swift ran the company founded by his father with a paternalistic concern for workers. Swift & Company paid the industry's highest wages, guaranteed long-term job security, worked closely with union officials to address worker grievances, and provided bonuses, pensions, and other benefits.

In 1960 Currier J. Holman and A. D. Anderson, two former Swift executives, decided to start their own meatpacking company, convinced that by slashing costs they could compete with the industry giants. The following year Iowa Beef Packers opened its first slaughterhouse — a meat factory that in its own way proved as influential as the first Speedee Service McDonald's in San Bernardino. Applying the same labor principles to meatpacking that the McDonald brothers had applied to making hamburgers, Holman and Anderson designed a production system for their slaughterhouse in Denison, Iowa, that eliminated the need for skilled workers. The new IBP plant was a one-story structure with a disassembly line. Each worker stood in one spot along the line, performing the same simple task over and over again, making the same knife cut thousands of times during an eight-hour shift. The gains that meatpacking workers had made since the days of

The Jungle stood in the way of IBP's new system, whose success depended upon access to a cheap and powerless workforce. At the dawn of the fast food era, IBP became a meatpacking company with a fast food mentality, obsessed with throughput, efficiency, centralization, and control. "We've tried to take the skill out of every step," A. D. Anderson later boasted.

In addition to creating a mass production system that employed a de-skilled workforce, IBP put its new slaughterhouses in rural areas close to the feedlots — and far away from the urban strongholds of the nation's labor unions. The new interstate highway system made it possible to rely upon trucks, instead of railroads, to ship meat. In 1967 IBP opened a large plant in Dakota City, Nebraska, that not only slaughtered cattle but also "fabricated" them into smaller cuts of meat — into primals (chucks, loins, ribs, rounds) and subprimals (such as chuck rolls). Instead of shipping whole sides of beef, IBP shipped these smaller cuts, vacuum-sealed and plastic-wrapped, as "boxed beef." This new way of marketing beef enabled supermarkets to fire most of their skilled, unionized butchers. It also left IBP with a great deal of leftover bones, blood, and scraps of meat that could be rendered into profitable byproducts such as dog food. IBP soon added "grinders" to its plants, machinery that made hamburger meat in enormous quantities, driving small processors and wholesalers out of business. The company's low wages and new production techniques transformed the entire beef industry, from the feedlot to the butcher counter.

The IBP revolution was guided by a hard, unsentimental view of the world. Amid a packinghouse culture that valued toughness, Currier J. Holman took pride in being tougher than anyone else. He didn't like unions and didn't hesitate to do whatever seemed necessary to break them. IBP should always conduct business, Holman argued, as though it were waging war. When workers at the IBP plant in Dakota City went on strike in 1969, Holman hired scabs to replace them. The striking workers responded by firing a bullet through Holman's office window, killing a suspected company spy, and bombing the home of IBP's general counsel. Confronted with a real war, Holman sought assistance from an unusually powerful ally.

In the spring of 1970 Holman and three other top IBP executives held secret meetings in New York City with Moe Steinman, a "labor consultant" who had close ties with La Cosa Nostra. Unionized butchers in New York were blocking the sale of IBP's boxed beef, out of solidarity with the striking workers and fear for their own jobs. IBP was eager to ship its products to the New York metropolitan area, the nation's largest market for beef. Moe Steinman offered to help end the butchers' boycott and in return demanded a five-cent "commission" on every ten pounds of beef that IBP sold in New York. IBP planned to ship hundreds of millions of pounds of beef to New York City every year. Currier J. Holman agreed to pay the mob its five-cent commission, and the leaders of New York's butcher union promptly withdrew their objections to IBP's boxed beef. Shipments of IBP meat were soon being unloaded in Manhattan.

After a lengthy investigation of mob involvement in the New York City meat business, Currier J. Holman and IBP were tried and convicted in 1974 for bribing union leaders and meat wholesalers. Judge Burton Roberts fined IBP $7,000, but did not punish Holman with any prison term or fine, noting that bribes were sometimes part of the cost of doing business in New York City. Holman's links to organized crime, however, extended far beyond the sort of payments that honest New York businessmen were often forced to make. He appointed one of Moe Steinman's friends to the board of IBP (a man who a decade earlier had been imprisoned for bribing meat inspectors and for selling tainted meat to the U.S. Army) and made Steinman's son-in-law a group vice president of IBP, head of the company's processing division (even though the son-in-law, in Judge Roberts's words, "knew virtually nothing about the meat business"). And Holman forced out four top IBP executives who opposed dealing with organized crime figures. Subsequent investigations by *Forbes* and the *Wall Street Journal* cited IBP as a prime example of how a mainstream corporation could be infiltrated by the mob.

The relentless low-cost competition from IBP presented old-line Chicago meatpackers with a stark choice: go west or go out of business. Instead of symbolizing democracy and freedom, going west meant getting cheap labor. One by one, the packinghouses in Chicago closed down, and slaughterhouses were built in rural states hostile toward labor unions. The new meatpacking plants in Iowa, Kansas, Texas, Colorado, and Nebraska followed IBP's example, paying wages that were sometimes more than 50 percent lower than what union workers earned in Chicago.

I recently drove through Chicago's Packingtown with Ruben Ramirez, president of the United Food and Commercial Workers (UFCW), Local 100A, the city's meatpacking union. Ramirez is in his early sixties, but still looks fit enough to work in a packing plant, with broad shoulders, a thick neck, and strong hands. His smoothly shaved head adds to his formidable appearance. When Ramirez arrived at the Chicago stockyards in 1956, cowboys on horseback still herded cattle from their pens to the slaughterhouses. He was seventeen years old at the time and did not speak any English. He'd just come from Guanajuato, Mexico, and found a job at an old processing plant operated by Swift & Company. He was one of the few Mexicans employed there; the other workers were Polish, Lithuanian, and African-American. They looked down at Mexicans, and so Ramirez was not allowed to use a knife or perform any skilled tasks. Supervisors gave him the lowest menial jobs in the plant. He carried heavy boxes and barrels of meat, getting soaked in blood that hardened and froze to his clothing during the winter. After a few years he went to work for a nearby processing company, Glenn & Anderson, where he worked in sanitation. Three years later Ramirez was finally promoted and allowed to cut meat. He saw friends get badly injured on the job, lost the middle finger on his right hand while using a saw, got knocked unconscious when a side of beef fell off a hook and struck him in the head. He married a young woman he met in church, and they later had six children. He woke up at four o'clock in the morning, worked eight hours a day at Glenn & Anderson, then took college courses at night. Life was far from easy, but his salary was good enough to let his wife stay home and look after the kids. All of their children went to college.

Ruben Ramirez became active in the union, first as a shop steward, then as an executive. He became an American citizen, loved this country, felt grateful for the opportunities it had given him, and took great pride in the accomplishments of his children. In 1993 he became the first Latino to head a local UFCW meatpacking union in the United States. But as Ramirez climbed to the top of Packingtown, the whole thing was crumbling right before his eyes. Any enjoyment of his own success had to be tempered by a hard, cold reality. While listening to Ruben Ramirez's life story, I looked out the car window at one poignant scene after another, at abandoned warehouses and slaughterhouses, at junkyards, slums, and parking lots where Chicago's stockyards once stood.

The world's biggest aggregation of labor and capital in one place has largely disappeared, with bits and pieces of its history lurking amid brick housing projects. The local meatpacking industry that once employed 40,000 people now employs about 2,000. Ninety-five percent of its jobs have moved elsewhere. The last of the Chicago stockyards closed in 1971. Today there's only one slaughterhouse left in Packingtown, an old hog plant. There's just a handful of meat processors: firms that make bacon, sausage, hamburger patties, and kosher products. When the large meatpackers departed, the soul of the place fled with them.

We got out of the car at the entrance to the Union Stockyards, built in 1875, a grand archway with two Victorian turrets on either side. Millions of men, horses, and cattle had passed through it over the years. A spot that had for generations been at the center of tumult and loud commotion now was desolate and quiet, except for an occasional car driving past to a nearby industrial park. The sculpted head of a steer gazed down from the center of the arch. Broken glass and an old sneaker lay on the ground beneath it. Weeds grew between the crumbling brick paving stones, and the pale beige surface of the arch was marred with cracks. The place felt like an archeological site, the ruins of a lost American civilization.

bags of money

DURING THE 1970s THE cordial relationship between Monfort executives and workers at the Greeley slaughterhouse came to an end. The underlying source of conflict was straightforward. Monfort wanted to reduce labor costs, but its workers thought that wages should not be cut at a time when the company was earning profits and the nation's annual inflation rate had reached double digits. In the midst of contract talks with Greeley workers in 1979, who were now represented by the UFCW, Ken Monfort purchased a slaughterhouse in Grand Island, Nebraska, from Swift & Company. Before handing over the plant, Swift shut it down and fired all of the workers, who also belonged to the UFCW. When Monfort took control of the slaughterhouse a few weeks later, he signed a sweetheart deal with the National Maritime Union — a group that had never before represented meatpacking workers and that quickly agreed to a large pay cut.

In November of 1979 the workers in Greeley went on strike. Monfort refused to meet their demands, and the dispute became ugly. The company began to hire scabs. Ken Monfort received death threats. Eight weeks after going on strike, the workers decided to return to their jobs without a contract, but riot police prevented them from entering the slaughterhouse. When the company allowed workers back into the plant, many of them disobeyed supervisors and committed acts of sabotage. After a few months of industrial anarchy, Monfort closed the Greeley slaughterhouse and fired all its workers. The days of paternalism were over in Greeley. Ken Monfort was no longer a liberal Democrat. He had become a pro-business Republican.

In 1982 the slaughterhouse in Greeley reopened without a union, paying wages that had been cut by 40 percent. Former workers were not offered jobs. Instead Monfort transferred some employees from its Grand Island plant and hired new ones. Although Ken Monfort decided to follow IBP's tough policy on labor unions, he strongly resisted the increasing consolidation of the meatpacking industry. During the early 1980s one independent meatpacker after another either went out of business or was purchased by a large corporate rival. In 1983, Monfort sued Excel — the nation's second-largest beef processor — to prevent it from acquiring Spencer Beef, the nation's third-largest beef processor. Monfort argued that the proposed acquisition would allow Excel to engage in predatory pricing and to reduce competition. A panel of federal judges ruled in favor of Monfort, but Excel appealed their decision to the U.S. Supreme Court. President Reagan's Justice Department submitted a brief in the case — and argued on behalf of Excel, claiming it had every right to buy a rival company.

The Reagan administration did not oppose the disappearance of hundreds of small meatpacking firms. On the contrary, it opposed using antitrust laws to stop the giant meatpackers. In 1986 the U.S. Supreme Court overturned the earlier ruling and approved the merger of America's second- and third-largest meatpacking companies. The following year, Monfort agreed to a friendly takeover by ConAgra. "It seemed to me that if the industry was going to be concentrated," Ken Monfort explained, "there should be at least three large players instead of just two." As part of the deal, he became a top executive at the company, head of the ConAgra Red Meat division, and his family received about $270 million in ConAgra stock.

By purchasing Monfort, ConAgra became the biggest meatpacker in the world. Today it is the largest foodservice supplier in North America. In addition to being the number-one producer of french fries (through its Lamb Weston subsidiary), ConAgra is also the nation's largest sheep and turkey processor, the largest distributor of agricultural chemicals, the second-largest manufacturer of frozen food, the second-largest flour miller, the third-largest chicken and pork processor, as well as a leading seed producer, feed producer, and commodity futures trader. The company sells its food under about one hundred consumer brand names, including Hunt's, Armour, La Choy, Country Pride, Swiss Miss, Orville Redenbacher's, Reddi-Wip, Taste O'Sea, Knott's Berry Farm, Hebrew National, and Healthy Choice. Although few Americans have heard of ConAgra, they are likely to eat at least one of its products every day.

Twenty years ago, ConAgra — a combination of two Latin words whose intended meaning is "partnership with the land" — was an obscure Nebraska company with annual revenues of about $500 million. Last year ConAgra's revenues exceeded $25 billion. The company's phenomenal growth over the past two decades was driven by the entrepreneurial spirit of its longtime chief executive, Charles "Mike" Harper. When Harper took over ConAgra in 1974, it was losing money, the market value of its stock was $10 million, and the value of its debt was $156 million. According to the company's official history, *ConAgra Who?* (1989), Harper promptly instituted a new corporate philosophy. "Harper told each general manager that he'd been given a bag of money," the company history explains, "and that at the end of the year he'd be expected to return it — plus a little extra." He gave each of his top executives a personalized, inspirational plaque. On it was a cartoon of two vultures sitting in a tree. "Patience, my ass," one vulture says to the other. "I'm gonna go kill somebody."

The intense pressure to return a bigger bag of money every year has prompted a number of ConAgra employees to break the law. In 1989, ConAgra was found guilty in federal court of having systematically cheated chicken growers in Alabama. During an eight-year period, 45,256 truckloads of full-grown birds were deliberately misweighed at a ConAgra processing plant in the state. ConAgra employees tampered with trucks and scales to make the birds seem lighter. The company was forced to pay $17.2 million in damages for the fraud.

In 1995, ConAgra agreed to pay $13.6 million to settle a class-action lawsuit that accused the company of having conspired with seven other firms to fix prices in the catfish industry. For more than a decade, ConAgra executives allegedly spoke on the phone to, or met at motels with, their ostensible rivals to set catfish prices nationwide. According to the plaintiffs in the case, ConAgra's price-fixing scheme gouged independent wholesalers, small retailers, and consumers.

In 1997, ConAgra paid $8.3 million in fines and pleaded guilty in federal court to charges involving wire fraud, the misgrading of crops, and the addition of water to grain. According to the Justice Department, ConAgra cheated farmers in Indiana for at least three years by doctoring samples of their crops, making the grain seem of lower quality in order to pay less for it. After buying the grain at an unfair price, ConAgra employees sprayed water on it and thereby fraudulently increased its weight, then sold it and cheated customers.

the new industrial migrants

HAVING BROKEN THE UNION at the Greeley slaughterhouse, Monfort began to employ a different sort of worker there: recent immigrants, many of them illegals. In the 1980s large numbers of young men and women from Mexico, Central America, and Southeast Asia started traveling to rural Colorado. Meatpacking jobs that had once provided a middle-class American life now offered little more than poverty wages. Instead of a waiting list, the slaughterhouse seemed to acquire a revolving door, as Monfort plowed through new hires to fill the roughly nine hundred jobs. During one eighteen-month period, more than five thousand different people were employed at the Greeley beef plant — an annual turnover rate of about 400 percent. The average worker quit or was fired every three months.

Today, roughly two-thirds of the workers at the beef plant in Greeley cannot speak English. Most of them are Mexican immigrants who live in places like the River Park Mobile Court, a collection of battered old trailers a quarter-mile down the road from the slaughterhouse. They share rooms in old motels, sleeping on mattresses that cover the floor. The basic pay at the slaughterhouse is now $9.25 an hour. Adjusted for inflation, today's hourly wage is more than a third lower than what Monfort paid forty years ago when the plant opened. Health insurance is now offered to workers after six months on the job; vacation pay, after a year. But most of the workers will never get that vacation. A spokesman for ConAgra recently acknowledged that the turnover rate at the Greeley slaughterhouse is about 80 percent a year. That figure actually represents a decline from the early 1990s.

Mike Coan candidly discussed the whole subject during a 1994 interview with *Business Insurance,* an industry trade journal. At the time, he was the corporate safety director of ConAgra Red Meat. "There is a 100 percent turnover rate annually," Coan said, in an article that applauded Monfort's skill at keeping its insurance costs low. Another

ConAgra meat executive agreed with Coan, noting that "turnover in our business is just astronomical." While Monfort did keep some long-term employees, many slaughterhouse jobs needed to be filled several times every year. "We're at the bottom of the literacy scale," Coan added; ". . . in some plants maybe a third of the people cannot read or write in any language."

During a federal hearing in the 1980s, Arden Walker, the head of labor relations at IBP for the company's first two decades, explained some of the advantages of having a high turnover rate:

> *Counsel:* With regard to turnover, since you [IBP] are obviously experiencing it, does that bother you?
> *Mr. Walker:* Not really.
> *Counsel:* Why not?
> *Mr. Walker:* We found very little correlation between turnover and profitability . . . For instance, insurance, as you know, is very costly. Insurance is not available to new employees until they've worked there for a period of a year or, in some cases, six months. Vacations don't accrue until the second year. There are some economies, frankly, that result from hiring new employees.

Far from being a liability, a high turnover rate in the meatpacking industry — as in the fast food industry — also helps maintain a workforce that is harder to unionize and much easier to control.

For more than a century, California agriculture has been dependent on migrant workers, on young men and women from rural villages in Mexico who travel north to pick by hand most of the state's fruits and vegetables. Migrant workers have long played an important role in the agricultural economy of other states, picking berries in Oregon, apples in Washington, and tomatoes in Florida. Today, the United States, for the first time in its history, has begun to rely on a migrant industrial workforce. Thousands of new migrants now travel north to work in the slaughterhouses and meat processing plants of the High Plains. Some of these new migrants save their earnings, then return home. Some try to establish roots and settle in meatpacking communities. And others wander the country, briefly employed in one state after another, looking for a meatpacking plant that treats its workers well. These migrants come mainly from Mexico, Guatemala, and El Salvador. Many were once farm workers in California, where steady jobs in the fields are now difficult to find. To farm workers who've labored outdoors, ten hours a day, for the nation's lowest wages, meatpacking jobs often sound too good to be true. Picking strawberries in California pays about $5.50 an hour, while cutting meat in a Colorado or Nebraska slaughterhouse can pay almost twice that amount. In many parts of rural Mexico and Guatemala, workers earn about $5 a day.

As in so many other aspects of meatpacking, IBP was a trailblazer in recruiting migrant labor. The company was among the first to recognize that recent immigrants would work for lower wages than American citizens — and would be more reluctant to join unions. To sustain the flow of new workers into IBP slaughterhouses, the company has for years dispatched recruiting teams to poor communities throughout the United States. It has recruited refugees and asylum-seekers from Laos and Bosnia. It has recruited homeless people living at shelters in New York, New Jersey, California, North Carolina, and Rhode Island. It has hired buses to import these workers from thousands of miles away. IBP now maintains a labor office in Mexico City, runs ads on Mexican radio stations offering jobs in the United States, and operates a bus service from rural Mexico to the heartland of America.

The Immigration and Naturalization Service estimates that about one-quarter of all meatpacking workers in Iowa and Nebraska are illegal immigrants. The proportion at some slaughterhouses can be much higher. Spokesmen for IBP and the ConAgra Beef Company adamantly deny that they in any way seek illegal immigrants. "We do not knowingly hire undocumented workers," an IBP executive told me. "IBP supports INS efforts to enforce the law and do[es] not want to employ people who are not authorized to work in the United States." Nevertheless, the recruiting efforts of the American meatpacking industry now target some of the most impoverished and most vulnerable groups in the Western Hemisphere. "If they've got a pulse," one meatpacking executive joked to the *Omaha World-Herald* in 1998, "we'll take an application."

The real costs of this migrant industrial workforce are being borne not by the large meatpacking firms, but by the nation's meatpacking communities. Poor workers without health insurance drive up local medical costs. Drug dealers prey on recent immigrants, and the large, transient population usually brings more crime. At times, the meatpacking firms have been especially brazen in assuming that public funds will cover their routine business costs. In September of 1994, GFI America, Inc. — a leading supplier of frozen hamburger patties to Dairy Queen, Cracker Barrel Old Country Store, and the federal school lunch program — needed workers for a plant in Minneapolis, Minnesota. It sent recruiters to Eagle Pass, Texas, near the Mexican border, promising steady work and housing. The recruiters hired thirty-nine people, rented a bus, drove the new workers from Texas to Minnesota, and then dropped them off across the street from People Serving People, a homeless shelter in downtown Minneapolis. Because the workers had no money, the shelter agreed to house them. GFI America offered to pay the facility $17 for each worker and to donate some free hamburgers, but the offer was declined. The company's plan to use a homeless shelter as worker housing soon backfired. Most of the new recruits refused to stay at the shelter; they had been promised rental apartments and now felt tricked and misled. The story was soon picked up by the local media. Advocates for the homeless were especially angry about GFI America's attempt to misuse the largest homeless shelter in Minneapolis. "Our job is not to provide subsidies to corporations that are importing low-cost labor," said a county official.

The high turnover rate in meatpacking is driven by the low pay and the poor working conditions. Workers quit one meatpacking job and float from town to town in the High Plains, looking for something better. Moving constantly is hard on their personal lives and their families. Most of these new industrial migrants would gladly stay in one job and settle in one spot, if the wages and the working conditions were good. The nation's meatpacking firms, on the other hand, have proven themselves to be far less committed to remaining in a particular community. They have successfully pitted one economically depressed region against another, using the threat of plant closures and the promise of future investment to obtain lucrative government subsidies. No longer locally owned, they feel no allegiance to any one place.

In January of 1987, Mike Harper told the newly elected governor of Nebraska, Kay Orr, that ConAgra wanted a number of tax breaks — or would move its headquarters out of Omaha. The company had been based in the state for almost seventy years, and Nebraska's tax rates were among the lowest in the United States. Nevertheless, a small group of ConAgra executives soon gathered on a Saturday morning at Harper's house, sat around his kitchen table, and came up with the basis for legislation that rewrote Nebraska's tax code. The bills, drafted largely by ConAgra, sought to lower the state taxes paid not only by large corporations, but also by wealthy executives. Mike Harper personally stood to gain about $295,000 from the proposed 30 percent reduction in the maximum tax rate on personal income. He was an avid pilot, and the new legislation also provided tax deductions for ConAgra's corporate jets. A number of state legislators called Harper's demands "blackmail." But the legislature granted the tax breaks, afraid that Nebraska might lose one of its largest private employers. Harper later described how easy it would have been for ConAgra to move elsewhere: "Some Friday night, we turn out the lights — click, click, click — back up the trucks and be gone by Monday morning."

IBP also benefited enormously from the legislation. Its corporate headquarters was located in Dakota City, Nebraska. One study has suggested that after the revision of the state's tax code every new job that ConAgra and IBP created there was backed by a taxpayer subsidy of between $13,000 and $23,000. Thanks to the 1987 legislation, IBP paid no corporate taxes in Nebraska for the next decade. Its executives paid state income taxes at a maximum rate of 7 percent. Despite all these financial benefits, IBP moved its headquarters out of Nebraska in 1997, relocating in South Dakota, a state with no corporate taxes — and no personal income tax. Robert L. Peterson, the chairman of IBP, said that moving to South Dakota was like giving his employees a 7 percent raise. "The move shows you how ungrateful corporate tax-break beneficiaries are," Don Weseley, a Nebraska state senator, told the *Omaha World-Herald*. "They take whatever you give them and then, if there's a better offer, leave you hanging and move on to the next best deal."

IBP had been based in Nebraska since 1967. From its inception, the company that started the revolution in meatpacking — by crushing labor unions and championing the ruthless efficiency of the market — has made ample use of government subsidies. In 1960, Currier J. Holman and A. D. Anderson launched Iowa Beef Packers with a $300,000 loan from the federal Small Business Administration.

the sweet smell

THE CHANGES THAT HAVE swept through Greeley, Colorado, have also occurred throughout the High Plains, wherever large meatpacking plants operate. Towns like Garden City, Kansas, Grand Island, Nebraska, and Storm Lake, Iowa, now have their own rural ghettos, drugs, poverty, rootlessness, and crime. Some of the most dramatic changes have occurred in Lexington, Nebraska, a small town about three hours west of Omaha. Lexington looks like the sort of place that Norman Rockwell liked to paint: shade trees, picket fences, modest Victorian homes, comfy chairs on front porches. The appearance is deceiving.

In 1990, IBP opened a slaughterhouse in Lexington. A year later, the town, with a population of roughly seven thousand, had the highest crime rate in the state of Nebraska. Within a decade, the number of serious crimes doubled; the number of Medicaid cases nearly doubled; Lexington became a major distribution center for illegal drugs; gang members appeared in town and committed drive-by shootings; the majority of Lexington's white inhabitants moved elsewhere; and the proportion of Latino inhabitants increased more than tenfold, climbing to over 50 percent. "Mexington" — as it is now called, affectionately by some, disparagingly by others — is an entirely new kind of American town, one that has been transfigured to meet the needs of a modern slaughterhouse. You would never think, driving past the IBP plant in Lexington, with its colorful children's playground out front, with Wal-Mart and Burger King across the street, that a single, innocuous-looking building could be responsible for so much sudden change, hardship, and despair.

In Lexington I met a cross-section of IBP workers. I met Guatemalan Indians who spoke no English and barely spoke Spanish, living in a dark basement strewn with garbage and used diapers. I met Mexican farm workers struggling to get used to the long Nebraska winters. I met one IBP worker who'd recently been a housekeeper in Santa Monica and another whose previous job was collecting manure from fields in rural Mexico and selling it as fertilizer. I met hard-working, illiterate, religious people willing to risk injury and endure pain for the benefit of their families.

The smell that permeates Lexington is even worse than the smell of Greeley. "We have three odors," a Lexington resident told a reporter: "burning hair and blood, that greasy smell, and the odor of rotten eggs." Hydrogen sulfide is the gas responsible for the rotten egg smell. It rises from slaughterhouse wastewater lagoons, causes respiratory problems and headaches, and at high levels can cause permanent damage to the nervous system. In January of 2000, the Justice Department sued IBP for violations of the Clean Air Act at its Dakota City plant, where as much as a ton of hydrogen sulfide was being released into the air every day. As part of a consent decree, IBP agreed to cover its wastewater lagoons there. "This agreement means that Nebraskans will no longer be forced to inhale IBP's toxic emissions," said a Justice Department official. As of this writing, IBP is also preparing to cover its Lexington wastewater lagoons.

On July 7, 1988, IBP held a public forum at a junior high school in Lexington, giving local citizens an opportunity to ask questions about the company's proposal to build a slaughterhouse there. The transcript of this meeting says a lot about how IBP views the rural communities where it operates. Would there be much turnover among workers at the new IBP plant, someone asked. Once the slaughterhouse was running, an IBP executive replied, it would have a stable workforce. "Ninety percent of our people," he said, "or 80 percent will be fairly stable." Would local people be hired for these jobs, someone else asked. "We will not bring in an hourly workforce," the IBP executive promised. A local IBP booster, who had just returned from a visit to the company's slaughterhouse in Emporia, Kansas, suggested there was little reason to worry about the "type of people" the plant might attract or the potential for increased crime. He said that in Emporia, apparently, "they work them so hard at IBP that they're tired and they go home and go to bed." An IBP executive, a vice president of public relations, confirmed that assessment. "And people who work on our lines work hard," he told the gathering. "As the chief of police [in Emporia] said, they go home at night and go to bed rather than carouse around town." Another IBP executive, a vice president of engineering, assured the audience that the new plant in Lexington would not foul the air. No odor would be noticeable, he promised, even "a few feet away" from the plant. In any event, the smell emitted by slaughterhouse lagoons would be "sweet," not objectionable. And the smell from the slaughterhouse itself, the IBP vice president said, would be "no different than that which you produce in your kitchen when you cook."

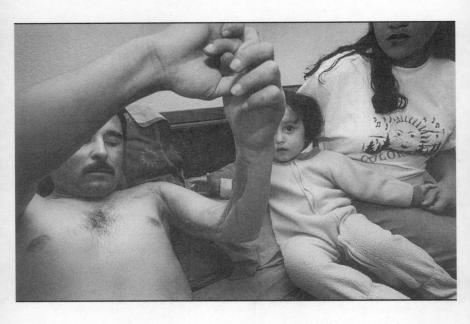

8 / the most dangerous job

ONE NIGHT I VISIT a slaughterhouse somewhere in the High Plains. The slaughterhouse is one of the nation's largest. About five thousand head of cattle enter it every day, single file, and leave in a different form. Someone who has access to the plant, who's upset by its working conditions, offers to give me a tour. The slaughterhouse is an immense building, gray and square, about three stories high, with no windows on the front and no architectural clues to what's happening inside. My friend gives me a chain-mail apron and gloves, suggesting I try them on. Workers on the line wear about eight pounds of chain mail beneath their white coats, shiny steel armor that covers their hands, wrists, stomach, and back. The chain mail's designed to protect workers from cutting themselves and from being cut by other workers. But knives somehow manage to get past it. My host hands me some Wellingtons, the kind of knee-high rubber boots that English gentlemen wear in the countryside. "Tuck your pants into the boots," he says. "We'll be walking through some blood."

I put on a hardhat and climb a stairway. The sounds get louder, factory sounds, the noise of power tools and machinery, bursts of compressed air. We start at the end of the line, the fabricating room. Workers call it "fab." When we step inside, fab seems familiar: steel catwalks, pipes along the walls, a vast room, a maze of conveyer belts. This could be the Lamb Weston plant in Idaho, except hunks of red meat ride the belts instead of french fries. Some machines assemble cardboard boxes, others vacuum-seal subprimals of beef in clear plastic. The workers look extremely busy, but there's nothing unsettling about this part of the plant. You see meat like this all the time in the back of your local supermarket.

The fab room is cooled to about 40 degrees, and as you head up the line, the feel of the place starts to change. The pieces of meat get bigger. Workers — about half of them women, almost all of them young and Latino — slice meat with long slender knives. They stand at a table that's chest high, grab meat off a conveyor belt, trim away fat, throw meat back on the belt, toss the scraps onto a conveyor belt above them, and then grab more meat, all in a matter of seconds. I'm now struck by how many workers there are, hundreds of them, pressed close together, constantly moving, slicing. You see hardhats, white coats, flashes of steel. Nobody is smiling or chatting, they're too busy, anxiously trying not to fall behind. An old man walks past me, pushing a blue plastic barrel filled with scraps. A few workers carve the meat with Whizzards, small electric knives that have spinning round blades. The Whizzards look like the Norelco razors that Santa rides in the TV ads. I notice that a few of the women near me are sweating, even though the place is freezing cold.

Sides of beef suspended from an overhead trolley swing toward a group of men. Each worker has a large knife in one hand and a steel hook in the other. They grab the meat with their hooks and attack it fiercely with their knives. As they hack away, using all their strength, grunting, the place suddenly feels different, primordial. The machinery seems beside the point, and what's going on before me has been going on for thousands of years — the meat, the hook, the knife, men straining to cut more meat.

On the kill floor, what I see no longer unfolds in a logical manner. It's one strange image after another. A worker with a power saw slices cattle into halves as though they were two-by-fours, and then the halves swing by me into the cooler. It feels like a slaughterhouse now. Dozens of cattle, stripped of their skins, dangle on chains from their hind legs. My host stops and asks how I feel, if I want to go any further. This is where some people get sick. I feel fine, determined to see the whole process, the world that's been deliberately hidden. The kill floor is hot and humid. It stinks of manure. Cattle have a body temperature of about 101 degrees, and there are a lot of them in the room. Carcasses swing so fast along the rail that you have to keep an eye on them constantly, dodge them, watch your step, or one will slam you and throw you onto the bloody concrete floor. It happens to workers all the time.

I see: a man reach inside cattle and pull out their kidneys with his bare hands, then drop the kidneys down a metal chute, over and over again, as each animal passes by him; a stainless steel rack of tongues; Whizzards peeling meat off decapitated heads, picking them almost as clean as the white skulls painted by Georgia O'Keeffe. We wade through blood that's ankle deep and that pours down drains into huge vats below us. As we approach the start of the line, for the first time I hear the steady *pop, pop, pop* of live animals being stunned.

Now the cattle suspended above me look just like the cattle I've seen on ranches for years, but these ones are upside down swinging on hooks. For a moment, the sight seems unreal; there are so many of them, a herd of them, lifeless. And then I see a few hind legs still kicking, a final reflex action, and the reality comes hard and clear.

For eight and a half hours, a worker called a "sticker" does nothing but stand in a river of blood, being drenched in blood, slitting the neck of a steer every ten seconds or so, severing its carotid artery. He uses a long knife and must hit exactly the right spot to kill the animal humanely. He hits that spot again and again. We walk up a slippery metal stairway and reach a small platform, where the production line begins. A man turns and smiles at me. He wears safety goggles and a hardhat. His face is splattered with gray matter and blood. He is the "knocker," the man who welcomes cattle to the building. Cattle walk down a narrow chute and pause in front of him, blocked by a gate, and then he shoots them in the head with a captive bolt stunner — a compressed-air gun attached to the ceiling by a long hose — which fires a steel bolt that knocks the cattle unconscious. The animals keep strolling up, oblivious to what comes next, and he stands over them and shoots. For eight and a half hours, he just shoots. As I stand there, he misses a few times and shoots the same animal twice. As soon as the steer falls, a worker grabs one of its hind legs, shackles it to a chain, and the chain lifts the huge animal into the air.

I watch the knocker knock cattle for a couple of minutes. The animals are powerful and imposing one moment and then gone in an instant, suspended from a rail, ready for carving. A steer slips from its chain, falls to the ground, and gets its head caught in one end of a conveyer belt. The production line stops as workers struggle to free the steer, stunned but alive, from the machinery. I've seen enough.

I step out of the building into the cool night air and follow the path that leads cattle into the slaughterhouse. They pass me, driven toward the building by workers with long white sticks that seem to glow in the dark. One steer, perhaps sensing instinctively what the other don't, turns and tries to run. But workers drive him back to join the rest. The cattle lazily walk single-file toward the muffled sounds, *pop, pop, pop,* coming from the open door.

The path has hairpin turns that prevent cattle from seeing what's in store and keep them relaxed. As the ramp gently slopes upward, the animals may think they're headed for another truck, another road trip — and they are, in unexpected ways. The ramp widens as it reaches ground level and then leads to a large cattle pen with wooden fences, a corral that belongs in a meadow, not here. As I walk along the fence, a group of cattle approach me, looking me straight in the eye, like dogs hoping for a treat, and follow me out of some mysterious impulse. I stop and try to absorb the whole scene: the cool breeze, the cattle and their gentle lowing, a cloudless sky, steam rising from the plant in the moonlight. And then I notice that the building does have one window, a small square of light on the second floor. It offers a glimpse of what's hidden behind this huge blank façade. Through the little window you can see bright red carcasses on hooks, going round and round.

sharp knives

KNOCKER, STICKER, SHACKLER, RUMPER, First Legger, Knuckle Dropper, Navel Boner, Splitter Top/Bottom Butt, Feed Kill Chain — the names of job assignments at a modern slaughterhouse convey some of the brutality inherent in the work. Meatpacking is now the most dangerous job in the United States. The injury rate in a slaughterhouse is about three times higher than the rate in a typical American factory. Every year more than one-quarter of the meatpacking workers in this country — roughly forty thousand men and women — suffer an injury or a work-related illness that requires medical attention beyond first aid. There is strong evidence that these numbers, compiled by the Bureau of Labor Statistics, understate the number of meatpacking injuries that occur. Thousands of additional injuries and illnesses most likely go unrecorded.

Despite the use of conveyer belts, forklifts, dehiding machines, and a variety of power tools, most of the work in the nation's slaughterhouses is still performed by hand. Poultry plants can be largely mechanized, thanks to the breeding of chickens that are uniform in size. The birds in some Tyson factories are killed, plucked, gutted, beheaded, and sliced into cutlets by robots and machines. But cattle still come in all sizes and shapes, varying in weight by hundreds of pounds. The lack of a standardized steer has hindered the mechanization of beef plants. In one crucial respect meatpacking work has changed little in the past hundred years. At the dawn of the twenty-first century, amid an era of extraordinary technological advance, the most important tool in a modern slaughterhouse is a sharp knife.

Lacerations are the most common injuries suffered by meatpackers, who often stab themselves or stab someone working nearby. Tendinitis and cumulative trauma disorders are also quite common. Meatpacking workers routinely develop back problems, shoulder problems, carpal tunnel syndrome, and "trigger finger" (a syndrome in which a finger becomes frozen in a curled position). Indeed, the rate of these cumulative trauma injuries in the meatpacking industry is far higher than the rate in any other American industry. It is roughly thirty-three times higher than the national average in industry. Many slaughterhouse workers make a knife cut every two or three seconds, which adds up to about 10,000 cuts during an eight-hour shift. If the knife has become dull, additional pressure is placed on the worker's tendons, joints, and nerves. A dull knife can cause pain to extend from the cutting hand all the way down the spine.

Workers often bring their knives home and spend at least forty minutes a day keeping the edges smooth, sharp, and sanded, with no pits. One IBP worker, a small Guatemalan woman with graying hair, spoke with me in the cramped kitchen of her mobile home. As a pot of beans cooked on the stove, she sat in a wooden chair, gently rocking, telling the story of her life, of her journey north in search of work, the whole time sharpening big knives in her lap as though she were knitting a sweater.

The "IBP revolution" has been directly responsible for many of the hazards that meatpacking workers now face. One of the leading determinants of the injury rate at a slaughterhouse today is the speed of the disassembly line. The faster it runs, the more likely that workers will get hurt. The old meatpacking plants in Chicago slaughtered about 50 cattle an hour. Twenty years ago, new plants in the High Plains slaughtered about 175 cattle an hour. Today some plants slaughter up to 400 cattle an hour — about half a dozen animals every minute, sent down a single production line, carved by workers desperate not to fall behind. While trying to keep up with the flow of meat, workers often neglect to resharpen their knives and thereby place more stress on their bodies. As the pace increases, so does the risk of accidental cuts and stabbings. "I could always tell the line speed," a former Monfort nurse told me, "by the number of people with lacerations coming into my office." People usually cut themselves; nevertheless, everyone on the line tries to stay alert. Meatpackers often work within inches of each other, wielding large knives. A simple mistake can cause a serious injury. A former IBP worker told me about boning knives suddenly flying out of hands and ricocheting off of machinery. "They're very flexible," she said, "and they'll spring on you . . . zwing, and they're gone."

Much like french fry factories, beef slaughterhouses often operate at profit margins as low as a few pennies a pound. The three meatpacking giants — ConAgra, IBP, and Excel — try to increase their earnings by maximizing the volume of production at each plant. Once a slaughterhouse is up and running, fully staffed, the profits it will earn are directly related to the speed of the line. A faster pace means higher profits. Market pressures now exert a perverse influence on the management of beef plants: the same factors that make these slaughterhouses relatively inefficient (the lack of mechanization, the reliance on human labor) encourage companies to make them even more dangerous (by speeding up the pace).

The unrelenting pressure of trying to keep up with the line has encouraged widespread methamphetamine use among meatpackers. Workers taking "crank" feel charged and self-confident, ready for anything. Supervisors have been known to sell crank to their workers or to supply it free in return for certain favors, such as working a second shift. Workers who use methamphetamine may feel energized and invincible, but are actually putting themselves at much greater risk of having an accident. For obvious reasons, a modern slaughterhouse is not a safe place to be high.

In the days when labor unions were strong, workers could complain about excessive line speeds and injury rates without fear of getting fired. Today only one-third of IBP's workers belong to a union. Most of the nonunion workers are recent immigrants; many are illegals; and they are generally employed "at will." That means they can be fired without warning, for just about any reason. Such an arrangement does not encourage them to lodge complaints. Workers who have traveled a great distance for this job, who have families to support, who are earning ten times more an hour in a meatpacking plant than they could possibly earn back home, are wary about speaking out and losing everything. The line speeds and labor costs at IBP's nonunion plants now set the standard for the rest of the industry. Every other company must try to produce beef as quickly and cheaply as IBP does; slowing the pace to protect workers can lead to a competitive disadvantage.

Again and again workers told me that they are under tremendous pressure not to report injuries. The annual bonuses of plant foremen and supervisors are often based in part on the injury rate of their workers. Instead of creating a safer workplace, these bonus schemes encourage slaughterhouse managers to make sure that accidents and injuries go unreported. Missing fingers, broken bones, deep lacerations, and amputated limbs are difficult to conceal from authorities. But the dramatic and catastrophic injuries in a slaughterhouse are greatly outnumbered by less visible, though no less debilitating, ailments: torn muscles, slipped disks, pinched nerves.

If a worker agrees not to report an injury, a supervisor will usually shift him or her to an easier job for a while, providing some time to heal. If the injury seems more serious, a Mexican worker is often given the opportunity to return home for a while, to recuperate there, then come back to his or her slaughterhouse job in the United States. Workers who abide by these unwritten rules are treated respectfully; those who disobey are likely to be punished and made an example. As one former IBP worker explained, "They're trying to deter you, period, from going to the doctor."

From a purely economic point of view, injured workers are a drag on profits. They are less productive. Getting rid of them makes a good deal of financial sense, especially when new workers are readily available and inexpensive to train. Injured workers are often given some of the most unpleasant tasks in the slaughterhouse. Their hourly wages are cut. And through a wide variety of unsubtle means they are encouraged to quit.

Not all supervisors in a slaughterhouse behave like Simon Legree, shouting at workers, cursing them, belittling their injuries, always pushing them to move faster. But enough supervisors act that way to warrant the comparison. Production supervisors tend to be men in their late twenties and early thirties. Most are Anglos and don't speak Spanish, although more and more Latinos are being promoted to the job. They earn about $30,000 a year, plus bonuses and benefits. In many rural communities, being a supervisor at a meatpacking plant is one of the best jobs in town. It comes with a fair amount of pressure: a supervisor must meet production goals, keep the number of recorded injuries low, and most importantly, keep the meat flowing down the line without interruption. The job also brings enormous power. Each supervisor is like a little dictator in his or her section of the plant, largely free to boss, fire, berate, or reassign workers. That sort of power can lead to all sorts of abuses, especially when the hourly workers being supervised are women.

Many women told me stories about being fondled and grabbed on the production line, and the behavior of supervisors sets the tone for the other male workers. In February of 1999, a federal jury in Des Moines awarded $2.4 million to a female employee at an IBP slaughterhouse. According to the woman's testimony, coworkers had "screamed obscenities and rubbed their bodies against hers while supervisors laughed." Seven months later, Monfort agreed to settle a lawsuit filed by the U.S. Equal Employment Opportunity Commission on behalf of fourteen female workers in Texas. As part of the settlement, the company paid the women $900,000 and vowed to establish formal procedures for handling sexual harassment complaints. In their lawsuit the women alleged that supervisors at a Monfort plant in Cactus, Texas, pressured them for dates and sex, and that male coworkers groped them, kissed them, and used animal parts in a sexually explicit manner.

The sexual relationships between supervisors and "hourlies" are for the most part consensual. Many female workers optimistically regard sex with their supervisor as a way to gain a secure place in American society, a green card, a husband — or at the very least a transfer to an easier job at the plant. Some supervisors become meatpacking Casanovas, engaging in multiple affairs. Sex, drugs, and slaughterhouses may seem an unlikely combination, but as one former Monfort employee told me: "Inside those walls is a different world that obeys different laws." Late on the second shift, when it's dark outside, assignations take place in locker rooms, staff rooms, and parked cars, even on the catwalk over the kill floor.

the worst

SOME OF THE MOST dangerous jobs in meatpacking today are performed by the late-night cleaning crews. A large proportion of these workers are illegal immigrants. They are considered "independent contractors," employed not by the meatpacking firms but by sanitation companies. They earn hourly wages that are about one-third lower than those of regular production employees. And their work is so hard and so horrendous that words seem inadequate to describe it. The men and women who now clean the nation's slaughterhouses may arguably have the worst job in the United States. "It takes a really dedicated person," a former member of a cleaning crew told me, "or a really desperate person to get the job done."

When a sanitation crew arrives at a meatpacking plant, usually around midnight, it faces a mess of monumental proportions. Three to four thousand cattle, each weighing about a thousand pounds, have been slaughtered there that day. The place has to be clean by sunrise. Some of the workers wear water-resistant clothing; most don't. Their principal cleaning tool is a high-pressure hose that shoots a mixture of water and chlorine heated to about 180 degrees. As the water is sprayed, the plant fills with a thick, heavy fog. Visibility drops to as little as five feet. The conveyer belts and machinery are running. Workers stand on the belts, spraying them, riding them like moving sidewalks, as high as fifteen feet off the ground. Workers climb ladders with hoses and spray the catwalks. They get under tables and conveyer belts, climbing right into the bloody muck, cleaning out grease, fat, manure, leftover scraps of meat.

Glasses and safety goggles fog up. The inside of the plant heats up; temperatures soon exceed 100 degrees. "It's hot, and it's foggy, and you can't see anything," a former sanitation worker said. The crew members can't see or hear each other when the machinery's running. They routinely spray each other with burning hot, chemical-laden water. They are sickened by the fumes. Jesus, a soft-spoken employee of DCS Sanitation Management, Inc., the company that IBP uses in many of its plants, told me that every night on the job he gets terrible headaches. "You feel it in your head," he said. "You feel it in your stomach, like you want to throw up." A friend of his vomits whenever they clean the rendering area. Other workers tease the young man as he retches. Jesus says the stench in rendering is so powerful that it won't wash off; no matter how much soap you use after a shift, the smell comes home with you, seeps from your pores.

One night while Jesus was cleaning, a coworker forgot to turn off a machine, lost two fingers, and went into shock. An ambulance came and took him away, as everyone else continued to clean. He was back at work the following week. "If one hand is no good," the supervisor told him, "use the other." Another sanitation worker lost an arm in a machine. Now he folds towels in the locker room. The scariest job, according to Jesus, is cleaning the vents on the roof of the slaughterhouse. The vents become clogged with grease and dried blood. In the winter, when everything gets icy and the winds pick up, Jesus worries that a sudden gust will blow him off the roof into the darkness.

Although official statistics are not kept, the death rate among slaughterhouse sanitation crews is extraordinarily high. They are the ultimate in disposable workers: illegal, illiterate, impoverished, untrained. The nation's worst job can end in just about the worst way. Sometimes these workers are literally ground up and reduced to nothing.

A brief description of some cleaning-crew accidents over the past decade says more about the work and the danger than any set of statistics. At the Monfort plant in Grand Island, Nebraska, Richard Skala was beheaded by a dehiding machine. Carlos Vincente — an employee of T and G Service Company, a twenty-eight-year-old Guatemalan who'd been in the United States for only a week — was pulled into the cogs of a conveyer belt at an Excel plant in Fort Morgan, Colorado, and torn apart. Lorenzo Marin, Sr., an employee of DCS Sanitation, fell from the top of a skinning machine while cleaning it with a high-pressure hose, struck his head on the concrete floor of an IBP plant in Columbus Junction, Iowa, and died. Another employee of DCS Sanitation, Salvador Hernandez-Gonzalez, had his head crushed by a pork-loin processing machine at an IBP plant in Madison, Nebraska. The same machine had fatally crushed the head of another worker, Ben Barone, a few years earlier. At a National Beef plant in Liberal, Kansas, Homer Stull climbed into a blood-collection tank to clean it, a filthy tank thirty feet high. Stull was overcome by hydrogen sulfide fumes. Two coworkers climbed into the tank and tried to rescue him. All three men died. Eight years earlier, Henry Wolf had been overcome by hydrogen sulfide fumes while cleaning the very same tank; Gary Sanders had tried to rescue him; both men died; and the Occupational Safety and Health Administration (OSHA) later fined National Beef for its negligence. The fine was $480 for each man's death.

don't get caught

DURING THE SAME YEARS when the working conditions at America's meatpacking plants became more dangerous — when line speeds increased and illegal immigrants replaced skilled workers — the federal government greatly reduced the enforcement of health and safety laws. OSHA had long been despised by the nation's manufacturers, who considered the agency a source of meddlesome regulations and unnecessary red tape. When Ronald Reagan was elected president in 1980, OSHA was already underfunded and understaffed: its 1,300 inspectors were responsible for the safety of more than 5 million workplaces across the country. A typical American employer could expect an OSHA inspection about once every eighty years. Nevertheless, the Reagan administration was determined to reduce OSHA's authority even further, as part of the push for deregulation. The number of OSHA inspectors was eventually cut by 20 percent, and in 1981 the agency adopted a new policy of "voluntary compliance." Instead of arriving unannounced at a factory and performing an inspection, OSHA employees were required to look at a company's injury log before setting foot inside the plant. If the records showed an injury rate at the factory lower than the national average for all manufacturers, the OSHA inspector had to turn around and leave at once — without entering the plant, examining its equipment, or talking to any of its workers. These injury logs were kept and maintained by company officials.

For most of the 1980s OSHA's relationship with the meatpacking industry was far from adversarial. While the number of serious injuries rose, the number of OSHA inspections fell. The death of a worker on the job was punished with a fine of just a few hundred dollars. At a gathering of meat company executives in October of 1987, OSHA's safety director, Barry White, promised to change federal safety standards that "appear amazingly stupid to you or overburdening or just not useful." According to an account of the meeting later published in the *Chicago Tribune,* the safety director at OSHA — the federal official most responsible for protecting the lives of meatpacking workers — acknowledged his own lack of qualification for the job. "I know very well that you know more about safety and health in the meat industry than I do," White told the executives. "And you know more about safety and health in the meat industry than any single employee at OSHA."

OSHA's voluntary compliance policy did indeed reduce the number of recorded injuries in meatpacking plants. It did not, however, reduce the number of people getting hurt. It merely encouraged companies, in the words of a subsequent congressional investigation, "to understate injuries, to falsify records, and to cover up accidents." At the IBP beef plant in Dakota City, Nebraska, for example, the company kept two sets of injury logs: one of them recording every injury and illness at the slaughterhouse, the other provided to visiting OSHA inspectors and researchers from the Bureau of Labor Statistics. During a three-month period in 1985, the first log recorded 1,800 injuries and illnesses at the plant. The OSHA log recorded only 160 — a discrepancy of more than 1,000 percent.

At congressional hearings on meatpacking in 1987, Robert L. Peterson, the chief executive of IBP, denied under oath that two sets of logs were ever kept and called IBP's safety record "the best of the best." Congressional investigators later got hold of both logs — and found that the injury rate at its Dakota City plant was as much as one-third higher than the average rate in the meatpacking industry. Congressional investigators also discovered that IBP had altered injury records at its beef plant in Emporia, Kansas. Another leading meatpacking company, John Morrell, was caught lying about injuries at its plant in Sioux Falls, South Dakota. The congressional investigation concluded that these companies had failed to report "serious injuries such as fractures, concussions, major cuts, hernias, some requiring hospitalization, surgery, even amputation."

Congressman Tom Lantos, whose subcommittee conducted the meatpacking inquiry, called IBP "one of the most irresponsible and reckless corporations in America." A Labor Department official called the company's behavior "the worst example of underreporting injuries and illnesses to workers ever encountered in OSHA's sixteen-year history." Nevertheless, Robert L. Peterson was never charged with perjury for his misleading testimony before Congress. Investigators argued that it would be difficult to prove "conclusively" that Peterson had "willfully" lied. In 1987 IBP was fined $2.6 million by OSHA for underreporting injuries and later fined an additional $3.1 million for the high rate of cumulative trauma injuries at the Dakota City plant. After the company introduced a new safety program there, the fines were reduced to $975,000 — a sum that might have appeared large at the time, yet represented about one one-hundredth of a percent of IBP's annual revenues.

Three years after the OSHA fines, a worker named Kevin Wilson injured his back at an IBP slaughterhouse in Council Bluffs, Iowa. Wilson went to see Diane Arndt, a nurse at the plant, who sent him to a doctor selected by the company. Wilson's injury was not serious, the doctor said, later assigning him to light duty at the plant. Wilson sought a second opinion; the new doctor said that he had a disk injury that required a period of absence from work. When Wilson stopped reporting for light duty, IBP's corporate security department began to conduct surveillance of his house. Eleven days after Wilson's new doctor told IBP that back surgery might be required, Diane Arndt called the doctor and said that IBP had obtained a videotape of Wilson engaging in strenuous physical activities at home. The doctor felt deceived, met with Wilson, accused him of being a liar, refused to provide him with any more treatment, and told him to get back to work. Convinced that no such videotape existed and that IBP had fabricated the entire story in order to deny him medical treatment, Kevin Wilson sued the company for slander.

The lawsuit eventually reached the Iowa Supreme Court. In a decision that received little media attention, the Supreme Court upheld a lower court's award of $2 million to Wilson and described some of IBP's unethical practices. The court found that seriously injured workers were required to show up at the IBP plant briefly each day so that the company could avoid reporting "lost workdays" to OSHA. Some workers were compelled to show up for work on the same day as a surgery or the day after an amputation. "IBP's management was aware of, and participated in, this practice," the Iowa Supreme Court noted. IBP nurses regularly entered false information into the plant's computer system, reclassifying injuries so that they didn't have to be reported to OSHA. Injured workers who proved uncooperative were assigned to jobs "watching gauges in the rendering plant, where they were subjected to an atrocious smell while hog remains were boiled down into fertilizers and blood was drained into tanks." According to evidence introduced in court, Diane Arndt had a low opinion of the workers whose injuries she was supposed to be treating. The IBP nurse called them "idiots" and "jerks," telling doctors that "this guy's a crybaby" and "this guy's full of shit." She later admitted that Wilson's back injury was legitimate. The Iowa Supreme Court concluded that the lies she told in this medical case, as well as in others, had been partly motivated by IBP's financial incentive program, which gave staff members bonuses and prizes when the number of lost workdays was kept low. The program, in the court's opinion, was "somewhat disingenuously called 'the safety award system.'"

IBP's attitude toward worker safety was hardly unique in the industry, according to Edward Murphy's testimony before Congress in 1992. Murphy had served as the safety director of the Monfort beef plant in Grand Island. After two workers were killed there in 1991, Monfort fired him. Murphy claimed that he had battled the company for years over safety issues and that Monfort had unfairly made him the scapegoat for its own illegal behavior. The company later paid him an undisclosed sum of money to settle a civil lawsuit over wrongful termination.

Murphy told Congress that during his tenure at the Grand Island plant, Monfort maintained two sets of injury logs, routinely lied to OSHA, and shredded documents requested by OSHA. He wanted Congress to know that the safety lapses at the plant were not accidental. They stemmed directly from Monfort's corporate philosophy, which Murphy described in these terms: "The first commandment is that only production counts . . . The employee's duty is to follow orders. Period. As I was repeatedly told, 'Do what I tell you, even if it is illegal . . . Don't get caught.'"

A lawsuit filed in May of 1998 suggests that little has changed since IBP was caught keeping two sets of injury logs more than a decade ago. Michael D. Ferrell, a former vice president at IBP, contends that the real blame for the high injury rate at the company lies not with the workers, supervisors, nurses, safety directors, or plant managers, but with IBP's top executives. Ferrell had ample opportunity to observe their decision-making process. Among other duties, he was in charge of the health and safety programs at IBP.

When Ferrell accepted the job in 1991, after many years as an industrial engineer at other firms, he believed that IBP's desire to improve worker safety was sincere. According to his legal complaint, Ferrell later discovered that IBP's safety records were routinely falsified and that the company cared more about production than anything else. Ferrell was fired by IBP in 1997, not long after a series of safety problems at a slaughterhouse in Palestine, Texas. The circumstances surrounding his firing are at the heart of the lawsuit. On December 4, 1996, an OSHA inspection of the Palestine plant found a number of serious violations and imposed a fine of $35,125. Less than a week later, a worker named Clarence Dupree lost an arm in a bone-crushing machine. And two days after that, another worker, Willie Morris, was killed by an ammonia gas explosion. Morris's body lay on the floor for hours, just ten feet from the door, as toxic gas filled the building. Nobody at the plant had been trained to use hazardous-materials gas masks or protective suits; the equipment sat in a locked storage room. Ferrell flew to Texas and toured the plant after the accidents. He thought the facility was in terrible shape — with a cooling system that violated OSHA standards, faulty wiring that threatened to cause a mass electrocution, and safety mechanisms that had deliberately been disabled with magnets. He wanted the slaughterhouse to be shut down immediately, and it was. Two months later, Ferrell lost his job.

In his lawsuit seeking payment for wrongful termination, Ferrell contends that he was fired for giving the order to close the Palestine plant. He claims that IBP had never before shut down a slaughterhouse purely for safety reasons and that Robert L. Peterson was enraged by the decision. IBP disputes this version of events, contending that Ferrell had never fit into IBP's corporate culture, that he delegated too much authority, and that he had not, in fact, made the decision to shut down the Palestine plant. According to IBP, the decision to shut it was made after a unanimous vote by its top executives.

IBP's Palestine slaughterhouse reopened in January of 1997. It was shut down again a year later — this time by the USDA. Federal inspectors cited the plant for "inhumane slaughter" and halted production there for one week, an extremely rare penalty imposed for the mistreatment of cattle. In 1999 IBP closed the plant. As of this writing, it sits empty, awaiting a buyer.

the value of an arm

WHEN I FIRST VISITED Greeley in 1997, Javier Ramirez was president of the UFCW, Local 990, the union representing employees at the Monfort beef plant. The National Labor Relations Board had ruled that Monfort committed "numerous, pervasive, and outrageous" violations of labor law after reopening the Greeley beef plant in 1982, discriminating against former union members at hiring time and intimidating new workers during a union election. Former employees who'd been treated unfairly ultimately received a $10.6 million settlement. After a long and arduous organizing drive, workers at the Monfort beef plant voted to join the UFCW in 1992. Javier Ramirez is thirty-one and knows a fair amount about beef. His father is Ruben Ramirez, the Chicago union leader. Javier grew up around slaughterhouses and watched the meatpacking industry abandon his hometown for the High Plains. Instead of finding another line of work, he followed the industry to Colorado, trying to gain better wages and working conditions for the mainly Latino workforce.

The UFCW has given workers in Greeley the ability to challenge unfair dismissals, file grievances against supervisors, and report safety lapses without fear of reprisal. But the union's power is limited by the plant's high turnover rate. Every year a new set of workers must be persuaded to support the UFCW. The plant's revolving door is not conducive to worker solidarity. At the moment some of the most pressing issues for the UFCW are related to the high injury rate at the slaughterhouse. It is a constant struggle not only to prevent workers from getting hurt, but also to gain them proper medical treatment and benefits once they've been hurt.

Colorado was one of the first states to pass a workers' compensation law. The idea behind the legislation, enacted in 1919, was to provide speedy medical care and a steady income to workers injured on the job. Workers' comp was meant to function much like no-fault insurance. In return for surrendering the right to sue employers for injuries, workers were supposed to receive immediate benefits. Similar workers' comp plans were adopted throughout the United States. In 1991, Colorado started another trend, becoming one of the first states to impose harsh restrictions on workers' comp payments. In addition to reducing the benefits afforded to injured employees, Colorado's new law granted employers the right to choose the physician who'd determine the severity of any work-related ailment. Enormous power over workers' comp claims was handed to company doctors.

Many other states subsequently followed Colorado's lead and cut back their workers' comp benefits. The Colorado bill, promoted as "workers' comp reform," was first introduced in the legislature by Tom Norton, the president of the Colorado State Senate and a conservative Republican. Norton represented Greeley, where his wife, Kay, was the vice president of legal and governmental affairs at ConAgra Red Meat.

In most businesses, a high injury rate would prompt insurance companies to demand changes in the workplace. But ConAgra, IBP, and the other large meatpacking firms are self-insured. They are under no pressure from independent underwriters and have a strong incentive to keep workers' comp payments to a bare minimum. Every penny spent on workers' comp is one less penny of corporate revenue.

Javier Ramirez began to educate Monfort workers about their legal right to get workers' comp benefits after an injury at the plant. Many workers don't realize that such insurance even exists. The workers' comp claim forms look intimidating, especially to people who don't speak any English and can't read any language: Filing a claim, challenging a powerful meatpacking company, and placing faith in the American legal system requires a good deal of courage, especially for a recent immigrant.

When a workers' comp claim involves an injury that is nearly impossible to refute (such as an on-the-job amputation), the meatpacking companies generally agree to pay. But when injuries are less visible (such as those stemming from cumulative trauma) the meatpackers often prolong the whole workers' comp process through litigation, insisting upon hearings and filing seemingly endless appeals. Some of the most painful and debilitating injuries are the hardest to prove.

Today it can take years for an injured worker to receive workers' comp benefits. During that time, he or she must pay medical bills and find a source of income. Many rely on public assistance. The ability of meatpacking firms to delay payment discourages many injured workers from ever filing workers' comp claims. It leads others to accept a reduced sum of money as part of a negotiated settlement in order to cover medical bills. The system now leaves countless unskilled and uneducated manual workers poorly compensated for injuries that will forever hamper their ability to earn a living. The few who win in court and receive full benefits are hardly set for life. Under Colorado's new law, the payment for losing an arm is $36,000. An amputated finger gets you anywhere from $2,200 to $4,500, depending on which one is lost. And "serious permanent disfigurement about the head, face, or parts of the body normally exposed to public view" entitles you to a maximum of $2,000.

As workers' comp benefits have become more difficult to obtain, the threat to workplace safety has grown more serious. During the first two years of the Clinton administration, OSHA seemed like a revitalized agency. It began to draw up the first ergonomics standards for the nation's manufacturers, aiming to reduce cumulative trauma disorders. The election of 1994, however, marked a turning point. The Republican majority in Congress that rose to power that year not only impeded the adoption of ergonomics standards but also raised questions about the future of OSHA. Working closely with the U.S. Chamber of Commerce and the National Association of Manufacturers, House Republicans have worked hard to limit OSHA's authority. Congressman Cass Ballenger, a Republican from North Carolina, introduced legislation that would require OSHA to spend at least half of its budget on "consultation" with businesses, instead of enforcement. This new budget requirement would further reduce the number of

OSHA inspections, which by the late 1990s had already reached an all-time low. Ballenger has long opposed OSHA inspections, despite the fact that near his own district a fire at a poultry plant killed twenty-five workers in 1991. The plant had never been inspected by OSHA, its emergency exits had been chained shut, and the bodies of workers were found in piles near the locked doors. Congressman Joel Hefley, a Colorado Republican whose district includes Colorado Springs, has introduced a bill that makes Ballenger's seem moderate. Hefley's "OSHA Reform Act" would essentially repeal the Occupational Safety and Health Act of 1970. It would forbid OSHA from conducting any workplace inspections or imposing any fines.

kenny

DURING MY TRIPS TO meatpacking towns in the High Plains I met dozens of workers who'd been injured. Each of their stories was different, yet somehow familiar, linked by common elements — the same struggle to receive proper medical care, the same fear of speaking out, the same underlying corporate indifference. We are human beings, more than one person told me, but they treat us like animals. The workers I met wanted their stories to be told. They wanted people to know about what is happening right now. A young woman who'd injured her back and her right hand at the Greeley plant said to me, "I want to get on top of a rooftop and scream my lungs out so that somebody will hear." The voices and faces of these workers are indelibly with me, as is the sight of their hands, the light brown skin criss-crossed with white scars. Although I cannot tell all of their stories, a few need to be mentioned. Like all lives, they can be used as examples or serve as representative types. But ultimately they are unique, individual, impossible to define or replace — the opposite of how this system has treated them.

Raoul was born in Zapoteca, Mexico, and did construction work in Anaheim before moving to Colorado. He speaks no English. After hearing a Monfort ad on a Spanish-language radio station, he applied for a job at the Greeley plant. One day Raoul reached into a processing machine to remove a piece of meat. The machine accidentally went on. Raoul's arm got stuck, and it took workers twenty minutes to get it out. The machine had to be taken apart. An ambulance brought Raoul to the hospital, where a deep gash in his shoulder was sewn shut. A tendon had been severed. After getting stitches and a strong prescription painkiller, he was driven back to the slaughterhouse and put back on the production line. Bandaged, groggy, and in pain, one arm tied in a sling, Raoul spent the rest of the day wiping blood off cardboard boxes with his good hand.

Renaldo was another Monfort worker who spoke no English, an older man with graying hair. He developed carpal tunnel syndrome while cutting meat. The injury got so bad that sharp pain shot from his hand all the way up to his shoulder. At night it hurt so much he could not fall asleep in bed. Instead he would fall asleep sitting in a chair beside the bed where his wife lay. For three years he slept in that chair every night.

Kenny Dobbins was a Monfort employee for almost sixteen years. He was born in Keokuk, Iowa, had a tough childhood and an abusive stepfather, left home at the age of thirteen, went in and out of various schools, never learned to read, did various odd jobs, and wound up at the Monfort slaughterhouse in Grand Island, Nebraska. He started working there in 1979, right after the company bought it from Swift. He was twenty-four. He worked in the shipping department at first, hauling boxes that weighed as much as 120 pounds. Kenny could handle it, though. He was a big man, muscular and six-foot-five, and nothing in his life had ever been easy.

One day Kenny heard someone yell, "Watch out!" then turned around and saw a ninety-pound box falling from an upper level of the shipping department. Kenny caught the box with one arm, but the momentum threw him against a conveyer belt, and the metal rim of the belt pierced his lower back. The company doctor bandaged Kenny's back and said the pain was just a pulled muscle. Kenny never filed for workers' comp, stayed home for a few days, then returned to work. He had a wife and three children to support. For the next few months, he was in terrible pain. "It hurt so fucking bad you wouldn't believe it," he told me. He saw another doctor, got a second opinion. The new doctor said Kenny had a pair of severely herniated disks. Kenny had back surgery, spent a month in the hospital, got sent to a pain clinic when the operation didn't work. His marriage broke up amid the stress and financial difficulty. Fourteen months after the injury, Kenny returned to the slaughterhouse. "GIVE UP AFTER BACK SURGERY? NOT KEN DOBBINS!!" a Monfort newsletter proclaimed. "Ken has learned how to handle the rigors of working in a packing plant and is trying to help others do the same. Thanks, Ken, and keep up the good work."

Kenny felt a strong loyalty to Monfort. He could not read, possessed few skills other than his strength, and the company had still given him a job. When Monfort decided to reopen its Greeley plant with a non-union workforce, Kenny volunteered to go there and help. He did not think highly of labor unions. His supervisors told him that unions had been responsible for shutting down meatpacking plants all over the country. When the UFCW tried to organize the Greeley slaughter-house, Kenny became an active and outspoken member of an anti-union group.

At the Grand Island facility, Kenny had been restricted to light duty after his injury. But his supervisor in Greeley said that old restrictions didn't apply in this new job. Soon Kenny was doing tough, physical la-bor once again, wielding a knife and grabbing forty- to fifty-pound pieces of beef off a table. When the pain became unbearable, he was transferred to ground beef, then to rendering. According to a former manager at the Greeley plant, Monfort was trying to get rid of Kenny, trying to make his work so unpleasant that he'd quit. Kenny didn't re-alize it. "He still believes in his heart that people are honest and good," the former manager said about Kenny. "And he's wrong."

As part of the job in rendering, Kenny sometimes had to climb into gigantic blood tanks and gut bins, reach to the bottom of them with his long arms, and unclog the drains. One day he was unexpectedly called to work over the weekend. There had been a problem with *Sal-monella* contamination. The plant needed to be disinfected, and some of the maintenance workers had refused to do it. In his street clothes, Kenny began cleaning the place, climbing into tanks and spraying a liquid chlorine mix. Chlorine is a hazardous chemical that can be in-haled or absorbed through the skin, causing a litany of health prob-lems. Workers who spray it need to wear protective gloves, safety gog-gles, a self-contained respirator, and full coveralls. Kenny's supervisor gave him a paper dust mask to wear, but it quickly dissolved. After eight hours of working with the chlorine in unventilated areas, Kenny went home and fell ill. He was rushed to the hospital and placed in an oxygen tent. His lungs had been burned by the chemicals. His body was covered in blisters. Kenny spent a month in the hospital.

Kenny eventually recovered from the overexposure to chlorine, but it left his chest feeling raw, made him susceptible to colds and sensitive to chemical aromas. He went back to work at the Greeley plant. He had remarried, didn't know what other kind of work to do, still felt loyal to the company. He was assigned to an early morning shift. He had to drive an old truck from one part of the slaughterhouse complex to another. The truck was filled with leftover scraps of meat. The headlights and the wipers didn't work. The windshield was filthy and cracked. One cold, dark morning in the middle of winter, Kenny became disoriented while driving. He stopped the truck, opened the door, got out to see where he was — and was struck by a train. It knocked his glasses off, threw him up in the air, and knocked both of his work boots off. The train was moving slowly, or he would've been killed. Kenny somehow made it back to the plant, barefoot and bleeding from deep gashes in his back and his face. He spent two weeks at the hospital, then went back to work.

One day, Kenny was in rendering and saw a worker about to stick his head into a pre-breaker machine, a device that uses hundreds of small hammers to pulverize gristle and bone into a fine powder. The worker had just turned the machine off, but Kenny knew the hammers inside were still spinning. It takes fifteen minutes for the machine to shut down completely. Kenny yelled, "Stop!" but the worker didn't hear him. And so Kenny ran across the room, grabbed the man by the seat of his pants, and pulled him away from the machine an instant before it would have pulverized him. To honor this act of bravery, Monfort gave Kenny an award for "Outstanding Achievement in CONCERN FOR FELLOW WORKERS." The award was a paper certificate, signed by his supervisor and the plant safety manager.

Kenny later broke his leg stepping into a hole in the slaughterhouse's concrete floor. On another occasion he shattered an ankle, an injury that required surgery and the insertion of five steel pins. Now Kenny had to wear a metal brace on one leg in order to walk, an elaborate, spring-loaded brace that cost $2,000. Standing for long periods caused him great pain. He was given a job recycling old knives at the plant. Despite his many injuries, the job required him to climb up and down three flights of narrow stairs carrying garbage bags filled with knives. In December of 1995 Kenny felt a sharp pain in his chest while lifting some boxes. He thought it was a heart attack. His union steward took him to see the nurse, who said it was just a pulled muscle and sent Kenny home. He was indeed having a massive heart attack. A friend rushed Kenny to a nearby hospital. A stent was inserted in his heart, and the doctors told Kenny that he was lucky to be alive.

While Kenny Dobbins was recuperating, Monfort fired him. Despite the fact that Kenny had been with the company for almost sixteen years, despite the fact that he was first in seniority at the Greeley plant, that he'd cleaned blood tanks with his bare hands, fought the union, done whatever the company had asked him to do, suffered injuries that would've killed weaker men, nobody from Monfort called him with the news. Nobody even bothered to write him. Kenny learned that he'd been fired when his payments to the company health insurance plan kept being returned by the post office. He called Monfort repeatedly to find out what was going on, and a sympathetic clerk in the claims office finally told Kenny that the checks were being returned because he was no longer a Monfort employee. When I asked company spokesmen to comment on the accuracy of Kenny's story, they would neither confirm nor deny any of the details.

Today Kenny is in poor health. His heart is permanently damaged. His immune system seems shot. His back hurts, his ankle hurts, and every so often he coughs up blood. He is unable to work at any job. His wife, Clara — who's half-Latina and half-Cheyenne, and looks like a younger sister of Cher's — was working as a nursing home attendant when Kenny had the heart attack. Amid the stress of his illness, she developed a serious kidney ailment. She is unemployed and recovering from a kidney transplant.

As I sat in the living room of their Greeley home, its walls decorated with paintings of wolves, Denver Broncos memorabilia, and an American flag, Kenny and Clara told me about their financial condition. After almost sixteen years on the job, Kenny did not get any pension from Monfort. The company challenged his workers' comp claim and finally agreed — three years after the initial filing — to pay him a settlement of $35,000. Fifteen percent of that money went to Kenny's lawyer, and the rest is long gone. Some months Kenny has to hock things to get money for Clara's medicine. They have two teenage children and live on Social Security payments. Kenny's health insurance, which costs more than $600 a month, is about to run out. His anger at Monfort, his feelings of betrayal, are of truly biblical proportions.

"They used me to the point where I had no body parts left to give," Kenny said, struggling to maintain his composure. "Then they just tossed me into the trash can." Once strong and powerfully built, he now walks with difficulty, tires easily, and feels useless, as though his life were over. He is forty-six years old.

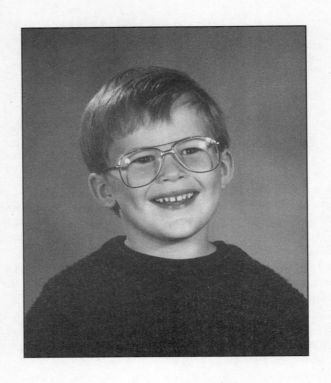

9 / what's in the meat

ON JULY 11, 1997, Lee Harding ordered soft chicken tacos at a Mexican restaurant in Pueblo, Colorado. Harding was twenty-two years old, a manager at Safeway. His wife Stacey was a manager at Wendy's. They were out to dinner on a Friday night. When the chicken tacos arrived, Harding thought there was something wrong with them. The meat seemed to have gone bad. The tacos tasted slimy and gross. An hour or so after leaving the restaurant, Harding began to experience severe abdominal cramps. It felt like something was eating away at his stomach. He was fit and healthy, stood six-foot-one, weighed two hundred pounds. He'd never felt pain this intense. The cramps got worse, and Harding lay in bed through the night, tightly curled into a ball. He developed bad diarrhea, then bloody diarrhea. He felt like he was dying, but was afraid to go to the hospital. If I'm going to die, he thought, I want to die at home.

The severe pain and diarrhea lasted through the weekend. On Monday evening Harding decided to seek medical attention; the cramps were getting better, but he was still passing a good deal of blood. He waited three hours in the emergency room at St. Mary-Corwin Hospital in Pueblo, gave a stool sample, and then finally saw a doctor. It's probably just a "summer flu," the doctor said. Harding was sent home with a prescription for an antibiotic. Tuesday afternoon, he heard a knock at his front door. When Harding opened it, nobody was there. But he found a note on the door from the Pueblo City–County Health Department. It said that his stool sample had tested positive for *Escherichia coli* 0157:H7, a virulent and potentially lethal foodborne pathogen.

The next morning Harding called Sandra Gallegos, a nurse with the Pueblo Health Department. She asked him to try and remember what foods he'd eaten during the previous five days. Harding mentioned the dinner at the Mexican restaurant and the foul taste of the chicken tacos. He was sure that was where he had gotten food poisoning. Gallegos disagreed. *E. coli* 0157:H7 was rarely found in chicken. She asked if Harding had consumed any ground beef lately. Harding recalled having eaten a hamburger a couple of days before visiting the Mexican restaurant. But he doubted that the hamburger could have made him ill. Both his wife and his wife's sister had eaten the same burgers, during a backyard barbecue, and neither had become sick. He and his wife had also eaten burgers from the same box the week before the barbecue without getting sick. They were frozen hamburgers he'd bought at Safeway. He remembered because it was the first time he'd ever bought frozen hamburgers. Gallegos asked if there were any left. Harding said there just might be, checked the freezer, and found the package. It was a red, white, and blue box that said "Hudson Beef Patties."

A Pueblo health official went to Harding's house, took the remaining hamburgers, and sent one to a USDA laboratory for analysis. State health officials had noticed a spike in the number of people suffering from *E. coli* 0157:H7 infections. At the time Colorado was one of only six states with the capability to perform DNA tests on samples of *E. coli* 0157:H7. The DNA tests showed that at least ten people had been sickened by the same strain of the bug. Investigators were searching for a common link between scattered cases reported in Pueblo, Brighton, Loveland, Grand Junction, and Colorado Springs. On July 28, the USDA lab notified Gallegos that Lee Harding's hamburger was contaminated with the same strain of *E. coli* 0157:H7. Here was the common link.

The lot number on Harding's package said that the frozen patties had been manufactured on June 5 at the Hudson Foods plant in Columbus, Nebraska. The plant seemed an unlikely source for an outbreak of food poisoning. Only two years old, it had been built primarily to supply hamburgers for the Burger King chain. It used state-of-the-art equipment and appeared to be spotlessly clean. But something had gone wrong. A modern factory designed for the mass production of food had instead become a vector for the spread of a deadly disease. The package of hamburger patties in Lee Harding's freezer and astute investigative work by Colorado health officials soon led to the largest recall of food in the nation's history. Roughly 35 million pounds of ground beef produced at the Columbus plant were voluntarily recalled by Hudson Foods in August of 1997. Although public health officials did a fine job of tracing the outbreak to its source, the recall proved less successful. By the time it was announced, about 25 million pounds of the ground beef had already been eaten.

an ideal system for new pathogens

EVERY DAY IN THE United States, roughly 200,000 people are sickened by a foodborne disease, 900 are hospitalized, and fourteen die. According to the Centers for Disease Control and Prevention (CDC), more than a quarter of the American population suffers a bout of food poisoning each year. Most of these cases are never reported to authorities or properly diagnosed. The widespread outbreaks that are detected and identified represent a small fraction of the number that actually occurs. And there is strong evidence not only that the incidence of food-related illness has risen in the past few decades, but also that the lasting health consequences of such illnesses are far more serious than was previously believed. The acute phase of a food poisoning — the initial few days of diarrhea and gastrointestinal upset — in many cases may simply be the most obvious manifestation of an infectious disease. Recent studies have found that many foodborne pathogens can precipitate long-term ailments, such as heart disease, inflammatory bowel disease, neurological problems, autoimmune disorders, and kidney damage.

Although the rise in foodborne illnesses has been caused by many complex factors, much of the increase can be attributed to recent changes in how American food is produced. Robert V. Tauxe, head of the Foodborne and Diarrheal Diseases Branch at the CDC, believes that entirely new kinds of outbreaks are now occurring. A generation ago, the typical outbreak of food poisoning involved a church supper, a family picnic, a wedding reception. Improper food handling or storage would cause a small group of people in one local area to get sick. Such traditional outbreaks still take place. But the nation's industrialized and centralized system of food processing has created a whole new sort of outbreak, one that can potentially sicken millions of people. Today a cluster of illnesses in one small town may stem from bad potato salad at a school barbecue — or it may be the first sign of an outbreak that extends statewide, nationwide, or even overseas.

Much like the human immunodeficiency virus (HIV) responsible for causing AIDS, the *E. coli* 0157:H7 bacterium is a newly emerged pathogen whose spread has been facilitated by recent social and technological changes. *E. coli* 0157:H7 was first isolated in 1982; HIV was discovered the following year. People who are infected with HIV can appear healthy for years, while cattle infected with *E. coli* 0157:H7 show few signs of illness. Although cases of AIDS date back at least to the late 1950s, the disease did not reach epidemic proportions in the United States until increased air travel and sexual promiscuity helped transmit the virus far and wide. *E. coli* 0157:H7 was most likely responsible for some human illnesses thirty or forty years ago. But the rise of huge feedlots, slaughterhouses, and hamburger grinders seems to have provided the means for this pathogen to become widely dispersed in the nation's food supply. American meat production has never before been so centralized: thirteen large packinghouses now slaughter most of the beef consumed in the United States. The meatpacking system that arose to supply the nation's fast food chains — an industry molded to serve their needs, to provide massive amounts of uniform ground beef so that all of McDonald's hamburgers would taste the same — has proved to be an extremely efficient system for spreading disease.

Although *E. coli* 0157:H7 has received a good deal of public attention, over the past two decades scientists have discovered more than a dozen other new foodborne pathogens, including *Campylobacter jejuni, Cryptosporidium parvum, Cyclospora cayetanensis, Listeria monocytogenes,* and Norwalk-like viruses. The CDC estimates that more than three-quarters of the food-related illnesses and deaths in the United States are caused by infectious agents that have not yet been identified. While medical researchers have gained important insights into the links between modern food processing and the spread of dangerous diseases, the nation's leading agribusiness firms have resolutely opposed any further regulation of their food safety practices. For years the large meatpacking companies have managed to avoid the sort of liability routinely imposed on the manufacturers of most consumer products. Today the U.S. government can demand the nationwide recall of defective softball bats, sneakers, stuffed animals, and foam-rubber toy cows. But it cannot order a meatpacking company to remove contaminated, potentially lethal ground beef from fast food kitchens and supermarket shelves. The unusual power of the large meatpacking firms has been sustained by their close ties and sizable donations to Republican members of Congress. It has also been made possible by a widespread lack of awareness about how many Americans suffer from food poisoning every year and how these illnesses actually spread.

The newly recognized foodborne pathogens tend to be carried and shed by apparently healthy animals. Food tainted by these organisms has most likely come in contact with an infected animal's stomach contents or manure, during slaughter or subsequent processing. A nationwide study published by the USDA in 1996 found that 7.5 percent of the ground beef samples taken at processing plants were contaminated with *Salmonella*, 11.7 percent were contaminated with *Listeria monocytogenes*, 30 percent were contaminated with *Staphylococcus aureus*, and 53.3 percent were contaminated with *Clostridium perfringens*. All of these pathogens can make people sick; food poisoning caused by *Listeria* generally requires hospitalization and proves fatal in about one out of every five cases. In the USDA study 78.6 percent of the ground beef contained microbes that are spread primarily by fecal material. The medical literature on the causes of food poisoning is full of euphemisms and dry scientific terms: coliform levels, aerobic plate counts, sorbitol, MacConkey agar, and so on. Behind them lies a simple explanation for why eating a hamburger can now make you seriously ill: There is shit in the meat.

the national dish

IN THE EARLY YEARS of the twentieth century, hamburgers had a bad reputation. According to the historian David Gerard Hogan, the hamburger was considered "a food for the poor," tainted and unsafe to eat. Restaurants rarely served hamburgers; they were sold at lunch carts parked near factories, at circuses, carnivals, and state fairs. Ground beef, it was widely believed, was made from old, putrid meat heavily laced with chemical preservatives. "The hamburger habit is just about as safe," one food critic warned, "as getting your meat out of a garbage can." White Castle, the nation's first hamburger chain, worked hard in the 1920s to dispel the hamburger's tawdry image. As Hogan notes in his history of the chain, *Selling 'Em by the Sack* (1997), the founders of White Castle placed their grills in direct view of customers, claimed that fresh ground beef was delivered twice a day, chose a name with connotations of purity, and even sponsored an experiment at the University of Minnesota in which a medical student lived for thirteen weeks on "nothing but White Castle hamburgers and water."

The success of White Castle in the East and the Midwest helped to popularize hamburgers and to remove much of their social stigma. The chain did not attract a broad range of people, however. Most of White Castle's customers were urban, working class, and male. During the 1950s, the rise of drive-ins and fast food restaurants in southern California helped turn the once lowly hamburger into America's national dish. Ray Kroc's decision to promote McDonald's as a restaurant chain for families had a profound impact on the nation's eating habits. Hamburgers seemed an ideal food for small children — convenient, inexpensive, hand-held, and easy to chew.

Before World War II, pork had been the most popular meat in the United States. Rising incomes, falling cattle prices, the growth of the fast food industry, and the mass appeal of the hamburger later pushed American consumption of beef higher than that of pork. By the early 1990s, beef production was responsible for almost half of the employment in American agriculture, and the annual revenues generated by beef were higher than those of any other agricultural commodity in the United States. The average American ate three hamburgers a week. More than two-thirds of those hamburgers were bought at fast food restaurants. And children between the ages of seven and thirteen ate more hamburgers than anyone else.

In January of 1993, doctors at a hospital in Seattle, Washington, noticed that an unusual number of children were being admitted with bloody diarrhea. Some were suffering from hemolytic uremic syndrome, a previously rare disorder that causes kidney damage. Health officials soon traced the outbreak of food poisoning to undercooked hamburgers served at local Jack in the Box restaurants. Tests of the hamburger patties disclosed the presence of *E. coli* 0157:H7. Jack in the Box issued an immediate recall of the contaminated ground beef, which had been supplied by the Vons Companies, Inc., in Arcadia, California. Nevertheless, more than seven hundred people in at least four states were sickened by Jack in the Box hamburgers, more than two hundred people were hospitalized, and four died. Most of the victims were children. One of the first to become ill, Lauren Beth Rudolph, ate a hamburger at a San Diego Jack in the Box a week before Christmas. She was admitted to the hospital on Christmas

Eve, suffered terrible pain, had three heart attacks, and died in her mother's arms on December 28, 1992. She was six years old.

The Jack in the Box outbreak received a great deal of attention from the media, alerting the public to the dangers of E. coli 0157:H7. The Jack in the Box chain almost went out of business amid all the bad publicity. But this was not the first outbreak of E. coli 0157:H7 linked to fast food hamburgers. In 1982 dozens of children were sickened by contaminated hamburgers sold at McDonald's restaurants in Oregon and Michigan. McDonald's quietly cooperated with investigators from the CDC, providing ground beef samples that were tainted with E. coli 0157:H7 — samples that for the first time linked the pathogen to serious illnesses. In public, however, the McDonald's Corporation denied that its hamburgers had made anyone sick. A spokesman for the chain acknowledged only "the possibility of a statistical association between a small number of diarrhea cases in two small towns and our restaurants."

In the eight years since the Jack in the Box outbreak, approximately half a million Americans, the majority of them children, have been made ill by E. coli 0157:H7. Thousands have been hospitalized, and hundreds have died.

a bug that kills children

E. coli 0157:H7 is a mutated version of a bacterium found abundantly in the human digestive system. Most E. coli bacteria help us digest food, synthesize vitamins, and guard against dangerous organisms. E. coli 0157:H7, on the other hand, can release a powerful toxin — called a "verotoxin" or a "Shiga toxin" — that attacks the lining of the intestine. Some people who are infected with E. coli 0157:H7 do not become ill. Others suffer mild diarrhea. In most cases, severe abdominal cramps are followed by watery, then bloody, diarrhea that subsides within a week or so. Sometimes the diarrhea is accompanied by vomiting and a low-grade fever.

In about 4 percent of reported E. coli 0157:H7 cases, the Shiga toxins enter the bloodstream, causing hemolytic uremic syndrome (HUS), which can lead to kidney failure, anemia, internal bleeding, and the destruction of vital organs. The Shiga toxins can cause seizures, neurological damage, and strokes. About 5 percent of the children who develop HUS are killed by it. Those who survive are often left with permanent disabilities, such as blindness or brain damage.

Children under the age of five, the elderly, and people with impaired immune systems are the most likely to suffer from illnesses caused by E. coli 0157:H7. The pathogen is now the leading cause of kidney failure among children in the United States. Nancy Donley, the president of Safe Tables Our Priority (STOP), an organization devoted to food safety, says it is hard to convey the suffering that E. coli 0157:H7 causes children. Her six-year-old son, Alex, was infected with the bug in July of 1993 after eating a tainted hamburger. His illness began with abdominal cramps that seemed as severe as labor pains. It progressed to diarrhea that filled a hospital toilet with blood. Doctors frantically tried to save Alex's life, drilling holes in his skull to relieve pressure, inserting tubes in his chest to keep him breathing, as the Shiga toxins destroyed internal organs. "I would have done anything to save my son's life," Donley says. "I would have run in front of a bus to save Alex." Instead, she stood and watched helplessly as he called out for her, terrified and in pain. He became ill on a Tuesday night, the night after his mother's birthday, and was dead by Sunday afternoon. Toward the end, Alex suffered hallucinations and dementia, no longer recognizing his mother or father. Portions of his brain had been liquefied. "The sheer brutality of his death was horrifying," Donley says.

As Lee Harding learned, adults in perfect health can be stricken by the pathogen, too. Six months after seemingly recovering from his bout of E. coli 0157:H7 food poisoning, Harding began to urinate blood. He was diagnosed as having a kidney infection, one that he believes was facilitated by residual tissue damage from the Shiga toxins. Although the infection soon passed, Harding still experiences occasional pain three years after eating a Hudson Beef hamburger. Nevertheless, he considers himself lucky.

Antibiotics have proven ineffective in treating illnesses caused by E. coli 0157:H7. Indeed the use of antibiotics may make such illnesses worse by killing off the pathogen and prompting a sudden release of its Shiga toxins. At the moment, little can be done for people with life-threatening E. coli 0157:H7 infections, aside from giving them fluids, blood transfusions, and dialysis.

Efforts to eradicate E. coli 0157:H7 have been complicated by the fact that it is an extraordinarily hearty microbe that is easy to transmit. *E. coli* 0157:H7 is resistant to acid, salt, and chlorine. It can live in fresh water or seawater. It can live on kitchen countertops for days and in moist environments for weeks. It can withstand freezing. It can survive heat up to 160 degrees Fahrenheit. To be infected by most foodborne pathogens, such as *Salmonella,* you have to consume a fairly large dose — at least a million organisms. An infection with *E. coli* 0157:H7 can be caused by as few as five organisms. A tiny uncooked particle of hamburger meat can contain enough of the pathogen to kill you.

The heartiness and minute infectious dose of *E. coli* 0157:H7 allow the pathogen to be spread in many ways. People have been infected by drinking contaminated water, by swimming in a contaminated lake, by playing at a contaminated water park, by crawling on a contaminated carpet. The most common cause of foodborne outbreaks has been the consumption of undercooked ground beef. But *E. coli* 0157:H7 outbreaks have also been caused by contaminated bean sprouts, salad greens, cantaloupe, salami, raw milk, and unpasteurized apple cider. All of those foods most likely had come in contact with cattle manure, though the pathogen may also be spread by the feces of deer, dogs, horses, and flies.

Person-to-person transmission has been responsible for a significant proportion of *E. coli* 0157:H7 illnesses. Roughly 10 percent of the people sickened during the Jack in the Box outbreak did not eat a contaminated burger, but were infected by someone who did. *E. coli* 0157:H7 is shed in the stool, and people infected with the bug, even those showing no outward sign of illness, can easily spread it through poor hygiene. Person-to-person transmission is most likely to occur among family members, at day care centers, and at senior citizen homes. On average, an infected person remains contagious for about two weeks, though in some cases *E. coli* 0157:H7 has been found in stool samples two to four months after an initial illness.

Some herds of American cattle may have been infected with *E. coli* 0157:H7 decades ago. But the recent changes in how cattle are raised, slaughtered, and processed have created an ideal means for the pathogen to spread. The problem begins in today's vast feedlots. A government health official, who prefers not to be named, compared the sanitary conditions in a modern feedlot to those in a crowded European city during the Middle Ages, when people dumped their chamber pots out the window, raw sewage ran in the streets, and epidemics raged.

The cattle now packed into feedlots get little exercise and live amid pools of manure. "You shouldn't eat dirty food and dirty water," the official told me. "But we still think we can give animals dirty food and dirty water." Feedlots have become an extremely efficient mechanism for "recirculating the manure," which is unfortunate, since *E. coli* 0157:H7 can replicate in cattle troughs and survive in manure for up to ninety days.

Far from their natural habitat, the cattle in feedlots become more prone to all sorts of illnesses. And what they are being fed often contributes to the spread of disease. The rise in grain prices has encouraged the feeding of less expensive materials to cattle, especially substances with a high protein content that accelerate growth. About 75 percent of the cattle in the United States were routinely fed livestock wastes — the rendered remains of dead sheep and dead cattle — until August of 1997. They were also fed millions of dead cats and dead dogs every year, purchased from animal shelters. The FDA banned such practices after evidence from Great Britain suggested that they were responsible for a widespread outbreak of bovine spongiform encephalopathy (BSE), also known as "mad cow disease." Nevertheless, current FDA regulations allow dead pigs and dead horses to be rendered into cattle feed, along with dead poultry. The regulations not only allow cattle to be fed dead poultry, they allow poultry to be fed dead cattle. Americans who spent more than six months in the United Kingdom during the 1980s are now forbidden to donate blood, in order to prevent the spread of BSE's human variant, Creutzfeldt-Jakob disease. But cattle blood is still put into the feed given to American cattle. Steven P. Bjerklie, a former editor of the trade journal *Meat & Poultry*, is appalled by what goes into cattle feed these days. "Goddamn it, these cattle are ruminants," Bjerklie says. "They're designed to eat grass and, maybe, grain. I mean, they have four stomachs for a reason — to eat products that have a high cellulose content. They are not designed to eat other animals."

The waste products from poultry plants, including the sawdust and old newspapers used as litter, are also being fed to cattle. A study published a few years ago in *Preventive Medicine* notes that in Arkansas alone, about 3 million pounds of chicken manure were fed to cattle in 1994. According to Dr. Neal D. Bernard, who heads the Physicians Committee for Responsible Medicine, chicken manure may contain dangerous bacteria such as *Salmonella* and *Campylobacter,* parasites such as tapeworms and *Giardia lamblia,* antibiotic residues, arsenic, and heavy metals.

The pathogens from infected cattle are spread not only in feedlots, but also at slaughterhouses and hamburger grinders. The slaughterhouse tasks most likely to contaminate meat are the removal of an animal's hide and the removal of its digestive system. The hides are now pulled off by machine; if a hide has been inadequately cleaned, chunks of dirt and manure may fall from it onto the meat. Stomachs and intestines are still pulled out of cattle by hand; if the job is not performed carefully, the contents of the digestive system may spill everywhere. The increased speed of today's production lines makes the task much more difficult. A single worker at a "gut table" may eviscerate sixty cattle an hour. Performing the job properly takes a fair amount of skill. A former IBP "gutter" told me that it took him six months to learn how to pull out the stomach and tie off the intestines without spillage. At best, he could gut two hundred consecutive cattle without spilling anything. Inexperienced gutters spill manure far more often. At the IBP slaughterhouse in Lexington, Nebraska, the hourly spillage rate at the gut table has run as high as 20 percent, with stomach contents splattering one out of five carcasses.

The consequences of a single error are quickly multiplied as hundreds of carcasses quickly move down the line. Knives are supposed to be cleaned and disinfected every few minutes, something that workers in a hurry tend to forget. A contaminated knife spreads germs to everything it touches. The overworked, often illiterate workers in the nation's slaughterhouses do not always understand the importance of good hygiene. They sometimes forget that this meat will eventually be eaten. They drop meat on the floor and then place it right back on the conveyer belt. They cook bite-sized pieces of meat in their sterilizers, as snacks, thereby rendering the sterilizers ineffective. They are directly exposed to a wide variety of pathogens in the meat, become infected, and inadvertently spread disease.

A recent USDA study found that during the winter about 1 percent of the cattle at feedlots carry *E. coli* 0157:H7 in their gut. The proportion rises to as much as 50 percent during the summer. Even if you assume that only 1 percent are infected, that means three or four cattle bearing the microbe are eviscerated at a large slaughterhouse every hour. The odds of widespread contamination are raised exponentially when the meat is processed into ground beef. A generation ago, local butchers and wholesalers made hamburger meat out of leftover scraps. Ground beef was distributed locally, and was often made from cattle slaughtered locally. Today large slaughterhouses and grinders dominate the nationwide production of ground beef. A modern processing plant can produce 800,000 pounds of hamburger a day, meat that will be shipped throughout the United States. A single animal infected with *E. coli* 0157:H7 can contaminate 32,000 pounds of that ground beef.

To make matters worse, the animals used to make about one-quarter of the nation's ground beef — worn-out dairy cattle — are the animals most likely to be diseased and riddled with antibiotic residues. The stresses of industrial milk production make them even more unhealthy than cattle in a large feedlot. Dairy cattle can live as long as forty years, but are often slaughtered at the age of four, when their milk output starts to decline. McDonald's relies heavily on dairy cattle for its hamburger supplies, since the animals are relatively inexpensive, yield low-fat meat, and enable the chain to boast that all its beef is raised in the United States. The days when hamburger meat was ground in the back of a butcher shop, out of scraps from one or two sides of beef, are long gone. Like the multiple sex partners that helped spread the AIDS epidemic, the huge admixture of animals in most American ground beef plants has played a crucial role in spreading *E. coli* 0157:H7. A single fast food hamburger now contains meat from dozens or even hundreds of different cattle.

all we care to pay

"THIS IS NO FAIRY STORY and no joke," Upton Sinclair wrote in 1906; "the meat would be shoveled into carts, and the man who did the shoveling would not trouble to lift out a rat even when he saw one — there were things that went into the sausage in comparison with which a poisoned rat was a tidbit." Sinclair described a long list of practices in the meatpacking industry that threatened the health of consumers: the routine slaughter of diseased animals, the use of chemicals such as borax and glycerine to disguise the smell of spoiled beef, the deliberate mislabeling of canned meat, the tendency of workers to urinate and defecate on the kill floor. After reading *The Jungle* President Theodore Roosevelt ordered an independent investigation of Sinclair's charges. When it confirmed the accuracy of the book, Roosevelt called for legislation requiring mandatory federal inspection of all meat sold through interstate commerce, accurate labeling and dating of canned meat products, and a fee-based regulatory system that made meatpackers pay the cost of cleaning up their own industry.

The powerful magnates of the Beef Trust responded by vilifying Roosevelt and Upton Sinclair, dismissing their accusations, and launching a public relations campaign to persuade the American people that nothing was wrong. "Meat and food products, generally speaking," J. Ogden Armour claimed in a *Saturday Evening Post* article, "are handled as carefully and circumspectly in large packing houses as they are in the average home kitchen." Testifying before Congress, Thomas Wilson, an executive at Morris & Company, said that blame for the occasional sanitary lapse lay not with the policies of industry executives, but with the greed and laziness of slaughterhouse workers. "Men are men," Wilson contended, "and it is pretty hard to control some of them." After an angry legislative battle, Congress narrowly passed the Meat Inspection Act of 1906, a watered-down version of Roosevelt's proposals that made taxpayers pay for the new regulations.

The meatpacking industry's response to *The Jungle* established a pattern that would be repeated throughout the twentieth century, whenever health concerns were raised about the nation's beef. The industry has repeatedly denied that problems exist, impugned the motives of its critics, fought vehemently against federal oversight, sought to avoid any responsibility for outbreaks of food poisoning, and worked hard to shift the costs of food safety efforts onto the general public. The industry's strategy has been driven by a profound antipathy to any government regulation that might lower profits. "There is no limit to the expense that might be put upon us," the Beef Trust's Wilson said in 1906, arguing against a federal inspection plan that would have cost meatpackers less than a dime per head of cattle. "[Our] contention is that in all reasonableness and fairness *we are paying all we care to pay.*"

During the 1980s, as the risks of widespread contamination increased, the meatpacking industry blocked the use of microbial testing in the federal meat inspection program. A panel appointed by the National Academy of Sciences warned in 1985 that the nation's meat inspection program was hopelessly outdated, still relying on visual and olfactory clues to find disease while dangerous pathogens slipped past undetected. Three years later, another National Academy of Sciences panel warned that the nation's public health infrastructure was in serious disarray, limiting its ability to track or prevent the spread of newly emerging pathogens. Without additional funding for public health measures, outbreaks and epidemics of new diseases were virtually inevitable. "Who knows what crisis will be next?" said the chairman of the panel.

Nevertheless, the Reagan and Bush administrations cut spending on public health measures and staffed the U.S. Department of Agriculture with officials far more interested in government deregulation than in food safety. The USDA became largely indistinguishable from the industries it was meant to police. President Reagan's first secretary of agriculture was in the hog business. His second was the president of the American Meat Institute (formerly known as the American Meat Packers Association). And his choice to run the USDA's Food Marketing and Inspection Service was a vice president of the National Cattleman's Association. President Bush later appointed the president of the National Cattleman's Association to the job.

Two months after the threat of deadly new outbreaks was outlined by the National Academy of Sciences, the USDA launched the Streamlined Inspection System for Cattle (SIS-C). The program was designed to reduce the presence of federal inspectors in the nation's slaughterhouses, allowing company employees to assume most of the food safety tasks. According to the Reagan administration, the Streamlined Inspection System for Cattle would help the USDA shrink its budget and deploy its manpower more efficiently. Freed from the hassles of continuous federal inspection, SIS-C also enabled meatpacking companies to increase their line speeds. Despite the fact that IBP and Morrell had just a year earlier been caught falsifying safety records and keeping two sets of injury logs, the meatpacking industry was given the authority to inspect its own meat. SIS-C was launched in 1988 as a pilot program at five major slaughterhouses that supplied about one-fifth of the beef consumed in the United States. The USDA hoped that within a decade the new system would extend nationwide and that the number of federal meat inspectors would be cut by half.

A 1992 USDA study of the Streamlined Inspection System for Cattle concluded that beef produced under the program was no dirtier than beef produced at slaughterhouses fully staffed by federal inspectors. But the accuracy of that study was thrown into doubt by the revelation that meatpacking firms had sometimes been told in advance when USDA investigators would be arriving at SIS-C slaughterhouses. The Monfort beef plant in Greeley, Colorado, was one of the original participants in the program. According to federal inspectors there, the meat produced under the Streamlined Inspection System "had never been filthier." At SIS-C slaughterhouses, visibly diseased animals — cattle infected with measles and tapeworms, covered with abscesses — were being slaughtered. Poorly trained company inspectors were allowing the shipment of beef contaminated with fecal material, hair, insects, metal shavings, urine, and vomit.

The Streamlined Inspection System for Cattle was discontinued in 1993, following the Jack in the Box outbreak. Cutbacks in federal inspection seemed difficult to justify, when hundreds of children had been made seriously ill by tainted hamburgers. Although the precise source of E. coli 0157:H7 contamination was never identified, some of the beef used by Jack in the Box came from an SIS-C plant — a Monfort slaughterhouse. The meatpacking industry's immediate reaction to the outbreak was an attempt to shift the blame elsewhere. As children continued to be hospitalized after eating Jack in the Box hamburgers, J. Patrick Boyle, the head of the American Meat Institute said, "This recent outbreak sheds light on a nationwide problem: inconsistent information about proper cooking temperatures for hamburger." The meat industry's allies at the USDA also seemed remarkably laissez-faire, noting that the contaminated hamburger patties had not violated any federal standards. According to Dr. Russell Cross, head of the USDA's Food Safety and Inspection Service, "The presence of bacteria in raw meat, including E. coli 0157:H7, although undesirable, is unavoidable, and not cause for condemnation of the product." Members of the newly elected Clinton administration disagreed. Dr. Cross, a Bush appointee, resigned. On September 29, 1993, his replacement, Michael R. Taylor, announced that E. coli 0157:H7 would henceforth be considered an illegal adulterant, that no ground beef contaminated with it could be sold, and that the USDA would begin random microbial testing to remove it from the nation's food supply. The American Meat Institute immediately filed a lawsuit in federal court to prevent the USDA from testing any ground beef for E. coli 0157:H7. Judge James R. Rowlin, a conservative and a cattleman, dismissed the meatpacking industry's arguments and allowed the testing to proceed.

a matter of will

WHILE THE MEATPACKING INDUSTRY sought to block implementation of a science-based inspection system, the owner of the Jack
in the Box chain, Foodmaker, Inc., struggled to recover from the bad
publicity surrounding the outbreak. Robert Nugent, the president of
Foodmaker, had waited a week before acknowledging that Jack in the
Box bore some responsibility for the illnesses. His first instinct had
been to blame the chain's ground beef supplier and Washington State
health officials. He claimed that Jack in the Box had never received a
thorough explanation of why hamburgers needed to be fully cooked.
Nugent soon recruited Jody Powell, President Jimmy Carter's former
press secretary, to help improve the company's image and hired David
M. Theno, a prominent food scientist, to prevent future outbreaks.

Theno had previously helped Foster Farms, a family-owned poultry
processor in California, eliminate most of the *Salmonella* from its
birds. He was a strong advocate of Hazard Analysis and Critical Control Points (HACCP) programs, embracing a food safety philosophy
that the National Academy of Sciences had promoted for years. The
essence of a HACCP program is prevention; it attempts to combine
scientific analysis with common sense. The most vulnerable steps in a
food production system are identified and then monitored. Stacks and
stacks of records are kept in order to follow what went where. Theno
quickly realized after arriving at Jack in the Box that the chain relied
upon the safety standards of its suppliers — instead of imposing its
own. He created the first HACCP plan in the fast food industry, a
"farm-to-fork" policy that scrutinized threats to food safety at every
level of production and distribution. Assuring Jack in the Box customers that their food was safe not only seemed the right thing to do, it
seemed essential for the chain's survival. In the years since the Jack in
the Box outbreak, David Theno has emerged as a fast food maverick,
applauded by consumer groups and considered "the Antichrist," he
says, by many in the meatpacking industry.

Theno insisted that every Jack in the Box manager attend a food
safety course, that every refrigerated delivery truck have a record-
keeping thermometer mounted inside it, that every kitchen grill be
calibrated to ensure an adequate cooking temperature, and that every
grill person use tongs to handle hamburger patties instead of bare
hands. An almost fanatical devotion to microbial testing, however, be-

came the key to Theno's food safety program. He discovered that the levels of contamination varied enormously in ground beef supplied by different meatpacking companies. Some slaughterhouses did a fine job; others were adequate; and a few were appalling. The companies that manufactured hamburger patties for Jack in the Box were required to test their beef every fifteen minutes for a wide range of dangerous microbes, including *E. coli* 0157:H7. Slaughterhouses that continued to ship bad meat were eliminated as suppliers.

Jack in the Box now buys all of its ground beef from two companies: SSI, a subsidiary of the J. R. Simplot Company, and Texas-American, a subsidiary of the family-owned American Food Service Corporation. Theno gave me a tour of the Texas-American plant in Fort Worth that makes hamburger patties for Jack in the Box. We were accompanied by the plant manager, Tim Biela. Much of Biela's work involved testing things repeatedly and maintaining records of the tests. "You can't manage what you don't measure," he said more than once. His records contain not only the date and time when a case of hamburger patties was produced, but also which employees worked that shift, which slaughterhouse provided that beef, and which feedlots sent cattle to the slaughterhouse that day. The hamburger patty plant looked new and clean. I saw huge vats of beef scraps — some shipped all the way from Australia — stacked high in a cooler. The beef was dumped from the vats into shiny stainless steel machines. It was ground into fine particles by giant augers, mixed into exact proportions of lean meat and fat, stamped into patties, perforated, frozen, passed through metal detectors and then sealed in plastic wrap. The frozen hamburger patties that came out of the machines looked like little pink waffles.

David Theno would like the meatpacking industry to adopt a system of "performance-based grading." Slaughterhouses that produced consistently clean meat would received a grade A. Plants that performed moderately well would receive a grade B, and so on. Microbial testing would determine the grades, and the marketplace would reward companies that ranked highest. Plants that earned only a C or a D would have to do better — or stick to making dog food.

Some people in the fast food industry resent the idea that Jack in the Box, which was involved in such a large outbreak of food poisoning, has assumed the mantle of leadership on the issue of food safety. Theno's support for tough food safety legislation in California made him unpopular with the state's restaurant association. The meatpacking industry is not fond of him, either. Theno says that the industry's long-standing resistance to microbial testing is a form of denial. "If you don't know about a problem," he explained, "then you don't have to deal with it." He thinks that the problem of *E. coli* 0157:H7 contamination in ground beef can be solved. He has an optimistic faith in the power of science and reason. "If you put in a score-keeping system and profile these meatpacking companies," Theno says, "you can fix this problem. You can actually fix this problem in six months . . . This is a matter of will, not technology." Despite the meatpacking industry's claims, the solution need not be enormously expensive. The entire Jack in the Box food safety program raises the cost of the chain's ground beef by about one penny per pound.

a lack of recall

THE CLINTON ADMINISTRATION'S EFFORTS to implement a tough, science-based food inspection system received an enormous setback when the Republican Party gained control of Congress in November of 1994. Both the meatpacking industry and the fast food industry have been major financial supporters of the Republican Party's right wing. Speaker of the House Newt Gingrich's Contract With America, stressing government deregulation and opposition to an increased minimum wage, fit perfectly with the legislative agenda of the large meatpackers and fast food chains. A study of campaign contributions between 1987 and 1996, conducted by the Center for Public Integrity, found that Gingrich received more money from the restaurant industry than any other congressman. Among the top twenty-five House recipients of restaurant industry funds, only four were Democrats. The meatpacking industry also directed most of its campaign contributions to conservative Republicans, providing strong support in the Senate to Mitch McConnell of Kentucky, Jesse Helms of North Carolina, and Orrin Hatch of Utah. Between 1987 and 1996, Phil Gramm, a Republican from Texas, received more money from the meatpacking industry than any other U.S. senator. Gramm is a member of the Senate Agriculture Committee, and his wife, Wendy Lee, sits on the board of IBP.

The meatpacking industry's allies in Congress worked hard in the 1990s to thwart modernization of the nation's meat inspection system.

A great deal of effort was spent denying the federal government any authority to recall contaminated meat or impose civil fines on firms that knowingly ship contaminated products. Under current law, the USDA cannot demand a recall. It can only consult with a company that has shipped bad meat and suggest that it withdraw the meat from interstate commerce. In extreme cases, the USDA can remove its inspectors from a slaughterhouse or processing plant, for all intents and purposes shutting down the facility. That step is rarely taken, however — and can be challenged by a meatpacker in federal court. In most cases, the USDA conducts negotiations with a meatpacking company over the timing and the scale of a proposed recall. The company has a strong economic interest in withdrawing as little meat as possible from the market (especially if the meat is difficult to trace) and in limiting publicity about the recall. And every day the USDA and the company spend discussing the subject is one more day in which Americans risk eating contaminated meat.

The Hudson Foods outbreak revealed many of the flaws in the current USDA policies on recall. Officials at Hudson Foods were informed late in July of 1997 that its frozen hamburger patties had infected Lee Harding with *E. coli* 0157:H7. Because Harding had saved the box, Hudson Foods knew the exact lot number and production code of the tainted meat. The company made no effort to warn the public or to recall the frozen patties for another three weeks, until the USDA found a second box of Hudson Foods patties contaminated with *E. coli* 0157:H7. On August 12 the company announced that it was *voluntarily* recalling 20,000 pounds of ground beef, an amount determined through negotiations with the USDA. The recall seemed surprisingly small, considering that the Hudson Foods plant in Columbus, Nebraska, could produce as much as 400,000 pounds of ground beef in a single shift — and that tainted patties had been manufactured, according to the product codes on their boxes, on at least three separate days in June. As food safety advocates and reporters began to question the size of the recall, it started to expand, reaching 40,000 pounds on August 13, 1.5 million pounds on August 15, and 25 million pounds on August 21. The recall eventually extended to 35 million pounds of ground beef, most of which had already been eaten.

The USDA had not only been forced to negotiate the Hudson Foods recall, it had to rely on company officials for information about how much meat needed to be recalled. Two of those officials suggested that just a few small lots of ground beef might have been contaminated. In reality, Hudson Foods had for months been using "rework" — ground beef left over from the previous day of production — as part of its routine processing supply. It had shipped hamburger meat potentially contaminated with the same strain of E. coli 0157:H7 from at least May of 1997 until the third week of August, when the company voluntarily agreed to shut the plant. Brent Wolke, the manager of the Hudson Foods plant in Columbus, and Michael Gregory, the company director of customer relations and quality control, were indicted in December of 1998. Federal prosecutors claimed that the pair had deliberately misled USDA inspectors and had falsified company documents to minimize the scale of the recall. Both men were later found innocent.

Once a company has decided voluntarily to pull contaminated meat from the market, it is under no legal obligation to inform the public — or even state health officials — that a recall is taking place. During the Jack in the Box outbreak, health officials in Nevada did not learn from the company that contaminated hamburger patties had been shipped there; they got the news when people noticed trucks pulling up to Jack in the Box restaurants in Las Vegas and removing the meat. Once the investigators realized that tainted ground beef had reached Nevada, a number of cases of severe food poisoning that might otherwise have been wrongly diagnosed were linked to E. coli 0157:H7. In 1994, Wendy's tried to recall about 250,000 pounds of ground beef without officially notifying state health officials, the USDA, or the public. The meat had been shipped to Wendy's restaurants in Illinois, Michigan, Minnesota, Missouri, and Wisconsin. When news of the recall leaked, Wendy's issued a press release claiming that only 8,000 pounds was being withdrawn, because it "had not been fully tested." The press release failed to mention that some ground beef from the same lot had indeed been tested — and had tested positive for E. coli 0157:H7.

A subsequent investigation by Cox News Service reporters Elliot Jaspin and Scott Montgomery found that the USDA does not inform the public when contaminated meat is recalled from fast food restaurants. "We live in a very litigious society," Jacque Knight, a USDA spokesman explained; if every meat recall was publicly announced, companies would face problems from "everybody with a stomachache." Between 1996 and 1999, the USDA didn't tell the public about more than one-third of the Class I recalls, cases in which consumers faced a serious and potentially lethal threat. The USDA now informs the public about every Class I recall, but will not reveal exactly where contaminated meat is being sold (unless it is being distributed under a brand name at a retail store). State health officials have attacked the USDA policy, arguing that it makes outbreaks much more difficult to trace and puts victims of food poisoning at much greater risk. Someone infected with *E. coli* 0157:H7, unsure about what has caused his or her symptoms and unaware of a local outbreak, may take over-the-counter medications that make the illness much worse.

Both the USDA and the meatpacking industry argue that details about where a company has distributed its meat must not be revealed in order to protect the firm's "trade secrets." In February of 1999, when IBP recalled 10,000 pounds of ground beef laced with small pieces of glass, the company would disclose only that the meat had been shipped to stores in Florida, Indiana, Michigan, and Ohio. Neither IBP, nor the USDA, would provide the names of those stores. "It's very frustrating for us," an Indiana health official told a reporter, explaining why the beef containing broken glass could not easily be removed from supermarket shelves. "If they don't give [the information] to us, there's not much we can do."

In addition to letting meatpacking executives determine when to recall ground beef, how much needs to be recalled, and who should be told about it, for years the USDA allowed these companies to help write the agency's own press releases about the recalls. After the Hudson Foods outbreak, Secretary of Agriculture Dan Glickman ended the policy of submitting USDA recall announcements to meatpacking companies for prior approval. Two years later, however, USDA officials proposed that the agency stop issuing any press releases about meat recalls, leaving that task entirely to the meatpacking industry. That proposal was never adopted. In January of 2000, the USDA decided to announce every meat recall with an official press release; the recalls are also noted on the agency's Web site. The new policy, however, has not made it any easier to learn where contaminated meat has been sold. "Press releases will not identify the specific recipients of product," the USDA directive says, "unless the supplier chooses to release the information to the public."

A recent IBP press release, announcing the recall of more than a quarter of a million pounds of ground beef possibly tainted with *E.*

coli 0157:H7, suggests that the industry's needs and those of consumers are not always the same. "In an abundance of caution, IBP is conducting this voluntary recall," the release said on June 23, 2000, implying that the move had been prompted mainly by a spirit of corporate generosity and good will. Hamburger meat potentially contaminated with the lethal pathogen had been shipped to wholesalers, distributors, and grocery stores in twenty-five states. At times, the press release reads more like an advertisement for IBP than an urgent health warning. It devotes more space to a description of the company's food safety program — with its "Triple Clean" slaughterhouse system and its "approved and accredited laboratories" — than to the details of how IBP managed to distribute nationwide enough suspect meat to make at least a million life-threatening hamburgers. Nowhere does the press release mention, for example, that the *E. coli* 0157:H7 in IBP's ground beef was first detected not by one of the firm's own accredited laboratories, not by employees at the Geneseo, Illinois, IBP plant where the meat was produced, not by USDA inspectors — but by investigators from the Arkansas Department of Health, who found the pathogen in a package of IBP ground beef at Tiger Harry's restaurant in El Dorado, Arkansas. Thirty-six people who'd recently eaten at Tiger Harry's had been sickened by *E. coli* 0157:H7. Despite the discovery of tainted ground beef in the restaurant freezer, the Arkansas Department of Health could not conclusively link IBP meat to the El Dorado *E. coli* 0157:H7 outbreak. "There have been no illnesses associated with this product," the company's press release brashly asserted. IBP's voluntary recall was issued about six weeks after the ground beef's production date. By then, almost all of the questionable meat had been eaten.

In the aftermath of the Jack in the Box outbreak, the Clinton administration backed legislation to provide the USDA with the authority to demand meat recalls and impose civil fines on meatpackers. Republicans in Congress failed to enact not only that bill, but also similar legislation introduced in 1996, 1997, 1998, and 1999. The inability of the USDA to seek monetary damages from the meatpacking industry is highly unusual, given the federal government's power to use fines as a means of regulatory enforcement in the airline, automobile, mining, steel, and toy industries. "We can fine circuses for mistreating elephants," Secretary of Agriculture Dan Glickman complained in 1997, "but we can't fine companies that violate food-safety standards."

our friend the atom

SURROUNDED BY PARENTS WHOSE children had died after eating hamburgers tainted with *E. coli* 0157:H7, President Clinton announced in July of 1996 that the USDA would finally adopt a science-based meat inspection system. Under the new regulations, every slaughterhouse and processing plant in the United States would by the end of the decade have to implement a government-approved HACCP plan and submit meat to the USDA for microbial testing. Clinton's announcement depicted the changes as the most sweeping reform of the federal government's food safety policies since the days of Theodore Roosevelt. The USDA plan, however, had been significantly watered down during negotiations with the meatpacking industry and Republican members of Congress. The new system would shift many food safety tasks to company employees. The records compiled by those employees — unlike the reports traditionally written by federal inspectors — would not be available to the public through the Freedom of Information Act. And meatpacking plants would not be required to test for *E. coli* 0157:H7, a pathogen whose discovery might lead to immediate condemnation of their meat. Instead, they could test for other bacteria as a broad measure of fecal contamination levels; the results of those tests would not have to be revealed to the government; and meat containing whatever organisms the tests found could still be sold to the public.

Many federal meat inspectors opposed the Clinton administration's new system, arguing that it greatly diminished their authority to detect and remove contaminated meat. Today the USDA's Food Safety and Inspection Service is demoralized and understaffed. In 1978, before the first known outbreak of *E. coli* 0157:H7, the USDA had 12,000 meat inspectors; now it has about 7,500. The federal inspectors I interviewed felt under enormous pressure from their USDA superiors not to slow down the line speeds at slaughterhouses. "A lot of us are feeling beaten down," one inspector told me. Job openings at the service are going unfilled for months. Federal inspectors warn that the new HACCP plans are only as good as the people running them — and that in the wrong hands HACCP stands for Have a Cup of Coffee and Pray. The Hudson Foods plant in Columbus, Nebraska, was operating under a HACCP plan in 1997 when it shipped 35 million pounds of potentially tainted meat.

"We give no serious validity to company-generated records," a long-time federal inspector told me. "There's a lot of falsification going on." His view was confirmed by other inspectors, and by former meatpacking workers who were in charge of quality control. According to Judy, a former "QC" at one of IBP's largest slaughterhouses, the HACCP plan at her plant was terrific on paper but much less impressive in real life: senior management cared much more about production than food safety. The quality control department was severely understaffed. A single QC had to keep an eye on two production lines simultaneously. "I had to check the sterilizer temperature, I had to check the Cryovac temperature, I had to look at packaging, I had to note the vats — did they have foreign objects in them or not? — I had to keep an eye on workers, so they wouldn't cheat," Judy said. "I was overwhelmed with work, it was just impossible to keep up with it all." She routinely falsified her checklist, as did the other QCs. The HACCP plan would have been "fantastic" if three people had been employed doing her job. There was no way that one person could get all the tasks on the list properly done.

Though the meatpacking industry has fought almost every federal effort to mandate food safety, it has also invested millions of dollars in new equipment to halt the spread of dangerous pathogens. IBP, for example, has installed expensive steam pasteurization cabinets at all of its beef slaughterhouses. Sides of beef enter the new contraption, which blow-dries them, bathes them in 220-degree steam for eight seconds, and then sprays them with cold water. When used properly, steam pasteurization cabinets can kill off most of the *E. coli* 0157:H7 and reduce the amount of bacteria on the meat's surface by as much as 90 percent. But an IBP internal corporate memo from 1997 suggests that the company's large investment in such technologies has been motivated less by a genuine concern for the health and well-being of American consumers than by other considerations.

"We have been informed that carcasses in your plant are occasionally being delayed for extended periods of time on the USDA outrail for final disposition (up to 6 hours)," the IBP memo began. It was sent by the company's vice president for quality control and food safety to the plant manager at the Lexington, Nebraska, slaughterhouse. It warned that the longer a carcass remains on the outrail, the harder it is to clean. With every passing minute, bacteria grows more firmly attached and difficult to kill. "This delayed carcass deposition," the memo emphasized, "is of concern and is cause for extraordinary actions regarding such affected carcasses." When carcasses sat for half an hour on the outrail, supervisors were instructed to find the cause for the delay. When carcasses sat for an hour, supervisors were told to spray the meat with a special acid wash. Carcasses that sat for longer than two hours, that were at highest risk for bacterial contamination, were not to be destroyed, or sent to rendering, or set aside for processing into precooked meats. "Such carcasses," IBP's top food safety executive advised, "are to be designated for outside (non-IBP) carcass sale." The dirtiest meat was to be shipped out and sold for public consumption — but not with an IBP label on it.

Instead of focusing on the primary causes of meat contamination — the feed being given to cattle, the overcrowding at feedlots, the poor sanitation at slaughterhouses, excessive line speeds, poorly trained workers, the lack of stringent government oversight — the meatpacking industry and the USDA are now advocating an exotic technological solution to the problem of foodborne pathogens. They want to irradiate the nation's meat. Irradiation is a form of bacterial birth control, pioneered in the 1960s by the U.S. Army and by NASA. When microorganisms are zapped with low levels of gamma rays or x-rays, they are not killed, but their DNA is disrupted, and they cannot reproduce. Irradiation has been used for years on some imported spices and domestic poultry. Most irradiating facilities have concrete walls that are six feet thick, employing cobalt 60 or cesium 137 (a waste product from nuclear weapons plants and nuclear power plants) to create highly charged, radioactive beams. A new technique, developed by the Titan Corporation, uses conventional electricity and an electronic accelerator instead of radioactive isotopes. Titan devised its SureBeam irradiation technology during the 1980s, while conducting research for the Star Wars antimissile program.

The American Medical Association and the World Health Organization have declared that irradiated foods are safe to eat. Widespread introduction of the process has thus far been impeded, however, by a reluctance among consumers to eat things that have been exposed to radiation. According to current USDA regulations, irradiated meat must be identified with a special label and with a radura (the internationally recognized symbol of radiation). The Beef Industry Food Safety Council — whose members include the meatpacking and fast food giants — has asked the USDA to change its rules and make the labeling of irradiated meat completely voluntary. The meatpacking industry is also working hard to get rid of the word "irradiation," much preferring the phrase "cold pasteurization."

One slaughterhouse engineer that I interviewed — who has helped to invent some of the most sophisticated food safety equipment now being used — told me that from a purely scientific point of view, irradiation may be safe and effective. But he is concerned about the introduction of highly complex electromagnetic and nuclear technology into slaughterhouses with a largely illiterate, non-English-speaking workforce. "These are not the type of people you want working on that level of equipment," he says. He also worries that the widespread use of irradiation might encourage meatpackers "to speed up the kill floor and spray shit everywhere." Steven Bjerklie, the former editor of *Meat & Poultry*, opposes irradiation on similar grounds. He thinks it will reduce pressure on the meatpacking industry to make fundamental and necessary changes in their production methods, allowing unsanitary practices to continue. "I don't want to be served irradiated feces along with my meat," Bjerklie says.

what kids eat

FOR YEARS SOME OF the most questionable ground beef in the United States was purchased by the USDA — and then distributed to school cafeterias throughout the country. Throughout the 1980s and 1990s, the USDA chose meat suppliers for its National School Lunch Program on the basis of the lowest price, without imposing additional food safety requirements. The cheapest ground beef was not only the most likely to be contaminated with pathogens, but also the most likely to contain pieces of spinal cord, bone, and gristle left behind by Automated Meat Recovery Systems (contraptions that squeeze the last shreds of meat off bones). A 1983 investigation by NBC News said that the Cattle King Packing Company — at the time, the USDA's largest supplier of ground beef for school lunches and a supplier to Wendy's — routinely processed cattle that were already dead before arriving at its plant, hid diseased cattle from inspectors, and mixed rotten meat that had been returned by customers into packages of hamburger meat. Cattle King's facilities were infested with rats and cockroaches. Rudy "Butch" Stanko, the owner of the company, was later tried and convicted for selling tainted meat to the federal government. He had been convicted just two years earlier on similar charges. That earlier felony conviction had not prevented him from supplying one-quarter of the ground beef served in the USDA school lunch program.

More recently, an eleven-year-old boy became seriously ill in April of 1998 after eating a hamburger at his elementary school in Danielsville, Georgia. Tests of the ground beef, which had been processed by the Bauer Meat Company, confirmed the presence of *E. coli* 0157:H7. Bauer Meat's processing plant in Ocala, Florida, was so filthy that on August 12, 1998, the USDA withdrew its inspectors, a highly unusual move. Frank Bauer, the company's owner, committed suicide the next day. The USDA later declared Bauer's meat products "unfit for human consumption," ordering that roughly 6 million pounds be detained. Nearly a third of the meat had already been shipped to school districts in North Carolina and Georgia, U.S. military bases, and prisons. Around the same time, a dozen children in Finley, Washington, were sickened by *E. coli* 0157:H7. Eleven of them had eaten undercooked beef tacos at their school cafeteria; the twelfth, a two-year-old, was most likely infected by one of the other children. The company that had supplied the USDA with the taco meat — Northern States Beef, a subsidiary of ConAgra — had in the previous eighteen months been cited for 171 "critical" food safety violations at its facilities. A critical violation is one likely to cause serious contamination and to harm consumers. Northern States Beef was also linked to a 1994 outbreak of *E. coli* 0157:H7 in Nebraska that sickened eighteen people. Nevertheless, the USDA continued to do business with the ConAgra subsidiary, buying about 20 million pounds of its meat for use in American schools.

In the summer and fall of 1999, a ground beef plant in Dallas, Texas, owned by Supreme Beef Processors failed a series of USDA tests for *Salmonella*. The tests showed that as much as 47 percent of the company's ground beef contained *Salmonella* — a proportion five times higher than what USDA regulations allow. Every year in the United States food tainted with *Salmonella* causes about 1.4 million illnesses and 500 deaths. Moreover, high levels of *Salmonella* in ground beef indicate high levels of fecal contamination. Despite the alarming test results, the USDA continued to purchase thousands of tons of meat from Supreme Beef for distribution in schools. Indeed, Supreme Beef Processors was one of the nation's largest suppliers to the school meals program, annually providing as much as 45 percent of its ground beef. On November 30, 1999, the USDA finally took action, suspending purchases from Supreme Beef and removing inspectors from the company's plant, effectively shutting it down.

Supreme Beef responded the next day by suing the USDA in federal court, claiming that *Salmonella* was a natural organism, not an adulterant. With backing from the National Meat Association, Supreme Beef challenged the legality of the USDA's science-based testing system and contended that the government had no right to remove inspectors from the plant. A. Joe Fish, a federal judge in Texas, heard Supreme Beef's arguments and immediately ordered USDA inspectors back into the plant, pending final resolution of the lawsuit. The plant shutdown — the first ever attempted under the USDA's new science-based system — lasted less than one day. A few weeks later, USDA inspectors detected *E. coli* 0157:H7 in a sample of meat from the Supreme Beef plant, and the company voluntarily recalled 180,000 pounds of ground beef that had been shipped to eight states. Nevertheless, just six weeks after that recall, the USDA resumed its purchases from Supreme Beef, once again allowing the company to supply ground beef for the nation's schools.

On May 25, 2000, Judge Fish issued a decision in the Supreme Beef case, ruling that the presence of high levels of *Salmonella* in the plant's ground beef was not proof that conditions there were "unsanitary." Fish endorsed one of Supreme Beef's central arguments: a ground beef processor should not be held responsible for the bacterial levels of meat that could easily have been tainted with *Salmonella* at a slaughterhouse. The ruling cast doubt on the USDA's ability to withdraw inspectors from a plant where tests revealed excessive levels of fecal contamination. Although Supreme Beef portrayed itself in the case as an innocent victim of forces beyond its control, much of the beef used at the plant had come from its own slaughterhouse in Ladonia, Texas. That slaughterhouse had repeatedly failed USDA tests for *Salmonella*.

Not long after the ruling, Supreme Beef failed another *Salmonella* test. The USDA moved to terminate its contract with the company and announced tough new rules for processors hoping to supply ground beef to the school lunch program. The rules sought to impose the same sort of food safety requirements that fast food chains demand from their suppliers. Beginning with the 2000–2001 school year, ground beef intended for distribution to schools would be tested for pathogens; meat that failed the tests would be rejected; and "downers"

— cattle too old or too sick to walk into a slaughterhouse — could no longer be processed into the ground beef that the USDA buys for children. The meatpacking industry immediately opposed the new rules.

your kitchen sink

DURING THE 1990s, the federal government (which is supposed to ensure food safety) applied standards to the meat it purchased for schools that were much less stringent than the standards applied by the fast food industry (which is responsible for much of the current threat to food safety). Having played a central role in the creation of a meatpacking system that can spread bacterial contamination far and wide, the fast food chains are now able to avoid many of the worst consequences. Much like Jack in the Box, the leading chains have in recent years forced their suppliers to conduct frequent tests for *E. coli* 0157:H7 and other pathogens. More importantly, the enormous buying power of the fast food giants has given them access to some of the cleanest ground beef. The meatpacking industry is now willing to perform the sort of rigorous testing for fast food chains that it refuses to do for the general public.

Anyone who brings raw ground beef into his or her kitchen today must regard it as a potential biohazard, one that may carry an extremely dangerous microbe, infectious at an extremely low dose. The current high levels of ground beef contamination, combined with the even higher levels of poultry contamination, have led to some bizarre findings. A series of tests conducted by Charles Gerba, a microbiologist at the University of Arizona, discovered far more fecal bacteria in the average American kitchen sink than on the average American toilet seat. According to Gerba, "You'd be better off eating a carrot stick that fell in your toilet than one that fell in your sink."

Although the fast food chains have belatedly made food safety a priority, their production and distribution systems remain vulnerable to newly emerging foodborne pathogens. A virus that carries the gene to produce Shiga toxins is now infecting previously harmless strains of *E. coli*. Dr. David Acheson, an associate professor of medicine at Tufts University Medical School, believes the spread of that virus is being encouraged by the indiscriminate use of antibiotics in cattle feed. In addition to *E. coli* 0157:H7, approximately sixty to one hundred other mutant *E. coli* organisms now produce Shiga toxins. Perhaps a third of them cause illnesses in human beings. Among the most dangerous are *E. coli* 0103, 0111, 026, 0121, and 0145. The standard tests being used to find *E. coli* 0157:H7 do not detect the presence of these other bugs. The CDC now estimates that roughly 37,000 Americans suffer food poisoning each year from non-0157 strains of *E. coli*, about 1,000 people are hospitalized, and about 25 die.

No matter how well executed the HACCP plan, no matter how highly automated the grills, no matter how many bursts of gamma radiation are fired at the meat, the safety of the food at any restaurant ultimately depends upon the workers in its kitchen. Dr. Patricia Griffin, one of the CDC's leading experts on *E. coli* 0157:H7, believes that food safety classes should be mandatory for fast food workers. "We place our lives in their hands," she says, "in the same way we entrust our lives to the training of airline pilots." Griffin worries that a low-paid, unskilled workforce composed of teenagers and recent immigrants may not always be familiar with proper food handling procedures.

Dr. Griffin has good reason to worry. A 1997 undercover investigation by KCBS-TV in Los Angeles videotaped local restaurant workers sneezing into their hands while preparing food, licking salad dressing off their fingers, picking their noses, and flicking their cigarettes into meals about to be served. In May of 2000, three teenage employees at a Burger King in Scottsville, New York, were arrested for putting spit, urine, and cleaning products such as Easy-Off Oven Cleaner and Comet with Bleach into the food. They had allegedly tampered with the Burger King food for eight months, and it was served to thousands of customers, until a fellow employee informed the management.

The teenage fast food workers I met in Colorado Springs, Colorado, told me other horror stories. The safety of the food seemed to be determined more by the personality of the manager on duty than by the written policies of the chain. Many workers would not eat anything at their restaurant unless they'd made it themselves. A Taco Bell employee said that food dropped on the floor was often picked up and served. An Arby's employee told me that one kitchen worker never washed his hands at work after doing engine repairs on his car. And several employees at the same McDonald's restaurant in Colorado Springs independently provided details about a cockroach infestation in the milk-shake machine and about armies of mice that urinated and defecated on hamburger rolls left out to thaw in the kitchen every night.

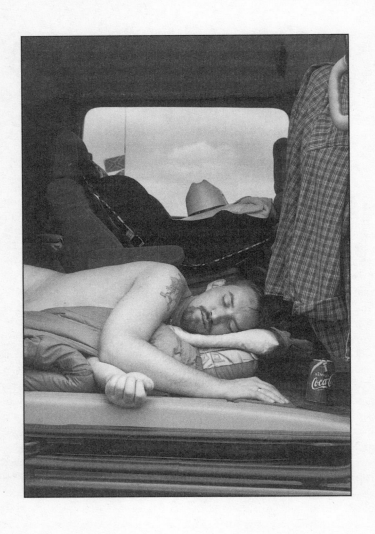

10 / global realization

WHENEVER I TOLD SOMEONE in Berlin that I was planning to visit Plauen, I got the same reaction. It didn't matter whom I told — someone old or young, hip or square, gay, straight, raised in West Germany, raised in the East — there'd always be a laugh, followed by a look of slight amazement. "Plauen?" they'd say. "Why would you ever want to go to Plauen?" The way the name was spoken, the long, drawn-out emphasis on the second syllable, implied that the whole idea was vaguely ridiculous. Located halfway between Munich and Berlin, in a part of Saxony known as the Vogtland, Plauen is a small provincial city surrounded by forests and rolling hills. To Berliners, whose city is the present capital of Germany and perhaps the future capital of Europe, Plauen is a sleepy backwater that sat for decades on the wrong side of the Berlin Wall. Berliners regard the place in much the same way that New Yorkers view Muncie, Indiana. But I found Plauen fascinating. The countryside around it is lush and green. Some of the old buildings have real charm. The people are open, friendly, unpretentious — and yet somehow cursed.

For decades Plauen has been on the margins of history, far removed from the centers of power; nevertheless, events there have oddly foreshadowed the rise and fall of great social movements. One after another, the leading ideologies of modern Europe — industrialism, fascism, communism, consumerism — have passed through Plauen and left their mark. None has completely triumphed or been completely erased. Bits and pieces of these worldviews still coexist uneasily, cropping up in unexpected places, from the graffiti on the wall of an apartment building to the tone of an offhand remark. There is nothing settled yet, nothing that can be assumed. All sorts of things, good and bad, are still possible. In the heart of the Vogtland, without much notice from the rest of the world, the little city of Plauen has been alternately punished, rewarded, devastated, and transformed by the great unifying systems of the twentieth century, by each new effort to govern all of mankind with a single set of rules. Plauen has been a battlefield for these competing ideologies, with their proudly displayed and archetypal symbols: the smokestack, the swastika, the hammer and sickle, the golden arches.

For centuries, Plauen was a small market town where Vogtland farmers came to buy and sell goods. And then, at the end of the nineteenth century, a local weaving tradition gave birth to a vibrant textile industry. Between 1890 and 1914, the city's population roughly tripled, reaching 118,000 on the eve of World War I. Its new textile mills specialized in lace and in embroidered fabrics, exporting most of their output to the United States. The doilies on dinner tables throughout the American Midwest came from Plauen, as well as the intricate lacework that set the tone of many upper-middle-class Victorian homes. Black-and-white postcards from Plauen before the Great War show lovely Art Nouveau and Neo-Romantic buildings that evoke the streets of Paris, elegant cafés and parks, electric streetcars, zeppelins in the air.

Life in Plauen became less idyllic after Germany's defeat. When the Victorian world and its values collapsed, so did the market for lace. Many of Plauen's textile mills closed, and thousands of people were thrown out of work. The social unrest that later engulfed the rest of Germany came early to Plauen. In the 1920s Plauen had the most millionaires per capita in Germany — and the most suicides. It also had the highest unemployment rate. Amid the misery, extremism thrived. Plauen was the first city outside of Bavaria to organize its own chapter of the Nazi party. In May of 1923, the Hitler Youth movement was launched in Plauen, and the following year, the little city became the Nazi headquarters for Saxony. Long before the Nazi reign of terror began elsewhere, union leaders and leftists were murdered in Plauen. Hitler visited the city on several occasions, receiving an enthusiastic welcome. Hermann Göring and Joseph Goebbels visited too, and Plauen became a sentimental favorite of the Nazi leadership. On the night of November 9, 1938, *Kristallnacht,* a crowd eagerly destroyed Plauen's only synagogue, a strikingly modern building designed by Bauhaus architect Fritz Landauer. Not long afterward, Plauen officially became *Jüden-frei* (Jew-free).

For most of World War II, Plauen remained strangely quiet and peaceful, an oasis of ordinary life. It provided safe haven to thousands of German refugees fleeing bombed-out cities. All sorts of rumors tried to explain why Plauen was being spared, while other towns in Saxony were being destroyed. On September 19, 1944, American bombers appeared over the city for the first time. Instead of rushing into shelters, people stood in the streets, amazed, watching bombs fall on the railway station and on a factory that built tanks for the German army. A few months later, Plauen appeared alongside Dresden on an Allied bombing list.

Plauen was largely deserted on April 10, 1945, when hundreds of British Lancaster bombers appeared over the city. Its inhabitants no longer felt mysteriously protected; they knew that Dresden had recently been fire-bombed into oblivion. During a single raid the Royal Air Force dropped 2,000 tons of high explosives on Plauen. Four days later, the U.S. Army occupied what was left of the town. The birthplace of the Hitler Youth, the most Nazified city in Saxony, gained another distinction only weeks before the war ended. More bombs were dropped on Plauen, per square mile, than on any other city in eastern Germany — roughly three times as many as were dropped on Dresden. Although the carnage was far worse in Dresden, a larger proportion of Plauen's buildings was destroyed. At the end of the war, about 75 percent of Plauen lay in ruins.

When the Allies divided their spheres of influence in Germany, Plauen's misfortune continued. The U.S. Army pulled out of the city and the Soviet army rolled in. Plauen became part of the communist German Democratic Republic (GDR), but just barely. The new border with West Germany was only nine miles away. Plauen languished under Communist rule. It lost one-third of its prewar population. Sitting in a remote corner of the GDR, it received little attention or investment from the Communist party leadership in East Berlin. Much of Plauen was never rebuilt; parking lots and empty lots occupied land where ornate buildings had once stood. One of the few successful factories, a synthetic wool plant, blanketed Plauen in some of East Germany's worst air pollution. According to historian John Connelly, the polluted air helped give the city an "unusually low quality of life, even for GDR standards."

On October 7, 1989, the first mass demonstration against East Germany's Communist rulers took place in Plauen. Small, scattered protests also occurred that day in Magdeberg, East Berlin, and other cities. The size of Plauen's demonstration set it apart. More than one-quarter of the city's population suddenly took to the streets. The level of unrest greatly surprised local government officials. The Stasi (East Germany's secret police) had expected about four hundred people to appear in the town center that day, the fortieth anniversary of the GDR's founding. Instead, about twenty thousand people began to gather, despite dark skies and a steady drizzle. The demonstration had no leadership, no organizers, no formal plan of action. It grew spontaneously, spreading through word of mouth.

The protesters in other East German cities were mainly college students and members of the intelligentsia; in Plauen they were factory workers and ordinary citizens. Some of the demonstration's most fervent supporters were long-haired, working-class fans of American heavy metal music, known in Plauen as *die Heavies,* who rode their motorcycles through town distributing antigovernment pamphlets. As the crowd grew, people began to chant Mikhail Gorbachev's nickname — "Gorby! Gorby!" — cheering the Soviet leader's policies of *glasnost* and *perestroika,* demanding similar reforms in East Germany, defiantly yelling "Stasi go home!" One large banner bore the words of the German poet Friedrich von Schiller. "We want freedom," it said, "like the freedom enjoyed by our forefathers."

Police officers and Stasi agents tried to break up the demonstration, arresting dozens of people, firing water cannons at the crowd, flying helicopters low over the rooftops of Plauen. But the protesters refused to disperse. They marched to the town hall and called for the mayor to come outside and address their demands. Thomas Küttler, the superintendent of Plauen's Lutheran church, volunteered to act as a mediator. Inside the town hall, he found Plauen's high-ranking officials cowering in fear. None would emerge to face the crowd. The equation of power had fundamentally changed that day. A mighty totalitarian system of rule, erected over the course of four decades, propped up by tanks and guns and thousands of Stasi informers, was crumbling before his eyes, as its rulers nervously chain-smoked in the safety of their offices. The mayor finally agreed to address the crowd, but a Stasi official prevented him from leaving the building. And so Küttler stood on the steps of the town hall with a megaphone, urging the soldiers not to fire their weapons and telling the demonstrators that their point had been made, now it was time to go home. As bells atop the Lutheran church rang, the crowd began to disperse.

A month later, the Berlin Wall fell. And a few months after that extraordinary event, marking the end of the Cold War, the McDonald's

Corporation announced plans to open its first restaurant in East Germany. The news provoked a last gasp of collectivism from Ernst Doerfler, a prominent member of the doomed East German parliament, who called for an official ban on "McDonald's and similar abnormal garbage-makers." McDonald's, however, would not be deterred; Burger King had already opened a mobile hamburger cart in Dresden. During the summer of 1990, construction quickly began on the first McDonald's in East Germany. It would occupy an abandoned lot in the center of Plauen, a block away from the steps of the town hall. The McDonald's would be the first new building erected in Plauen since the coming of a new Germany.

uncle mcdonald

AS THE FAST FOOD industry has grown more competitive in the United States, the major chains have looked to overseas markets for their future growth. The McDonald's Corporation recently used a new phrase to describe its hopes for foreign conquest: "global realization." A decade ago, McDonald's had about three thousand restaurants outside the United States; today it has about seventeen thousand restaurants in more than 120 foreign countries. It currently opens about five new restaurants every day, and at least four of them are overseas. Within the next decade, Jack Greenberg, the company's chief executive, hopes to double the number of McDonald's. The chain earns the majority of its profits outside the United States, as does KFC. McDonald's now ranks as the most widely recognized brand in the world, more familiar than Coca-Cola. The values, tastes, and industrial practices of the American fast food industry are being exported to every corner of the globe, helping to create a homogenized international culture that sociologist Benjamin R. Barber has labeled "McWorld."

The fast food chains have become totems of Western economic development. They are often the first multinationals to arrive when a country has opened its markets, serving as the avant-garde of American franchising. Fifteen years ago, when McDonald's opened its first restaurant in Turkey, no other foreign franchisor did business there. Turkey now has hundreds of franchise outlets, including 7-Eleven, Nutra Slim, Re/Max Real Estate, Mail Boxes Etc., and Ziebart Tidy Car. Support for the growth of franchising has even become part of American foreign policy. The U.S. State Department now publishes detailed studies of overseas franchise opportunities and runs a Gold Key Program at many of its embassies to help American franchisors find overseas partners.

The anthropologist Yunxiang Yan has noted that in the eyes of Beijing consumers, McDonald's represents "Americana and the promise of modernization." Thousands of people waited patiently for hours to eat at the city's first McDonald's in 1992. Two years later, when a McDonald's opened in Kuwait, the line of cars waiting at the drive-through window extended for seven miles. Around the same time, a Kentucky Fried Chicken restaurant in Saudi Arabia's holy city of Mecca set new sales records for the chain, earning $200,000 in a single week during Ramadan, the Muslim holy month. In Brazil, McDonald's has become the nation's largest private employer. The fast food chains are now imperial fiefdoms, sending their emissaries far and wide. Classes at McDonald's Hamburger University in Oak Brook, Illinois, are taught in more than two dozen languages. Few places on earth seem too distant or too remote for the golden arches. In 1986, the Tahiti Tourism Promotion Board ran an ad campaign featuring pristine beaches and the slogan "Sorry, No McDonald's." A decade later, one opened in Papeete, the Tahitian capital, bringing hamburgers and fries to a spot thousands of miles, across the Pacific, from the nearest cattle ranches or potato fields.

As the fast food chains have moved overseas, they have been accompanied by their major suppliers. In order to diminish fears of American imperialism, the chains try to purchase as much food as possible in the countries where they operate. Instead of importing food, they import entire systems of agricultural production. Seven years before McDonald's opened its first restaurant in India, the company began to establish a supply network there, teaching Indian farmers how to grow iceburg lettuce with seeds specially developed for the nation's climate. "A McDonald's restaurant is just the window of a much larger system comprising an extensive food-chain, running right up to the farms," one of the company's Indian partners told a foreign journalist.

In 1987, ConAgra took over Australia Meat Holdings, the largest beef company in the country that exports more beef than any other in the world. Over the past decade, Cargill and IBP have gained control of the beef industry in Canada. Cargill has established large-scale poultry operations in China and Thailand. Tyson Foods is planning to build chicken-processing plants in China, Indonesia, and the Philippines. ConAgra's Lamb Weston division now manufactures frozen french fries in Holland, India, and Turkey. McCain, the world's biggest french fry producer, operates fifty processing plants scattered across four continents. In order to supply McDonald's, J. R. Simplot began to grow Russet Burbank potatoes in China, opening that nation's first french fry factory in 1993. A few years ago Simplot bought eleven processing plants in Australia, aiming to increase sales in the East Asian market. He also purchased a 3-million-acre ranch in Australia, where he hopes to run cattle, raise vegetables, and grow potatoes. "It's a great little country," Simplot says, "and there's nobody in it."

As in the United States, the fast food companies have targeted their foreign advertising and promotion at a group of consumers with the fewest attachments to tradition: young children. "Kids are the same regarding the issues that affect the all-important stages of their development," a top executive at the Gepetto Group told the audience at a recent KidPower conference, "and they apply to any kid in Berlin, Beijing, or Brooklyn." The KidPower conference, attended by marketing executives from Burger King and Nickelodeon, among others, was held at the Disneyland outside of Paris. In Australia, where the number of fast food restaurants roughly tripled during the 1990s, a survey found that half of the nation's nine- and ten-year-olds thought that Ronald McDonald knew what kids should eat. At a primary school in Beijing, Yunxiang Yan found that all of the children recognized an image of Ronald McDonald. The children told Yan they liked "Uncle McDonald" because he was "funny, gentle, kind, and . . . he understood children's hearts." Coca-Cola is now the favorite drink among Chinese children, and McDonald's serves their favorite food. Simply eating at a McDonald's in Beijing seems to elevate a person's social status. The idea that you are what you eat has been enthusiastically promoted for years by Den Fujita, the eccentric billionaire who brought McDonald's to Japan three decades ago. "If we eat McDonald's hamburgers and potatoes for a thousand years," Fujita once promised his countrymen, "we will become taller, our skin will become white, and our hair will be blonde."

The impact of fast food is readily apparent in Germany, which has become one of McDonald's most profitable overseas markets. Germany is not only the largest country in Europe, but also the most Americanized. Although the four Allied powers occupied it after World War II, the Americans exerted the greatest lasting influence, perhaps because their nationalism was so inclusive, and their nation so distant. Children in West German schools were required to study English, facilitating the spread of American pop culture. Young people who sought to distance themselves from the wartime behavior of their parents found escape in American movies, music, and novels. "For a child growing up in the turmoil of [postwar] Berlin . . . the Americans were angels," Christa Maerker, a Berlin filmmaker, wrote in an essay on postwar Germany's infatuation with the United States. "Anything from them was bigger and more wonderful than anything that preceded it."

The United States and Germany fought against each other twice in the twentieth century, but the enmity between them has often seemed less visceral than other national rivalries. The recent takeover of prominent American corporations — such as Chrysler, Random House, and RCA Records — by German companies provoked none of the public anger that was unleashed when Japanese firms bought much less significant American assets in the 1980s. Despite America's long-standing "special relationship" with Great Britain, the underlying cultural ties between the United States and Germany, though less obvious, are equally strong. Americans with German ancestors far outnumber those with English ancestors. Moreover, during the past century both American culture and German culture have shown an unusually strong passion for science, technology, engineering, empiricism, social order, and efficiency. The electronic paper-towel dispenser that I saw in a Munich men's room is the spiritual kin of the gas-powered ketchup dispensers at the McDonald's in Colorado Springs.

The traditional German restaurant — serving schnitzel, bratwurst, knackwurst, sauerbraten, and large quantities of beer — is rapidly disappearing in Germany. Such establishments now account for less than one-third of the German foodservice market. Their high labor costs have for the most part been responsible for their demise, along with the declining popularity of schnitzel. McDonald's Deutschland, Inc., is by far the biggest restaurant company in Germany today, more than twice as large as the nearest competitor. It opened the first German McDonald's in 1971; at the beginning of the 1990s it had four hundred restaurants, and now it has more than a thousand. The company's main dish happens to be named after Hamburg, a German city where ground-beef steaks were popular in the early nineteenth century. The hamburger was born when Americans added the bun. McDonald's Deutschland uses German potatoes for its fries and Bavarian dairy cows for its burgers. It sends Ronald McDonald into hospitals and schools. It puts new McDonald's restaurants in gas stations, railway stations, and airports. It battles labor unions and — according to Siegfried Pater, author of *Zum Beispiel McDonald's* — has repeatedly fired union sympathizers. The success of McDonald's, Pizza Hut, and T.G.I. Fridays in Germany has helped spark a franchising boom. Since 1992, the number of franchised outlets there has doubled, and about five thousand more are being added every year. In August of 1999, McDonald's Deutschland announced that it would be putting restaurants in Germany's new Wal-Mart stores. "The partnership scheme will undoubtedly be a success," a German financial analyst told London's *Evening Standard*. "The kiddie factor alone — children urging their parents to shop at Wal-Mart because they have a McDonald's inside the store — could generate an upsurge in customers."

The golden arches have become so commonplace in Germany that they seem almost invisible. You don't notice them unless you're looking for them, or feeling hungry. One German McDonald's, however, stands out from the rest. It sits on a nondescript street in a new shopping complex not far from Dachau, the first concentration camp opened by the Nazis. The stores were built on fields where Dachau's inmates once did forced labor. Although the architecture of the shopping complex looks German and futuristic, the haphazard placement of the buildings on the land seems distinctively American. They would not seem out of place near an off-ramp of I-25 in Colorado. Across the street from the McDonald's there's a discount supermarket. An auto parts store stands a few hundred yards from the other buildings, separated by fields that have not yet vanished beneath concrete. In 1997, protests were staged against the opening of a McDonald's so close to a concentration camp where gypsies, Jews, homosexuals, and political opponents of the Nazis were imprisoned, where Luftwaffe scientists performed medical experiments on inmates and roughly 30,000 people died. The McDonald's Corporation denied that it was trying to profit from the Holocaust and said the restaurant was at least a mile from the camp. After the curator of the Dachau Museum complained that McDonald's was distributing thousands of leaflets among tourists in the camp's parking lot, the company halted the practice. "Welcome to Dachau," said the leaflets, "and welcome to McDonald's."

The McDonald's at Dachau is one-third of a mile from the entrance to the concentration camp. The day I went there, the restaurant was staging a "Western Big Mac" promotion. It was decorated in a Wild West theme, with paper place mats featuring a wanted poster of

"Butch Essidie." The restaurant was full of mothers and small children. Teenagers dressed in Nikes, Levis, and Tommy Hilfiger T-shirts sat in groups and smoked cigarettes. Turkish immigrants worked in the kitchen, seventies disco music played, and the red paper cups on everyone's tray said "Always Coca-Cola." This McDonald's was in Dachau, but it could have been anywhere — anywhere in the United States, anywhere in the world. Millions of other people at that very moment were standing at the same counter, ordering the same food from the same menu, food that tasted everywhere the same.

at the circus

THE MOST SURREAL EXPERIENCE that I had during three years of research into fast food took place not at the top-secret air force base that got its Domino's pizzas delivered, not at the flavor factory off the New Jersey Turnpike, not at the Dachau McDonald's. It occurred on March 1, 1999, at the Mirage Hotel in Las Vegas. Like an epiphany, it revealed the strange power of fast food in the new world order. The Mirage — with its five-story volcano, its shark tank, dolphin tank, indoor rain forest, Lagoon Saloon, DKNY boutique, and Secret Garden of Siegfried & Roy — is a fine place for the surreal. Even its name suggests the triumph of illusion over reality, a promise that you won't believe your eyes. On that day in March, as usual, Las Vegas was full of spectacles and name acts. George Carlin was at Bally's, and David Cassidy was at the MGM Grand, starring in *EFX*, a show billed as a high-tech journey through space and time. *The History of Sex* was at the Golden Nugget, *The Number One Fool Contest* was at the Comedy Stop, Joacquin Ayala (Mexico's most famous magician) was at Harrah's, the Radio City Rockettes were at the Flamingo Hilton, "the Dream King" (Elvis impersonator Trent Carlini) was at the Boardwalk. And Mikhail Gorbachev (former president of the Supreme Soviet of the USSR, winner of the Orders of Lenin, the Red Banner of Labor, and the Nobel Peace Prize) was at the Grand Ballroom of the Mirage, giving the keynote speech before a fast food convention.

The convention and its setting were an ideal match. In many ways Las Vegas is the fulfillment of social and economic trends now sweeping from the American West to the farthest reaches of the globe. Las Vegas is the fastest-growing major city in the United States — an entirely man-made creation, a city that lives for the present, that has little connection to its surrounding landscape, that cares little about its own past. Nothing in Las Vegas is built to last, hotels are routinely demolished as soon as they seem out of fashion, and the city limits seem as arbitrary as its location, with plastic bags and garbage littering the open land where the lawns end, the desert not far from the Strip.

Las Vegas began as an overnight camp for travelers going to California on the Old Spanish Trail. It later became a ranching town, notable in the early 1940s mainly for its rodeo, its Wild West tourist attractions, and a nightclub called the Apache Bar. The population was about 8,000. The subsequent growth of Las Vegas was made possible by the federal government, which spent billions of dollars to erect the Hoover Dam and build military bases near the city. The dam supplied water and electricity, while the bases provided the early casinos with customers. When authorities in southern California cracked down on illegal gambling after World War II, the gamblers headed for Nevada. As in Colorado Springs, the real boom in Las Vegas began toward the end of the 1970s. Over the past twenty years the population of Las Vegas has nearly tripled.

Today there are few remaining traces of the city's cowboy past. Indeed, the global equation has been reversed. While the rest of the world builds Wal-Marts, Arby's, Taco Bells, and other outposts of Americana, Las Vegas has spent the past decade recreating the rest of the world. The fast food joints along the Strip seem insignificant compared to the new monuments towering over them: recreations of the Eiffel Tower, the Statue of Liberty, and the Sphinx, enormous buildings that evoke Venice, Paris, New York, Tuscany, medieval England, ancient Egypt and Rome, the Middle East, the South Seas. Las Vegas is now so contrived and artificial that it has become something authentic, a place unlike any other. The same forces that are homogenizing other cities have made Las Vegas even more unique.

At the heart of Las Vegas is technology: machinery that cools the air, erupts the volcano, and powers the shimmering lights. Most important of all is the machinery that makes money for the casinos. While Las Vegas portrays itself as a free-wheeling, entrepreneurial town where anyone can come and strike it rich, life there is more tightly regulated, controlled, and monitored by hidden cameras than just about anywhere else in the United States. The city's principal industry is legally protected against the workings of the free market, and operates according to strict rules laid down by the state. The Nevada Gaming Control Board determines not only who can own a casino, but who can enter one. In a town built on gambling, where fortunes were once earned with a roll of the dice, it is remarkable how little is now left to chance. Until the late 1960s, about three-quarters of a typical casino's profits came from table games, from poker, blackjack, baccarat, roulette. During the last twenty-five years table games, which are supervised by dealers and offer gamblers the best odds, have been displaced by slot machines. Today about two-thirds of a typical casino's profits now come from slots and video poker — machines that are precisely calibrated to take your money. They guarantee the casino a profit rate of as much as 20 percent — four times what a roulette wheel will bring.

The latest slot machines are electronically connected to a central computer, allowing the casino to track the size of every bet and its outcome. The music, flashing lights, and sound effects emitted by these slots help disguise the fact that a small processor inside them is deciding with mathematical certainty how long you will play before you lose. It is the ultimate consumer technology, designed to manufacture not a tangible product, but something much more elusive: a brief sense of hope. That is what Las Vegas really sells, the most brilliant illusion of all, a loss that feels like winning.

Mikhail Gorbachev was in town to speak at the Twenty-sixth Annual Chain Operators Exchange, a convention sponsored by the International Foodservice Manufacturers Association. Executives from the major fast food companies had gathered to discuss, among other things, the latest labor-saving machinery and the prospects of someday employing a workforce that needed "zero training." Representatives from the industry's leading suppliers — ConAgra, Monfort, Simplot, and others — had come to sell their latest products. The Grand Ballroom at the Mirage was filled with hundreds of middle-aged white men in expensive business suits. They sat at long tables beneath crystal chandeliers, drinking coffee, greeting old friends, waiting for the morning program to begin. A few of them were obviously struggling to recover from whatever they'd done in Las Vegas the night before.

On the surface, Mikhail Gorbachev seemed an odd choice to address a group so resolutely opposed to labor unions, minimum wages, and workplace safety rules. "Those who hope we shall move away from the socialist path will be greatly disappointed," Gorbachev had written in *Perestroika* (1987), at the height of his power. He had never sought the dissolution of the Soviet Union and never renounced his fundamental commitment to Marxism-Leninism. He still believed in the class struggle and "scientific socialism." But the fall of the Berlin Wall had thrown Gorbachev out of power and left him in a precarious financial condition. He was beloved abroad, yet despised in his own land. During Russia's 1996 presidential election he received just 1 percent of the vote. The following year he expressed great praise for America's leading fast food chain. "And the merry clowns, the Big Mac signs, the colourful, unique decorations and ideal cleanliness," Gorbachev wrote in the foreword of *To Russia with Fries,* a memoir by a McDonald's executive, "all of this complements the hamburgers whose great popularity is well deserved."

In December of 1997, Gorbachev appeared in a Pizza Hut commercial, following in the footsteps of Cindy Crawford and Ivana Trump. A group of patrons at a Moscow Pizza Hut thanked him in the ad for bringing the fast food chain to Russia and then shouted "Hail to Gorbachev!" In response Gorbachev saluted them by raising a slice of pizza. He reportedly earned $160,000 for his appearance in the sixty-second spot, money earmarked for his nonprofit foundation. A year later Pizza Hut announced that it was pulling out of Russia as the country's economy collapsed, and Gorbachev told a German reporter that "all my money is gone." For his hour-long speech at the Mirage, Gorbachev was promised a fee of $150,000 and the use of a private jet.

The Twenty-sixth Annual Chain Operators Exchange officially opened with a video presentation of the national anthem. As the song boomed from speakers throughout the Grand Ballroom, two huge screens above the stage displayed a series of patriotic images: the Statue of Liberty, the Lincoln Memorial, amber waves of grain. In one of the morning's first speeches, an executive hailed the restaurant industry's record profits the previous year, adding without irony, "As if things weren't good enough, consumers also dropped all pretense of wanting healthy food." An ongoing industry survey had found that public concerns about salt, fat, and food additives were at their lowest level since 1982, when the survey began — one more bit of news to justify the industry's "current state of bliss." Another executive, a self-described "sensory evaluation specialist," emphasized the importance of pleasant smells. He noted that Las Vegas resorts were now experimenting with "signature scents" in their casinos, hoping the subtle aromas would subconsciously make people gamble more money.

Robert Nugent, the head of Jack in the Box and honorary chairman of the Twenty-sixth Annual Chain Operators Exchange, broke the cheery mood with an ominous, unsettling speech. He essentially accused critics of the fast food industry of being un-American. "A growing number of groups who represent narrow social and political interests," Nugent warned, "have set their sights on our industry in an effort to legislate behavioral change." Enjoying a great meal at a restaurant was "the very essence of freedom," he declared, a ritual now being threatened by groups with an agenda that was "anti-meat, anti-alcohol, anti-caffeine, anti-fat, anti-chemical additives, anti-horseradish, anti-non-dairy creamer." The media played a central role in helping these "activist fearmongers," but the National Restaurant Association had recently launched a counterattack, working closely with journalists to dispel myths and gain better publicity. Nugent called upon the fast food executives to respond even more forcefully to their critics, people who today posed "a real danger to our industry — and more broadly to our way of life."

Not long afterward Mikhail Gorbachev appeared onstage and received a standing ovation. Here was the man who'd ended the Cold War, who'd brought political freedom to hundreds of millions, who'd opened vast new markets. At the age of sixty-nine Gorbachev looked remarkably unchanged from his appearance during the Reagan years. His hair was white, but he seemed vigorous and strong, still capable of running a mighty empire. He spoke quickly in Russian and then waited patiently for the translator to catch up. His delivery was full of energy and passion. "I like America," Gorbachev said with a broad smile. "And I like American people." He wanted to give the audience a sense of what was happening in Russia today. Few people in the United States seemed to care much about events in Russia, a dangerous state of affairs. He asked the crowd to learn about his country, to form partnerships and make investments there. "You must have a lot of money," Gorbachev said. "Send it to Russia."

A few minutes into Gorbachev's speech, the audience began to lose interest. He had badly misjudged the crowd. His speech might have been a success at the Council on Foreign Relations or at the United Nations General Assembly, but at the Grand Ballroom of the Mirage it was a bomb. As Gorbachev explained why the United States must strongly support the policies of Yevgeny Primakov (the Russian prime minister who was fired not long afterward) row after row of eyes began to glaze. He earnestly asked why there was "some kind of a dislike of Primakov that is widespread in this country," unaware that few Americans knew who Yevgeny Primakov was and even fewer cared about him, one way or the other. I counted at least half a dozen people seated near me in the Grand Ballroom who fell asleep during Gorbachev's speech. The executive right beside me suddenly awoke in the middle of a long anecdote about how the Mongol invasion had affected the Russian character in the Middle Ages. The executive seemed startled and unaware of his surroundings, then glanced at the podium for a moment, felt reassured, and drifted back to sleep, his chin resting flat on his chest.

Gorbachev sounded like a politician from a distant era, from a time before sound bites. He was serious, long-winded, and sometimes difficult to follow. His mere presence at the Mirage was far more important to this crowd than anything he said. The meaning hit me as I looked around at all the fast food executives, the sea of pinstriped suits and silk ties. In ancient Rome, the leaders of conquered nations were put on display at the Circus. The symbolism was unmistakable; the submission to Rome, complete. Gorbachev's appearance at the Mirage seemed an Americanized version of that custom, a public opportunity for the victors to gloat — though it would have been even more fitting if the fast food convention had been down the road at Caesars Palace.

As a Soviet leader, Mikhail Gorbachev never learned when to leave the stage, a flaw that led to his humiliating defeat in the election of 1996. He made the same mistake in Las Vegas; people got up and left the Grand Ballroom while he was still speaking. "Margaret Thatcher was a lot better," I heard one executive say to another as they headed for the door. Thatcher had addressed the previous year's Chain Operators Exchange.

The day after Gorbachev's speech at the Mirage, Bob Dylan performed at the grand opening of the new Mandalay Bay casino. And billboards along the interstate announced that Peter Lowe's Success 1999 was coming to Las Vegas, with special appearances by Elizabeth Dole and General Colin Powell.

an empire of fat

FOR MOST OF THE twentieth century, the Soviet Union stood as the greatest obstacle to the worldwide spread of American values and the American way of life. The collapse of Soviet Communism has led to an unprecedented "Americanization" of the world, expressed in the growing popularity of movies, CDs, music videos, television shows, and clothing from the United States. Unlike those commodities, fast food is the one form of American culture that foreign consumers literally consume. By eating like Americans, people all over the world are beginning to look more like Americans, at least in one respect. The United States now has the highest obesity rate of any industrialized nation in the world. More than half of all American adults and about one-quarter of all American children are now obese or overweight. Those proportions have soared during the last few decades, along with the consumption of fast food. The rate of obesity among American adults is twice as high today as it was in the early 1960s. The rate of obesity among American children is twice as high as it was in the late 1970s. According to James O. Hill, a prominent nutritionist at the University of Colorado, "We've got the fattest, least fit generation of kids ever."

The medical literature classifies a person as obese if he or she has a Body Mass Index (BMI) of 30 or higher — a measurement that takes into account both weight and height. For example, a woman who is five-foot-five and weighs 132 pounds has a BMI of 22, which is considered normal. If she gains eighteen pounds, her BMI rises to 25, and she's considered overweight. If she gains fifty pounds, her BMI reaches 30, and she's considered obese. Today about 44 million American adults are obese. An additional 6 million are "super-obese"; they weigh about a hundred pounds more than they should. No other nation in history has gotten so fat so fast.

A recent study by half a dozen researchers at the Centers for Disease Control and Prevention found that the rate of American obesity was increasing in every state and among both sexes, regardless of age, race, or educational level. In 1991, only four states had obesity rates of 15 percent or higher; today at least thirty-seven states do. "Rarely do chronic conditions such as obesity," the CDC scientists observed, "spread with the speed and dispersion characteristic of a communicable disease epidemic." Although the current rise in obesity has a number of complex causes, genetics is not one of them. The American gene pool has not changed radically in the past few decades. What has changed is the nation's way of eating and living. In simple terms: when people eat more and move less, they get fat. In the United States, people have become increasingly sedentary — driving to work instead of walking, performing little manual labor, driving to do errands, watching television, playing video games, and using a computer instead of exercising. Budget cuts have eliminated physical education programs at many schools. And the growth of the fast food industry has made an abundance of high-fat, inexpensive meals widely available.

As people eat more meals outside the home, they consume more calories, less fiber, and more fat. Commodity prices have fallen so low that the fast food industry has greatly increased its portion sizes, without reducing profits, in order to attract customers. The size of a burger has become one of its main selling points. Wendy's offers the Triple Decker; Burger King, the Great American; and Hardee's sells a hamburger called the Monster. The Little Caesars slogan "Big! Big!" now applies not just to the industry's portions, but to its customers. Over the past forty years in the United States, per capita consumption of carbonated soft drinks has more than quadrupled. During the late 1950s the typical soft drink order at a fast food restaurant contained about eight ounces of soda; today a "Child" order of Coke at McDonald's is twelve ounces. A "Large" Coke is thirty-two ounces — and about 310 calories. In 1972, McDonald's added Large French Fries to its menu; twenty years later, the chain added Super Size Fries, a serving three times larger than what McDonald's offered a generation ago. Super Size Fries have 610 calories and 29 grams of fat. At Carl's Jr. restaurants, an order of CrissCut Fries and a Double Western Bacon Cheeseburger boasts 73 grams of fat — more fat than ten of the chain's milk shakes.

A number of attempts to introduce healthy dishes (such as the McLean Deluxe, a hamburger partly composed of seaweed) have proven unsuccessful. A taste for fat developed in childhood is difficult to lose as an adult. At the moment, the fast food industry is heavily promoting menu items that contain bacon. "Consumers savor the flavor while operators embrace [the] profit margin," *Advertising Age* noted. A decade ago, restaurants sold about 20 percent of the bacon consumed in the United States; now they sell about 70 percent. "Make It Bacon" is one of the new slogans at McDonald's. With the exception of Subway (which promotes healthier food), the major chains have apparently decided that it's much easier and much more profitable to increase the size and the fat content of their portions than to battle eating habits largely formed by years of their own mass marketing.

The cost of America's obesity epidemic extends far beyond emotional pain and low self-esteem. Obesity is now second only to smoking as a cause of mortality in the United States. The CDC estimates that about 280,000 Americans die every year as a direct result of being overweight. The annual health care costs in the United States stemming from obesity now approach $240 billion; on top of that Americans spend more than $33 billion on various weight-loss schemes and diet products. Obesity has been linked to heart disease, colon cancer, stomach cancer, breast cancer, diabetes, arthritis, high blood pressure, infertility, and strokes. A 1999 study by the American Cancer Society found that overweight people had a much higher rate of premature death. Severely overweight people were four times more likely to die young than people of normal weight. Moderately overweight people were twice as likely to die young. "The message is we're too fat and it's killing us," said one of the study's principal authors. Young people who are obese face not only long-term, but also immediate threats to their health. Severely obese American children, aged six to ten, are now dying from heart attacks caused by their weight.

The obesity epidemic that began in the United States during the late 1970s is now spreading to the rest of the world, with fast food as one of its vectors. Between 1984 and 1993, the number of fast food restaurants in Great Britain roughly doubled — and so did the obesity rate among adults. The British now eat more fast food than any other nationality in Western Europe. They also have the highest obesity rate. Obesity is much less of a problem in Italy and Spain, where spending on fast food is relatively low. The relationship between a nation's fast food consumption and its rate of obesity has not been definitively established through any long-term, epidemiological study. The growing popularity of fast food is just one of many cultural changes that have been brought about by globalization. Nevertheless, it seems wherever America's fast food chains go, waistlines start expanding.

In China, the proportion of overweight teenagers has roughly tripled in the past decade. In Japan, eating hamburgers and french fries has not made people any blonder, though it has made them fatter. Overweight people were once a rarity in Japan. The nation's traditional diet of rice, fish, vegetables, and soy products has been deemed one of the healthiest in the world. And yet the Japanese are rapidly abandoning that diet. Consumption of red meat has been rising in Japan since the American occupation after World War II. The arrival of McDonald's in 1971 accelerated the shift in Japanese eating habits. During the 1980s, the sale of fast food in Japan more than doubled; the rate of obesity among children soon doubled, too. Today about one-third of all Japanese men in their thirties — members of the nation's first generation raised on Happy Meals and "Bi-gu Ma-kus" — are overweight. Heart disease, diabetes, colon cancer, and breast cancer, the principal "diseases of affluence," have been linked to diets low in fiber and high in animal fats. Long common in the United States, these diseases are likely to become widespread in Japan as its fast food generation ages. More than a decade ago a study of middle-aged Japanese men who had settled in the United States found that their switch to a Western diet doubled their risk of heart disease and tripled their risk of stroke. For the men in the study, embracing an American way of life meant increasing the likelihood of a premature death.

Obesity is extremely difficult to cure. During thousands of years marked by food scarcity, human beings developed efficient physiological mechanisms to store energy as fat. Until recently, societies rarely enjoyed an overabundance of cheap food. As a result, our bodies are far more efficient at gaining weight than at losing it. Health officials have concluded that prevention, not treatment, offers the best hope of halting the worldwide obesity epidemic. European consumer groups are pushing for a complete ban on all television advertising directed at children. In 1991 Sweden banned all TV advertising directed at children under the age of twelve. Restrictions on ads during children's programming have been imposed in Greece, Norway, Denmark, Austria and the Netherlands. The eating habits of American kids are widely considered a good example of what other countries must avoid. American children now get about one-quarter of their total vegetable servings in the form of potato chips or french fries. A survey of children's advertising in the European Union (EU) found that 95 percent of the food ads there encouraged kids to eat foods high in sugar, salt, and fat. The company running the most ads aimed at children was McDonalds.

mclibel

"RESIST AMERICA BEGINNING with Cola," said a banner at Beijing University in May of 1999. "Attack McDonald's, Storm KFC." The U.S. Air Force had just bombed the Chinese Embassy in Belgrade, Yugoslavia, and anti-American demonstrations were erupting throughout China. At least a dozen McDonald's and four Kentucky Fried Chicken restaurants were damaged by Chinese protesters. For some reason, no Pizza Huts were harmed. "Maybe they think it's Italian," said a Pizza Hut spokesman in Shanghai.

A generation ago American embassies and oil companies were the most likely targets of overseas demonstrations against "U.S. imperialism." Today fast food restaurants have assumed that symbolic role, with McDonald's a particular favorite. In 1995, a crowd of four hundred Danish anarchists looted a McDonald's in downtown Copenhagen, made a bonfire of its furniture in the street, and burned the restaurant to the ground. In 1996, Indian farmers ransacked a Kentucky Fried Chicken restaurant in Bangalore, convinced that the chain threatened their traditional agricultural practices. In 1997, a McDonald's in the Colombian city of Cali was destroyed by a bomb. In 1998, bombs destroyed a McDonald's in St. Petersburg, Russia, two McDonald's in suburban Athens, a McDonald's in the heart of Rio de Janeiro, and a Planet Hollywood in Cape Town, South Africa. In 1999, Belgian vegetarians set fire to a McDonald's in Antwerp, and a year later, May Day protesters tore the sign off a McDonald's in London's Trafalgar Square, destroyed the restaurant, and handed out free hamburgers to the crowd. Fearing more violence, McDonald's temporarily closed all fifty of its London restaurants.

In France, a French sheep farmer and political activist named Jose Bove led a group that demolished a McDonald's under construction in his hometown of Millau. Bove's defiant attitude, brief imprisonment, and impassioned speeches against "lousy food" have made him a hero in France, praised by socialists and conservatives, invited to meetings with the president and the prime minister. He has written a French bestseller entitled *The World Is Not for Sale — And Nor Am I!* In a society where food is a source of tremendous national pride, the McDonald's Corporation has become an easy target, for reasons that are not entirely symbolic. McDonald's is now the largest purchaser of agricultural commodities in France. Bove's message — that Frenchmen should not become "servile slaves at the service of agribusiness" — has struck a chord. During July of 2000 an estimated thirty thousand demonstrators gathered in Millau when Jose Bove went on trial, some carrying signs that said "Non à McMerde."

The overseas critics of fast food are far more diverse than America's old Soviet bloc adversaries. Farmers, leftists, anarchists, nationalists, environmentalists, consumer advocates, educators, health officials, labor unions, and defenders of animal rights have found common ground in a campaign against the perceived Americanization of the world. Fast food has become a target because it is so ubiquitous and because it threatens a fundamental aspect of national identity: how, where, and what people choose to eat.

The longest-running and most systematic assault on fast food overseas has been waged by a pair of British activists affiliated with London Greenpeace. The loosely organized group was formed in 1971 to oppose French nuclear weapon tests in the South Seas. It later staged demonstrations in support of animal rights and British trade unions. It protested against nuclear power and the Falklands War. The group's membership was a small, eclectic mix of pacifists, anarchists, vegetarians, and libertarians brought together by a commitment to nonviolent political action. They ran the organization without any formal leadership, even refusing to join the International Greenpeace movement.

A typical meeting of London Greenpeace attracted anywhere from three people to three dozen. In 1986 the group decided to target McDonald's, later explaining that the company "epitomises everything we despise: a junk culture, the deadly banality of capitalism." Members of London Greenpeace began to distribute a six-page leaflet called "What's Wrong with McDonald's? Everything they don't want you to know." It accused the fast food chain of promoting Third World poverty, selling unhealthy food, exploiting workers and children, torturing animals, and destroying the Amazon rain forest, among other things. Some of the text was factual and straightforward; some of it was pure agitprop. Along the top of the leaflet ran a series of golden arches punctuated by slogans like "McDollars, McGreedy, McCancer, McMurder, McProfits, McGarbage." London Greenpeace distributed the leaflets for four years without attracting much attention. And then in September of 1990 McDonald's sued five members of the group for libel, claiming that every statement in the leaflet was false.

The libel laws in Great Britain are far more unfavorable to a defendant than those in the United States. Under American law, an accuser must prove that the allegations at the heart of a libel case are not only false and defamatory, but also have been recklessly, negligently, or deliberately spread. Under British law, the burden of proof is on the defendant. Allegations that may harm someone's reputation are presumed to be false. Moreover, the defendant in a British court has to use primary sources, such as firsthand witnesses and official documents, to prove the accuracy of a published statement. Secondary sources, including peer-reviewed articles in scientific journals, are deemed inadmissible as evidence. And the defendant's intentions are irrelevant — a British libel case can be lost because of a truly innocent mistake.

The McDonald's Corporation had for years taken advantage of British libel laws to silence its critics. During the 1980s alone, McDonald's threatened to sue at last fifty British publications and organizations, including Channel 4, the Sunday *Times*, the *Guardian*, student publications, a vegetarian society, and a Scottish youth theater group. The tactic worked, prompting retractions and apologies. The cost of losing a libel case, in both legal fees and damages, could be huge.

The London Greenpeace activists being sued by McDonald's had not written the leaflet in question; they had merely handed it to people. Nevertheless, their behavior could be ruled libelous. Fearing the potential monetary costs, three of the activists reluctantly appeared in court and apologized to McDonald's. The other two decided to fight.

Helen Steel was a twenty-five-year-old gardener, minibus driver, and bartender who'd been drawn to London Greenpeace by her devotion to vegetarianism and animal rights. Dave Morris was a thirty-six-year-old single father, a former postal worker interested in labor issues and the power of multinational corporations. The two friends seemed to stand little chance in court against the world's largest fast food chain. Steel had left school at seventeen, Morris at eighteen; and neither could afford a lawyer. McDonald's, on the other hand, could afford armies of attorneys and had annual revenues at the time of about $18 billion. Morris and Steel were denied legal aid and forced to defend themselves in front of a judge, instead of a jury. But with some help from the secretary of the Haldane Society of Socialist Lawyers, the pair turned the "McLibel case" into the longest trial in British history and a public relations disaster for McDonald's.

The McDonald's Corporation had never expected the case to reach the courtroom. The burden on the defendants was enormous: Morris and Steel had to assemble witnesses and official documents to support the broad assertions in the leaflet. The pair proved to be indefatigable researchers, aided by the McLibel Support Campaign, an international network of activists. By the end of the trial, the court record included 40,000 pages of documents and witness statements, as well as 18,000 pages of transcripts.

McDonald's had made a huge tactical error by asserting that everything in the leaflet was libelous — not only the more extreme claims ("McDonald's and Burger King are . . . using lethal poisons to destroy vast areas of Central American rainforest"), but also the more innocuous ones ("a diet high in fat, sugar, animal products, and salt . . . is linked with cancers of the breast and bowel, and heart disease"). The blunder allowed Steel and Morris to turn the tables, putting McDonald's on trial and forcing a public examination of the chain's labor, marketing, environmental, nutrition, food safety, and animal welfare policies. Some of the chain's top executives were forced to appear on the stand and endure days of cross-examination by the pair of self-taught attorneys. The British media seized upon the David-and-Goliath aspects of the story and made the trial front-page news.

After years of legal wrangling, the McLibel trial formally began in March of 1994. It ended more than three years later, when Justice Rodger Bell submitted an 800-page Judgement. Morris and Steel were found to have libeled McDonald's. The judge ruled that the two had failed to prove most of their allegations — but had indeed proved some. According to Justice Bell's decision, McDonald's did "exploit" children through its advertising, endanger the health of customers who eat there several times a week, pay its restaurant workers unreasonably low wages, and bear responsibility for the cruelty inflicted upon animals by many of its suppliers. Morris and Steel were fined £60,000. The two promptly announced they would appeal the decision. "McDonald's don't deserve a penny," Helen Steel said, "and in any event we haven't got any money."

Evidence submitted during the McLibel trial disclosed much about the inner workings of the McDonald's Corporation. Many of its labor, food safety, and advertising practices had already been publicly criticized in the United States for years. Testimony in the London courtroom, however, provided new revelations about the company's attitude toward civil liberties and freedom of speech. Morris and Steel were stunned to discover that McDonald's had infiltrated London Greenpeace with informers, who regularly attended the group's meetings and spied on its members.

The spying had begun in 1989 and did not end until 1991, nearly a year after the libel suit had been filed. McDonald's had used subterfuge to find out who'd distributed the leaflets, and also learnt from its spies how Morris and Steel reacted to the company's legal action. The company had employed at least seven different undercover agents. During some London Greenpeace meetings, about half the people in attendance were corporate spies. One spy broke into the London Greenpeace office, took photographs, and stole documents. Another had a six-month affair with a member of London Greenpeace while informing on his activities. McDonald's spies inadvertently spied on each other, unaware that the company was using at least two different detective agencies. They participated in demonstrations against McDonald's and gave out anti-McDonald's leaflets.

During the trial, Sidney Nicholson — the McDonald's vice president who'd supervised the undercover operation, a former police officer in South Africa and former superintendent in London's Metropolitan Police — admitted in court that McDonald's had used its law enforcement connections to obtain information on Steel and Morris from Scotland Yard. Indeed, it was officers belonging to Special Branch, an elite British unit that tracks "subversives" and organized crime figures, who informed McDonald's of the pair's identity. One of the company's undercover agents later had a change of heart and testified on behalf of the McLibel defendants. "At no time did I believe they were dangerous people," said Fran Tiller, following her conversion to vegetarianism. "I think they genuinely believed in the issues they were supporting."

For Dave Morris, perhaps the most disturbing moment of the trial was hearing how McDonald's had obtained his home address. One of its spies admitted in court that a gift of baby clothes had been a ruse to find out where Morris lived. Morris had unwittingly accepted the gift, believing it to be an act of friendship — and was disgusted to learn that his infant son had for months worn outfits supplied by McDonald's as part of its surveillance.

I visited Dave Morris one night in February of 1999, as he prepared for an appearance the next day before the Court of Appeal. Morris lives in a small flat above a carpet shop in North London. The apartment lacks central heating, the ceilings are sagging, and the place is crammed with books, boxes, files, transcripts, leaflets, and posters announcing various demonstrations. The place feels like everything McDonald's is not — lively, unruly, deeply idiosyncratic, and organized according to a highly complex scheme that only one human being could possibly understand. Morris spent about an hour with me, as his son finished homework upstairs. He spoke intensely about McDonald's, but stressed that its arrogant behavior was just one manifestation of a much larger problem now confronting the world: the rise of powerful multinationals that shift capital across borders with few qualms, that feel no allegiance to any nation, no loyalty to any group of farmers, workers, or consumers.

The British journalist John Vidal, in his book on the McLibel trial, noted some of the similarities between Dave Morris and Ray Kroc. As Morris offered an impassioned critique of globalization, the comparison made sense — both men true believers, charismatic, driven by ideas outside the mainstream, albeit championing opposite viewpoints. During the McLibel trial, Paul Preston, the president of McDonald's UK, had said, "Fitting into a finely working machine, that's what McDonald's is about." And here was Morris, in the living room of his North London flat, warmed by a gas heater in the fireplace, surrounded by stacks of papers and files, caring nothing for money, determined somehow to smash that machine.

On March 31, 1999, the three Court of Appeal justices overruled parts of the original McLibel verdict, supporting the leaflet's assertions that eating too much McDonald's food can cause heart disease and ruling that it was 'fair comment' to say that workers are treated badly. The court reduced the damages owed by Steel and Morris to about £40,000. The McDonald's Corporation had previously announced that it had no intention of collecting the money and would no longer try to stop London Greenpeace from distributing the leaflet (which by then had been translated into twenty-seven languages). McDonald's was tired of the bad publicity and wanted this case to go away. But Morris and Steel were not yet through with McDonald's. They appealed the Court of Appeal decision to the British House of Lords and sued the police for providing information about them to McDonalds. Scotland Yard settled the case out of court, apologizing to the pair and paying them £10,000 in damages. When the House of Lords refused to hear their case, Morris and Steel filed an appeal with the European Court of Human Rights, challenging the validity not only of the verdict, but also of the British libel laws. As of this writing, the McLibel case is entering its eleventh year. After intimidating British critics for years, the McDonald's Corporation picked on the wrong two people.

back at the ranch

WHEN THE FIRST McDonald's opened in East Germany, in December of 1990, the company was unsure how American food would be received there. On opening day the McDonald's in Plauen served potato dumplings, a Vogtland favorite, along with hamburgers and fries. Today hundreds of McDonald's restaurants dot the landscape of eastern Germany. In town after town, statues of Lenin have come down and statues of Ronald McDonald have gone up. One of the largest is in Bitterfeld, where a three-story-high, illuminated Ronald can be seen from the autobahn for miles.

During my first visit to Plauen, in October of 1998, McDonald's was the only business open in the central market square. It was Reunification Day, a national holiday, and everything else was closed, the small shops selling used clothing and furniture, the pseudo-Irish pub on one corner, the pizzeria on another. McDonald's was packed, overflowing not just with children and their parents, but with teenagers, seniors, young couples, a cross-section of the town. The restaurant was brightly lit and spotlessly clean. Cheerful middle-aged women took orders behind the counter, worked in the kitchen, delivered food to tables, scrubbed the windows. Most of them had worked at this McDonald's for years. Some had been there since the day it opened. Across the street stood an abandoned building once occupied by a branch of the East German army; a few blocks away the houses were dilapidated and covered in graffiti, looking as though the Wall had never fallen. That day McDonald's was the nicest, cleanest, brightest place in all of Plauen. Children played with the Hot Wheels and Barbies that came with their Happy Meals, and smiling workers poured free refills of coffee. Outside the window, three bright red flags bearing the golden arches fluttered in the wind.

Life after Communism has not been easy in Plauen. At first there was an outpouring of great optimism and excitement. As in other East German towns, people quickly used their new liberty to travel overseas for the first time. They borrowed money to buy new cars. According to Thomas Küttler, the hero of Plauen's 1989 uprising, thoughts about Friedrich von Schiller and the freedom of their forefathers soon gave way to a hunger for Western consumer goods. Küttler is disappointed by how fast the idealism of 1989 vanished, but feels little nostalgia for the old East Germany. Under Communist rule in Plauen, a person could be arrested for watching television broadcasts from the West or for listening to American rock 'n' roll. Today in Plauen you can get dozens of channels on cable and even more via satellite. MTV is popular there, and most of the songs on the radio are in English. Becoming part of the larger world, however, has had its costs. Plauen's economy has suffered as one after another, old and inefficient manufacturing plants closed, throwing people out of work. Since the fall of the Berlin Wall, Plauen has lost about 10 percent of its population, as people move away in search of a better life. The town seems unable to break free from its past. Every year a few unexploded bombs from World War II are still discovered and defused.

At the moment, Plauen's unemployment rate is about 20 percent — twice the rate in Germany as a whole. You see men in their forties, a lost generation, too young to retire but too old to fit into the new scheme, staggering drunk in the middle of the day. The factory workers who bravely defied and brought down the old regime are the group who've fared worst, the group with the wrong skills and the least hope. Others have done quite well.

Manfred Voigt, the McDonald's franchisee in Plauen, is now a successful businessman who, with his wife, Brigitte, vacations in Florida every year. In an interview with the *Wall Street Journal,* Manfred Voigt attributed his recent success to forces beyond his control. "It was dumb luck," Voigt explained; "fate." He and his wife had no money and could not understand why McDonald's had chosen them to own its first restaurant in East Germany, why the company had trained and financed them. One explanation, never really explored in the *Wall Street Journal* profile, might be that the Voigts were one of the most powerful couples in Plauen under the old regime. They headed the local branch of Konsum, the state-controlled foodservice monopoly. Today the Voigts are one of Plauen's wealthiest couples; they own two other McDonald's in nearby towns. Throughout the former Eastern bloc, members of the old Communist elite have had the easiest time adjusting to Western consumerism. They had the right connections and many of the right skills. They now own some of the most lucrative franchises.

The high unemployment rate in Plauen has created social and political instability. What seems lacking is a stable middle ground. Roughly a third of the young people in eastern Germany now express support for various nationalist and neo-Nazi groups. Right-wing extremists have declared large parts of the east to be "foreigner-free" zones, where immigrants are not welcome. The roads leading into Plauen are decorated with signs posted by the Deutschland Volks Union, a right-wing party. "Germany for the Germans," the signs say. "Jobs for Germans, Not Foreigners." Neo-Nazi skinheads have thus far not caused much trouble in Plauen, though a black person today needs real courage to walk the city's streets at night. The opposition to American fast food voiced by many environmentalists and left-wing groups does not seem to be shared by German groups on the far right. When I asked an employee at the McDonald's in Plauen if the restaurant had ever been the target of neo-Nazis, she laughed and said there'd never been any threats of that kind. People in the area did not consider McDonald's to be "foreign."

Around the time that Plauen got its McDonald's in 1990, a new nightclub opened in a red brick building on the edge of town. "The Ranch" has an American flag and a Confederate flag hanging out front. Inside there's a long bar, and the walls are decorated with old-fashioned farm implements, saddles, bridles, and wagon wheels. Frieder Stephan, the owner of The Ranch, was inspired by photographs of the American West, but gathered all the items on the walls from nearby farms. The place looks like a bar in Cripple Creek, circa 1895. Before the fall of the Berlin Wall, Frieder Stephan was a disc jockey on an East German tourist ferry. He secretly listened to Creedance Clearwater, the Stones, and the Lovin' Spoonful. Now forty-nine years old, he is the leading impresario in Plauen's thriving country-western scene, booking local bands (like the Midnight Ramblers and C.C. Raider) at his club. The city's country-western fans call themselves "Vogtland Cowboys," put on their western boots and ten-gallon hats at night, and hit the town, drinking at The Ranch or joining the Square Dance Club at a bar called the White Magpie. The Square Dance Club is sponsored by Thommy's Western Store on Friedrich Engels Avenue. Plauen now has a number of small western-wear shops like Thommy's that sell imported cowboy boots, cowboy posters, fancy belt buckles, work shirts with snaps, and Wrangler jeans. While teenagers in Colorado Springs today could not care less about cowboys, kids in Plauen are sporting bolo ties and cowboy hats.

Every Wednesday night, a few hundred people gather at The Ranch for line dancing. Members of Plauen's American Car Club pull up in their big Ford and Chevy trucks. Others come from miles away, dressed in their western best, ready to dance. Most of them are working class, and many are unemployed. Their ages range from seven years old to seventy. If somebody doesn't know how to line-dance, a young woman named Petra gives lessons. People wear their souvenir T-shirts from Utah. They smoke Marlboros and drink beer. They listen to Willie Nelson, Garth Brooks, Johnny Cash — and they dance, kicking up their boots, twirling their partners, waving their cowboy hats in the air. And for a few hours the spirit of the American West fills this funky bar deep in the heart of Saxony, in a town that has seen too much history, and the old dream lives on, the dream of freedom without limits, self-reliance, and a wide-open frontier.

epilogue: have it your way

WORLDS AWAY from The Ranch, Dale Lasater stands in a corral full of huge bulls, feeding them treats from his hand. Behind him on this warm spring day, the Rockies are still white with snow. Lasater is in his early fifties, with a handlebar mustache and wire-rimmed glasses. He wears worn-out jeans and boots, and a well-ironed, button-down shirt, looking part-cowboy, part–Ivy Leaguer. The bulls that crowd around him seem almost sweet, acting more like a bunch of Ferdinands than like fierce symbols of machismo. They were bred to be gentle, never dehorned, and never roped. The Lasater Ranch occupies about 30,000 acres of shortgrass prairie near the town of Matheson, Colorado. It is a profitable, working ranch that for half a century has not used pesticides, herbicides, poisons, or commercial fertilizers on the land, has not killed local predators such as coyotes, has not administered growth hormones, anabolic steroids, or antibiotics to the cattle. The Lasaters are by no means typical, but have worked hard to change how American beef is produced. Their philosophy of cattle ranching is based upon a simple tenet: "Nature is smart as hell."

Dale Lasater's iconoclasm seems bred in the bone. One of his grandfathers headed a Texas cattleman's association during the early 1900s and led the fight against the Beef Trust, testifying before Congress and calling for strict enforcement of the antitrust laws. In retaliation, the Beef Trust refused for years to buy Lasater cattle. Dale Lasater's father, Tom, dropped out of Princeton after the Wall Street crash of 1929 to become a full-time rancher. Hard times forced him to seek ways of raising cattle inexpensively. He decided to let nature do most of the work. He bred cattle to be gentle, fertile, and strong, not caring in the least how they looked. He combined Herefords,

Shorthorns, and Brahmans to make a whole new breed, only the second new breed of cattle registered in the United States. And he gave the breed an appropriately American name: the Beefmaster. In 1948, Tom Lasater moved his family from Texas to eastern Colorado. Despite the anger and disbelief of his neighbors, he refused to kill predators or to allow hunting on his land, permitting animals that other ranchers exterminated — rattlesnakes, coyotes, badgers, ground squirrels, gophers, and prairie dogs — to flourish. He thought cattle benefited more from the challenges of a natural ecosystem than from any human efforts to control the environment.

Tom Lasater is ninety years old now, and his memory is failing, but he still has the aura of a strong patriarch. As Dale bounces an old cream-colored Suburban Custom Deluxe along one of the ranch's dirt roads, his father sits in the back seat, wearing a cowboy hat, a bolo tie, and thick black glasses, silently staring at the Beefmasters scattered across the prairie. He scrutinizes them, and every so often asks Dale about a particular animal. The cattle roam a landscape that appears vast and unspoiled. The Lasater Ranch is a wildlife sanctuary. The native grasses are thriving, tall cottonwoods grow along the stream banks, and herds of antelope graze alongside the cattle. Dale parks the truck, and I walk a short distance to a rocky outcropping. The Suburban now seems like a small, insignificant speck compared to what surrounds it. Pikes Peak and Cheyenne Mountain rise to the west, and in every other direction the prairie extends to the horizon, the shortgrass moving in waves, blown by a steady wind.

Beyond the Lasater property line, the land is not faring so well. Smaller farms and ranches in the area have been disappearing for years. A population loss that began in the 1950s has recently slowed, but too late. Many small towns have become virtual ghost towns. In the little commercial district of Matheson, along a dirt road named Broadway, the feed store, the general store, and a repair shop have all been abandoned. The whitewashed buildings have quaint, fading signs, and stand empty. The large, brick elementary school that Dale Lasater attended — built at the turn of the century, its architecture full of American optimism — is now used by a local rancher to store grain.

Before taking over the family ranch, Dale Lasater spent a year in Argentina as a Fulbright scholar, ran a feedlot company in Kansas, and managed cattle ranches in Texas, Florida, and New Mexico. He has come to believe that our industrialized system of cattle production cannot be sustained. Rising grain prices may someday hit ranchers and feedlots hard. More importantly, Lasater finds it hard to justify feeding millions of tons of precious grain to American cattle while elsewhere in the world millions of people starve. He respects the decision to become a vegetarian, but has little tolerance for the air of moral superiority that often accompanies it. Growing up on the prairie gave him a view of Mother Nature that is somewhat different from the Disney version. Cattle that are not eaten by people, that are simply allowed to grow old and weak, still get eaten — by coyotes and turkey buzzards, and it's not a pretty sight.

Dale Lasater recently set up a company to sell organic, free-range, grass-fed beef. None of the cattle used in Lasater Grasslands Beef spent any time at a feedlot. The meat is much lower in fat than grain-fed beef, and has a much stronger, more distinctive flavor. Lasater says that most Americans have forgotten what real beef tastes like. Argentine beef is considered a gourmet item, served at expensive restaurants, and almost all of the cattle in Argentina are grass-fed. Recent findings that grass-fed cattle may be less likely to spread *E. coli* 0157:H7 have strengthened Lasater's determination to follow a different path. Along with a number of other innovative ranchers in Colorado, he is trying to raise cattle in a way that does not harm consumers or the land. Hank was a dear friend of his, in many ways a kindred spirit. Lasater doesn't think that his little company will revolutionize the American beef industry; but it's a start.

Sixty miles away, on South Nevada Avenue in Colorado Springs, Rich Conway helps run a family business that's also bucking the tide. Conway's Red Top Restaurant occupies a modest brick building on a street full of old western motels, the kind with animated neon Indian chiefs on their signs, the kind where the U in the 4-U Motel is a golden horseshoe. Rich Conway's been through a lot. He's had a motorcycle accident and a bad car accident, later slipped on some ice and broke his back. Now in his early fifties, Conway walks slowly with a cane, but has a handsome, weathered face, a Zen-like calm and a tough, independent streak that keeps him going, against the odds. He's a survivor. When I asked why the Conway family provides health insurance to all the full-time workers at the restaurant, he smiled politely, as though the answer was pretty obvious, and said, "We want to have healthy employees."

Rich Conway's parents started working at the Red Top not long after it opened in 1944 and bought the restaurant in 1961. He grew up working there, along with his nine brothers and sisters. Conway's Red Top — with a little spinning top on its yellow sign — became a local favorite, thanks to its large, oval hamburgers, homemade fries, and friendly atmosphere. The restaurant continued to thrive in the 1970s, despite an invasion by national fast food chains that landed up and down South Nevada. But Conway's almost closed in the early 1980s, after the death of Rich's father. The restaurant's local suppliers helped keep it afloat until new financing could be arranged, a story whose details bring to mind *It's a Wonderful Life*. Conway's Red Top now has four locations in Colorado Springs. Rich Conway was president of the family business until 1999; his younger brother Jim now has that job. Their brother Dan is the finance director, their sister Mary Kaye is the marketing director; another brother, Mike, is the operations manager; another sister, Patty Jo, is an assistant manager — and many of the thirty-seven Conways in the next generation work at various Red Top restaurants. The family has an intense, personal commitment to their work, and it shows. According to food critics Jane and Michael Stern, Conway's Red Top sells some of the best hamburgers in the United States.

At the Conway's on South Nevada, hamburger patties are still formed every day by hand, using fresh, not frozen, ground beef. The meat is obtained from GNC Packing, a small, independent processor in Colorado Springs. The buns come from a bakery in Pueblo. Two hundred pounds of potatoes are peeled every morning in the kitchen and then sliced with an old crank-operated contraption. The burgers and fries are made to order by cooks who earn $10 an hour. They wear baseball caps that say "Conway's Red Top: One's a Meal." The workers are not told what to do by fancy computer software, there's take-out but no drive-through, and the food is only slightly more expensive than what's served in the half-empty Wendy's across the street. One day I met a customer at Conway's who has regularly been having lunch there for fifty years.

The Conway family is now debating how to expand the business without compromising the values responsible for its success. Opening new restaurants could provide financial opportunities for the dozens of Conway offspring, but could also involve a good deal of risk. The timing may be right, however, for a few more Red Tops to open. As the rest of Colorado grows more bland and homogenous, Colorado Springs seems to be getting more independent and open-minded. The quirkiness of the downtown may indeed overcome the uniformity of the outlying sprawl.

In the 1999 Colorado Springs mayoral race, Mary Lou Makepeace — a single mother with a fine surname for consensus-building — was elected to a second term, soundly defeating a right-wing candidate backed by Focus on the Family. Mayor Makepeace had helped persuade the voters of Colorado Springs, perhaps the nation's most Republican city, to vote for a tax increase. The additional revenue was used to protect open land from development. She has also spearheaded new investment in public parks. And she has helped launch the redevelopment of fifty-eight acres of land near the downtown business district, an area that was once a thriving neighborhood but has been largely abandoned for years. The project embraces the goals of the "new urbanism," a movement opposed to mindless sprawl, combining residential buildings with commercial and retail space in a way that encourages walking and discourages driving. The aim of the Lowell Neighborhood is not to get rid of cars, says architect Morey Bean, but to put them in their proper place: preferably out of sight in underground parking lots.

It may be tempting to dismiss Conway's Red Top as a holdover from an earlier era, a business whose low-tech methods are quaint but obsolete. And yet one of America's most profitable fast food chains operates much like Conway's. In 1948, the year that the McDonald brothers introduced the Speedee Service System, Harry and Esther Snyder opened their first In-N-Out Burger restaurant on the road between Los Angeles and Palm Springs. It was the nation's first drive-through hamburger stand. Today there are about 150 In-N-Outs in California and Nevada, generating more than $150 million in annual revenues. Harry Snyder died in 1976 — but at the age of eighty, Esther still serves as president of the family-owned company. The Snyders have declined countless offers to sell the chain, refuse to franchise it, and have succeeded by rejecting just about everything the rest of the fast food industry has done.

In-N-Out has followed its own path: there are verses from the Bible on the bottom of its soda cups. More importantly, the chain pays the highest wages in the fast food industry. The starting wage of a part-time worker at In-N-Out is $8 an hour. Full-time workers get a benefits package that includes medical, dental, vision, and life insurance. The typical salary of an In-N-Out restaurant manager is more than

$80,000 a year. The managers have, on average, been with the chain for more than thirteen years. The high wages at In-N-Out have not led to higher prices or lower-quality food. The most expensive item on the menu costs $2.45. There are no microwaves, heat lamps, or freezers in the kitchens at In-N-Out restaurants. The ground beef is fresh, potatoes are peeled every day to make the fries, and the milk shakes are made from ice cream, not syrup.

In March of 2000, the annual *Restaurants and Institutions* Choice in Chains survey found that among the nation's fast food hamburger chains, In-N-Out ranked first in food quality, value, service, atmosphere, and cleanliness. In-N-Out has ranked highest in food quality every year that the chain has been included in the survey. According to the consumers polled by *Restaurants and Institutions* in 2000, the lowest-quality food of any major hamburger chain was served at McDonald's.

scientific socialists

THERE IS NOTHING INEVITABLE about the fast food nation that surrounds us — about its marketing strategies, labor policies, and agricultural techniques, about its relentless drive for conformity and cheapness. The triumph of McDonald's and its imitators was by no means preordained. During the past two decades, rhetoric about the "free market" has cloaked changes in the nation's economy that bear little relation to real competition or freedom of choice. From the airline industry to the publishing business, from the railroads to telecommunications, American corporations have worked hard to avoid the rigors of the market by eliminating and absorbing their rivals. The strongest engines of American economic growth in the 1990s — the computer, software, aerospace, and satellite industries — have been heavily subsidized by the Pentagon for decades. Indeed, the U.S. defense budget has long served as a form of industrial policy, a quasi-socialist system of planning that frequently yields unplanned results. The Internet at the heart of today's "New Economy" began as the ARPANET, a military communications network created in the late 1970s. For better or worse, legislation passed by Congress has played a far more important role in shaping the economic history of the postwar era than any free market forces.

The market is a tool, and a useful one. But the worship of this tool is a hollow faith. Far more important than any tool is what you make with it. Many of America's greatest accomplishments stand in complete defiance of the free market: the prohibition of child labor, the establishment of a minimum wage, the creation of wilderness areas and national parks, the construction of dams, bridges, roads, churches, schools, and universities. If all that mattered were the unfettered right to buy and sell, tainted food could not be kept off supermarket shelves, toxic waste could be dumped next door to elementary schools, and every American family could import an indentured servant (or two), paying them with meals instead of money.

Much like the workings of the market, technology is just one means toward an end, not something to be celebrated for its own sake. The Titan II missiles built at the Lockheed Martin plant northwest of Colorado Springs were originally designed to carry nuclear warheads. Today they carry weather satellites into orbit. The missiles are equally efficient at both tasks. There is nothing inexorable about the use of such technology. Its value cannot be judged without considering its purpose and likely effects. The launch of a Titan II can be beautiful, or horrific, depending upon the aim of the missile and what it carries. No society in human history worshipped science more devoutly or more blindly than the Soviet Union, where "scientific socialism" was considered the highest truth. And no society has ever suffered so much environmental devastation on such a massive scale.

The history of the twentieth century was dominated by the struggle against totalitarian systems of state power. The twenty-first will no doubt be marked by a struggle to curtail excessive corporate power. The great challenge now facing countries throughout the world is how to find a proper balance between the efficiency and the amorality of the market. Over the past twenty years the United States has swung too far in one direction, weakening the regulations that safeguard workers, consumers, and the environment. An economic system promising freedom has too often become a means of denying it, as the narrow dictates of the market gain precedence over more important democratic values.

Today's fast food industry is the culmination of those larger social and economic trends. The low price of a fast food hamburger does not reflect its real cost — and should. The profits of the fast food chains have been made possible by losses imposed on the rest of society. The annual cost of obesity alone is now twice as large as the fast food industry's total revenues. The environmental movement has forced companies to curtail their pollution, and a similar campaign must induce the fast food chains to assume responsibility for their business practices and minimize their harmful effects.

what to do

IN 1995, THE American Academy of Pediatrics declared that "advertising directed at children is inherently deceptive and exploits children under eight years of age." The academy did not recommend a ban on such advertising because it seemed impractical and would infringe upon advertisers' freedom of speech. Today the health risks faced by the nation's children far outweigh the needs of its mass marketers. Congress should immediately ban all advertisements aimed at children that promote foods high in fat and sugar. Thirty years ago Congress banned cigarette ads from radio and television as a public health measure — and those ads were directed at adults. Smoking has declined ever since. A ban on advertising unhealthy foods to children would discourage eating habits that are not only hard to break, but potentially life-threatening. Moreover, such a ban would encourage the fast food chains to alter the recipes for their children's meals. Greatly reducing the fat content of Happy Meals, for example, could have an immediate effect on the diet of the nation's kids. Every month more than 90 percent of the children in the United States eat at McDonald's.

Congress cannot require fast food chains to provide job training to their workers. But it can eliminate the tax breaks that reward chains for churning through their workers and keeping job skills to a minimum. Job training schemes subsidized by the federal government should insist that companies employ workers for at least a year — and actually provide some training. Strict enforcement of minimum wage, overtime, and child labor laws would improve the lives of fast food workers, as would OSHA regulations on workplace violence at restaurants. Passing new laws to facilitate union organizing might not lead to picket lines in front of every McDonald's, but it would encourage the fast food industry to treat workers better and listen to their complaints. Teenagers should be rewarded, not harmed, by the decision to work after school. And if the nation is genuinely interested in their future, it will adequately fund their education, instead of inviting advertisers into the schools.

As for the food now served at school cafeterias, it should be safer to eat than what is sold at fast food restaurants, not less safe. The USDA should insist upon the highest possible food safety standards from every company that supplies ground beef to the school lunch program — or it should stop purchasing ground beef. American taxpayers shouldn't be paying for food that might endanger their children. The USDA's recent decision to perform *E. coli* 0157:H7 tests on the ground beef it buys for schools, though commendable, was made more than seven years after the Jack in the Box outbreak. It was made after countless children were needlessly sickened. The meatpacking industry's ability to sell questionable meat, for years, to the federal agency responsible for ensuring safe food is just one more symptom of a much broader problem — of a government food safety system that is poorly structured, underfunded, and unable to detect most outbreaks of food poisoning.

Federal officials and meatpacking executives often claim that the United States has the safest food supply in the world. There is little evidence to support that contention. Other countries have enacted much tougher food safety laws and implemented much more thorough food inspection systems. Sweden began a program to eliminate *Salmonella* from its livestock more than forty years ago. Today about 0.1 percent of Swedish cattle harbor *Salmonella,* a proportion vastly lower than the rate in the United States. The Netherlands began to test ground beef for *E. coli* 0157:H7 in 1989. The Dutch food safety program is administered not by agriculture officials, but by public health officials. Strict regulations cover every aspect of meat production, prohibiting the inclusion of animal wastes in feed, banning the use of hormones as growth stimulants, limiting the stress that cattle endure during transport (and thereby reducing the amount of bacteria shed in their stool), and confiscating tainted meat. At Dutch slaughterhouses the speed of the production line is determined by food safety considerations.

At the moment, a dozen federal agencies in the United States are responsible for food safety, and twenty-eight congressional committees oversee them. The welter of competing bureaucracies leads to confusion, gaps in enforcement, and numerous food safety absurdities. The USDA has the power to conduct microbial tests on cattle that have already been slaughtered, but cannot test live cattle in order to keep infected animals out of slaughterhouses. The manufacture of frozen cheese pizzas is regulated by the FDA, but if a pizza has pepperoni on it, the USDA has food safety jurisdiction. Eggs are regulated by the FDA, but chickens are regulated by the USDA, and a lack of cooperation between the two agencies has hampered efforts to reduce the levels of *Salmonella* in American eggs. *Salmonella* has been almost entirely eliminated from Swedish and Dutch eggs. Every year in the United States, however, more than half a million people become ill after eating eggs contaminated with *Salmonella,* and more than 300 people die.

Congress should create a single food safety agency that has sufficient authority to protect the public health. The two main tasks currently assigned to the USDA — to promote American agriculture and to police it — are incompatible. The nation's other leading food safety agency, the FDA, spends much of its budget regulating prescription drugs. An American food processor can expect a visit from an FDA inspector, on average, once every ten years. The new food safety agency should be given the power to track commodities throughout the production cycle, from their origin on ranches and farms to their sale at restaurants and supermarkets. At the moment, the nation's roughly 200,000 fast food restaurants are not subject to any oversight by federal health authorities. The war on foodborne pathogens deserves the sort of national attention and resources that has been devoted to the war on drugs. Far more Americans are severely harmed every year by food poisoning than by illegal drug use. And the harms caused by food poisoning are usually inadvertent and unanticipated. People who smoke crack know the potential dangers; most people who eat hamburgers don't. Eating in the United States should no longer be a form of high-risk behavior.

The steps taken to improve sanitary conditions at the nation's slaughterhouses can have the added benefit of lowering the injury rate among meatpacking workers. The line speeds at Dutch slaughterhouses average less than one hundred cattle an hour; the American average is more than three times as high. IBP workers that I met in Lexington, Nebraska, told me that they always liked days when their plant was processing beef for shipment to the European Union, which imposes tough standards on imported meat. They said IBP slowed down the line so that work could be performed more carefully. The IBP workers liked EU days because the pace was less frantic and there were fewer injuries.

The working conditions and food safety standards in the nation's

meatpacking plants should not improve on days when the beef is being processed for export. American workers and consumers deserve at
least the same consideration as overseas customers. Toughening the
food safety laws could also reduce the number of slaughterhouse
workers who get hurt. The greatest gains in worker safety, however,
will come when state and federal authorities look at the meatpacking
industry's injury rate from a new perspective. Almost any workplace
injury, viewed in isolation, can be described as an "accident." Workers
are routinely made to feel responsible for their own injuries, and many
do indeed make mistakes. But when at least one-third of meatpacking
workers are injured every year, when the causes of those injuries are
well known, when the means to prevent those injuries are readily
available and yet not applied, there is nothing accidental about the lacerations, amputations, cumulative traumas, and deaths in the meatpacking industry. These injuries do not stem from individual mistakes. They are systematic, and they are caused by greed.

OSHA fines imposed on meatpacking companies have done little to
change the safety practices of the industry. At the moment, the maximum OSHA fine for a death caused by willful employer negligence is
$70,000. That amount does not strike fear in the hearts of agribusiness
executives, whose firms annually earn tens of billions of dollars. Much
tougher sanctions should be imposed on behalf of the thousands of
meatpacking workers who are needlessly injured each year. These injuries are by no means impossible to foresee or prevent. The new penalties should include greatly increased OSHA fines, mandatory plant
closures, and criminal charges for negligence. The prosecution of a
few meatpacking executives for the deaths or injuries of their workers
will serve as a wake-up call for the industry. It will convey a blunt message that most Americans would instinctively support: allowing innocent people to be maimed and killed is a crime.

The working conditions in America's slaughterhouses demonstrate
what can happen when employers wield virtually unchecked power
over their workers. When labor unions have too much influence, they
can become corrupt and encourage inefficiencies. But the absence of
unions can permit corporations to behave like continuing criminal
enterprises, to violate labor laws with impunity. If the meatpacking industry is allowed to continue its recruitment of poor, illiterate, often
illegal immigrants, many other industries will soon follow its example.
The rise of a migrant industrial workforce poses a grave threat to de-

mocracy. Workers who are illegal immigrants cannot vote and have little ability to defend their legal rights. Without the countervailing force of labor unions, companies will increasingly seek out and exploit the most vulnerable members of society. As in the meatpacking industry, the progress made by American workers over the course of a century will literally vanish overnight. The rural ghettos of Lexington and Greeley should not represent the future of America's heartland.

Any reform of the current system of industrialized agriculture will have to address the needs of independent ranchers and farmers. They are more than just a sentimental link to America's rural past. They are a unique source of innovation and long-term stewardship of the land. Throughout the Cold War, America's decentralized system of agriculture, relying upon millions of independent producers, was depicted as the most productive system in the world, as proof of capitalism's inherent superiority. The perennial crop failures in the Soviet Union were attributed to a highly centralized system run by distant bureaucrats. Today the handful of agribusiness firms that dominate American food production are championing another centralized system of production, one in which livestock and farmland are viewed purely as commodities, farmers are reduced to the status of employees, and crop decisions are made by executives far away from the fields. Although competition between the large processors has indeed led to lower costs for consumers, price fixing and collusion have devastated independent ranchers and farmers. The antitrust laws outlawing such behavior need to be vigorously enforced. More than a century ago, during the congressional debate on the Sherman Antitrust Act, Henry M. Teller, a Republican senator from Colorado, dismissed the argument that lower consumer prices justified the ruthless exercise of monopoly power. "I do not believe," Teller argued, "that the great object in life is to make everything cheap."

Having centralized American agriculture, the large agribusiness firms are now attempting, like Soviet commissars, to stifle criticism of their policies. Over the past decade, "veggie libel laws" backed by agribusiness have been passed in thirteen states. The laws make it illegal to criticize agricultural commodities in a manner inconsistent with "reasonable" scientific evidence. The whole concept of "veggie libel" is probably unconstitutional; nevertheless, these laws remain on the books. Oprah Winfrey, among others, has been sued for making disparaging remarks about food. In Texas, a man was sued by a sod company for criticizing the quality of its lawns. In Georgia and Alabama, the veggie libel laws have been framed in imitation of British libel law, placing the burden of proof upon the defendant. In Colorado, violating the veggie libel law is now a criminal, not a civil, offense. Criticizing the ground beef produced at the Greeley slaughterhouse could put you behind bars.

how to do it

CONGRESS SHOULD BAN ADVERTISING that preys upon children, it should stop subsidizing dead-end jobs, it should pass tougher food safety laws, it should protect American workers from serious harm, it should fight against dangerous concentrations of economic power. Congress should do all those things, but it isn't likely to do any of them soon. The political influence of the fast food industry and its agribusiness suppliers makes a discussion of what Congress should do largely academic. The fast food industry spends millions of dollars every year on lobbying and billions on mass marketing. The wealth and power of the major chains make them seem impossible to defeat. And yet those companies must obey the demands of one group — consumers — whom they eagerly flatter and pursue. As the market for fast food in the United States becomes increasingly saturated, the chains have to compete fiercely with one another for customers. According to William P. Foley II, the chairman of the company that owns Carl's Jr., the basic imperative of today's fast food industry is "Grow or die." The slightest drop in a chain's market share can cause a large decline in the value of its stock. Even the McDonald's Corporation is now vulnerable to the changing whims of consumers. It is opening fewer McDonald's in the United States and expanding mainly through pizza, chicken, and Mexican food chains that do not bear the company name.

The right pressure applied to the fast food industry in the right way could produce change faster than any act of Congress. The United Students Against Sweatshops and other activist groups have brought widespread attention to the child labor, low wages, and hazardous working conditions in Asian factories that make sneakers for Nike. At first, the company disavowed responsibility for these plants, which it claimed were owned by independent suppliers. Nike later changed course, forcing its Asian suppliers to improve working conditions and pay higher wages. The same tactics employed by the antisweatshop groups can be used to help workers much closer to home — workers in the slaughterhouses and processing plants of the High Plains.

As the nation's largest purchaser of beef, the McDonald's Corporation must be held accountable for the behavior of its suppliers. When McDonald's demanded ground beef free of lethal pathogens, the five companies that manufacture its hamburger patties increased their investment in new equipment and microbial testing. If McDonald's were to demand higher wages and safer working conditions for meatpacking workers, its suppliers would provide them. As the nation's largest purchaser of potatoes, McDonald's could also use its clout on behalf of Idaho farmers. And as the second-largest purchaser of chicken, McDonald's could demand changes in the way poultry growers are compensated by their processors. Small increases in the cost of beef, chicken, and potatoes would raise fast food menu prices by a few pennies, if at all. The fast food chains insist that suppliers follow strict specifications regarding the sugar content, fat content, size, shape, taste, and texture of their products. The chains could just as easily enforce a strict code of conduct governing the treatment of workers, ranchers, and farmers.

McDonald's has already shown a willingness to act quickly when confronted with consumer protests. In the late 1960s, African-American groups attacked the McDonald's Corporation for opening restaurants in minority neighborhoods without giving minority businessmen the opportunity to become franchisees. The company responded by actively recruiting African-American franchisees, a move that defused tensions and helped McDonald's penetrate urban markets. A decade ago, environmentalists criticized the chain for the amount of polystyrene waste it generated. At the time, McDonald's served hamburgers in little plastic boxes that were briefly used and then discarded, making it one of the nation's largest purchasers of polystyrene. In order to counter the criticism, McDonald's formed an unusual alliance with the Environmental Defense Fund in August of 1990 and later announced that the chain's hamburgers would no longer be served in polystyrene boxes. The decision was portrayed in the media as the "greening" of McDonald's and a great victory for the environmental movement. The switch from plastic boxes to paper ones did not, however, represent a sudden and profound change in corporate philosophy. It was a response to bad publicity. McDonald's no longer uses polystyrene boxes in the United States — but it continues to use them overseas, where the environmental harms are no different.

Even the anticipation of consumer anger has prompted McDonald's to demand changes from its suppliers. In the spring of 2000, McDonald's informed Lamb Weston and the J. R. Simplot Company that it would no longer purchase frozen french fries made from genetically engineered potatoes. As a result, the two large processors told their growers to stop planting genetically engineered potatoes — and sales of Monsanto's New Leaf, the nation's only biotech potato, instantly plummeted. McDonald's had stopped serving genetically engineered potatoes a year earlier in Western Europe, where the issue of "Frankenfoods" had generated enormous publicity. In the United States, there was relatively little consumer backlash against genetic engineering. Nevertheless, McDonald's decided to act. Just the fear of controversy swiftly led to a purchasing change with important ramifications for American agriculture.

The challenge of overcoming the fast food giants may seem daunting. But it's insignificant compared to what the ordinary citizens, factory workers, and heavy-metal fans of Plauen once faced. They confronted a system propped up by guns, tanks, barbed wire, the media, the secret police, and legions of informers, a system that controlled every aspect of state power — except popular consent. Without leaders or a manifesto, the residents of a small East German backwater decided to seek the freedom of their forefathers. And within months a wall that had seemed impenetrable fell.

Nobody in the United States is forced to buy fast food. The first step toward meaningful change is by far the easiest: stop buying it. The executives who run the fast food industry are not bad men. They are businessmen. They will sell free-range, organic, grass-fed hamburgers if you demand it. They will sell whatever sells at a profit. The usefulness of the market, its effectiveness as a tool, cuts both ways. The real power of the American consumer has not yet been unleashed. The heads of Burger King, KFC, and McDonald's should feel daunted; they're outnumbered. There are three of them and almost three hundred million of you. A good boycott, a refusal to buy, can speak much louder than words. Sometimes the most irresistible force is the most mundane.

Pull open the glass door, feel the rush of cool air, walk inside, get in line, and look around you, look at the kids working in the kitchen, at the customers in their seats, at the ads for the latest toys, study the backlit color photographs above the counter, think about where the food came from, about how and where it was made, about what is set in motion by every single fast food purchase, the ripple effect near and far, think about it. Then place your order. Or turn and walk out the door. It's not too late. Even in this fast food nation, you can still have it your way.

afterword: the meaning of mad cow

Fast Food Nation was published on April 26, 2001, as an outbreak of foot-and-mouth disease spread across Great Britain, providing ghastly televised images of sheep and cattle burning in funeral pyres. At the same time, European governments were beginning to slaughter hundreds of thousands of cattle potentially infected with mad cow disease (BSE). These two calamities no doubt generated interest in the book and its critique of industrialized agriculture. Long after mad cow and foot-and-mouth receded from the news, however, *Fast Food Nation* continued to attract readers. Its success should not be attributed to my literary style, my storytelling ability, or the novelty of my arguments. Had the same book been published a decade ago, with the same words in the same order, it probably wouldn't have attracted much attention. Not just in the United States, but throughout western Europe and Japan, people are beginning to question the massive, homogenizing systems that produce, distribute, and market their food. The unexpected popularity of *Fast Food Nation*, I believe, has a simple, yet profound, explanation. The times are changing.

Aside from a brief mention on page 202, *Fast Food Nation* did not address mad cow disease or its implications. When I started working on the book a few years ago, the threat of BSE in the United States seemed largely hypothetical. *E. coli* 0157:H7, on the other hand, was sickening tens of thousands of Americans every year. Those illnesses were often linked to the consumption of tainted ground beef, and the meatpacking industry's refusal to deal effectively with the problem of fecal contamination seemed a good example of the weaknesses in America's food safety system. The harms caused by *E. coli* 0157:H7 have not diminished since the publication of *Fast Food Nation*. But mad cow disease now poses an even greater potential threat to anyone who loves hamburgers — and to the companies that sell them. Among other things, this afterword provides a brief account of the risks that BSE may pose, the government efforts to reduce those risks, and the remarkable power that the major fast food chains wield over the meatpacking industry. Mad cow disease is important today, not just as a deadly foodborne illness, but also as a powerful symbol of all that is wrong about the industrialization of farm animals.

On March 29, 1996, the Food and Drug Administration announced that in order to prevent an outbreak of BSE in the United States, the agency would "expedite" new rules prohibiting the use of certain animal proteins in cattle feed. American consumer groups had been demanding tough feed restrictions for years and were planning to sue the FDA if it refused to take action. Nine days earlier, Stephen Dorrell, the British health minister, had surprised Parliament by acknowledging for the first time that mad cow disease might cross the species barrier and infect human beings — a possibility that his government had vehemently denied for years. Great Britain was soon engulfed in a mad cow panic. Ten young people had developed a previously unknown ailment, called new variant Creutzfeldt-Jakob disease (vCJD), that literally destroyed their brains. The disease was tentatively linked to the consumption of tainted beef. Cattle that had eaten feed containing the remains of infected animals now seemed responsible for transmitting the pathogen to human beings. Some of the young people with vCJD, *Science* magazine noted, had been "keen consumers of beef burgers." The McDonald's Corporation promptly announced that it was suspending the purchase of British beef.

The FDA's vow to act quickly soon encountered resistance from the American cattle, meatpacking, meat-processing, feed-manufacturing, and rendering industries. Animal protein was an inexpensive feed additive that promoted growth, and slaughterhouses produced huge volumes of waste that needed to go somewhere. At the time, American cattle were eating about 2 billion pounds of animal protein every year — mainly the remains of other cattle. About three-quarters of all American cattle were being fed animal protein, and dairy cattle were the most likely to eat it in significant amounts. They were also the most likely to wind up as fast food hamburgers one day.

The National Renderers Association, the American Feed Industry Association, the Fats & Protein Research Foundation, and the Animal Protein Producers Industry opposed an FDA ban. Spokesmen for the rendering industry asserted that the link between mad cow disease and human illness was "totally unsupported by any scientific evidence." They said that a ban on feeding dead cattle to cattle would be "unfeasible, impractical, and unenforceable." They thought any feed change should remain voluntary; strict new FDA regulations would bring little real benefit and cause great economic harm. The National Cattlemen's Beef Association opposed a total ban on animal proteins, suggesting instead that feed restrictions should be limited to certain organs known to transmit mad cow: brains, spinal cords, eyeballs. The American Meat Institute called for muscle meat to be exempted from any FDA ban, along with fats, blood, blood products, and intestinal material. The National Pork Producers Council said there was absolutely no harm in allowing cattle to continue eating dead pigs.

Consumer groups and public health officials wanted strict controls on what livestock could be fed. The Consumers Union demanded a total ban on the feeding of "all mammal remains to all food animals." Such a ban was now being imposed in Great Britain; scientists there had demonstrated in 1990 that pigs could be infected, through injection, with a variant of mad cow disease. Moreover, a British ban on the feeding of ruminants (goats, sheep, cattle, elk, deer) to other ruminants had not been entirely successful at halting the spread of BSE. Prohibited material intended for poultry and hogs had, one way or another, still wound up being fed to cattle. The Centers for Disease Control and Prevention advised that, at a bare minimum, the feeding of ruminants to ruminants had to be outlawed in order to prevent an outbreak of BSE.

On August 4, 1997, almost a year and a half after the FDA promised a speedy response to the threat of mad cow, new animal-feed restrictions took effect. "The United States has no BSE," the agency declared, "and the final rule provides the necessary feed controls ... should BSE occur here." The FDA described its new ban as "mammalian-to-ruminant, with exceptions.' Dead sheep, goats, cattle, deer, mink, elk, dogs and cats could no longer be fed to cattle. Rendering plants and feed mills would have to prevent these banned ingredients from mingling with feedstuffs that cattle were still allowed to eat: dead horses, pigs, and poultry; cattle blood, gelatin, and tallow; and plate waste collected from restaurants, regardless of what kind of meat those leftovers contained. Extensive records had to be kept on the disposition of various animal proteins, and feeds that were now prohibited for cattle had to be clearly labeled as such. There were no new restrictions, however, on what could be fed to poultry, hogs, zoo animals, or pets. Indeed, the Grocery Manufacturers of America, the National Food Processors Association, and the Pet Food Institute successfully lobbied against any new labeling requirement for pet foods. These industry groups rightly worried that the FDA's proposed warning label — "Do not feed to ruminants" — might alarm consumers about what their pets were actually being fed.

The dire predictions of the meat, feed, and rendering industries — their claims that new FDA rules would create havoc and cost them hundreds of millions of dollars — proved unfounded. Cattle remains that had previously been fed to cattle were instead fed to pets, hogs, and poultry. Aside from slightly higher transportation costs, the new feed restrictions had a negligible economic effect. One rendering industry supplier told *Meat Marketing & Technology* magazine that the whole rule-making process had proven to be "a remarkable example of cooperation between the industry and the FDA." That cooperation, another rendering executive said, had "protected the beef industry and the rendering industry" without creating "a mood in the country that recycled protein ingredients would be harmful." The trade journal noted that some of the wording of the new FDA rules had been taken "verbatim" from the rendering industry's own recommendations.

In the United States, mad cow gradually receded from the headlines — until January, 2001. For more than a decade, countries in the European Union had assured the public that BSE had not been detected in their cattle. Which was true, because relatively few of their cattle had been tested for the disease. Once widespread testing began in Europe, the actual scale of the mad cow epidemic started to become clear. Switzerland was the first to begin routine testing; the number of BSE cases there soon doubled. Then Denmark began testing and discovered its first infected animal, followed by new cases in Spain and Germany. After widespread testing began in France, the number of BSE cases there increased fivefold. On January 1, 2001, the European Union launched a program that required BSE testing for all cattle older than 30 months. Intended to calm fears of mad cow, the EU program had the opposite effect, as more and more infected cattle were discovered. On January 15, the first case of BSE was found in Italy. The infected animal was discovered at a slaughterhouse near Modena that supplied ground beef to McDonald's restaurants in a number of European countries.

The fear of mad cow disease caused beef sales in the EU to plummet by as much as 50 percent, and news from the United States was hardly reassuring to consumers there. A federal investigation of American feed mills and rendering plants found that many companies had not been taking the threat of mad cow — or the FDA's new feed regulations — very seriously. More than one-quarter of the firms handling "prohibited" feed neglected to add a label warning that it should never be given to cattle. One-fifth of the firms handling both prohibited feeds and feeds approved for cattle had no system in place to prevent commingling or cross-contamination. And about one out of every ten rendering firms was completely unaware that the FDA had passed feed restrictions to prevent the spread of mad cow. In Colorado, more than one-quarter of the cattle-feed producers had somehow never heard about the new rules.

The federal government's apparent inability to keep prohibited feed away from cattle prompted the McDonald's Corporation to take action. The company's sales in Europe had already fallen by 10 percent, and American publicity about mad cow was raising doubts about the wisdom of eating any hamburgers, let alone Big Macs. Officials from the FDA and the USDA, as well as representatives from the leading meatpacking and rendering companies, were quietly invited to discuss the feed issue at McDonald's corporate headquarters in Oak Brook, Illinois. On March 13, the McDonald's Corporation announced that its ground beef suppliers would be required to supply documentation showing that FDA feed rules were being strictly followed — or McDonald's would no longer buy their beef.

IBP, Excel, and ConAgra immediately agreed to follow McDonald's directive, vowing that no cattle would be purchased without proper certification. Every rancher and feedlot would have to supply signed affidavits promising that banned feeds had never been given to their cattle. The American Meat Institute, which routinely fought against any mandatory food-safety measures proposed by the federal government, made no complaint about these new rules. "If McDonald's is requiring something of their suppliers, it has a pretty profound effect," said an AMI spokeswoman. What the FDA had failed to achieve — after nearly five years of industry consultation and half-hearted regulation — the McDonald's Corporation accomplished in a matter of weeks. "Because we have the world's biggest shopping cart," a McDonald's spokesman explained, "we can use that leadership to provide more focus and more order throughout the beef system."

wrong wrong wrong

FOR THIS PAPERBACK EDITION Penguin has included quotations from some favorable reviews of *Fast Food Nation*. In the interest of balance, I'd like to quote a few contrary opinions. "McGarbage," wrote a correspondent for the *National Review Online*. "Schlosser wears many hats, a few of which are conical and contain the word 'dunce.'" I was described, moreover, as a "health fascist," and "economics ignoramus," a "banjo-strumming performer at Farm Aid," and a "hectoring taskmaster of the nanny state." The book was reviewed in the *Wall Street Journal* not by one of the paper's fine investigative journalists, but by a right-wing member of its editorial staff. Among other things, she accused me of producing a "hodgepodge of impressions, statistics, anecdotes, and prejudices." A spokeswoman for the American Meat Institute said that my evidence of worker safety problems in meatpacking plants was "anecdotal," and that I had "vilified the industry in a way that is very unfair." The restaurant industry did not like *Fast Food Nation*, either. "In addition to acting like the 'food police', and trying to coerce the American consumer never to eat fast food again," the National Restaurant Association said, "[Schlosser] recklessly disparages an industry that has contributed tremendously to our nation."

The McDonald's Corporation also gave *Fast Food Nation* an unfavorable review. "The real McDonald's bears no resemblance to anything described in [Schlosser's] book," said a company statement. "He's wrong about our people, wrong about our jobs, and wrong about our food." Contrary to what McDonald's executives may believe, a sincere passion for accuracy led me to document every assertion in this book. Although *Fast Food Nation* has been strongly attacked, thus far its critics have failed to cite any errors in the text. Spokesmen for the meatpacking industry and the fast food industry have shied away from specifics, offering general denouncements of my work and leaving it at that. I am grateful to those readers who've taken the time to inform me about typos, misspellings, and other small mistakes. Mike Callicrate — an iconoclastic feedlot owner in Kansas who would make a fine copy editor — pointed out that I'd miscalculated some cattle manure statistics. The error has been corrected.

There is one criticism of *Fast Food Nation* that needs to be addressed. A number of people have said that I was too hard on the Republican Party, that an anti-Republican bias seems to pervade the book. *Fast Food Nation* has no hidden partisan agenda; the issues that it addresses transcend party politics. In retrospect, I could have been more critical of the Clinton administration's ties to agribusiness. Had I devoted more space to the poultry industry, for example, I would have examined the close links between Bill Clinton and the Tyson family. The FDA's failure to investigate the health risks of biotech foods and its lackadaisical effort to keep cattle remains out of cattle feed also occurred during the Clinton years.

Nevertheless, it is a sad but undeniable fact that for the past two decades the right wing of the Republican Party has worked closely with the fast food industry and the meatpacking industry to oppose food safety laws, worker safety laws, and increases in the minimum wage. One of President George W. Bush's first acts in office was to rescind a new ergonomics standard, backed by the Occupational Safety and Health Administration (OSHA), that would have protected millions of workers from cumulative trauma injuries. The National Restaurant Association and the American Meat Institute applauded Bush's move. The newly appointed chairman of the House Subcommittee on Workforce Protections, which oversees all legislation pertaining to OSHA, is Representative Charles Norwood, a Republican from Georgia. During the 1990s Norwood sponsored legislation that would have prevented OSHA from inspecting unsafe workplaces or fining negligent employers. He has publicly suggested that some workers may actually be getting their repetitive stress injuries from skiing and playing too much tennis, not from their jobs.

One of the Bush administration's first food-safety decisions was to stop testing the National School Lunch Program's ground beef for *Salmonella*. The meatpacking industry's lobbyists were delighted; they had worked hard to end the testing, which the industry considered expensive, inconvenient, and unnecessary. But consumer groups were outraged. In the ten months that the USDA had been testing ground beef intended for schoolchildren, roughly 5 million pounds were rejected because of *Salmonella* contamination. The decision to halt the tests generated a fair amount of bad publicity. Three days after it was announced, Secretary of Agriculture Ann M. Veneman said that she'd never authorized the new policy, reversed course, and promised that the school-lunch program's *Salmonella* testing would continue.

Ideally, food safety would be a non-partisan issue. It doesn't matter if you're a Democrat or a Republican, Labour or Conservative, Social Democrat or Christian Democrat — you still have to eat. In recent years the Democrats have been far more willing than the Republicans to support tough food-safety legislation in the United States. But that was not always the case. It was a Republican president, Theodore Roosevelt, who had the nerve to condemn dangerous concentrations of economic power, battle the meatpacking industry, and win passage of the nation's first food-safety law. Should that sort of spirit guide the Republican Party once again, there will be fewer reasons for criticizing its policies.

Of the many reactions to *Fast Food Nation*, the most surprising were the international events partly set in motion by Chapter 5, "Why the Fries Taste Good." A couple of months after the book's publication, Hitesh Shah, a software designer in Los Angeles, contacted McDonald's to find out if their french fries really did contain animal products. He was a regular customer at McDonald's, a vegetarian, and a devout Jain. His religion, Jainism, prohibits not just eating animal products but also wearing them. Jainist monks cover their noses and mouths with cloth to avoid inhaling any insects. Hitesh Shah was upset by the e-mail that McDonald's Home Office Customer Satisfaction Department sent him on March 28. "For flavor enhancement, McDonald's french fry suppliers use a minuscule amount of beef flavoring as an ingredient in the raw product," it said. "... (W)e are sorry if this has caused any confusion." McDonald's fries did in fact contain some beef; that's why they taste so good. Shah forwarded the e-mail to Viji Sundaram, a reporter at *India-West*, a California weekly with a large Hindu readership. Cows are considered sacred animals by Hindus and cannot legally be slaughtered in India. Sundaram briefly conducted her own investigation, confirmed the pertinent details of my french fry chapter and of Hitesh Shah's e-mail, then wrote an article for *India-West* ("Where's the Beef? It's in Your French Fries") that outraged Hindus and vegetarians worldwide.

After reading the *India-West* article, Harish Bharti, a Seattle attorney, filed a class-action lawsuit against the McDonald's Corporation, alleging that the chain had deliberately misled vegetarians about the true content of its fries, causing great emotional damage and endangering the souls of Hindu consumers. "Eating a cow for a Hindu," Bharti later explained, "would be like eating your own mother."

When news of the lawsuit reached India, a crowd of five hundred Hindu nationalists marched to a McDonald's in a suburb of Bombay and ransacked the restaurant. At another McDonald's in Bombay, an angry crowd smeared cow dung on a statue of Ronald McDonald. In New Delhi, activists from the nationalist Shiv Sena party staged a demonstration in front of McDonald's Indian headquarters. "We came to warn them to shut down the restaurants," a Shiv Sena leader said, calling upon the McDonald's Corporation to leave India immediately. The timing of the protests was unfortunate for the company. McDonald's was planning to triple the number of restaurants in India over the next few years and had just opened the nation's first drive-through, near the Taj Mahal.

"If you visit McDonald's anywhere in the world, the great taste of our world famous French Fries and Big Mac is the same," a company Web site declared. "At McDonald's we have a saying, 'One Taste Worldwide.'" Given such pronouncements, the outrage among Hindus in India seemed justified. The dispute over beef in the fries soon revealed, however, that McDonald's was in fact using different ingredients in different countries. McDonald's India assured customers and protesters that its fries were never cooked in oil containing animal products, a fact that Bombay health authorities later confirmed through chemical analysis. Nor was beef added to the fries at McDonald's in Great Britain, a country with a sizeable Hindu population. The company was quietly adjusting its french fry recipe to suit varying cultural preferences and taboos. In Canada, Japan, Mexico, and Australia, McDonald's still made fries the macho, old-fashioned way, cooking them in beef tallow.

In the United States, the McDonald's Corporation took the highly unusual step of issuing an apology. "We regret if customers felt that the information provided [about the fries] was not complete enough to meet their needs," the company said. "If there was confusion, we apologize." The statement did not satisfy Harish Bharti or the other attorneys who'd filed class-action lawsuits on behalf of America's 1 million Hindus and 15 million vegetarians. Bharti argued that "confusion" was the wrong word; McDonald's had been lying to Hindus and vegetarians for years, telling them it used "100 percent vegetable oil" when it didn't. Bharti refused to drop the lawsuit, hoping to punish McDonald's for its insensitivity toward religious minorities and to teach it a lesson that other American companies would not ignore. "We apologize for any confusion," a McDonald's spokesman responded, "but again, we have never made any vegetarian claims about our french fries — never."

Not long afterward, Bharti received a letter from a woman in Florida. The letter had been written on May 5, 1993, by a manager at McDonald's Customer Satisfaction Department. The letter was a response to the woman's inquiry. It said: "Thank you for contacting us regarding McDonald's menu selections for vegetarians. We appreciate your thoughts, and hope the following information will interest you ... we presently serve several items that vegetarians can enjoy at McDonald's — garden salads, french fries and hash browns (cooked in 100 percent vegetable oil) ..."

decline and fall

THE YEAR 2000 may some day be regarded as a milestone for the fast food industry. It may be remembered as the year that the leading chains began to unravel. According to NPD Foodworld, a market research firm, during 2000 the fast food industry did not gain any new customers in the United States. The stagnant sales preceded the headlines about mad cow disease and extended throughout most of the industry. Fewer people visited not only hamburger chains, but also pizza and Mexican food chains. Business did not improve in the first half of 2001. McDonald's profits fell in Europe, Asia, Latin America, and the United States. Customer traffic fell at Burger King restaurants worldwide. Burger King's new french fries proved a marketing disaster and were scrapped, at a cost of more than $70 million. And its parent company, Diageo PLC, had to spend millions to keep some large Burger King franchisees afloat, while searching for ways to unload the chain.

Taco Bell — a brand that in many ways perfected the art of selling inexpensive, mass-produced, highly industrialized foods — has lately encountered some financial difficulties. In 1989 Taco Bell introduced a "K minus" program. The K stood for "kitchens", which the chain strove to eliminate from its restaurants. Precooking the beef and the beans at central locations allowed Taco Bell to offer low prices, with most of the core menu items selling for less than a dollar. The strategy was a success during the 1990s, but eventually backfired, as Taco Bell gained a reputation for cheap, bland food. Sales at its company-owned restaurants fell by 9 percent in the fourth quarter of 2000, causing financial problems for as many as a thousand Taco Bell franchisees. Tricon Global Restaurants, the chain's parent company, had to set aside millions of dollars to help struggling franchisees, and PepsiCo Inc. sent them early "soda-rebate" checks worth additional millions to keep them in the business of selling Pepsi. A major recall of taco shells — sold under the Taco Bell name only at supermarkets and containing genetically engineered corn not approved for human consumption — no doubt also hurt the brand.

Taco Bell's problems, however, extend far beyond passing fears of tainted tacos. "We are not doing a great job in terms of quality, in terms of speed, in terms of cleanliness in the store," Emil Brolick, the chain's new president, confessed. The speed at which Taco Bell's financial health deteriorated, with relatively minor sales declines threatening widespread restaurant closures, shows how vulnerable the world's largest fast food chains have become. A 2 percent decline in sales is enough to send their stock prices spiralling downward.

The glory days of the major chains seem to be over. Smaller, regional restaurant companies are the ones now enjoying rapid growth in the United States, as many larger ones lose customers. Although the McDonald's Corporation continues to hunt for promising new American locations (a McDonald's recently opened at the Brentwood Baptist Church in Houston), the chain's problems increasingly resemble those of the British Empire a century ago. For imperial Britain, rapid expansion overseas was a sign not of economic strength, but of underlying weaknesses at home. An empire that looked impressive and invincible on the map later proved to be remarkably fragile, shrinking much faster than it had grown. During the 1990s McDonald's opened restaurants overseas at a furious pace, distracting attention from the fact that it was gaining few new customers in the United States. The mad cow epidemic in Europe, combined with economic downturns in Asia and Latin America, have created doubts on Wall Street about McDonald's imperial strategy. It costs a great deal of money to open new restaurants on distant continents. The McDonald's Corporation remains profitable, but now intends to grow by doubling its sales within the United States over the next decade. That goal may be unrealistic. A recent survey of American consumers found enormous dissatisfaction with McDonald's. Among the two hundred national organizations examined in the study, McDonald's ranked just a couple of places from the bottom.

Ever since the débâcle of the McLibel trial, the McDonald's

Corporation has tried to improve its public image and at times behave in a more socially responsible manner. During the spring of 2001 it began to offer discounts on health insurance and other benefits to employees at company-owned restaurants in the United States, which comprise about one-seventh of the chain. During the summer of 2001 it disclosed the basic ingredients of its natural flavors (and, perhaps in deference to Hindus, has taken the beef extract out of its McNuggets). In addition to forcing compliance with the FDA's feed regulations, McDonald's has required that its meatpacking suppliers handle and slaughter animals more humanely. For years, excessive line speeds and improper stunning have led to cattle and hogs being dismembered while fully conscious. McDonald's new policy on humane slaughter did not arise in a vacuum. Animal rights groups, such as People for the Ethical Treatment of Animals, were staging protests at McDonald's, asking the company to seek changes from its suppliers. Whatever the true motive, McDonald's acted decisively and hired Temple Grandin — one of the nation's foremost experts on animal welfare and proper livestock handling — to devise an auditing system for the slaughterhouses that provide the chain's beef and pork. According to Grandin, McDonald's threat to stop purchasing meat from companies that mistreat animals changed many of the industry's practices within a year. Although McDonald's auditors are employed by the same companies that manufacture its hamburger patties, Grandin says they seem genuinely committed to the new policy, making unannounced visits to slaughterhouses and observing whether animals are properly handled and stunned. When advocated by animal rights groups, such an inspection program had gone nowhere; demanded by McDonald's, it received the enthusiastic support of the meatpacking industry and the American Meat Institute.

Having shown a strong commitment to the ethical treatment of animals, the McDonald's Corporation should now demonstrate the same level of concern for the ethical treatment of the human beings who work in the nation's slaughterhouses. After the publication of *Fast Food Nation*, the photographer Eugene Richards and I visited meatpacking communities in Texas for *Mother Jones* magazine. We were appalled by what we found: conditions even worse than those in Nebraska or Colorado, conditions that bring to mind the worst abuses of the nineteenth-century Beef Trust. In Texas, the big meatpacking companies don't have to manipulate the workers' compensation system — they don't even have to participate in it. Texas is the only state in the union that allows a company to leave the workers' comp system and set up its own process for dealing with workplace injuries. Taking advantage of that unique opportunity, IBP has established a remarkable system there. When a worker is injured at an IBP plant in Texas, he or she is immediately presented with a waiver. Signing the waiver means forever surrendering the right to sue IBP on any grounds. Workers who sign the waiver may receive medical care under IBP's Workplace Injury Settlement Program. Or they may not. Once they sign, IBP and its company-approved doctors have control over the job-related medical treatment — for life. Under the program's terms, seeking treatment from an independent physician can be grounds for losing all medical benefits. Workers who refuse to sign the IBP waiver not only risk getting no medical care from the company, but also risk being fired on the spot. The Texas Supreme Court has ruled that companies operating outside the workers' comp system can fire workers simply because they're injured.

Today an IBP worker who gets hurt on the job in Texas faces a cruel dilemma: sign the waiver, perhaps receive medical attention, and remain beholden, forever, to IBP. Or refuse to sign, risk losing your job, receive no help with your medical bills, file a lawsuit, and hope to win a big judgement against the company years from now. Injured workers almost always sign the waiver. The pressure to do so is immense. An IBP medical case manager will literally bring the waiver to a hospital emergency room in order to obtain an injured worker's signature. When Lonita Leal's right hand was mangled by a hamburger grinder at the IBP plant in Amarillo, a case manager talked her into signing the waiver with her left hand, as she waited in the hospital for surgery. When Duane Mullin had both hands crushed in a hammer mill at the same plant, an IBP representative persuaded him to sign the waiver with a pen held in his mouth.

The recent purchase of IBP by Tyson Foods has created the world's biggest and most powerful meatpacking firm, with the largest market share in beef and poultry, the second-largest in pork. The Tyson/IBP merger fulfills every independent rancher's worst nightmare about being reduced to the status of a poultry grower — and may portend even faster line speeds at meatpacking plants. In order to complete the purchase, Tyson Foods had to assume $1.7 billion in debt. As a result, the new meatpacking colossus will likely be under great pressure to ship as much meat as possible out the door.

Over the past year, the McDonald's Corporation has proven,

beyond any doubt, that it can force its meatpacking suppliers to make fundamental changes quickly. If McDonald's insisted that the large meatpackers improve working conditions and reduce injury levels, these companies would do so. The cost of slowing down their production lines would be insignificant compared to the cost of losing their biggest customer. If McDonald's can send auditors into slaughterhouses to monitor the ethical treatment of cattle, it can certainly do the same for poor immigrant workers. As to the company's ability to influence this sort of behavior, I agree wholeheartedly with the American Meat Institute: "If McDonald's is requiring something of their suppliers, it has a pretty profound effect." Unlike compliance with the FDA's feed rules, which required an elaborate new system of paperwork and affidavits, it wouldn't take weeks to make America's slaughterhouses safer. If McDonald's were to demand that the line speeds be slowed down, preventing untold misery and harm, it could be accomplished in an instant.

dog eat dog

AS OF THIS WRITING, about a hundred people have died from vCJD, the human form of mad cow disease. Although every one of those deaths was tragic and unnecessary, they must be viewed in a larger perspective. Roughly the same number of people die every day in the United States from automobile accidents — and yet we do not live in fear of cars. At the moment there is no cure for vCJD, and it is impossible to predict how many people will get the disease by eating tainted meat. A great deal of scientific uncertainty still surrounds various attributes of the pathogen, such as the degree of infectivity among humans and the size of an infectious dose. About 800,000 cattle with mad cow disease were unwittingly eaten by people in Great Britain. One crucial determinant of the eventual death toll is the average incubation period for vCJD. That statistic is currently unknown. If it takes about ten years for most infected people to develop the disease, then we are now in the middle of the epidemic, and perhaps a thousand or so will die. If the average incubation period is twenty, thirty, or forty years — as the latest science suggests — then the epidemic is just beginning, and hundreds of thousands may die. Time will tell.

Regardless of whether mad cow causes a small outbreak among

humans or a deadly modern plague, it will haunt the beef industry for years, much as Three Mile Island and Chernobyl changed attitudes toward nuclear power. The spread of BSE in Europe has revealed how secret alliances between agribusiness and government can endanger the public health. It has shown how the desire for profit can overrule every other consideration. British agricultural officials were concerned as early as 1987 that eating meat from BSE-infected cattle might pose a risk to human beings. That information was suppressed for years, and the possibility of any health risk was strenuously denied, in order to protect exports of British beef. Scientists who disagreed with the official line were publicly attacked and kept off government committees investigating BSE. Official denials of the truth delayed important health measures and led to some absurdities. The British decision to keep some of the most infective cattle parts (brains, spleens, spinal materials, thymus glands, and intestines) out of the human food supply was prompted not by health or agricultural officials, but by a leading manufacturer of pet foods. Worried by mounting evidence that mad cow disease might have the ability to cross species barriers, Pedigree Master Foods decided to keep cattle offal out of its products and told the Ministry of Agriculture that it was a good idea to do the same with food intended for human consumption. Meanwhile, British children were being served some of the nation's cheapest meats — hamburgers, sausages, and mince pies full of potentially contaminated offal — because the 1980 Education Act had eliminated government subsidies for nutritious school meals.

A great many British pets were eating safer food than the British people, until November of 1989, when the government banned the sale of cattle offal and its use in the manufacture of ground beef. Seven months later, the worst fears of Pedigree Master Foods were confirmed; a Siamese cat named Max died in Bristol from a feline variant of BSE, after eating contaminated cat food. The death of "Mad Max," as the tabloids dubbed him, proved that mad cow could indeed cross the species barrier. Nevertheless, the British government denied for six more years that the disease posed any risk to human beings.

Governments throughout Europe ignored the interests of consumers while protecting those of agribusiness. A recent report by the French senate found that from 1988 to 2000 the agriculture ministry in that country minimized the danger of mad cow and "constantly sought to prevent or delay the introduction of precautionary measures." Health officials were repeatedly ignored in order to block decisions that "might have had an adverse effect on the competitiveness of the agri-foodstuffs industry." Great Britain banned the feeding of ruminants to ruminants in 1988, but continued to export animal feed potentially contaminated with BSE for another eight years — shipping about 150 million pounds of the stuff to dozens of countries and thereby turning a local outbreak of mad cow into one with worldwide ramifications. Other countries in the European Union imported the cheap British feed and then exported it to North Africa and the Middle East.

The recent outbreak of mad cow disease in Japan was most likely caused by infected feed from Europe. Japanese agricultural officials displayed remarkable incompetence in responding to the threat of BSE. Five years after the British government acknowledged the link between BSE and serious illness in human beings, Japanese farmers were still feeding meat-and-bonemeal to their cattle, without violating any law. When the Scientific Steering Commission of the European Commission warned in June of 2001 that such practices created a high risk of a BSE outbreak, the Japanese Ministry of Agriculture, Forestry and Fisheries (MAFF) strongly denied the risk and blocked publication of the EU report. Three months later, a Japanese cow tested positive for BSE. A senior MAFF official assured the public that the animal's carcass had been "disposed of." In fact, MAFF had inadvertently allowed the tainted meat to be rendered into animal feed.

Today nations with BSE must not only confront the prospect of slaughtering millions of potentially infected cattle, but must also figure out what to do with their remains. In Great Britain, about a billion pounds of rendered cattle sit at waste sites, vast mounds of fine brown powder, awaiting incineration. In Japan, plans are being made to blend rendered cattle with concrete — and use the mixture as a building material. In Denmark, a company is now erecting the world's first power plant that generates electricity by burning cattle.

Thanks to the McDonald's Corporation, the FDA's animal feed restrictions are most likely being obeyed in the United States. But those prohibitions may not be strict enough to prevent the spread of BSE. The feeding of all animal proteins to all farm animals has been banned throughout the European Union. Such a ban was justified as a means of preventing hog and poultry feed from winding up in cattle troughs. The ban will also, however, halt the transmission of mad cow through new and unexpected means. John Collinge — a professor at London's Imperial College School of Medicine and a prominent member of the British government's Spongiform Encephalopathy Advisory Committee — believes that BSE may easily cross the species barrier and survive undetected in animals that outwardly show no symptoms of the disease. If pigs or poultry were to be found silently carrying mad cow, the FDA's feed restrictions would prove futile. The continued use of cattle blood in cattle feed seems especially unwise. "All cannibalistic recycling is potentially dangerous," Collinge warns, "and I have said that repeatedly."

The USDA, the FDA, and the American Meat Institute oppose any additional prohibition on what can be fed to livestock. They argue that new restrictions are unnecessary, because mad cow disease has never been detected in the United States. Their argument on behalf of continuing to feed animal proteins to livestock is a risky form of denial, an exercise in wishful thinking. By the time Great Britain discovered its first two cows with BSE, at least 60,000 other cattle there were already infected. The claim that mad cow disease has never been detected in the United States is accurate, as of this writing. The USDA, however, has not tried very hard to find it. "If you don't look, you won't find," says Dr Perluigi Gambetti, a BSE expert who heads the National Prion Disease Surveillance Center at Case Western Reserve University. "Unless we test more, we will never know if we have it here." Since 1990, approximately 375 million cattle have been slaughtered in the United States, and about 15,000 of them were tested for mad cow. Belgium, with a cattle herd roughly one-thirtieth the size of ours, plans to test 400,000 for mad cow disease every year.

The current FDA feed rules are primarily concerned with efficiency and utility, not public health. They allow cattle to be fed pigs, pigs to be fed cattle, cattle to be fed poultry, and poultry to be fed cattle. They allow dogs and cats to be fed dogs and cats. Although leading American manufacturers promise never to put rendered pets into their pet food, it is still legal to do so. A Canadian company, Sanimal Inc., was putting 40,000 pounds of dead dogs and dead cats into its dog and cat food every week, until discontinuing the practice in June, 2001. "This food is healthy and good," said the company's vice president of procurement, responding to critics, "but some people don't like to see meat meal that contains any pets."

Perhaps the most effective action taken by the federal government to prevent the introduction of BSE to the United States — a 1989 ban on imports of livestock and feed from Great Britain — was the one action that threatened no economic harm to the American meat industry. The ban on imports, like any protectionist measure, helped American producers. But a strict FDA prohibition of all animal protein in animal feeds would reduce some of the profit that American agribusiness firms can derive from vertical integration. At the moment, the most common source of animal protein in poultry feed isn't hogs or cattle. It's poultry. Tyson Foods takes leftover chicken meat and skin and intestines from its poultry slaughterhouses, ships them to Tyson feed plants, adds them to chicken feed, and then provides the feed to Tyson growers, so that baby chicks can eat their ancestors. The Tyson feed mill in Buzzard Bluff, Arkansas, processes about 10 million pounds of chicken parts every week.

The mad cow epidemic has greatly reduced beef consumption in Europe and Japan, devastating farmers who raise cattle. Livestock practices that once seemed to be cost-efficient turned out to be disastrously inefficient. Feelings of anger and betrayal among consumers have prompted a fundamental reappraisal of agricultural policies. Food safety, animal welfare, and environmental concerns are gaining precedence over the traditional agribusiness emphasis on production levels. The Scandinavian countries, Italy, and Austria are seeking basic, structural changes in how European food is produced. Even Great Britain now seems to be questioning its reliance on high-volume, industrialized farming. For years the Labour government of Tony Blair had forged close ties with leading food processing, supermarket, and fast food companies. Blair's handling of the foot-and-mouth epidemic seemed more influenced by the export needs of Nestlé, the world's largest food company, than by the latest scientific evidence on the efficacy of vaccines. His unapologetic defense of a £15,000 political donation from the McDonald's Corporation prompted critics to call the majority party "McLabour." His appointee to serve as Rural Recovery Coordinator, Chris Haskins, headed a large food processing firm, ran a dairy that supplied the milk for McDonald's milkshakes, and publicly belittled the prospects for small farms and organic agriculture. Nevertheless, even Lord Haskins proposed a shift of EU agricultural policy in October of 2001, arguing that subsidies should be awarded to farms whose production methods do not harm the environment.

The German government has taken the lead on this issue in the

EU, calling for the de-industrialization of agriculture and planning to make 20 percent of its farmland organic by the year 2010. "Things will no longer be the way they are," declared Renate Kuenast, who serves as the German minister for agriculture — and for consumer protection. Kuenast says that Germans must develop the same reverence for their food that they've always had for their beer. Under a German law that dates back to the early sixteenth century, no additives can be put into beer, which must be made using only water, hops, and barley. Vowing to outlaw the use of antibiotics and other additives in animal feed, Kuenast offers a revolutionary alternative: "Our cows should get only water, grain, and grass."

Future historians, I hope, will consider the American fast food industry a relic of the twentieth century — a set of attitudes, systems, and beliefs that emerged from postwar southern California, that embodied its limitless faith in technology, that quickly spread across the globe, flourished briefly, and then receded, once its true costs became clear and its thinking became obsolete. We cannot ignore the meaning of mad cow. It is one more warning about unintended consequences, about human arrogance and the blind worship of science. The same mindset that would add 4-methylacetophenone and solvent to your milkshake would also feed pigs to cows. Whatever replaces the fast food industry should be regional, diverse, authentic, unpredictable, sustainable, profitable — and humble. It should know its limits. People can be fed without being fattened or deceived. This new century may bring an impatience with conformity, a refusal to be kept in the dark, less greed, more compassion, less speed, more common sense, a sense of humor about brand essences and loyalties, a view of food as more than just fuel. Things don't have to be the way they are. Despite all evidence to the contrary, I remain optimistic.

PHOTO CREDITS

NOTES

BIBLIOGRAPHY

ACKNOWLEDGMENTS

INDEX

photo credits

INTRODUCTION: Cheyenne Mountain. © 2000 by Greg Skinner.

CHAPTER 1: Carl Karcher holding his daughter Anne Marie beside his first hot dog stand, 1942. Courtesy of CKE, Inc.

CHAPTER 2: Ronald McDonald in the classroom. © 1989 by Evan Johnson/Impact Visuals.

CHAPTER 3: Working at Wendy's. © 2000 by Skylar Nielsen.

CHAPTER 4: Signs at night. © 2000 by Skylar Nielsen.

CHAPTER 5: J. R. Simplot. © 1995 by Louis Psihoyos/Matrix.

CHAPTER 6: Cattle in eastern Colorado. © 2000 by Rob Buchanan.

CHAPTER 7: Welcome to Greeley. © 2000 by Eugene Richards.

CHAPTER 8: Injured ConAgra Beef worker and his family. © 2000 by Eugene Richards.

CHAPTER 9: Alex Donley. Courtesy of Nancy Donley.

CHAPTER 10: A Vogtland cowboy. © 1999 by Franziska Heinze.

EPILOGUE: Fast food nation. © 2000 by Mark Mann.

notes

Introduction

Although I did a great deal of firsthand reporting and research for this book, I also benefited from the hard work of others. In these notes I've tried to give credit to the many people whose writing and research helped mine. Robert L. Emerson's *The New Economics of Fast Food* (New York: Van Nostrand Reinhold, 1990) offers a fine overview of the business. Though many of its statistics are out of date, the book's analysis of relative labor, marketing, and franchising costs remains useful. *Fast Food: Roadside Restaurants in the Automobile Age*, by John A. Jakle and Keith A. Sculle (Baltimore: John Hopkins University Press, 1999), is less concerned with the workings of the industry than with its impact on the American landscape and "sense of place." McDonald's has played a central role in the creation of this industry, and half a dozen books about the company provide a broad perspective of its impact on the world. Ray Kroc's memoir with Robert Anderson, *Grinding It Out: The Making of McDonald's* (New York: St. Martin's Paperbacks, 1987) conveys the sensibility of its charismatic founder, an outlook that still pervades the chain. John F. Love's *McDonald's: Behind the Arches* (New York: Bantam Books, 1995) is an authorized corporate history, but an unusual one — fascinating, thoughtful, sometimes critical, and extremely well researched. *Big Mac: The Unauthorized Story of McDonald's* (New York: E. P. Dutton, 1976), by Max Boas and Steve Chain, looks behind the McDonald's PR machine and finds a company whose behavior is frequently cynical and manipulative. John Vidal's *McLibel: Burger Culture on Trial* (New York: New Press, 1997) uses a narrative of the McLibel case to provide an indictment of McDonald's and globalization. George Ritzer's *The McDonaldization of Society: An Investigation into the Changing Character of Contemporary Social Life* (Thousand Oaks, Calif.: Pine Ridge Press, 1996) applies the theories of Max Weber to contemporary America, tracing the wide-ranging effects of McDonald's zeal for efficiency and uniformity. *McDonaldization Revisited: Critical Essays on Consumer Culture* (Westport, Conn.: Praeger, 1998), edited by Mark Alfino, John S. Caputo, and Robin Winyard, attests to the current influence of Ritzer's work in the field of sociology. With a much less theoretical emphasis, Stan Luxenberg's *Roadside Empires: How the Chains Franchised America* (New York: Viking, 1985) examines the fast food industry's role in helping to create America's postwar service economy. I found a great deal of interesting material in trade publications such as *Restaurant Business, Restaurants and Institutions, Nation's Restaurant News,* and *ID: The Voice of Foodservice.* For years some of the best reporting on the fast food industry has appeared in the *Wall Street Journal.*

Page

1 *Cheyenne Mountain sits:* The description of Cheyenne Mountain Air Force Station is based upon my visit to the facility, and I am grateful to Major Mike Birmingham of the U.S. Space Command for his subsequent help in obtaining additional information.

3 *about $6 billion on fast food . . . more than $110 billion:* Both of these estimates were provided by the National Restaurant Association.

more money on fast food than on higher education: My calculation is based on figures contained in "Personal Consumption Expenditures in Millions of Current Dollars," U.S. Commerce Department, 2000. According to the Commerce Department, 1999 consumer spending on fast food exceeded spending on higher education ($75.6 billion); personal computers and peripherals ($25.9 billion); computer software ($8.4 billion); new cars ($101 billion); movies ($6.7 billion); books and maps ($29.5 billion); magazines and sheet music ($19 billion); newspapers ($16.7 billion); video rentals ($8.6 billion); and records, tapes, and disks ($12.2 billion).

about one-quarter of the adult population: This is my own estimate, based on the following information from the National Restaurant Association: about half of the adult population visits a restaurant on any given day, and more than half of the restaurant industry's annual revenues now come from fast food. Since the average check at a fast food restaurant is much lower that that at a full-service restaurant, my estimate may be too conservative (and the actual number of daily fast food visits may be higher).

4 *the hourly wage of the average U.S. worker:* By "average" I mean workers assigned to nonsupervisory tasks. See "Real Average Weekly and Hourly Earnings of Production and Non-Supervisory Workers, 1967–98 (1998 Dollars)," Economic Policy Institute, 1999; "Average Hourly and Weekly Earnings by Private Industry Group, 1980–1998," *Statistical Abstract of the United States* (Washington, D.C.: U.S. Census Bureau, 1999), p. 443.

about one-third of American mothers . . . today almost two-thirds: See "Labor Force Participation Rates for Wives, Husbands Present, by Age of Own Youngest Child, 1975–1998," *Statistical Abstract,* p. 417.

Cameron Lynne Macdonald and Carmen Sirianni: See *Working in the Service Society* (Philadelphia: Temple University Press, 1996), edited by Cameron Lynne Macdonald and Carmen Sirianni, p. 2.

A generation ago, three-quarters of the money . . . Today about half of the money: The comparison is between money spent on food for consumption at home and money spent on foodservice. See Charlene Price, "Fast Food Chains Penetrate New Markets: Industry Overview," *USDA Food Review,* January 1993; "Personal Consumption Expenditures," U.S. Commerce Department.

90 percent of the country's new jobs: Cited in Macdonald and Sirianni, *Service Society,* p. 1.

4 *An estimated one out of every eight workers in the United States:* Cited in "Welcome to McDonald's," McDonald's Corporation, 1996.

annually hires about one million people: This is my own estimate, based on the following: McDonald's has about 14,000 restaurants in the United States, each employing about 50 crew members; a conservative estimate of the turnover rate among McDonald's crew members is about 150 percent; having a workforce of roughly 700,000 and an annual turnover rate of 150 percent requires the hiring of about 1 million new workers every year. In its promotional literature, the McDonald's Corporation claims to have "surpassed the U.S. Army as the nation's largest training organization." Given how McDonald's actually "trains" its workers, I have used the word "hires" as a synonym. See "Welcome to McDonald's."

the nation's largest purchaser of beef, pork, and potatoes . . . the second largest purchaser of chicken: See Love, *Behind the Arches,* pp. 3–4; Mark D. Jekanowski, "Causes and Consequences of Fast Food Sales Growth; Statistical Data Included," *USDA Food Review,* January 1, 1999. McDonald's role as the leading pork purchaser was described to me by a pork industry executive who prefers not to be named.

the largest owner of retail property in the world: See Bruce Upbin, "Beyond Burgers," *Forbes,* November 1, 1999; Love, *Behind the Arches,* p. 4.

earns the majority of its profits: McDonald's has an unusual franchise arrangement, serving as landlord for its franchisees and adjusting lease payments according to sales levels. About 85 percent of the McDonald's in the United States are operated by franchisees. See Emerson, *New Economics of Fast Food,* pp. 59–62; Love, *Behind the Arches,* pp. 154–57; "Welcome to McDonald's."

spends more money on advertising and marketing: Interview with Lynn Fava, Competitive Media Reporting.

the world's most famous brand: See "McDonald's Wins Top Spot in Global Brand Ratings," *Brand Strategy,* November 22, 1996.

more playgrounds than any other private entity: Its nearest rival, Burger King, operates about one-quarter the number of playgrounds.

one of the nation's largest distributors of toys: According to the British newspaper the *Evening Standard,* in 1998 McDonald's purchased 1.3 billion toys from Chinese manufacturers. Cited in Lachlan Colquhoun, "McDonald's Soars to Success in Chinese Fast Food Market," *Evening Standard,* October 21, 1999.

96 percent could identify Ronald McDonald: Cited in "Welcome to McDonald's."

The only fictional character with a higher degree: Max Boas and Steve Chain express some reservations about the accuracy of this study, which was conducted by McDonald's, but I find it credible. A more recent study, conducted by an independent market research firm, found that at least 80 percent of the children in the nine foreign countries surveyed could recognize Ronald McDonald. See Boas and Chain, *Big Mac,* p. 115; Love, *Behind the Arches,* p. 2; and "Barbie, McDonald's Find Common Ground," *Selling to Kids,* September 30, 1998.

more widely recognized than the Christian cross: A survey by a marketing firm called Sponsorship Research International — conducted among 7,000 people in the United States, the United Kingdom, Germany, Australia, India, and Japan — found that 88 percent could identify the golden arches and that 54 percent could identify the Christian cross. The most widely recognized symbol was the interlocking rings of the Olympics. See "Golden Arches More Familiar Than the Cross," *Plain Dealer*, August 26, 1995.

5 *"the McDonaldization of America"*: Jim Hightower, *Eat Your Heart Out: Food Profiteering in America* (New York: Crown, 1975), p. 237.

"bigger is not better": Ibid., p. 3.

the final remains of one out of every nine Americans: Cited in Erin Kelly, "Death Takes a Holiday," *Fortune*, March 15, 1999.

"We have found out . . . that we cannot trust": Quoted in Love, *Behind the Arches*, p. 144.

6 *America's largest private employer*: The health care industry employs more workers, but a large proportion of them work at publicly owned and operated facilities. See "Employment by Selected Industry, with Projections 1986–2006," *Statistical Abstract*, p. 429.

the real value of wages in the restaurant industry: See Patrick Barta, "Rises in Many Salaries Barely Keep Pace with Inflation," *Wall Street Journal*, February 1, 2000.

roughly 3.5 million fast food workers: The figure was supplied by the National Restaurant Association.

by far the largest group of minimum wage earners in the United States: Interview with Alan B. Krueger, professor of politics and economics at Princeton University.

The only Americans who consistently earn: Fast food workers are at the bottom of the restaurant industry's pay scale, and the industry pays the lowest wages of any nonagricultural endeavor. Similarly, migrant farm workers are at the bottom of the agricultural pay scale. Although some farm laborers earn a decent hourly wage, many are paid the minimum wage — or less. See "Non-Farm Industries — Employees and Earnings, 1980–1998," *Statistical Abstract*, p. 436; and Eric Schlosser, "In the Strawberry Fields," *Atlantic Monthly*, November 1995.

approximately three hamburgers: My estimate is based on the following: Per capita consumption of ground beef is now about thirty pounds a year, with the vast majority consumed as hamburgers. A regular hamburger patty at McDonald's weighs 1.6 ounces; using that as a standard, Americans eat about three hundred burgers a year (five to six a week). Using a Quarter Pounder as the standard, Americans eat about 120 hamburgers a year (at least two a week). The consumption figure that I've used assumes an average patty weight somewhere between 1.6 and 4 ounces. See "Hamburger Consumption Takes a Hit, But a Reversal of Fortune Is in Offing," *National Provisioner*, August 1999.

four orders of french fries every week: Per capita consumption of frozen potato products (a category that is almost entirely french fries) is about 30 pounds a year. A regular order of french fries at McDonald's weighs 68 grams. Converting the pounds to kilograms and then dividing that number by 68 leaves you with the number of annual french fry servings: 205 (about four per week). See "Potatoes: U.S. Per Capita Utilization by Category, 1991–1999," USDA Economic Research Service, 2000.

new restaurants are opening there at a faster pace: See "1999 to Mark Eighth Consecutive Year of Growth for Restaurant Industry," news release, National Restaurant Association, December 22, 1998.

8 *"interstate socialism":* Stephen B. Goddard, *Getting There: The Epic Struggle between Road and Rail in the American Century* (New York: Basic Books, 1994), p. 179.

the inflation-adjusted value of the minimum wage: Between 1968 and and 1989 the real value of the minimum wage fell from $7.21 to $4.24; in 1995, it stood at $4.38. See "Federal Minimum Wage Rates: 1954–1996," *Statistical Abstract,* p. 447.

more prison inmates than full-time farmers: Today there are fewer than 1 million full-time farmers in the United States. And there are about 1.3 million people in the nation's prisons. For the number of full-time farmers, see "Appendix Table 21 — Characteristics of Farms and Their Operators, by Farm Typology Group, 1996," *Rural Conditions and Trends,* USDA Economic Research Service, February 1999. For the number of prison inmates, see "Nation's Prison and Jail Population Reaches 1,860,520," press release, Bureau of Justice Statistics, April 19, 2000.

9 *"the irrationality of rationality":* See Ritzer, *The McDonaldization of America,* pp. 121–42.

1. The Founding Fathers

I spent an afternoon with Carl Karcher at his Anaheim office. My account of his life is largely based on that interview and on a pair of corporate histories: B. Carolyn Knight, *Making It Happen: The Story of Carl Karcher Enterprises* (Anaheim, Calif.: Carl Karcher Enterprises, 1981); and Carl Karcher with B. Carolyn Knight, *Never Stop Dreaming: 50 Years of Making It Happen* (San Marcos, Calif.: Robert Erdmann Publishing, 1991). For the history of Anaheim, I relied on John Westcott, *Anaheim: City of Dreams* (Chatsworth, Calif.: Windsor Publications, 1990). My view of early Los Angeles has been greatly influenced by the work of Carey McWilliams, one of the twentieth century's finest and most underappreciated journalists. His *Southern California Country* (New York: Duell, Sloan & Pearce, 1946) and *California: The Great Exception* (Berkeley: University of California Press, 1999) are still vibrant and insightful, though first published more than fifty years ago. Mike Davis is in many ways carrying forward the aims and ideals of McWilliams; *City of Quartz* (New York: Vintage Books, 1992), especially the material on San Bernardino and Fontana, was both useful and inspiring. Kevin Starr's *The Dream Endures: California Enters the 1940s* (New York: Oxford University Press, 1997) gave me a strong sense of life there before the "fabulous boom." Richard White's *"It's Your Misfortune and None of My Own": A New History of the American West* (Norman: University of Oklahoma Press, 1991) provides a good overview of a region where free enterprise has long been celebrated more in theory than in practice. Marc Reisner's *Cadillac Desert: The American West and Its Disappearing Water* (New York: Penguin Books, 1987) aptly describes how water was brought to Los Angeles, and the rest of the arid West, at public expense. "Aerospace Capital of the World: Los Angeles" — a chapter in *The Rise of the Gunbelt: The Military Remapping of Industrial America* (New York: Oxford University Press, 1991), by Ann Markuson et al. — outlines how military spending fueled southern California's postwar economy. For California's role in the spread of the car culture, I relied on Kenneth T. Jackson's classic *Crabgrass Frontier: The Suburbanization of the United States* (New York: Oxford University Press, 1985). In *Getting There*, Stephen B. Goddard shows how the free market had little to do with the triumph of the automobile. Jonathan Kwitny's "The Great Transportation Conspiracy," published in *Harper's* during February of 1981, is a fine piece of investigative journalism.

The fast food memoir is a growing literary genre; in addition to Carl Karcher's, I relied on Ray Kroc's *Grinding It Out*; James W. McLamore, *The Burger King: Jim McLamore and the Building of an Empire* (New York: McGraw-Hill, 1998); Tom Monaghan, with Robert Anderson, *Pizza Tiger* (New York: Random House, 1986); Colonel Harland Sanders, *Life As I Have Known It Has Been "Finger Lickin' Good"* (Carol Stream, Ill.: Creation House, 1974); R. David Thomas, *Dave's Way: A New Approach to Old-Fashioned Success* (New York: G. P. Putnam's Sons, 1991). Richard J. McDonald, one of the founders of the chain with that name, contributed the foreword to Ronald J. McDonald's interesting book, *The Complete Hamburger: The History of America's Favorite Sandwich* (New York: Birch Lane Press, 1997). I learned a great deal from two other books that have similar themes and many evocative photographs: Jeffrey Tennyson, *Hamburger Heaven: The Illustrated History of the Hamburger* (New York: Hyperion, 1993); and Michael Karl Witzel, *The American Drive-In: History and Folklore of the Drive-In Restaurant in American Car Culture* (Osceola, Wis.: Motorbooks International, 1994). Stan Luxenberg's *Roadside Empires* has much information on the early days of the fast food industry, as do John Love's *Behind the Arches* and *Big Mac*, by Max Boas and Steve Chain. William Whitworth's profile of Colonel Sanders, "Kentucky Fried," published in the *New Yorker* on February 14, 1970, remains my favorite piece of writing on fast food.

Page

13 *"The harder you work"*: Interview with Carl Karcher.
"This is heaven": Ibid.
the heart of southern California's citrus belt: See McWilliams, *Southern California Country*, p. 206. The chapter titled "The Citrus Belt" is a good account of the region's cultural and economic life.

14 *the leading agricultural counties in the United States*: Ibid., p. 213. See also Reisner, *Cadillac Desert*, p. 87.
about 70,000 acres: Cited in Westcott, *Anaheim*, p. 67.
the acronym "KIGY": Ibid., p. 54.

15 *"I'm in business for myself now"*: Karcher interview.
the population of southern California nearly tripled: Cited in McWilliams, *Southern California*, p. 14.
About 80 percent of the population: Cited ibid., p. 165.

16 *about a million cars in Los Angeles*: Cited ibid., p. 236.
Lobbyists from the oil, tire, and automobile industries: See Jackson, *Crabgrass Frontier*, pp. 163–68.
General Motors secretly began to purchase: For the story of the American trolley's demise, see Kwitny, "The Great Transportation Conspiracy"; Jackson, *Crabgrass Frontier*, pp. 168–71; and Goddard, *Getting There*, pp. 120–37. For a contrary

view, much more benign toward General Motors, see Martha J. Bianco, "Techno-logical Innovation and the Rise and Fall of Urban Mass Transit," *Journal of Urban History*, March 1999.

17 *"People with cars are so lazy"*: Quoted in Witzel, *American Drive-In*, p. 24.
"circular meccas of neon": Ibid., p. 47.

18 *"fabulous boom"*: McWilliams, *The Great Exception*, p. 233.
federal government spent nearly $20 billion . . . federal spending was responsible for nearly half: Cited in White, *Your Misfortune*, p. 498.
the second-largest manufacturing center: Ibid., p. 498.
the focus of the local economy: Ibid., p. 515.

19 *"Worship as you are"*: Quoted in Jackson, *Crabgrass Frontier*, p. 264.
the fastest-growing city: Cited in Wescott, *Anaheim*, p. 71.
Richard and Maurice McDonald: For the story of the McDonald brothers, I have relied on Kroc, *Grinding It Out*; McDonald, *Complete Hamburger*; Love, *Behind the Arches*; Tennyson, *Hamburger Heaven*; Boas and Chain, *Big Mac*.

20 *"Imagine — No Car Hops"*: The ad is reprinted in Tennyson, *Hamburger Heaven*, p. 62.
"Working-class families": Love, *Behind the Arches*, p. 41.

21 *The same year the McDonald brothers opened*: For the founding of the Hell's Angels and the fiftieth anniversary celebration, see Phillip W. Browne, "Ventura Event a 'Milestone' for Hell's Angels," *Ventura County Star*, March 15, 1998.
"They get angry when they read": Hunter S. Thompson, *Hell's Angels: A Strange and Terrible Saga* (New York: Ballantine Books, 1995), p. 45.

22 *impressed by Adolf Hitler's Reichsautobahn*: See Goddard, *Getting There*, p. 181; "1956: Interstate," *Business Week: 100 Years of Innovation*, Summer 1999.
46,000 miles of road: "1956: Interstate."
"Our food was exactly the same": George Clark, one of the founders of Burger Queen, made this admission. Quoted in Luxenberg, *Roadside Empires*, p. 76.
William Rosenberg: For the story of Dunkin' Donuts, see Luxenberg, *Roadside Empires*, pp. 18–20.
Glenn W. Bell, Jr.: For the story of Taco Bell, see Love, *Behind the Arches*, pp. 26–7; Jakle and Sculle, *Fast Food*, pp. 257–58.
Keith G. Cramer: For the story of Burger King, see McLamore, *The Burger King*.
Dave Thomas: For the story of Wendy's, see Thomas, *Dave's Way*.

23 *Thomas S. Monaghan*: For the story of Domino's, see Monaghan, *Pizza Tiger*.
Harland Sanders: For the story of KFC, see Sanders, *Life As I Have Known It*; and Whitworth, "Kentucky Fried."
"not to call a no-good, lazy": Sanders, *Life As I Have Known It*, p. 141.

24 *The Motormat*: See Witzel, *American Drive-In*, p. 121.
the Biff-Burger chain: See Tennyson, *Hamburger Heaven*, p. 73.
"Miracle Insta Machines": See McLamore, *The Burger King*, photo insert between pp. 126 and 127.

25 *one of the largest privately owned fast food chains*: Karcher, *Never Stop Dreaming*, p. 79.
accused of insider trading: See Karcher, *Never Stop Dreaming*, pp. 123–24; Bruce Horovitz and Keith Bradsher, "Carl's Jr. Founder Accused of Insider Trading

Scheme," *Los Angeles Times,* April 15, 1988; and Richard Martin, "Karchers Pay $664,000 Fine in Stock Case," *Nation's Restaurant News,* August 7, 1989.

25 *Carl's real estate investments proved unwise:* My account of Carl Karcher's financial difficulties is based primarily on my interview with him. I confirmed the details through a variety of printed sources, including "Carl Karcher Board Rejects Founder's Bid to Take Firm Private," *Wall Street Journal,* December 21, 1992; Thomas R. King, "Chairman of Carl Karcher Enterprises May Seek to Oust Some Board Members," *Wall Street Journal,* September 2, 1993; Peggy Hesketh, "Karcher's 'Godfather': Board Says Pizza Baron's Offer Is One It Can Refuse," *Orange County Business Journal,* September 20, 1993; David J. Jefferson, "Fast Food Firm Ousts Karcher as Chairman," *Wall Street Journal,* October 4, 1993; Jim Gardner, "Foley-Karcher: Tentative Team in Control of CKE," *Orange County Business Journal,* December 20, 1993; Richard Martin, "Carl N. Karcher: CKE's Founder Reflects on His Past, Looks Toward His Future," *Nation's Restaurant News,* August 3, 1998.

2. Your Trusted Friends

For the story of Ray Kroc, I relied mainly on his memoir, *Grinding It Out;* Max Boas and Steven Chain, *Big Mac;* and John Love, *Behind the Arches.* My visit to the Ray A. Kroc museum provided many useful insights into the man. Steven Watts's *The Magic Kingdom: Walt Disney and the American Way of Life* (Boston: Houghton Mifflin, 1997), is by far the best biography of Disney, drawing extensively upon material from the Disney archive and interviews with Disney's associates. Although I disagree with some of Watts's conclusions, his research is extraordinary. Richard Schickel's *The Disney Version: The Life, Times, Art, and Commerce of Walt Disney* (New York: Avon Books, 1968) remains provocative and highly relevant more than three decades after its publication. Leonard Mosley's *Disney's World* (New York: Stein and Day, 1985) and Marc Eliot's *Walt Disney: Hollywood's Dark Prince* (London: Andre Deutsch, 1993) offer a counterpoint to the hagiographies sponsored by the Walt Disney Company. My view of American attitudes toward technology was greatly influenced by two books: Leo Marx's *The Machine in the Garden: Technology and the Pastoral Ideal in America* (New York: Oxford University Press, 1970) and David E. Nye's *American Technological Sublime* (Cambridge, Mass.: MIT Press, 1994).

In the growing literature on marketing to children, three books are worth mentioning for what they (often inadvertently) reveal: Dan S. Acuff with Robert H. Reiher, *What Kids Buy and Why: The Psychology of Marketing to Kids* (New York: Free Press, 1997); Gene Del Vecchio, *Creating Ever-Cool: A Marketer's Guide to a Kid's Heart* (Gretna, La.: Pelican Publishing, 1998); and James U. McNeal, *Kids As Customers: A Handbook of Marketing to Children* (New York: Lexington Books, 1992). Some of the articles in children's marketing journals, such as *Selling to Kids* and *Entertainment Marketing Letter,* are remarkable documents for future historians. Two fine reports introduced me to the whole subject of marketing in America's schools: Consumers Union Education Services, "Captive Kids: A Report on Commercial Pressures on Kids at School," Consumers Union, 1998; and Alex Molnar, "Sponsored Schools and Commercialized Classrooms: Schoolhouse Commercializing Trends in the 1990s," Center for the Analysis of Commercialism in Education, University of Wisconsin-Milwaukee, August 1998. The Center for Science in the Public Interest has been battling for food safety and proper nutrition for more than thirty years. Michael Jacobson's report "Liquid Candy: How Soft Drinks Are Harming Americans' Health," October 1998, is another fine example of the center's work. The corporate memos from the McDonald's advertising campaign were given to me by someone who thought I'd find them "enlightening," and indeed they are.

Page
32 *"One of the highlights of my sixty-first birthday"*: Exhibit, Ray A. Kroc Museum.
33 *"to order, control, and keep clean"*: Schickel, *Disney Version*, p. 24.
    even more famous than Mickey Mouse: According to John Love, Ronald McDonald is the most widely recognized commercial character in the United States. Love, *Behind the Arches*, p. 222.
34 *"That was where I learned"*: Kroc, *Grinding It Out*, p. 17.
    "If you believe in it": Voice recording, Ray A. Kroc Museum.
35 *"When I saw it"*: Kroc, *Grinding It Out*, p. 71.
    "through the eyes of a salesman": Ibid., pp. 9–10, 72.
    $100,000 a year in profits: Love, *Behind the Arches*, p. 19.
    "This little fellow comes in": Voice recording, Ray A. Kroc Museum.
    "Dear Walt": Quoted in Leslie Doolittle, "McDonald's Plan Cooked Up Decades Ago," *Orlando Sentinel*, January 8, 1998.
    According to one account: See Boas and Chain, *Big Mac*, p. 25.
36 *"He was regarded as a strange duck"*: Kroc, *Grinding It Out*, p. 19.
    describes Walt Disney's efforts: See Watts, *Magic Kingdom*, pp. 164–74.
    "fun factory": Ibid., p. 167.
    "Hundreds of young people were being trained": Quoted ibid., p. 170.
37 *"Don't forget this"*: Quoted ibid., p. 223.
    "Look, it is ridiculous to call this an industry": Quoted in Boas and Chain, *Big Mac*, pp. 15–16.
    gave $250,000 to President Nixon's reelection campaign: For varying interpretations of Kroc's donation, see Kroc, *Grinding It Out*, p. 191–2; Love, *Behind the Arches*, pp. 357–9; Boas and Chain, *Big Mac*, pp. 198–206; and Luxenberg, *Roadside Empires*, pp. 246–48.
    "sons of bitches": Kroc, *Grinding It Out*, p. 191.
38 *more than 90 percent of his studio's output*: See Watts, *Magic Kingdom*, p. 235.
39 *an early and enthusiastic member of the Nazi Party*: For von Braun's political affiliations, the conditions at Dora-Nordhausen, and the American recruitment of Nazi scientists, I have relied on Tom Bower, *The Paperclip Conspiracy: The Hunt for Nazi Scientists* (Boston: Little, Brown, 1987); Linda Hunt, *Secret Agenda: The United States Government, Nazi Scientists, and Project Paperclip, 1945 to 1990* (New York: St. Martin's Press, 1991); Michael J. Neufeld, *The Rocket and the Reich: Peenemünde and the Coming of the Ballistic Missile Era* (New York: Free Press, 1995); and Dennis Piszkiewicz, *Wernher von Braun: The Man Who Sold the Moon* (Westport, Conn.: Praeger, 1998).

39 *von Braun was giving orders to Disney animators:* For a brief account of Disney and von Braun, see the chapter "Disneyland" in Piszkiewicz, *von Braun*, pp. 83–91.

another key Tomorrowland adviser: I stumbled upon Heinz Haber's unusual career path while doing research on another project. Haber was a protégé of Dr. Hubertus Strughold, the director of the Luftwaffe Institute for Aviation Medicine. Strughold later became chief scientist at the U.S. Air Force's Aerospace Medical Division, had a U.S. Air Force library named after him, and was hailed as "the father of U.S. space medicine." I pieced together Heinz Haber's wartime behavior from the following: Otto Gauer and Heinz Haber, "Man Under Gravity-Free Conditions," in *German Aviation Medicine, World War II*, vol. 1 (Washington, D.C.: U.S. Air Force, 1950), pp. 641-43; Henry G. Armstrong, Heinz Haber, and Hubertus Strughold, "Aero Medical Problems of Space Travel" (panel meeting, School of Aviation Medicine), *Journal of Aviation Medicine*, December 1949; "Clinical Factors: USAF Aerospace Medicine," in Mae Mills Link, *Space Medicine in Project Mercury* (NASA SP-4003, 1965); "Beginnings of Space Medicine," "Zero G," and "Multiple G," in Loyds Swenson, Jr., James M. Grimwood, and Charles C. Alexander, *This New Ocean: A History of Project Mercury* (NASA SP-4201, 1966); "History of Research in Subgravity and Zero-G at the Air Force Missile Development Center 1948–1958," in *History of Research in Space Biology and Biodynamics at the US Air Force Missile Development Center, Holloman Air Force Base, New Mexico, 1946–1958* (Historical Division, Air Force Missile Development Center, Holloman Air Force Base).

the Luftwaffe Institute for Aviation Medicine: Accounts of the concentration camp experiments administered by the Luftwaffe can be found in Bower, *Paperclip Conspiracy*, pp. 214–32, and Hunt, *Secret Agenda*, pp. 78–93.

When the Eisenhower administration asked Walt Disney: See Mark Langer, "Disney's Atomic Fleet," *Animation World Magazine*, April 1998.

a popular children's book: Heinz Haber, *The Walt Disney Story of Our Friend the Atom* (New York: Simon and Schuster, 1956).

40 *Disney had signed seventy licensing deals:* See Watts, *Magic Kingdom*, pp. 161–62.

41 *"A child who loves our TV commercials":* Kroc, *Grinding It Out*, p. 114.

An ad agency designed the outfit: For the story of Willard Scott and Ronald McDonald, see Love, *Behind the Arches*, pp. 218–22, 244–45.

"If they were drowning to death": Quoted in Penny Moser, "The McDonald's Mystique," *Fortune*, July 4, 1988.

42 *park, tentatively called Western World:* For Kroc's amusement park schemes, see Love, *Behind the Arches*, pp. 411–13.

43 *"the decade of the child consumer":* McNeal, *Kids as Customers*, p. 6.

as early as the age of two: Cited in "Brand Aware," *Children's Business*, June 2000.

children often recognize a brand logo: See "Brand Consciousness," *IFF on Kids: Kid Focus*, no. 3.

a 1991 study . . . found: Paul Fischer et al., "Brand Logo Recognition by Children Aged 3 to 6 Years: Mickey Mouse and Old Joe the Camel," *Journal of the American Medical Association*, December 11, 1991.

43 *Another study found:* See Judann Dagnoli, "JAMA Lights New Fire Under Camel's Ads," *Advertising Age,* December 16, 1991.

the CME KidCom Ad Traction Study II: Cited in "Market Research Ages 6–17: Talking Chihuahua Strikes Chord with Kids," *Selling to Kids,* February 3, 1999.

"It's not just getting kids to whine": Quoted in "Market Research: The Old Nagging Game Can Pay off for Marketers," *Selling to Kids,* April 15, 1998.

Vance Packard described children as "surrogate salesmen": See Boas and Chain, *Big Mac,* p. 127; Vance Packard, *The Hidden Persuaders* (New York: D. McKay, 1957), pp. 158–61.

44 *"children's requesting styles and appeals":* McNeal, *Kids as Customers,* pp. 72–75.

"Kid Kustomers": Ibid., p. 4.

"The key is getting children to see a firm": Ibid., p. 98.

learn about their tastes: For a sense of the techniques now being used by marketers, see Tom McGee, "Getting Inside Kids' Heads," *American Demographics,* January 1997.

45 *roughly 80 percent of children's dreams:* Cited in Acuff, *What Kids Buy and Why,* pp. 45–46.

"Marketing messages sent through a club": McNeal, *Kids As Customers,* p. 175.

increased the sales of children's meals: Cited in Karen Benezra, "Keeping Burger King on a Roll," *Brandweek,* January 15, 1996.

a federal investigation of Web sites aimed at children: Cited in "Children's Online Privacy Proposed Rule Issued by FTC," press release, Federal Trade Commission, April 20, 1999.

"the ultimate authority in everything": Quoted in "Is Your Kid Caught Up in the Web?" *Consumer Reports,* May 1997.

The site encouraged kids: See Matthew McAllester, "Life in Cyberspace: What's McDonald's Doing with Kids' E-mail Responses?" *Newsday,* July 20, 1997.

46 *"They cannot protect themselves":* Quoted in Linda E. Demkovich, "Pulling the Sweet Tooth of Children's TV Advertising," *National Journal,* January 7, 1978.

"We are delighted by the FTC's reasonable recommendation": Quoted in A. O. Sulzberger, Jr., "FTC Staff Urges End to Child-TV Ad Study," *New York Times,* April 3, 1981.

about 80 percent of all television viewing by kids: Cited in Steve McClellan and Richard Tedesco, "Children's TV Market May Be Played Out," *Broadcasting & Cable,* March 1, 1999.

about twenty-one hours a week: Cited in "Policy Statement: Media Education," American Academy of Pediatrics, August 1999.

more time watching television than doing: Cited in "Policy Statement: Children, Adolescents, and Television," American Academy of Pediatrics, October 1995.

more than thirty thousand TV commercials: Cited in Mary C. Martin, "Children's Understanding of the Intent of Advertising: A Meta-Analysis," *Journal of Public Policy & Marketing,* Fall 1997

one-quarter of American children: Cited in Lisa Jennings, "Baby, Hand Me the Remote," *Scripps Howard News Service,* October 13, 1999.

47 *annually spend about $3 billion on television:* Interview with Lynn Fava, Competitive Media Reporting.

47 *now operates more than eight thousand playgrounds . . . Burger King has more than two thousand:* Cited in "Fast Food and Playgrounds: A Natural Combination," promotional material, Playlandservices, Inc.

"Playlands bring in children": Ibid.

about 90 percent of American children: Cited in Rod Taylor, "The Beanie Factor," *Brandweek,* June 16, 1997.

"But when it gets down to brass tacks": Sam Bradley and Betsey Spethmann, "Subway's Kid Pack: The Ties That Sell," *Brandweek,* October 10, 1994.

According to a publication called Tomart's*:* Meredith Williams, *Tomart's Price Guide to McDonald's Happy Meal Collectibles* (Dayton, Ohio: Tomart Publications, 1995).

one of the most successful promotions: The story of McDonald's Teenie Beanie Baby promotion can be found in Taylor, "The Beanie Factor."

48 *"We see this as a great opportunity":* Quoted in "McDonald's Launches Second Animated Video in Series Starring Ronald McDonald," press release, McDonald's Corporation, January 21, 1999.

Ball told the Hollywood Reporter: See T. L. Stanley, *Hollywood Reporter,* May 26, 1998.

49 *Some industry observers thought Disney:* See Thomas R. King, "Mickey May Be the Big Winner in Disney-McDonald's Alliance," *Wall Street Journal,* May 24, 1996.

the McDonald's Corporation had turned away offers: See Monci Jo Williams, "McDonald's Refuses to Plateau," *Fortune,* November 12, 1984.

"A lot of people can't get used to the fact": Quoted in James Bates, "You Want First-Run Features with Those Fries?" *Newsday,* May 11, 1997.

51 *gaining it just $37,500 a year:* Cited in Eric Dexheimer, "Class Warfare," *Denver Westword,* February 6, 1997.

For $12,000, a company got . . . Within a year, DeRose had nearly tripled: Ibid.

52 *"Discover your own river of revenue":* Quoted in Molnar, "Sponsored Schools and Commercialized Classrooms," p. 28.

"if it weren't for the acute need for funds": Quoted in Brian McTaggart, "Selling Our Schools," *Houston Chronicle,* August 10, 1997.

53 *"You've reached Grapevine-Colleyville":* Quoted in G. Chambers Williams III, "Fliers May Be Seeing Ads on Roofs of Grapevine-Colleyville Schools," *Fort Worth Star-Telegram,* March 4, 1997.

Dan DeRose tells reporters: See "The Art of the Deal," *Food Management,* February 1998.

"In Kansas City they were getting 67 cents a kid": Quoted in Constance L. Hays, "Today's Lesson: Soda Rights," *New York Times,* May 21, 1999.

"There are critics to penicillin": Quoted in Tracy Correa, "Campus Market: Corporate America Is Coming to Fresno-Area Schools with Ads That Target Children and Their Parents," *Fresno Bee,* November 9, 1998.

Thus far, DeRose has been responsible for: Voice mail from Dan DeRose.

control 90.3 percent of the U.S. market: Cited in G. Pascal Zachary, "Let's Play Oligopoly! Why Giants Like Having Other Giants Around," *Wall Street Journal,* March 8, 1999.

53 *about fifty-six gallons per person:* Cited in Greg W. Prince, "The Year of Living Dangerously," *Beverage World,* March 15, 2000.

Coca-Cola has set itself the goal: See Dean Foust, "Man on the Spot: Nowadays Things Go Tougher at Coke," *Business Week,* May 3, 1999.

"Influencing elementary school students": Kent Steinriede, "Sponsorship scorecard 1999," *Beverage Industry,* January 1999.

54 *"We at McDonald's are thankful":* Quoted in Ernest Holsendorph, "Keeping McDonald's Out in Front: 'Gas' Is No Problem; Chicken May Be Served," *New York Times,* December 30, 1973.

McDonald's sells more Coca-Cola: Cited in "Welcome to McDonald's."

about $4.25 a gallon: According to *Business Week,* Burger King annually pays Coke $170 million for 40 million gallons of syrup. That works out to a cost of about $4.25 a gallon — or 3.3 cents an ounce. It is safe to assume that McDonald's, an even larger customer, buys its syrup at a price that is equivalent, if not lower. See Foust, "Man on the Spot."

A medium Coke that sells for $1.29: The standard soft drink ratio is one part syrup to five parts carbonated water. A small Coke at McDonald's contains about 2.6 ounces of syrup; a medium Coke, about 3.5 ounces. For the composition of soft drinks, see Lauren Curtis, "Pop Art," *Food Product Design,* January 1998.

55 *A 1997 study:* Cited in Jacobson, "Liquid Candy," p. 10.

"It's our responsibility to make it clear": Quoted in Martha Groves, "Serving Kids . . . Up to Marketers," *Los Angeles Times,* July 14, 1999.

The principal said Cameron could have been suspended: See Frank Swoboda, "Pepsi Prank Fizzles at School's Coke Day," *Washington Post,* March 26, 1998.

"I don't consider this a prank": Quoted ibid.

"the earth could benefit rather than be harmed": Quoted in Consumers Union, "Captive Kids."

56 *About twenty million elementary school students:* Cited in "Pizza Hut Book It! Awards $50,000 to Elementary Schools," *PR Newswire,* June 6, 2000.

The group claims that its publications: See Consumers Union, "Captive Kids."

"Now you can enter the classroom": Quoted in Alex Molnar, "Advertising in the Classroom," *San Diego Union-Tribune,* March 10, 1993.

"Through these materials, your product": Quoted in Consumers Union, "Captive Kids."

eight million of the nation's middle, junior, and high school: Cited in "Prepared Testimony of Ralph Nader before the Senate Committee on Health, Education, Labor, and Pensions," *Federal New Service,* May 20, 1999.

At least twenty school districts: Cited in Diane Brockett, "School Cafeterias Selling Brand-Name Junk Food," *Education Digest,* October 1, 1998.

The American School Food Service Association estimates: Cited in Dan Morse, "School Cafeterias are Enrolling as Fast-Food Franchisees," *Wall Street Journal,* July 28, 1998.

"We try to be more like the fast food places": Quoted in Janet Bingham, "Corporate Curriculum: And Now a Word, Lesson, Lunch, from a Sponsor," *Denver Post,* February 22, 1998.

57 *The Coca-Cola deal that DD Marketing negotiated:* For the story of District 11's

shortfall, see Cara DeGette, "The Real Thing: Corporate Welfare Comes to the Classroom," *Colorado Springs Independent,* November 25–December 1, 1998.

3. Behind the Counter

For the history of the Pikes Peak region, I relied on Carl Ubbelohde, Maxine Benson, and Duane A. Smith, *A Colorado History* (Boulder, Colo.: Pruett Publishing, 1995); Patricia Farris Skolout, *Colorado Springs History A to Z* (Colorado Springs: Patricia Farris Skolout, 1992); Judith Reid Finley, *Time Capsule 1900: Colorado Springs a Century Ago* (Colorado Springs: Pastword Publishing, 1998); and two entertaining books by Marshall Sprague, *Money Mountain: The Story of Cripple Creek Gold* (Lincoln: University of Nebraska Press, 1979), and *Newport in the Rockies: The Life and Good Times of Colorado Springs* (Athens, Ohio: Swallow Press, 1987). Markusen et al., *The Rise of the Gunbelt,* contains an excellent chapter entitled "Space Mountain: Generals and Boosters Build Colorado Springs," pp. 174–210.

For the driving forces behind sprawl, I relied principally on: F. Caid Benfield, Matthew D. Raimi, Donald D. T. Chen, *Once There Were Greenfields: How Urban Sprawl Is Undermining America's Environment, Economy, and Social Fabric* (Washington, D.C.: National Resources Defense Council, 1999); James Howard Kunstler, *The Geography of Nowhere: The Rise and Decline of America's Man-Made Landscape* (New York: Touchstone, 1994); Philip Langdon, *A Better Place to Live: Reshaping the American Suburb* (Amherst: University of Massachusetts Press, 1994). John C. Melaniphy's *Restaurant and Fast Food Site Selection* (New York: John Wiley & Sons, 1992) helped me see how the economic needs of the fast food chains have directly contributed to the nationwide spread of sprawl. Two site selection experts explained how the latest geographic information systems combine satellite data, census data, and market research to determine the best location for a new fast food restaurant: Libby Duane, the marketing director at SRC LLC, whose "Site Analyzer" is used by Church's Chicken and Popeye's, among other chains; and Elliott Olson, the chairman of the Dakota Worldwide Corporation, which distributes a PC version of the Quintillion software developed by McDonald's. Mr. Olson was kind enough to send me a demonstration disk of Quintillion.

Space does not permit me to list all of the people whom I interviewed about the economic, cultural, and social life of Colorado Springs today. Some people, however, were especially helpful or insightful: guidance counselors Cheryl Griesinger at Cheyenne Mountain High School, Mike Foreman and Nancy Martinez at Manitou Springs High School, Jane Trogdon at Harrison High School, and Chris Christian at Palmer High School; Elisa, Carlos, and Cynthia Zamot; the architect Morey Bean; Richard Conway of Conway's Red Top Restaurant; Richard and Judy Noyes at the Chinook Bookshop; Rocky Scott, president of the Greater Colorado Springs Economic Development Corporation; Cara DeGette, news editor of the *Colorado Springs Independent;* Amy D. Haimerl, editor of the *Colorado Springs Business Journal;* Major Mike Birmingham at the U.S. Space Command; Joe Brady, co-owner of The Hide & Seek; Toast and Marcea, proprietors of the Holey Rollers Tattoo Parlor; and the lovely elderly woman who gave me a guided tour of the Focus on the Family headquarters complex, whose name I will not mention. For a sense of James Dobson's philosophy, I read his child-rearing guide *The New Dare to Discipline* (Wheaton, Ill.: Tyndale House Publishers, 1992) and Gil Alexander-Moegerle, *James Dobson's War on America* (Amherst, N.Y.: Prometheus Books, 1997).

Robert Emerson's *The New Economics of Fast Food* has useful material on the labor costs and policies of the major chains, as do John Love's *Behind the Arches* and *Big Mac*, by Max Boas and Steve Chain. Robin Leidner and Ester Reiter are sociologists who worked at chain restaurants in order to write about the nature of such employment. Reiter's *Making Fast Food: From the Frying Pan into the Fryer* (Montreal: McGill–Queen's University Press, 1991) focuses on Burger King, while Leidner's *Fast Food, Fast Talk: Service Work and the Routinization of Everyday Life* (Berkeley: University of California Press, 1993) looks at McDonald's. *Quick Service that Sells!: The Art of Profitable Hospitality for Quick-Service Restaurants* (Denver: Pencom International, 1997), written by Phil "Zoom" Roberts and Christopher O'Donnell, reveals some motivational tricks of the trade.

Working in the Service Society, edited by Lynn Macdonald and Carmen Sirianni, suggests how the labor policies of the fast food industry are now being adopted throughout the American economy. Alan B. Krueger, a professor of economics and public affairs at Princeton University, outlined for me some of his research on the fast food industry and the minimum wage. I also found the book that he wrote with David Card, *Myth and Measurement: The New Economics of the Minimum Wage* (Princeton: Princeton University Press, 1995), to be useful. A recent study by the USDA Economic Research Service cogently refutes the argument that higher wages will harm the fast food industry. The study, written by Chinkook Lee and Brian O'Roark, is titled "The Impact of Minimum Wage Increases on Food and Kindred Products Prices: An Analysis of Price Pass-Through" (Washington, D.C.: Food and Rural Economics Division, USDA Economic Research Service, Technical Bulletin No. 1877, July 1999). A report by the Institute of Medicine's Committee on the Health and Safety Implications of Child Labor — *Protecting Youth at Work: Health, Safety, and Development of Working Children and Adolescents in the United States* (Washington, D.C.: National Academy Press, 1998) — outlines the social consequences of a teenage workforce. Many of its conclusions were foreshadowed by a National Safe Workplace Institute report, *Sacrificing America's Youth: The Problem of Child Labor and the Response of Government* (Chicago: National Safe Workplace Institute, 1992). Two other reports were useful: Janice Windau, Eric Sygnatur, and Guy Toscano, "Profile of Work Injuries Incurred by Young Workers," *Monthly Labor Review*, June 1, 1999; and *Report on the Youth Labor Force* (Washington, D.C., U.S. Department of Labor, June 2000). For the section on fast food crime, I interviewed law enforcement officers in Colorado Springs, Los Angeles, and Omaha — as well as Joseph A. Kinney, president of the National Safe Workplace Institute, and Jerald Greenberg, an expert on workplace theft and a professor of ethics and business management at the University of Ohio.

Page

61 *About a third of the city's inhabitants:* Cited in "Colorado Springs Facts," Colorado Springs Chamber of Commerce.

the population of the Colorado Springs metropolitan area: See "Colorado Springs Fact Sheet," Greater Colorado Springs Economic Development Corporation,

June 1998; and "Metropolitan Area Population Estimates for July 1, 1998, and Population Change for April 1990 to July 1998," U.S. Census Bureau, September 30, 1999.

61 *Denver's population is about four times larger:* See "Metropolitan Area Population Estimates," and Terry Cotten, "Springs Council Adopts Budget," *Denver Post,* November 29, 1999.

about one-fifth of the city's housing sat vacant: Cited in Markusen et al., *Rise of the Gunbelt,* p. 178.

a direct capital investment of $30 million: Ibid., p. 178.

62 *nearly half the jobs in Colorado Springs:* Interview with Rocky Scott, president of the Greater Colorado Springs Economic Development Corporation.

"In Your Face from Outer Space": The unit is the U.S. Air Force Space Warfare Center.

the rate of union membership: Cited in "Colorado Springs: The Pikes Peak Region," Greater Colorado Springs Development Agency, 1997.

Hoiles was politically conservative: See James S. Granelli, "The Fight for Freedom Newspapers," *Los Angeles Times,* November 17, 1985.

advocates spanking disobedient children: See Dobson, *The New Dare to Discipline,* pp. 1–7, 50, 64.

generates much larger annual revenues: See Alexander-Moegerle, *Dobson's War on America,* p. 13.

64 *more staunchly Republican than the American South:* See Valerie Richardson, "Population Flow Upends West's Politics," *Washington Times,* February 28, 1999.

approximately one million people: Cited in William H. Frey, "Immigrant and Native Migrant Magnets," *American Demographics,* November 1996. See also William G. Deming, "A decade of economic change and population shifts in U.S. regions," *Monthly Labor Review,* November 1996.

"the new white flight": William H. Frey, "The New White Flight," *American Demographics,* April 1994.

about 100,000 people: Cited in Donald Blount, "Colorado's Pace of Growth Likely to Taper Off in 1999," *Denver Post,* February 7, 1999.

ranked forty-ninth in the nation: The ranking, by *Education Week* magazine in 1998, took into account the state's per capita spending on schools, cost of living, and personal income. Cited in Janet Bingham, "Schools Get Lower Marks," *Denver Post,* January 8, 1999.

three times the number of cars: Cited in Terri Cotten, "Colorado Springs: City Grapples with Gridlock," *Denver Post,* May 23, 1999.

annual surplus of about $700 million: Cited in Burt Hubbard, "Tax Cut Feeding Frenzy," *Rocky Mountain News,* April 18, 1999.

one-third of the surface area: See White, *It's Your Misfortune,* p. 550.

65 *the largest private employer in the state today:* Cited in "1998 Menu of Facts," Colorado Restaurant Association.

restaurant industry has grown much faster than the population: To determine the rate of growth, I counted the number of restaurants listed in the Colorado Springs Yellow Pages in 1967 and 1997.

66 *more than 70 percent of fast food visits:* Cited in J. P. Donlon, "Quinlan Fries

Harder: Interview with McDonald's CEO Michael Quinlan," *Chief Executive,* January 11, 1998. See also Judith Waldrop, "Most Restaurant Meals Are Bought on Impulse," *American Demographics,* February 1994.

66 *Ray Kroc flew in a Cessna . . . McDonald's later used helicopters:* See Kroc, *Grinding It Out,* p. 176.

one of the world's leading purchasers of commercial satellite: Interview with Elliott Olson.

"spy on their customers": William Dunn, "Skycams Drain Floods, Save Lives, Sell Burgers," *American Demographics,* July 1992.

68 *two-thirds of the nation's fast food workers:* Cited in Robert W. Van Giezen, "Occupational Wages in the Fast Food Industry," *Monthly Labor Review,* August 1994; and Alan Liddle, "Diversity at Work: Teenagers," *Nation's Restaurant News,* May 24, 1999.

Business historian Alfred D. Chandler has argued: Alfred D. Chandler, Jr., *The Visible Hand: The Managerial Revolution in American Business* (Cambridge, Mass.: Belknap Press of Harvard University Press, 1977), pp. 241–42.

69 *The guacamole isn't made by workers:* See Joel Millman, "These Days, Mexico Serves as a Giant Offshore Kitchen," *Wall Street Journal,* January 19, 2000.

70 *"Smile with a greeting":* Quoted in Reiter, *Making Fast Food,* p. 85.

"When management determines exactly": Leidner, *Fast Food, Fast Talk,* p. 3.

English is now the second language: Cited in Rita Rousseau, "Employing the New America," *Restaurants and Institutions,* March 15, 1997.

71 *a 1999 conference on foodservice equipment:* The conference was COEX '99, the Twenty-sixth Annual Chain Operators Exchange. The panel was Breakout Session C: "Too Many Cooks . . . Cutting Labor Cost in the Kitchen." The participants were Larry Behm, vice president, restaurant systems engineering, Taco Bell Corporation; Dave Brewer, vice president, engineering KFC-Tricon; Jane Gannaway, vice president, restaurant planning, design and procurement, Hardee's; Jerry Sus, home office director, equipment systems engineering, McDonald's Corporation; and John Reckert, director of strategic operations and research & development, Burger King Corporation. The session was recorded by Convention Tapes International, Miami, Florida.

72 *an investigation by the U.S. Department of Labor:* Cited in L. M. Sixel, "Giving Tax Break a Second Chance; Credit to Hire Disadvantaged Returns," *Houston Chronicle,* October 16, 1996. See also Ben Wildavsky, "Taking Credit," *National Journal,* March 29, 1997.

as much as $385 million in subsidies: Cited in Sixel, "Giving Tax Break a Second Chance."

"They've got to crawl": Quoted ibid.

about 1 million migrant farm workers: See Schlosser, "In the Strawberry Fields."

73 *about 300 to 400 percent:* The lower figure is cited in Jennifer Waters, "R&I Executive of the Year: Robert Nugent," *Restaurants and Institutions,* July 1, 1998. The higher figure, remarkably, comes from Denise Fugo, treasurer of the National Restaurant Association, quoted in Lornet Turnbull, "Restaurants Feeding Off Fit Economy," February 23, 1999.

a higher proportion of its workers: Interview with Alan B. Krueger.

73 *the real value of the U.S. minimum wage:* See Krueger, *Myth and Measurement,* p. 6.

In the late 1990s, the real value: Cited in Aaron Bernstein, "A Perfect Time to Raise the Minimum Wage," *Business Week,* May 17, 1999.

a federal guest worker program: See Jerd Smith, "Undocumented Workers Enliven State's Economy, But at What Costs to Other Residents and Agencies?" *Rocky Mountain News,* April 18, 1999.

a 1997 survey in Nation's Restaurant News: Alan Liddle, "Demand Fuels Salary, Bonus Surge; Wages Still Lag," *Nation's Restaurant News,* August 18, 1997.

Increasing the federal minimum wage by a dollar: According to economists Chinkook Lee and Brian O'Roark, every fifty cent increase in the minimum wage leads to a 1 percent price increase at restaurants. A McDonald's hamburger costs 99 cents; a 2 percent increase in price is about 2 cents. See Lee and O'Roark, "Impact of Minimum Wage Increases."

Roughly 90 percent of the nation's fast food workers: Of the roughly fifty to sixty employees at a a typical McDonald's, only four or five are full-time, salaried managers. See Leidner, *Fast Food, Fast Talk,* p. 50–54.

74 *an average of thirty hours a week:* Cited in Robert W. Van Giezen, "Occupational Wages in the Fast-Food Restaurant Industry," *Monthly Labor Review,* August 1994.

earn about $23,000 a year: Cited in Liddle, "Demand Fuels Salary, Bonus Surge."

training in "transactional analysis": See Boas and Chain, *Big Mac,* pp. 91–93; Ben Wildavsky, "McJobs: Inside America's Largest Youth Training Program," *Policy Review,* Summer 1989.

75 *forced to clean restaurants . . . compensated with food:* See Gillian Flynn, "Pizza As Pay? Compensation Gets Too Creative," *Workforce,* August 1998.

As many as 16,000 current and former employees . . . a high school dropout named Regina Jones: See E. Scott Reckard, "Jury: Taco Bell Short-changed Its Employees," *Los Angeles Times,* April 9, 1997; Steve Miletich, "Taco Bell Is Found Guilty of Worker Abuses," *Seattle Post-Intelligencer,* April 9, 1997; Stephanie Armour, "One Woman's Story: More and More Workers Are Being Asked to Work Overtime Without Pay," *USA Today,* April 22, 1998.

the trait most valued: Reiter, *Making Fast Food,* p. 129.

76 *A "flying squad" of experienced managers:* See Love, *Behind the Arches,* pp. 394–95; Boas and Chain, *Big Mac,* pp. 94–112.

amid a bitter organizing drive in San Francisco: For the events in San Francisco, see Boas and Chain, *Big Mac,* pp. 104–12

77 *employed fifteen attorneys:* Cited in Bill Tieleman, "Did Somebody Say McUnion? Not If They Want to Keep Their McJob," *National Post,* March 29, 1999.

"one of the most anti-union companies on the planet": Quoted in Mike King, "McDonald's Workers Win the Union War But Lose Jobs," *Ottawa Citizen,* March 3, 1998.

a money-loser: See Mike King, "McDonald's to Go," *Montreal Gazette,* February 15, 1998.

77 *about 300 to 1:* Roughly three McDonald's closed per year in Canada during the early 1990s, while about eighty new ones annually opened. Cited in King, "McDonald's to Go."

"Did somebody say McUnion?": Tieleman, "McUnion?"

80 *Numerous studies have found:"* See *Protecting Youth at Work,* pp. 225–26.

Teenage boys who work longer hours: Ibid., p. 132.

"IT'S TIME FOR BRINGING IN THE GREEN!": The ad appeared in the *Colorado Springs Gazette* on March 20, 1999. My account of the working conditions at FutureCall is based on conversations with former employees. For more on FutureCall, see Jeremy Simon, "Telemarketing," *Colorado Springs Gazette,* February 15, 1999.

82 *George, a former Taco Bell employee:* Whenever a person is identified only by a first name in this book, the name is a pseudonym. All of the people described really exist; none is a composite.

83 *The injury rate of teenage workers:* Cited in *Protecting Youth at Work,* p. 4.

about 200,000 are injured on the job: Ibid., p. 68.

Roughly four or five fast food workers are now murdered . . . more restaurant workers were murdered on the job: In 1998, the most recent year for which figures are available, fifty-two police officers and detectives were murdered on the job — and sixty-nine restaurant workers were murdered on the job, mainly during robberies. The vast majority of restaurant robberies occur at fast food restaurants, because they are open late, staffed by teenagers, full of cash, and convenient. The homicide figures are cited in Eric F. Sygnatur and Guy A. Toscano, "Work-Related Homicides: The Facts," *Compensation and Working Conditions,* Spring 2000.

more attractive to armed robbers than convenience stores: See Laurie Grossman, "Easy Marks: Fast-Food Industry is Slow to Take Action Against Growing Crime," *Wall Street Journal,* September 22, 1994; Kerry Lydon, "Prime Crime Targets; Highly Publicized Restaurant Crimes Have Drawn Both Criminal and Customer Attention to Security Lapses," *Restaurants and Institutions,* June 15, 1995; Milford Prewitt, Naomi R. Kooker, Alan J. Liddle, and Robin Lee Allen, "Taking Aim at Crime: Barbaric to Bizarre, Crime Robs Operators' Peace of Mind, Profits," *Nation's Restaurant News,* May 22, 2000.

at 7–Eleven stores the average robbery: Cited in Scot Lins and Rosemary J. Erickson, "Stores Learn to Inconvenience Robbers: 7–Eleven Shares Many of Its Robbery Deterrence Strategies," *Security Management,* November 1998.

84 *about two-thirds of the robberies at fast food restaurants:* Cited in Grossman, "Easy Marks"; and Lydon, "Prime Crime Targets."

about half of all restaurant workers: Cited in Ed Rubinstein, "High-Tech Systems Look to Head Off Restaurant Shrinkage," *Nation's Restaurant News,* January 11, 1999.

The typical employee stole about $218: Cited in "NCS Reports Employee Theft Doubled in Restaurant/Fast Food Industry," press release, NCS and National Food Service Security Council, July 9, 1999.

"It may be common sense": Interview with Jerald Greenberg.

OSHA was prompted: See Ralph Vartabedian, "Big Business, Big Bucks: The Rising Tide of Corporate Political Donations," *Los Angeles Times*, September 23, 1997; Joan Oleck, "Who's Afraid of OSHA?" *Restaurant Business*, February 10, 1995.

84 *OSHA recommended:* See "Recommendations for Workplace Violence Prevention Programs in Late-Night Retail Establishments," U.S. Department of Labor, OSHA 3153, 1998

85 *"Who would oppose putting out guidelines":* Quoted in Vartabedian, "Big Business."

"potentially damaging" robbery statistics: Quoted in Jack Hayes, "Industry Execs Nix OSHA Guidelines at 'Security Summit,'" *Nation's Restaurant News*, May 19, 1997.

"No other American industry": Interview with Joseph A. Kinney.

86 *Hundreds of fast food restaurants are robbed:* This is my own estimate. The Los Angeles Police Department is one law enforcement agency that does track restaurant robberies, of which the vast majority are fast food robberies. The population of Los Angeles is about one-eightieth the total U.S. population. In 1998, 520 L.A. restaurants were robbed. Even if you assume, conservatively, that L.A. restaurants are four times more likely to be robbed than restaurants elsewhere in the country, that still leaves an estimated 10,000 U.S. restaurant robberies every year. The actual number is most likely higher. The FBI does compile statistics on convenience store robberies, and during the mid-1990s about 28,000 of them were robbed every year (more than 500 a week). According to the LAPD's 1998 robbery statistics, restaurants were robbed nearly twice as often as minimarts. See "Restaurant Robberies in L.A. from 01/01/98 to 12/31/98" and "Mini-Mart Robberies in L.A. from 01/01/98 to 12/31/98," Los Angeles Police Department; and Greg Warchoi, "Workplace Violence, 1992–96," Bureau of Labor Statistics Special Report, July 1998.

88 *"Cynics need to be in some other industry":* The speeches and panel discussions at the Thirty-eighth Annual Multi-Unit Foodserver Operator Conference were tape-recorded by the Sound of Knowledge, Inc., San Diego, California.

4. Success

Mahmood A. Khan's *Restaurant Franchising* (New York: Van Nostrand Reinhold, 1992) provides a straightforward examination of the subject, much like a textbook. Stan Luxenberg's *Roadside Empires* is less thorough but much more interesting, examining the franchise boom in the context of American postwar culture. *Big Mac*, by Max Boas and Steven Chain, John Love's *Behind the Arches*, and Ray Kroc's *Grinding It Out* also contain good material on the early days of franchising in the fast food industry. A number of articles published in academic journals helped me understand some of franchising's finer details: Francine Lafontaine, "Pricing Decisions in Franchised Chains: A Look at the Restaurant and Fast-Food Industry," Working Paper 5247, National Bureau of Economic Research, September 1995; Scott A. Shane, "Hybrid Organizational Arrangements and their Implications for Firm Growth and Survival: A Study of New Franchisors," *Academy of Management Journal*, February 1996; H. G.

Parsa, "Franchisee-Franchisor Relationships in Quick-Service-Restaurant Systems," *Cornell Hotel & Restaurant Administration Quarterly*, June 1996; Scott A. Shane and Chester Spell, "Factors for New Franchise Success," *Sloan Management Review*, March 22, 1998; Robert W. Emerson, "Franchise Terminations: Legal Rights and Practical Effects When Franchisees Claim the Franchisor Discriminates," *American Business Law Journal*, June 22, 1998. The *Franchise Opportunities Guide*, published annually by the International Franchise Association, gives a rosy view of "the success story of the 1990s." *The Franchise Fraud: How to Protect Yourself Before and After You Invest* (New York: John Wiley & Sons, 1994), by Robert L. Purvin, Jr., regards the promises of franchisors with more suspicion. Mr. Purvin — an attorney who serves as chairman of the board of trustees of the American Association of Franchisees and Dealers — helped to ensure the accuracy of my legal analysis. Susan Kezios, president of the American Franchisee Association, spoke with me at length about the legislative reforms being sought by her organization. Richard Adams, the president of Consortium Members, Inc., an alliance of disgruntled McDonald's franchisees, described some of the franchising practices of the world's largest fast food chain. Rieva Lesonsky, the editorial director of *Entrepreneur* magazine (which annually publishes the "Franchise 500: Best Franchises to Start Now!") gave me a much brighter view of the industry. Peter Lowe took time from his hectic schedule to discuss success. In addition to Dave Feamster, I interviewed a number of other fast food franchisees who shall remain unnamed. I am grateful to Feamster not only for giving me free rein at his restaurant, but also for allowing me to spend an evening delivering Little Caesars pizzas in Pueblo.

Page

94 *"Instead of the company paying the salesmen"*: Luxenberg, *Roadside Empires*, p. 13.

95 *often earned more money than the company's founder*: See Emerson, *Economics of Fast Food*, p. 59; Love, *Behind the Arches*, pp. 171–75.

"common sense": Kroc, *Grinding It Out*, p. 111.

"any unusual aptitude or intellect": Ibid., p. 111.

96 *"We are not basically in the food business"*: Quoted in Love, *Behind the Arches*, p. 199. See also Kroc, *Grinding It Out*, p. 109.

more than $180 million a year: By 1998, the year of Richard McDonald's death, the annual system-wide sales of McDonald's exceeded $36 billion. Cited in "The Annual," McDonald's Corporation 1998 Annual Report.

"grinding it out": Kroc, *Grinding It Out*, p. 123.

97 *"Eventually I opened a McDonald's"*: Ibid., p. 123.

The distinctive architecture of each chain: For the use of chain architecture as "packaging" and Louis Cheskin's advice to McDonald's, see Thomas Hines, *The Total Package: The Evolution and Secret Meanings of Boxes, Bottles, Cans, and Tubes* (New York: Little, Brown, 1995), pp. 121–24.

98 *"mother McDonald's breasts"*: Quoted in "Brand Iconography: The Secret to Creating Lasting Brands?" *Brand Strategy*, February 20, 1999.

an IFA survey claimed that 92 percent: Cited in Dan Morse and Jeffrey A. Tannenbaum, "Poll on High Success Rate for Franchises Raises Eyebrows," *Wall Street Journal*, March 17, 1998. For the results of a similar, equally dubious IFA poll, see

Joan Oleck, "The Numbers Game: Retail Franchise Failure Rates," *Restaurant Business*, June 10, 1993.

98 *38.1 percent of new franchised businesses:* Cited in testimony of Dr. Timothy Bates to the Subcommittee on Commercial and Administrative Law, Judiciary Committee, U.S. House of Representatives, June 24, 1999.

According to another study: Despite the high failure rate, the study's author, Scott A. Shane, believes that franchising is still the best way to expand a company quickly, though the financial risks are often understated. See Scott A. Shane, "Hybrid Organizational Arrangements and Their Implications for Firm Growth and Survival: A Study of New Franchisors," *Academy of Management Journal*, February 1996.

"In short": Testimony of Dr. Timothy Bates.

99 *Ralston-Purina once terminated:* See Boas and Chain, *Big Mac*, pp. 162–63.

100 *more legal disputes with franchisees:* Cited in Richard Behar, "Why Subway Is 'The Biggest Problem in Franchising,'" *Fortune*, March 16, 1998.

the "worst" franchise in America: Quoted in Jennifer Lanthier, "Subway Bites," *Financial Post*, November 25, 1995. For other accounts of Subway's questionable business practices, see Barbara Marsh, "Franchise Realities: Sandwich Shop Chain Surges, but to Run One Can Take Heroic Effort," *Wall Street Journal*, September 16, 1992; Jeffrey A. Tannenbaum, "Right to Retake Subway Shops Spurs Outcry," *Wall Street Journal*, February 2, 1995.

"Subway is the biggest problem in franchising": Quoted in Behar, "Subway."

"almost as geared to selling franchises": Lanthier, "Subway Bites."

A top Subway executive has acknowledged: See Behar, "Subway."

101 *30 to 50 percent of Subway's new franchisees:* Cited ibid.

Coble's bill would for the first time: For a detailed analysis of the legislation and strong criticism of its proposals, see Harold Brown, "The Proposed Federal Legislation in 1999," *New York Law Journal*, January 28, 1999; Rochelle B. Spandorf, "Federal Regulating Legislation," *Franchising Business and Law Alert*, November 1999.

"We are not seeking to penalize anyone": Testimony of Howard Coble to the Subcommittee on Commercial and Administrative Law, House Judiciary Committee, June 29, 1999.

"whiny butts": For this quote and Ireland's views on franchise reform, see Kirk Victor, "Franchising Fracas," *National Journal*, September 26, 1992; Deirdre Shesgreen, "Franchisees Seek Protection on Hill," *Legal Times*, January 4, 1999.

"free enterprise contract negotiations": Quoted in "Small Business Franchise Partnerships Feared Endangered if Federal Government Muscles In," *PR Newswire*, July 1, 1999.

"Small businesses and franchising succeed": Quoted ibid.

102 *A 1981 study by the General Accounting Office:* For the GAO study and the congressional investigation that prompted it, see Luxenberg, *Roadside Empires*, pp. 256–59.

The chain was "experimenting": Quoted ibid., p. 258.

a recent study by the Heritage Foundation: See Scott A. Hodge, "For Big Franchisers, Money to Go: Is the SBA Dispensing Corporate Welfare?" *Washington Post*, November 30, 1997.

5. Why the Fries Taste Good

Food: A Culinary History (New York: Columbia University Press, 1999), edited by Jean-Louis Flandrin and Massimo Montanari, traces the cultural and technological changes in food preparation from prehistoric campfires to the kitchens at McDonald's. A good account of the history of American food processing can be found in John M. Connor and William A. Schiek, *Food Processing: An Industrial Powerhouse in Transition* (New York: John Wiley & Sons, 1997). Harvey Levenstein's *Paradox of Plenty: A Social History of Eating in Modern America* (New York: Oxford University Press, 1993) has a fine chapter on the implications of postwar advances in food processing. For consolidation in the food processing industry and its effects on American farmers, I learned a great deal from the following sources: Charles R. Handy and Alden C. Manchester, "Structure and Performance of the Food System Beyond the Farm Gate," Commodities Economics Division White Paper, USDA Economic Research Service, April 1990; Alden C. Manchester, "The Transformation of U.S. Food Marketing," in *Food and Agricultural Markets: The Quiet Revolution,* edited by Lyle P. Schertz and Lynn M. Daff (Washington, D.C.: National Planning Association, 1994); *Concentration in Agriculture, A Report of the USDA Advisory Committee on Agricultural Concentration* (Washington, D.C.: USDA Agricultural Marketing Service, June 1996); *A Time to Act: Report of the USDA National Commission on Small Farms* (Washington, D.C.: United States Department of Agriculture, 1998); and William Heffernan, "Consolidation in the Food and Agriculture System," Report to the National Farmers Union, February 5, 1999. A telephone interview, extending for hours, with J. R. Simplot provided much information on the details of his life and the origins of the potato industry in Idaho. Simplot was blunt, charismatic, entertaining, and seemingly tireless. Fred Zerza, the vice president for public and government relations at the J. R. Simplot Company, helped confirm the accuracy of Simplot's remarks. I also relied on "Origins of the J. R. Simplot Company," J. R. Simplot Company, 1997; and James W. Davis, *Aristocrat in Burlap: A History of the Potato in Idaho* (Boise: Idaho Potato Commission, 1992). Paul Patterson, an extension professor of agricultural economics at the University of Idaho, graciously explained to me how potatoes are grown, processed, and sold today. Bert Moulton, at the Potato Growers of Idaho, gave me a sense of the challenges that farmers in his state must now confront. I am grateful to Ben Strand, at the Simplot Food Group, and Bud Mandeville, at Lamb Weston, for giving me tours of their french fry facilities.

The reference books on flavor technology were a pleasure to read; they reminded me of medieval texts on the black arts. Among the works I consulted were *Fenaroli's Handbook of Flavor Ingredients,* vol. 2 (Ann Arbor, Mich.: CRC Press, 1995); Henry B. Heath, *Source Book of Flavors* (Westport, Conn.: Avi Publishing, 1981); Martin S. Peterson and Arnold H. Johnson, *Encyclopedia of Food Science* (Westport, Conn.: Avi Publishing, 1978); Y. H. Hui, *Encyclopedia of Food Science and Technology,* vol. 2 (New York: John Wiley & Sons, 1992); Carl W. Hall, A. W. Farrall, and A. L. Rippen, *Encyclopedia of Food Engineering* (Westport, Conn.: Avi Publishing, 1986); *Flavor Science: Sensible Principles and Techniques,* edited by Terry E. Acree and Roy Teranishi (Washington, D.C.: American Chemical Scoiety, 1993); *Biotechnology for Improved Foods and Flavors,* edited by Gary R. Takeoka, Roy Teranishi, Patrick J. Williams, and Akio

Kobayashi (Washington, D.C.: American Chemical Society, 1995); *Flavor Analysis: Developments in Isolation and Characterization*, edited by Cynthia J. Mussinan and Michael J. Novello (Washington, D.C.: American Chemical Society, 1998). I found many useful articles on the flavor industry in journals such as *Food Product Design, Food Engineering, Food Processing, Food Manufacture, Chemistry and Industry, Chemical Market Reporter*, and *Soap-Cosmetics-Chemical Specialties* (now published as *Soap & Cosmetics*). A good overview of the flavor business can be found in *Industry and Trade Summary: Flavor and Fragrance Materials* (Washington, D.C.: U.S. International Trade Commission, USITC Publication 3162, March 1999). Ellen Ruppel Shell wrote a fine article on the work of flavorists more than a decade ago: "Chemists Whip Up a Tasty Mess of Artificial Flavors," *Smithsonian*, May 1986. Terry Acree, a professor of food science technology at Cornell University, was a wonderful resource on the subjects of smell, taste, flavor, and the flavor industry. Bob Bauer, executive director of the National Association of Fruits, Flavors, and Syrups, outlined when and where the flavor industry settled in New Jersey. At International Flavors & Fragrances, I am grateful to Nancy Ciancaglini, Diane Mora, and Brian Grainger, who patiently answered many questions. The flavorists at other firms whom I interviewed shall remain anonymous.

Page

113 *"gold dust"*: Interview with J. R. Simplot.
     "the Golden Age of Food Processing": Levenstein's chapter on the postwar era entitled "The Golden Age of Food Processing: Miracle Whip *Über Alles*," in Levenstein, *Paradox of Plenty*, pp. 104–18.

114 *"Potato salad from a package!"*: Quoted ibid.
     tableside microwave ovens: Cited ibid., p. 128.
     Although Thomas Jefferson had brought the Parisian recipe: See "The French Fries," a chapter in Elizabeth Rozin's *The Primal Cheeseburger* (New York: Penguin Books, 1994), pp. 133–52.
     "That's a helluva thing": Simplot interview.
     "The french fry [was] . . . almost sacrosanct": Kroc, *Grinding It Out*, p. 10.

115 *thinly sliced Russet Burbanks in special fryers*: See Love, *Behind the Arches*, p. 123.
     about 175 different local suppliers: Ibid., p. 329.
     the typical American ate eighty-one pounds: The figures on fresh potato and french fry consumption come from the USDA Economic Research Service.
     Ninety percent of those fries: Potato statistics, USDA Economic Research Service.
     the most widely sold foodservice item: Cited in Lisa Bocchino, "Frozen Potato Products," *ID: The Voice of Foodservice Distribution*, January 1995.

116 *bigger than the state of Delaware*: Delaware has about 1.6 million acres of land.
     "It's big and it's real": Simplot interview.
     the J. R. Simplot Company supplies the majority: Interview with Fred Zerza.

117 *Simplot, Lamb Weston, and McCain now control*: This is a conservative estimate, based on discussions with a variety of industry sources.
     a $70 million advertising campaign: See Constance L. Hays, "Burger King Campaign Is Promoting New Fries," *New York Times*, December 11, 1997.
     Idaho's potato output surpassed Maine's: Potato Statistics, Economic Research Service, USDA.

117 *Since 1980, the tonnage of potatoes grown in Idaho:* Figures for 1980 courtesy of Paul Patterson; 1999 figures from the National Agricultural Statistical Service.

Out of every $1.50 spent: A large order of fries weighs about one-quarter of a pound. It takes about a half pound of fresh potatoes to make a quarter pound of fries. A typical farm price for fresh processing potatoes is $4 to $5 per hundredweight — or 4 to 5 cents a pound.

It costs about $1,500 an acre: Interview with Paul Patterson.

118 *needs to receive about $5 per hundredweight:* Ibid.

as low as $1.50 per hundredweight: Ibid.

Idaho has lost about half: Interview with Bert Moulton.

the amount of land devoted to potatoes: Idaho Agricultural Statistics Service.

119 *roughly 1,100 potato farmers:* Bert Moulton estimates there are between 1,000 and 1,200; Don Gehrhardt, at the Idaho Agricultural Statistics Service, believes there are about 1,100.

120 *America's agricultural economy now resembles:* See Heffernan, "Consolidation in the Food and Agricultural System," p. 1.

The taste of McDonald's french fries: Since the publication of *Fast Food Nation*, the McDonald's Corporation has been more forthcoming about the ingredients in their fries. For the origins of the new policy, see pages 278–80 of the Afterword.

James Beard loved McDonald's fries: See Elizabeth Mehren, "From Whisks to Molds, James Beard's Personal Possessions to Be Auctioned," *Los Angeles Times*, September 12, 1985.

The taste of a fast food fry is largely determined: See Olivia Wu, "Fats and Oils in a New Light," *Restaurants and Institutions*, January 15, 1997; and Candy Sagon, "Fry, Fry Again: The Secret of Great French Fries? Frying and more Frying," *Washington Post*, July 9, 1997.

more saturated beef fat per ounce: A small McDonald's hamburger weighed 102 grams and had 3.6 grams of saturated fat; a small order of fries weighed 68 grams and had 5.05 grams of saturated fat. See "Where's the Fat," *USA Today*, April 5, 1990; Marian Burros, "The Slimming of Fat Fast Food," *New York Times*, July 25, 1990; and Michael F. Jacobson and Sarah Fritscher, *The Completely Revised and Updated Fast-Food Guide* (New York: Workman Publishing, 1991).

A look at the ingredients now used: See "McDonald's Nutrition Facts," McDonald's Corporation, July 1997.

About 90 percent of the money that Americans spend on food: See "Personal Consumption Expenditures Table, 1999," Bureau of Economic Analysis, U.S. Department of Commerce.

the area produces about two-thirds of the flavor additives: Cited in Joyce Jones, "Labs Conjure Up Fragrances and Flavors to Add Allure," *New York Times*, December 26, 1993.

122 *six of the ten best-selling fine perfumes . . . the smell of Estée Lauder's Beautiful:* Interview with Nancy Ciancaglini, International Flavors & Fragrances.

The aroma of a food can be responsible: Cited in Ruth Sambrook, "Do You Smell What I Smell? The Science of Smell and Taste," Institute of Food Research, March 1999.

123 *a rich and full sense of deliciousness:* See Marilynn Larkin, "Truncated Glutamate Receptor Holds Key to the Fifth Primary Taste," *Lancet,* January 29, 2000; and Andy Coghlan, "In Good Taste," *New Scientist,* January 29, 2000.

Babies like sweet tastes: See Julie A. Mennella and Gary K. Beauchamp, "Early Flavor Experiences: When Do They Start?" *Nutrition Today,* September 1994.

like those of the chain's "heavy users": See Jennifer Ordonez, "Hamburger Joints Call Them 'Heavy Users' — But Not to Their Faces," *Wall Street Journal,* January 12, 2000.

124 *annual revenues of about $1.4 billion:* Interview with Nancy Ciancaglini.

Approximately ten thousand new processed food products: Cited in Susan Carroll, "Flavors Market Is Poised for Recovery This Year," *Chemical Market Report,* July 19, 1999.

And about nine out of every ten . . . fail: Cited in Andrew Bary, "Take a Whiff: Why International Flavors & Fragrances Looks Tempting Right Now," *Barron's,* July 20, 1998.

125 *Its annual revenues have grown almost fifteenfold:* IFF's sales were about $103 million in 1970 and about $1.4 billion in 1999. The first figure comes from "Company History," IFF Advertising and Public Relations. The second is cited in Catherine Curan, "Perfume Company Banks on CEO's Nose for Business," *Crain's NY Business,* June 26, 2000.

the dominant flavor of bell pepper: The chemical is isobutylmethoxy pyrazine. Its minute taste recognition threshold is noted in "Flavor Chemistry Seminar," International Flavors & Fragrances.

The flavor in a twelve-ounce can of Coke: An industry source, who shall go unnamed, provided me with the cost of the flavor in a six-pack of Coke, and I did the rest of the math.

A typical artificial strawberry flavor: This recipe comes from *Fenaroli's Handbook of Flavor Ingredients,* vol. 2, p. 831.

127 *"A natural flavor":* Interview with Terry Acree.

"consumer likeability": Quoted in "What Is Flavor? An IFF Consumer Insights Perspective."

128 *The TA.XT2i Texture Analyzer:* For a description of similar devices, see Ray Marsili, "Texture and Mouthfeel: Making Rheology Real," *Food Product Design,* August 1993.

the ones being synthesized by funguses: See Leticia Mancini, "Expanding Flavor Horizons," *Food Engineering,* November 1991; and Kitty Kevin, "A Brave New World: Capturing the Flavor Bug: Flavors from Microorganisms," *Food Processing,* March 1995.

McDonald's did acknowledge: See Jeanne-Marie Bartas, "Vegan Menu Items at Fast Food and Family-Style Restaurants — Part 2," *Vegetarian Journal,* January/ February 1998.

Wendy's Grilled Chicken Sandwich: See "Wendy's Nutrition/Ingredient Guide," Wendy's International, Inc., 1997.

Burger King's BK Broiler: See "Nutritional Information," Burger King, 1999.

6. On the Range

Sam Bingham, *The Last Ranch: A Colorado Community and the Coming Desert* (New York: Harcourt Brace, 1996), and Peter R. Decker, *Old Fences, New Neighbors* (Tucson: University of Arizona Press, 1998), are two fine books about the current struggles of Colorado ranchers. "The Rancher's Code," a chapter in Charles F. Wilkinson's *Crossing the Next Meridian* (Washington, D.C.: Island Press, 1992), outlines the steps progressive ranchers are taking both to preserve and to remain profitably on the land. Among the many interviews I conducted in the ranching community, a number deserve mention. Dave Carlson, at the Resource Analysis Section of the Colorado Department of agriculture, helped me understand the economic forces now changing the state's landscape. Dave Carter, president of the Rocky Mountain Farmer's Union, outlined many of the development pressures and well-entrenched political interests that ranchers now confront. Dean Preston, the *Pueblo Chieftain's* agriculture correspondent for nearly three decades, described the changes he's witnessed in rural Colorado. Lee Pitts, the editor of *Livestock Market Digest,* helped place the experience of Rocky Mountain ranchers in a broader national perspective. Over the years his work for the *Digest* has represented independent American journalism at its finest.

For the history of cattle ranching and the Beef Trust I relied mainly upon Willard F. Williams and Thomas T. Stout, *Economics of the Livestock-Meat Industry* (New York, Macmillan, 1964); Mary Yeager, *Competition and Regulation: The Development of Oligopoly in the Meat Packing Industry* (Greenwich, Conn.: Jai Press, 1981); and Jimmy M. Skaggs, *Prime Cut: Livestock Raising and Meatpacking in the United States, 1607–1983* (College Station: Texas A&M University Press, 1986). John Crabtree, at the Center for Rural Affairs in Walt Hill, Nebraska, helped me see today's formula pricing arangements in the proper historical context. Two of the center's publications were especially useful: *Competition and the Livestock Market* (April 1990) and *From the Carcass to the Kitchen: Competition and the Wholesale Meat Market* (November 1995), the latter written by Marty Strange and Annette Higby. *Concentration in Agriculture, A Report of the USDA Advisory Committee on Agricultural Concentration* (Washington, D.C.: USDA Agricultural Marketing Service, June 1996) is an official and belated acknowledgment of the problems faced by American ranchers and farmers. *A Time to Act,* the report of the USDA's National Commission on Small Farms, does an even better job of portraying the harms of concentrated power in agriculture.

Mike Callicrate, one of the plaintiffs in *Pickett v. IBP, Inc.,* provided a great deal of information about the misbehavior of the large meatpacking firms and the rural unrest now growing in response to it. And Dave Domina, one of the attorneys representing Cállicrate et al., explained the legal basis for the case and supplied hundreds of pages of documents. *Industry and Trade Summary: Poultry* (Washington, D.C.: U.S. International Trade Commission, USITC Publication 3148, December 1998) gives a thorough overview of the American poultry industry. Marc Linder, a professor at the University of Iowa Law School, introduced me to the subject of poultry growers, poultry workers, and their misfortunes. Linder's article "I Gave My Employer a Chicken That Had No Bone: Joint Firm-State Responsibility for Line-Speed-Related Occupational Injuries," *Case Western Reserve Law Review* 46, no. 1 (Fall 1995), contains an excellent history of the industry and its labor relations. Steve Bjerklie's three-part article on contract poultry growing, which appeared in *Meat & Poultry* (August, October, and December 1994), is a scathing indictment of the large processors by a longtime observer of the industry. The investigative reports by Dan Fesperman and Kate Shatzin, published by the *Baltimore Sun* in February and March of 1999, chronicle the latest processor abuses. For the story of the McNugget, I largely relied on Laura Konrad Jereski's account in "McDonald's Strikes Gold with Chicken McNuggets," *Marketing and Media Decisions,* March 22, 1985; Timothey K. Smith, "Changing Tastes: By End of the Year Poultry Will Surpass Beef in the U.S. Diet; Price, Health Concerns Propel Move Toward Chicken; The Impact of McNuggets," *Wall Street Journal,* September 17, 1987; and John F. Love, *Behind the Arches,* pp. 338–43.

Page

133 *Hank was the first person:* At the request of Hank's family, I have not used his real name.

136 *about half a million ranchers sold off:* Based on numbers provided by the National Agricultural Statistics Service.

In 1968, McDonald's bought ground beef: For the consolidation of the chain's beef purchasing, see Love, *Behind the Arches,* pp. 333–38.

137 *at the height of the Beef Trust:* Cited in *Competition and the Livestock Market,* Report of a Task Force Commissioned by the Center for Rural Affairs (Walt Hill, Neb.: April 1990), p. 31.

In 1970 the top four meatpacking firms: Cited ibid., p. 31.

Today the top four meatpacking firms: The figure comes from a USDA study, cited in George Anthan, "2 Reports Focus on Packers' Profits," *Des Moines Register,* May 30, 1999.

138 *the rancher's share of every retail dollar:* Estimate cited in "Prepared Statement of Keith Collins, Chief Economist, U.S. Department of Agriculture, Before the House Committee on Agriculture," *Federal News Service,* February 10, 1999.

control about 20 percent of the live cattle in the United States: 1997 estimate of the Grain Inspection, Packers and Stockyards Administration, cited in "Prepared Statement of Keith Collins." See also "Captive Supplies — Who, What, When, Where, and Why," *Colorado Farmer,* October 1997.

as much as 80 percent of the cattle being exchanged: Cited in *Concentration in Agriculture,* p. 31.

"A free market requires": Competition and the Livestock Market, p. v.

139 *Eight chicken processors now control:* Cited in *Industry and Trade Summary: Poultry,* p. 8.

Alabama, Arkansas, Georgia, and Mississippi now produce: Ibid., p. A-3.

"I have an idea": Quoted in Monci Jo Williams, "McDonald's Refuses to Plateau," *Fortune,* November 12, 1984.

140 *a new breed of chicken:* See Love, *Behind the Arches,* p. 342.

the second-largest purchaser of chicken: Cited in Williams, "McDonald's Refuses to Plateau."

A chemical analysis of McNuggets: The researcher was Dr. Frank Sacks, assistant professor of medicine at the Harvard University Medical School, and he utilized gas chromatography to analyze McNuggets for *Science Digest.* See "Study Raises Beef over Fast-Food Frying," *Chicago Tribune,* March 11, 1986, and Irvin

Molotsky, "Risk Seen in Saturated Fats Used in Fast Foods," *New York Times,* November 15, 1985.

140 *still derive much of their flavor from beef additives:* The ingredients and fat profile of McNuggets can be found in "McDonald's Nutrition Facts," McDonald's Corporation, 1997.

"The impact of McNuggets": Quoted in Smith, "Changing Tastes."

Twenty years ago, most chicken was sold whole: Industry and Trade Summary: Poultry, p. 21.

In 1992 American consumption of chicken: Cited in Linder, "I Gave My Employer a Chicken That Had No Bone," p. 53.

Tyson now manufactures: Cited in Sheila Edmundson, "Real Home of the McNugget Is Tyson," *Memphis Business Journal,* July 9, 1999.

and sells chicken to ninety of the one hundred largest restaurant chains: Cited in Douglas McInnis, "Super Chicken," *Beef,* February 2000.

A Tyson chicken grower never owns: Interview with Larry Holder, executive director of the National Contract Poultry Growing Association.

141 *Most growers must borrow:* See Steven Bjerklie, "Dark Passage," *Meat & Poultry,* (August 1994), as well as Dan Fesperman and Kate Shatzkin, "The Plucking of the American Chicken Farmer; From the Big Poultry Companies Comes a New Twist on Capitalism," *Baltimore Sun,* February 28, 1999.

A 1995 survey by Louisiana Tech: "Economic Returns for U.S. Broiler Producers," National Contract Growers Institute study, completed with cooperation of researchers in the Department of Agricultural Sciences, Louisiana Tech University, October 11, 1995.

About half of the nation's chicken growers: Cited in Sheri Venena, "Growing Pains," *Arkansas Democrat-Gazette,* October 18, 1998.

"We get the check first": Quoted ibid.

when the United States had dozens of poultry firms: See Marj Charlier, "Chicken Economics: The Broiler Industry Consolidates, and That Is Bad News to Farmers," *Wall Street Journal,* January 4, 1990.

142 *"Our relationship with our growers":* Quoted in Venena, "Growing Pains."

A number of studies by the U.S. Department of Agriculture: The most recent study, issued by the USDA's Economic Research Service in May 1999, found "no evidence . . . that increasing [packer] concentration results in lower farm prices" — a finding considered absurd and ridiculed by a number of ranchers and economists. Quoted in Anthan, "2 Reports Focus on Packers' Profits." See also "Meatpacking: Where's the Big Beef?" *Bismarck Tribune,* May 9, 1999.

Annual beef consumption in the United States: See Chris Bastian and Glen Whipple, "Trends in Supply and Demand of Beef," *Western Beef Producer,* October 1997.

A pound of chicken costs: Cited in *Industry and Trade Summary: Poultry,* p. 19.

"alternative methods for selling fed cattle": Quoted in Alan Guebert, "Chew on This: USDA, Congress, Take on Meatpackers with Little Success," *Pantagraph,* June 7, 1998.

143 *Three of Archer Daniels Midland's top officials:* For the prison terms, see Sharon Walsh, "Three Former Officials at ADM Get Jail Terms," *Washington Post,* July 10, 1999. For the cost to farmers, see Sharon Walsh, "ADM Officials Found

Guilty of Price Fixing," *Washington Post*, September 18, 1998. For a detailed account of the conspiracy, see Angela Wissman, "ADM Execs Nailed on Price-Fixing, May Do Time, Government Gets Watershed Convictions, But Company Still Dominates Lysine Market," *Illinois Legal Times*, October 1998.

143 *"We have a saying at this company":* Quoted in Kurt Eichenwald, "Videotapes Take Star Role at Archers Daniels Midland Trial," *New York Times*, August 4, 1998.
many ranchers were afraid to testify: See *Concentration in Agriculture*, pp. 7, 29–30.

144 *"It makes no sense for us":* Quoted in Kevin O' Hanlon, "Judge Clears Way for Alabama Lawsuit Against Nation's Largest Meatpacker," *Associated Press*, May 4, 1999.
Colorado has lost roughly 1.5 million acres: Cited in "A Report on the Conversion of Agricultural Land in Colorado," Colorado Department of Agriculture and the Governor's Task Force on Agricultural Lands, 1997.
eight of the nation's top ten TV shows: Cited in White, *It's Your Misfortune and None of My Own*, p. 613.

145 *The median age of Colorado's ranchers and farmers:* Cited in Sam Bingham, "Cattlemen Organize Land Trust: Ranchers' Group Works to Keep Colorado Properties Agricultural," *Denver Post*, June 22, 1997.
thus far protected about 40,000 acres: Interview with Lynne Sherrod, executive director, Colorado Cattlemen's Agricultural Land Trust.
vanishing at the rate of about 90,000 acres a year: Cited in "Loss of Agricultural Land Figures for Colorado," Memorandum by David Carlson, resource analyst, Colorado Department of Agriculture, January 8, 1998.

146 *The suicide rate among ranchers and farmers:* The statistic comes from Florence Williams, "Farmed Out," *New Republic*, August 16, 1999.

147 *"To fail several generations of relatives":* Osha Gray Davidson, *Broken Heartland: The Rise of America's Rural Ghetto* (Iowa City: University of Iowa Press, 1996), p. 95.

7. Cogs in the Great Machine

Upton Sinclair's *The Jungle* (1906; reprint, New York: Bantam Books, 1981) unfortunately remains the essential starting point for an understanding of America's meatpacking industry today. Nearly a century after the book's publication, many of the descriptive passages still ring true. Sinclair's prescription for reform, however — his call for a centralized, socialized, highly industrialized agriculture — shows how even the best of intentions can lead to disaster. For a contemporary view of nineteenth-century meatpacking, I relied mainly on Yeager, *Competition and Regulation* and Skaggs, *Prime Cut*. For the struggle to improve working conditions in Chicago's Packingtown, see *Unionizing the Jungles: Labor and Community in the Twentieth Century Meatpacking Industry*, edited by Shelton Stromquist and Marvin Bergman (Iowa City: University of Iowa Press, 1997). One of the essays in the book, "The Swift Difference," by Paul Street, gives a strong sense of the corporate paternalism and decent working conditions that were later eliminated by the "IBP revolution." For an account of that revolution's leadership, see Jonathan Kwitny, *Vicious Circles: The Mafia in the Marketplace*

(New York: W. W. Norton, 1979); James Cook and Jane Carmichael, "The Mob's Legitimate Connections," *Forbes*, November 24, 1980; and James Cook, "Those Simple, Barefoot Boys from Iowa Beef," *Forbes*, June 22, 1981. Also see the inadvertently revealing corporate history by Jane E. Limprecht, *ConAgra Who? $15 Billion and Growing* (Omaha: ConAgra, 1989). Jeremy Rifkin's *Beyond Beef: The Rise and Fall of the Cattle Culture* (New York: Penguin, 1993) is a provocative diatribe against "the industrialization of beef." Kathleen Meister's response to Rifkin, "The Beef Controversy," *American Council on Science and Health Special Reports*, August 31, 1993, is less convincing, but makes a number of good points. Osha Gray Davidson's *Broken Heartland* does a fine job of explaining the root causes and social implications of the rising poverty in America's meatpacking towns. Carol Andreas's *Meatpackers and Beef Barons: Company Town in a Global Economy* (Niwot: University Press of Colorado, 1994) examines the recent transformation of Greeley. I am grateful to Ms. Andreas for discussing her work at length with me.

In Greeley, many former and current Monfort employees — some at the managerial level — shared their perspective on changes at the company after its sale to ConAgra; at their request, I have not included their names. I am grateful to Javier and Ruben Ramirez for the many hours they spent with me discussing the labor histories of Greeley and Chicago. For a straightforward analysis of structural changes in the cattle business, see James M. MacDonald and Michael Ollinger, "U.S. Meat Slaughter Consolidating Rapidly," *USDA Food Review*, May 1, 1997. The best book on today's meatpacking industry is *Any Way You Cut It: Meat Processing and Small-Town America* (Lawrence: University Press of Kansas, 1995), edited by Donald D. Stull, Michael J. Broadway, and David Griffith. The essays by Lourdes Gouveia, Donald D. Stull, Mark Grey, and Steve Bjerklie were especially useful to me. I am indebted to Ms. Gouveia, a professor of sociology at the University of Nebraska–Omaha, whose work on the recent changes in Lexington, Nebraska, is exemplary and who helped me contact people there. Her essay "Global Strategies and Local Linkages: The Case of the U.S. Meatpacking Industry" is well worth reading, as is the rest of the book in which it appears: *From Columbus to ConAgra: The Globalization of Agriculture and Food*, edited by Alessandro Bonanno, Lawrence Busch, William H. Friedland, Lourdes Gouveia, and Enzo Mingione (Lawrence: University Press of Kansas, 1994). For a government report that belatedly confirms many of the findings made by Stull, Grey, Davidson, Gouveia, and others, see "Community Development: Changes in Nebraska's and Iowa's Counties With Large Meatpacking Plant Workforces," *Report to Congressional Requesters*, United States General Accounting Office, February 1998. Milo Muungard, the executive director of Nebraska's Appleseed Center, gave me useful material on the social and environmental effects of a migrant industrial workforce. Greg Lauby, an attorney whose family has lived in Lexington, Nebraska, for generations, graciously shared his knowledge of the town's history, its residents, its recent changes — and the reasons for its smell. I am particularly grateful to the many IBP workers who invited me into their homes and told me their stories.

Page

150 *earns more money every year from livestock products: 1997 Census of Agriculture* (Washington, D.C.: U.S. Department of Commerce), p. 36.

150 *the largest private employer in Weld County:* Indeed, a recent study by two Colorado State University economists found that ConAgra's facilities are "practically synonymous with Greeley and Weld County." Andrew Seidl and Stephan Weiler, "The Estimated Value of ConAgra Packing Plants in Weld County, CO," *Agricultural and Resource Policy Report,* Colorado State University Cooperative Extension, Fort Collins, February 2000, p. 3.

A typical steer will consume: Interview with Mike Callicrate, Kansas feedlot operator.

deposits about fifty pounds of manure: The figure was determined by researchers at Colorado State University. Cited in Mark Obmascik, "As Greeley Ponders Tax, Cows Keep On Doing Their Thing," *Denver Post,* July 29, 1995.

produce more excrement than the cities: According to O. W. Charles, of the Extension Poultry Science Department of the University of Georgia, one head of cattle generates the same amount of waste as 16.4 people. Cited in Eric R. Haapapuro, Neal D. Barnard, and Michele Simon, "Animal Waste Used as Livestock Feed: Dangers to Human Health," *Preventive Medicine,* September/October 1997. Using that ratio, the roughly 200,000 cattle in Monfort's two Weld County feedlots produce an amount of waste equivalent to that of about 3.2 million people. The combined populations of Denver (about 500,000), Boston (about 550,000), Atlanta (about 400,000), and St. Louis (about 375,00) produce much less excrement than Greeley's cattle.

it was a utopian community: My account of early Greeley is based on Mike Peters, "Meeker Killed on Western Slope," *Greeley Tribune,* 1998; Mike Peters, "Controversy over Cattle Ranches Leads to 'The Fence,'" *Greeley Tribune,* 1998; and Carl Ubbelohde, Maxine Benson, Duane A. Smith, *A Colorado History* (Boulder, Colo.: Pruett Publishing Company, 1995), pp. 123–32.

151 *started his business in the 1930s with eighteen head:* See Curt Olsen, "Monforts: Changing the Way the World Is Fed," *National Cattlemen,* August 1997.

a place on President Nixon's "enemies list": See "Beef Baron," *Rocky Mountain News Sunday Magazine,* May 3, 1987.

"If I can ever be of help": Quoted in Andreas, *Meatpackers and Beef Barons,* p. 37.

152 *"the greatest aggregation":* Sinclair, *Jungle,* p. 40.

"cogs in the great packing machine": Ibid., p. 78.

"conditions that are entirely unnecessary": Quoted in Yeager, *Competition and Regulation,* p. 200.

153 *"I aimed for the public's heart":* Quoted in Skaggs, *Prime Cut,* p. 118.

paid the industry's highest wages: See Stromquist and Bergman, *Unionizing the Jungles,* pp. 25–33.

154 *"We've tried to take the skill out":* Quoted in Stull et al., *Any Way You Cut It,* p. 19.

as though it were waging war: Holman is quoted in Christopher Drew, "A Chain of Setbacks for Meat Workers," *Chicago Tribune,* October 25, 1988.

close ties with La Cosa Nostra: Steinman was a central figure in New York City's meat business, dominated at the time by the Lucchese and Gambino crime families. See Kwitny, *Vicious Circles,* pp. 252–53.

155 *a five-cent "commission":* The arrangement, technically, was a fifty-cent commission for every hundred pounds. Ibid., p. 301.

155 *"knew virtually nothing about the meat business"*: Quoted ibid., p. 375.

investigations by Forbes *and the* Wall Street Journal: Jonathan Kwitny, the *Journal* reporter, and James Cook and Jane Carmichael, writing for *Forbes*, drew some- what different conclusions about the meaning of the IBP case. Kwitny was out- raged, arguing that it was as though "the Mafia had moved into . . . the oil indus- try, bringing Exxon to its knees." Cook and Carmichael were more detached and pragmatic. "The ordeal of Iowa Beef Processors shows as clearly as any- thing can," they wrote, "how legitimate business can become linked with orga- nized crime, to their mutual benefit." Kwitny, *Vicious Circles*, p. 252; Cook and Carmichael, "Mob's Legitimate Connections."

wages that were sometimes more than 50 percent lower: While Swift and Armour were paying $17 to $18 an hour, IBP was paying just $8. See Winston Williams, "An Upheaval in Meatpacking," *New York Times*, June 20, 1983. See also Cook, "Those Simple, Barefoot Boys."

once employed 40,000 people: According to Erin Troya of the Chicago Historical Society, Packingtown employed about 40,000 workers at its peak during the 1920s. The current estimate of 2,000 comes from Ruben Ramirez. Dot McGrier, at the U.S. Census Bureau, says that Chicago now has a total of 6,000 meat- packing workers, but most of them are employed in the Watermarket area on the western edge of the city.

157 *a sweetheart deal with the National Maritime Union:* See Bill Saporito, "Unions Fight the Corporate Sell-Off," *Fortune*, July 11, 1983; Jim Morris, "Easy Prey: Harsh work for Immigrants," *Houston Chronicle*, June 26, 1995; Andreas, *Meat- packers and Beef Barons*, p. 68.

158 *wages that had been cut by 40 percent:* Andreas, *Meatpackers and Beef Barons*, p. 98.

"if the industry was going to be concentrated": Quoted ibid., p. 76.

the largest foodservice supplier: Interview with Karen Savinski, director of corpo- rate communications, ConAgra.

159 *annual revenues of about $500 million:* Cited in Limprecht, *ConAgra Who?*, p. 98.

the market value of its stock: Ibid., p. 7.

"Harper told each general manager": Quoted ibid., p. 12.

"Patience, my ass": Ibid., p. 120.

45,256 truckloads: See Tom Hughes, "Alabama Growers' Court Settlement Not Chicken Feed," *Montgomery Advertiser*, October 7, 1992. See also Richard Gib- son, "ConAgra Settles Case of Cheating By Bird Weighers," *Wall Street Journal*, October 9, 1992.

ConAgra agreed to pay $13.6 million: Cited in Richard Gibson, "ConAgra, Hormel Pay a Pretty Penny in an Ugly Catfish Price-Fixing Case," *Wall Street Journal*, December 29, 1995.

ConAgra paid $8.3 million in fines: See *"ConAgra Pays* $8.3 Million in Penalties for Fraud Scheme," *Federal Department and Agency Documents*, March 19, 1997. See also Scott Kilman, "ConAgra to Pay $8.3 Million to Settle Fraud Charges in Grain-Handling Case," *Wall Street Journal*, March 20, 1997.

160 *more than five thousand different people were employed:* Cited in "Here's the Beef: Underreporting of Injuries, OSHA's Policy of Exempting Companies from Pro-

grammed Inspections Based on Injury Records, and Unsafe Conditions in the Meatpacking Industry," *Forty-Second Report by the Committee on Government and Operations* (Washington, D.C.: U.S. Government Printing Office, 1988), p. 12.

160 *roughly two-thirds of the workers at the beef plant:* Interview with Javier Ramirez, former president of UFCW Local 990, Greeley, Colorado.

A spokesman for ConAgra recently acknowledged: Interview with Brett Fox, director of industry affairs and media relations, ConAgra Beef Company.

"There is a 100 percent turnover rate annually": Quoted in James M. Burcke, "1994 Risk Manager of the Year: Meatpacker's Losses Trimmed Down to Size," *Business Insurance,* April 18, 1994.

161 *Arden Walker, the head of labor relations at IBP:* Quoted in "Here's the Beef," p. 11.

162 *Picking strawberries in California pays:* For the role and the wages of Latino migrants in California agriculture, see Schlosser, "In the Strawberry Fields."

refugees and asylum-seekers . . . homeless people living at shelters: See "IBP; Meat Processing Plant Fails to Uphold Social Contract with Waterloo, Iowa; Crime and Homelessness Increase," *60 Minutes,* CBS News transcripts, March 9, 1997; "IBP's Hiring Reflects Evolution of Meatpacking Industry," *Quad-City Times,* June 30, 1997; Marc Cooper, "The Heartland's Raw Deal: How Meatpacking Is Creating a New Immigrant Underclass," *Nation,* February 3, 1997; and George Rodrigue, "Packing Them In: Meat Processing Firm's Hiring of Ex-Welfare Recipients Questioned," *Dallas Morning News,* September 25, 1997.

a labor office in Mexico City: See Laurie Cohen, "Free Ride: With Help from INS, U.S. Meatpacker Taps Mexican Work Force," *Wall Street Journal,* October 15, 1998.

one-quarter of all meatpacking workers in Iowa: Cited in "Changes in Nebraska's and Iowa's Counties with Large Meatpacking Plant Workforces," *GAO Reports,* p. 15.

Spokesmen for IBP and the ConAgra Beef Company: Fox interview; interview with Gary Mickelson, IBP Public Affairs Department.

"If they've got a pulse": Quoted in Rick Ruggles, "INS: Undocumented Workers Face New Meat-Plant Tactics," *Omaha World-Herald,* September 11, 1998.

In September of 1994, GFI America: See Joe Rigert and Richard Meryhew, "Food Company Takes Hired Workers to Homeless Shelter," *Minneapolis Star Tribune,* September 14, 1994; Tony Kennedy, "International Dairy Queen to Review Its Relationship with Meat Supplier GFI," *Minneapolis Star-Tribune,* September 15, 1994; and "GFI's Frugal Ways Led to Problems for Some Workers," *Minneapolis Star-Tribune,* December 9, 1994.

163 *"Our job is not to provide":* Quoted in Rigert and Meryhew, "Food Company Takes Hired Workers."

Mike Harper personally stood to gain: Cited in "Capital Gains Exclusion Would Benefit Key Backers," *UPI,* April 19, 1987.

164 *called Harper's demands "blackmail":* See Limprecht, *ConAgra Who?,* p. 269.

"Some Friday night, we turn out the lights": Quoted in Dennis Farney, "Nebraska, Hungry of Jobs, Grants Big Business Big Tax Breaks Despite Charges of 'Blackmail,'" *Wall Street Journal,* June 23, 1987.

164 *after the revision of the state's tax code:* See Henry J. Cordes, "Did It Prime the Pump? Report Questions Economic Incentives," *Omaha World-Herald,* December 28, 1997. Ernie Goss, an economist at Creighton University, thinks the estimate of $13,000 to $23,000 is fair. Interview with Ernie Goss.

like giving his employees a 7 percent raise . . . "The move shows you how ungrateful": Quoted in John Taylor, "IBP's Move Prompts Look at Tax Policy," *Omaha World-Herald,* June 13, 1996.

a $300,000 loan: See Kenneth B. Noble, "Signs of Violence in Meat Plant's Lockout," *New York Times,* January 18, 1987.

165 *the highest crime rate in the state of Nebraska:* See Robert A. Hackenberg, David Griffith, Donald Stull, and Lourdes Gouveia, "Creating a Disposable Labor Force," *Aspen Institute Quarterly* 5, no. 2 (Spring 1993), p. 92.

the number of serious crimes doubled: Cited in "Changes in Nebraska's and Iowa's Counties with Large Meatpacking Plant Workforces," *GAO Report,* p. 39.

the number of Medicaid cases nearly doubled: Ibid., p. 36.

a major distribution center for illegal drugs; gang members appeared in town: See Richard A. Serrano, "Mexican Drug Cartels Target U.S. Heartland: Officials Say Illegal Immigrants are Using Interstates as Pipeline to Bring Cocaine, Methamphetamines to Midwest and Rocky Mountain Areas Where Abuse Is Burgeoning," *Los Angeles Times,* December 10, 1997; Jennifer Dukes Lee, "Meatpacking Towns Seen As Key Funnel for Meth," *Des Moines Register,* March 7, 1999.

the majority of Lexington's white inhabitants . . . the proportion of Latino inhabitants: Lexington is the principal city in Dawson County, and in 1990, 4.7 percent of the county's population was Latino, according to census figures. A recount in 1993 found the Latino population to be almost 30 percent and expected to reach 50 percent within three years. Cited in Lourdes Gouveia, "From the Beet Fields to the Kill Floors: Latinos in Nebraska's Meatpacking Communities," unpublished manuscript.

"Mexington": For some of the positive effects of the new immigration wave, see Edwin Garcia and Ben Stocking, "Latinos on the Move to a New Promised Land," *San Jose Mercury News,* August 16, 1998.

"We have three odors": Quoted in Melody M. Loughry, "Issues Now," *North Platte Resident,* January 15, 1996.

the Justice Department sued IBP: See Elliot Blair Smith, "Stench Chokes Meatpacking Towns," *USA Today,* February 14, 2000; "U.S. Sues Meatpacking Giant for Violating Numerous Environmental Laws in Midwest," press release, Environmental Protection Agency, January 12, 2000.

"This agreement means": Quoted in "Meatpacker Must Cut Hydrogen Sulfide Emissions at Nebraska Plant," press release, Environmental Protection Agency, May 24, 2000.

166 *The transcript of this meeting:* "Presenting IBP, Inc., to Lexington, Nebraska: A Public Forum Conducted by the Dawson County Council for Economic Development, July 7, 1988, at the Junior High School Auditorium," transcription by the staff of the Lauby Law Office, Lexington, Nebraska.

8. The Most Dangerous Job

This chapter is based largely on interviews that I conducted with dozens of Latino meatpacking workers in Colorado and Nebraska. I also interviewed a former slaughterhouse safety director, a former slaughterhouse nurse, former plant supervisors, and a physician whose medical practice was for years devoted to the treatment of slaughterhouse workers. All of these managerial personnel had left the meatpacking industry by choice; none had been fired; and their reluctance to use their real names in this book stems from the widespread fear of the meatpackers in rural communities where they operate. I am grateful to those who spoke with me and showed me around.

Deborah E. Berkowitz, the former director of health and safety at the UFCW, was an invaluable source of information about the workings of a modern slaughterhouse and the dangers that workers face there. Her article on meatpacking and meat processing in *The Encyclopaedia of Occupational Health and Safety* (Geneva, Switzerland: International Labour Organization, 1998), cowritten with Michael J. Fagel, is a good introduction to the subject. Curt Brandt, the president of UFCW Local 22 in Fremont, Nebraska, described the various tactics he's seen meatpacking firms use over the years to avoid compensating injured workers. Two Colorado attorneys, Joseph Goldhammer and Dennis E. Valentine, helped me understand the intricacies of their state's workers' comp law and described their work on behalf of injured Monfort employees. Rod Rehm, an attorney based in Lincoln, Nebraska, spent many hours depicting the conditions in his state and arranged for me to meet some of his clients. Rehm is an outspoken advocate for poor Latinos in a state where they have few political allies. Bruce L. Braley, one of the attorneys in *Ferrell v. IBP*, told me a great deal about the company's behavior and sent me stacks of documents pertaining to the case. "Killing Them Softly: Work in Meatpacking Plants and What It Does to Workers," by Donald D. Stull and Michael J. Broadway, in *Any Way You Cut It*, is one of the best published accounts of America's most dangerous job. "Here's the Beef: Underreporting of Injuries, OSHA's Policy of Exempting Companies from Programmed Inspections Based on Injury Record, and Unsafe Conditions in the Meatpacking Industry," *Forty-Second Report by the Committee on Government Operations* (Washington, D.C.: U.S. Government Printing Office, 1988), shows the extraordinary abuses that can occur when an industry is allowed to regulate itself. After the congressional investigation, Christopher Drew wrote a terrific series of articles on meatpacking, published by the *Chicago Tribune* in October of 1988. The fact that working conditions have changed little since then is remarkably depressing. Gail A. Eisnitz's *Slaughterhouse: The Shocking Story of Greed, Neglect, and Inhumane Treatment Inside the U.S. Meat Industry* (Amherst, N.Y.: Prometheus Books, 1997), suggests that many cattle are needlessly brutalized prior to slaughter. Nothing that these sources reveal would come as a surprise to readers of Upton Sinclair.

Page

172 *The injury rate in a slaughterhouse:* In 1999, the most recent year for which statistics are available, the injury and illness rate in the nation's meatpacking industry was 26.7 per 100 hundred workers. For the rest of U.S. manufacturing, it was 9.2

per hundred workers. See "Industries with the Highest Nonfatal Total Cases, Incidence Rates for Injuries and Illnesses, Private Industry, 1999," Bureau of Labor Statistics, December 2000; and "Incidence Rates of Nonfatal Occupational Injuries and Illnesses by Selected Industries and Case Types, 1999," Bureau of Labor Statistics, U.S. Department of Labor, December 2000.

172 *roughly forty thousand men and women:* The meatpacking industry now has about 147,600 workers, and at least 26.7 percent of them suffer workplace injuries and illnesses. See "Industries with the Highest Nonfatal Total Cases."

Thousands of additional injuries and illnesses: At some plants, as many as half of the workers may be hurt each year. You need spend only an hour or so with a roomful of poor Latino meatpacking workers to get a sense of how many serious injuries are never reported.

Poultry plants can be largely mechanized: Despite the higher level of mechanization, workers in the poultry industry have one of the nation's highest rates of injury and illness, largely due to the repetitive nature of the work and the speed of the production line.

173 *roughly thirty-three times higher than the national average:* In 1999 the incidence of repeated trauma injuries in private industry was 27.3 per 10,000 workers; in the poultry industry the rate was 337.1; and in the meatpacking industry it was 912.5. See "Industries with the Highest Nonfatal Illness Incidence Rate of Disorders Associated with Repeated Trauma and the Number of Cases in These Industries," Bureau of Labor Statistics, U.S. Department of Labor, December 2000.

adds up to about 10,000 cuts: According to Berkowitz and Fagel, some production jobs can require 20,000 cuts a day. Berkowitz and Fagel, *Encyclopaedia of Occupational Health and Safety,* p. 67.14.

174 *beef slaughterhouses often operate at profit margins:* According to Steve Bjerklie, the profit margin for slaughter is about 1 percent, with additional earnings from processing and the sale of byproducts. See Steve Bjerklie, "On the Horns of a Dilemma," in *Any Way You Cut It,* p. 42.

widespread methamphetamine use: Many workers told me stories about methamphetamine use. See also Lee, "Meatpacking towns seen as key funnel for meth."

only one-third of IBP's workers belong to a union: Cited in Cohen, "Free Ride with Help from INS."

176 *awarded $2.4 million to a female employee . . . "screamed obscenities and rubbed their bodies":* A federal judge later reduced the award to $1.75 million. See Lynn Hicks, "IBP Worker Awarded $2.4 Million by Jury," *Des Moines Register,* February 27, 1999; Lynn Hicks, "Worker: Sexism, Racism at IBP," *Des Moines Register,* February 3, 1999; "IBP Told to Pay Attorney's Fees," *Des Moines Register,* December 30, 1999.

the company paid the women $900,000: See "Monfort Beef to Pay $900,000 to Settle Sexual Harassment Suit," *Houston Chronicle,* September 1, 1999.

pressured them for dates and sex: Ibid.

They are considered "independent contractors": As a result, the meatpacking firms are not liable for the work-related injuries of the slaughterhouse employees who face the greatest risks. When OSHA tried to penalize IBP for the death of a sanitation worker, IBP appealed the decision, with the backing of the National Association of Manufacturers, before a federal appeals court in 1998 — and won. Although the meatpackers own the slaughterhouses and the slaughterhouse equipment, they are not legally responsible for the immigrants who clean them. See Stephan C. Yohay and Arthur G. Sapper, "Liability on Multi-Employer Worksites," *Occupational Hazards*, October 1998.

178 *Richard Skala was beheaded:* See Jim Morris, "Easy Prey: Harsh Work for Immigrants," *Houston Chronicle*, June 26, 1995.

Carlos Vincente: See "Guatemalan Man Dies after Falling into Machinery of Beef Processing Plant," *AP*, November 3, 1998; "Ft. Morgan Firm Faces $350,000 in OSHA Fines," *AP*, May 4, 1999.

Lorenzo Marin, Sr.: See Mark P. Couch, "IBP Told to Pay Damages to Family," *Des Moines Register*, June 7, 1995.

Another employee of DCS Sanitation . . . The same machine: See Jim Rasmussen, "Company Expecting Fines Today; Death at IBP Plant May Cost Ohio Firm," *Omaha World-Herald*, October 7, 1993.

Homer Stull climbed into a blood-collection tank: See Allen Freedman, "Workers Stiffed: Death and Injury Rates among American Workers Soar, and the Government Has Never Cared Less," *Washington Monthly*, November 1992.

Henry Wolf had been overcome: See "Liberal Packing Plant Fined $960," *UPI*, October 19, 1983.

179 *its 1,300 inspectors:* See Kenneth B. Noble, "The Long Tug-of-War over What Is How Hazardous; For OSHA, Balance Is Hard to Find," *New York Times*, January 10, 1988; and Christopher Drew, "Regulators Slow Down as Packers Speed Up," *Chicago Tribune*, October 26, 1988.

more than 5 million workplaces: Cited in "Here's the Beef," p. 4.

A typical American employer: Cited in Susannah Zak Figura, "The New OSHA," *Government Executive*, May 1997.

The number of OSHA inspectors: See Noble, "The Long Tug of War"; and Drew, "Regulators Slow Down."

a new policy of "voluntary compliance": See "Here's the Beef," p. 3.

While the number of serious injuries rose: See Christopher Drew, "A Chain of Setbacks for Meat Workers," *Chicago Tribune*, October 25, 1988.

"appear amazingly stupid to you" . . . "I know very well that you know": Quoted in Drew, "Regulators Slow Down."

"to understate injuries, to falsify records": "Here's the Beef," p. 21.

180 *every injury and illness at the slaughterhouse:* Ibid., pp. 3, 14.

the first log recorded 1,800 injuries . . . The OSHA log: Ibid., p. 14.

denied under oath: Ibid., p. 15. See also Philip Shabecoff, "OSHA Seeks $2.59 Million Fine for Meatpacker's Injury Reports," *New York Times*, July 22, 1987.

"the best of the best": Quoted in "Here's the Beef," p. 9.

as much as one-third higher: Ibid., p. 9.

investigators also discovered: Ibid., p. 21.

Another leading meatpacking company: Ibid., pp. 21–22.

"serious injuries such as fractures": Ibid., p. 8.

180 *"one of the most irresponsible and reckless"*: Quoted in Donald Woutat, "Meat-packer IBP Fined $3.1 Million in Safety Action; Health Problem Disabled More than 600, OSHA Says," *Los Angeles Times,* May 12, 1988.

"the worst example of underreporting": Assistant Labor Secretary John A. Pender-grass, quoted in Shabecoff, "OSHA Seeks $2.59 Million Fine."

difficult to prove "conclusively": "Here's the Beef," p. 19.

fined $2.6 million by OSHA: Shabecoff, "OSHA Seeks $2.59 Million."

fined an additional $3.1 million: Woutat, "Meatpacker IBP Fined $3.1 Million."

fines were reduced to $975,000: See Christopher Drew, "IBP Agrees to Injury Plan," *Chicago Tribune,* November 23, 1988; Marianne Lavelle, "When Fines Collapse: Critics Target OSHA's Settlements," *National Law Journal,* December 4, 1989.

about one one-hundredth of a percent: According to Robert L. Peterson, IBP's rev-enues that year were about $8.8 billion. "IBP's Presentation at the New York So-ciety of Security Analysts," *Business Wire,* October 28, 1988.

a worker named Kevin Wilson: My account of the Wilson case is based upon John Taylor, "Ex-IBP Worker Gets $15 Million in Damage Award," *Omaha World-Herald,* December 3, 1994; "Opinion," *Kevin Wilson v IBP, Inc., and Diane Arndt,* Supreme Court of Iowa, no. 258/95–477, February 14, 1997; "$2 Million Puni-tive Award Won by Injured Employee," *Managing Risk,* March 1997; and "IBP's Appeal of $2 Million Punitive Award Rejected," *Omaha World-Herald,* October 7, 1997

181 *The IBP nurse called them "idiots" and "jerks"*: Quoted in *Wilson v IBP and Arndt,* Iowa Supreme Court.

182 *The company later paid him an undisclosed sum:* See Morris, "Easy Prey."

"The first commandment is that only production counts": A transcript of Murphy's testimony appears in Andreas, Meatpackers and Beef Barons, pp. 171–83.

little has changed since IBP was caught: For Ferrell's side of the case, I have relied upon "Plaintiff's Statement of Specific Disputed Facts and Additional Material Facts," *Michael D. Ferrell v IBP, Inc.,* United States District Court for the North-ern District of Iowa, Western Division, May 7, 1999.

183 *IBP disputes this version:* For IBP's version of events, I have relied upon "State-ment of Undisputed Facts in Support of Defendant's Motion for Summary Judgment," *Michael D. Ferrell v IBP, Inc.,* United States District Court for the Northern District of Iowa, Western Division, March 6, 1999.

"numerous, pervasive, and outrageous": Quoted in "Labor Board Charges Mon-fort with Discrimination; Orders Reinstatement, Back Pay, and Union Election," *PR Newswire,* April 12, 1990. See also James M. Biers, "Monfort Flouted Labor Laws," *Denver Post,* November 4, 1995.

184 *Colorado was one of the first states:* See Ben Wear, "Lawmakers Seek Cure, Not Band-Aid; All Sides Cry Foul in Fight to Protect Interests," *Colorado Springs Ga-zette Telegraph,* February 3, 1991; Karen Bowers, "The Big Hurt: Truth Is the First Casualty in the Political War over Amendment 11," *Denver Westword,* Octo-ber 19, 1994; and Stuart Steers, "Injured Workers Have Borne the Brunt of Workers' Comp 'Reform' in Colorado," *Denver Westword,* July 19, 1996.

185 *Under Colorado's new law:* The figures on missing digits and other injuries are from the 1999 Workers' Compensation Act, State of Colorado.

Congressman Cass Ballenger: See "Congressman Argues for an Overhaul of OSHA," *Business Insurance,* July 10, 1995; David Maraniss and Michael Weisskopf, "OSHA's Enemies Find Themselves in High Places," *Washington Post,* July 24, 1995; and Figura, "New OSHA."

by the late 1990s had already reached an all-time low: See "Study Finds Decline in Workplace Inspections," *AP,* September 5, 1998.

The plant had never been inspected by OSHA: See Maraniss and Weisskopf, "OSHA's Enemies."

Congressman Joel Hefley: See "Congressman Argues for an Overhaul"; "Hutchison, Hefley Introduce Proposals in House, Senate to Overhaul OSHA," *Asbestos and Lead Abatement Report,* April 7, 1997; and Erin Emery, "Political Novice Alford Faces Hefley," *Denver Post,* October 14, 1998.

9. What's in the Meat

Interviews with two of the nation's leading experts on Shiga toxin–producing *E. coli* — Dr. David Acheson, an associate professor of medicine in the Division of Infectious Diseases at Tufts University Medical School, and Dr. Patricia M. Griffin, chief of the Foodborne Diseases Epidemiology Section, Foodborne and Diarrheal Diseases Branch, Centers for Disease Control and Prevention — helped me understand some of the distinctive characteristics and potential dangers of these organisms. A pair of journal articles greatly influenced my view of the role of the fast food and meatpacking industries in spreading disease: Gregory L. Armstrong, Jill Hollingsworth, and J. Glenn Morris, Jr., "Emerging Foodborne Pathogens: *Escherichia coli* 0157:H7 as a Model of Entry of a New Pathogen into the Food Supply of the Developed World," *Epidemiologic Reviews* 18, no. 1 (1996); and Robert V. Tauxe, "Emerging Foodborne Diseases: An Evolving Public Health Challenge," *Emerging Infectious Diseases* 3, no. 4 (October/December 1997). Tauxe is the chief of the Foodborne and Diarrheal Diseases Branch at the CDC. Throughout this chapter, the figures on the annual incidence of various foodborne pathogens — as well as on the number of deaths, hospitalizations, and so on — come from the most thorough nationwide study of food poisonings to date: Paul S. Mead, Laurence Slutsker, Vance Dietz, Linda F. McCaig, Joseph S. Bresee, Craig Shapiro, Patricia M. Griffin, and Robert V. Tauxe, "Food-Related Illness and Death in the United States," *Emerging Infectious Diseases* 5, no. 5 (September/October 1999).

For the general reader, the two best books on foodborne pathogens are *Spoiled: The Dangerous Truth about a Food Chain Gone Haywire* (New York: Basic Books, 1997) and *It Was Probably Something You Ate: A Practical Guide to Avoiding and Surviving Foodborne Illness* (New York: Penguin, 1999). Nicols Fox is the author of both, and she was extremely generous about sharing her unsettling knowledge with me. Dr. Neal D. Bernard, at the Physicians Committee for Responsible Medicine, told me in gruesome detail what America's livestock are being fed today. I am grateful to Lee Harding, Nancy Donley, and Mary Heersink — three people whose lives were changed in varying degrees by E. coli 0157:H7 — for speaking to me about their experiences. Donna Rosenbaum, one of the founders of Safe Tables Our Priority, provided much useful information about the meatpacking industry's role in outbreaks. Heather Klinkhamer, the former program director at STOP, graciously let me rummage through her files and borrow literally hundreds of them.

David Theno and Tim Biela spent a day with me, explaining how currently available technology has helped Jack in the Box reduce the threat of foodborne illness. Steve Bjerklie shared his expertise on the meat industry's response to food safety issues. For the Hudson Beef outbreak and federal meat recall policy, I relied heavily on the transcripts of two USDA meetings: the National Advisory Committee on Meat and Poultry Inspection meeting held in Washington, D.C., September 10, 1997, and the FSIS Recall Policy Public Meeting held in Arlington, Virginia, September 24, 1997. Jan Sharp, one of the U.S. attorneys in the Hudson Foods case, and Steve Kay, the editor of *Cattle Buyers Weekly*, were also helpful. David Kroeger, the president of the Midwest Council of the National Joint Council of Food Inspection Locals, spoke to me about the effects of the Streamlined Inspection System during the late 1980s and of the reduced inspections under today's new HACCP plans. The other USDA meat inspectors that I interviewed were equally informative but preferred not to be named. Felicia Nestor, at the Government Accountability Project, sent me a thick stack of USDA inspection reports given to her by federal whistleblowers. A straightforward account of the effort to create a science-based system of meat inspection can be found in *Food Safety: Risk-Based Inspections and Microbial Monitoring Needed for Meat and Poultry* (GAO Reports, June 1, 1994). The Center for Public Integrity has done a fine job investigating the meatpacking industry's close ties to members of Congress. One of its reports, *Safety Last: The Politics of E. coli and other Food-Borne Pathogens* (Washington, D.C.: Center for Public Integrity, 1998) outlines how public health measures have in recent years been framed to suit the needs of well-funded private interests.

Page

193   *called Sandra Gallegos:* For the investigation of Harding's illness, I relied on interviews with Lee Harding and Sandra Gallegos, as well as on Julie Collins, "Hudson Beef Recall: How the Link Was Discovered," *Journal of Environmental Health*, December 1, 1997; Tom Kenworthy, "Friendly Barbecue May Have Led to Meat Recall," *Washington Post*, August 24, 1997; Tom Morgenthau, "Health Pros' Detective Work Helps Arrest Villain E. coli," *Portland Oregonian*, August 31, 1997; Ann Schrader, "Tracing E. coli to Meat Earns Awards for Workers," *Denver Post*, September 18, 1997; and the transcript of the NAC Meat and Poultry Inspection Hearing, September 10, 1997.

194   *Colorado was one of only six states:* Meat and Poultry Inspection Hearing transcript, p. 396.

     primarily to supply hamburgers for the Burger King chain: See Melanie Warner, "How Tyson Ate Hudson," *Fortune*, October 27, 1997.

     Roughly 35 million pounds of ground beef: See Steve Kay, "Hudson Recall Was Larger Than Reported," *Cattle Buyers Weekly*, September 29, 1997. Kay's estimate may in fact be too conservative, since it is based on a production rate of 400,000 pounds a day. The Hudson Beef plant could actually produce twice that amount daily.

195 *roughly 200,000 people are sickened:* Derived from the annual numbers cited in Mead et al., "Food-Related Illness and Death": 76 million illnesses, 325,000 hospitalizations, and 5,000 deaths.

more than a quarter of the American population: Ibid.

can precipitate long-term ailments: See James A. Lindsay, "Chronic Sequelae of Foodborne Disease," *Emerging Infectious Diseases* 3, no. 4 (October/December 1997).

entirely new kinds of outbreaks are now occurring: See Tauxe, "Emerging Foodborne Diseases."

196 *a newly emerged pathogen:* See Armstrong et al., "Emerging Foodborne Pathogens."

thirteen large packinghouses now slaughter: Cited in James M. MacDonald and Michael Ollinger, "U.S. Meat Slaughter Consolidating Rapidly," *USDA Food Review,* May 1, 1997.

more than a dozen other new foodborne pathogens: Cited in Tauxe, "Emerging Foodborne Diseases."

infectious agents that have not yet been identified: See "Food-Related Illness and Death."

defective softball bats, sneakers, stuffed animals: See Consumer Product Safety Commission, press releases, June 1997–June 1999.

197 *7.5 percent of the ground beef samples:* The figures on ground beef contamination are from "Nationwide Federal Plant Raw Ground Beef Microbiological Survey, August 1993–March 1994," United States Deartment of Agriculture, Food Safety and Inspection Service, Science and Technology, Microbiology Division, April 1996.

fatal in about one out of . . . cases: Mead et al., "Food-Related Illness and Death."

"a food for the poor": David Gerard Hogan, *Selling 'Em by the Sack* (New York: New York University Press, 1997), p. 22.

"The hamburger habit is just about as safe": Quoted ibid., p. 32.

198 *"nothing but White Castle Hamburgers and water":* By the end of the experiment the student was eating up to two dozen hamburgers a day. Quoted ibid., p. 33; Tennyson, *Hamburger Heaven,* p. 24.

pork had been the most popular: Interview with James Ratchford, American Meat Institute.

almost half of the employment in American agriculture . . . annual revenues generated by beef: National Cattlemen's Beef Association Fact Sheet.

More than two-thirds of those hamburgers were bought: Cited in David Theno, "Raising the Bar to Ensure Safer Burgers," *San Diego Union-Tribune,* August 27, 1997.

children between the ages of seven and thirteen ate: A survey by McDonald's once found that children under the age of seven ate 1.7 hamburgers a week; those from seven to thirteen ate 6.2. People from thirteen to thirty ate 5.2; from thirty to thirty-five, 3.3; from thirty-five to sixty, 2.6; and over sixty, 1.3. Cited in Boas and Chain, *Big Mac,* p. 218.

more than seven hundred people in at least four states: See "Update: Multistate Outbreak of *Escherichia coli* 0157:H7 Infections from Hamburgers — Western

United States, 1992–1993," *Morbidity and Mortality Weekly Report,* Centers for Disease Control and Prevention, April 16, 1993; and Fox, *Spoiled,* pp. 246–68.

199 *In 1982 dozens of children were sickened:* Nicols Fox offers the best account of this outbreak. See Fox, *Spoiled,* pp. 220–29.

"the possibility of a statistical association": Quoted ibid., p. 227.

In the eight years since the Jack in the Box outbreak: I have taken the annual *E. coli* 0157:H7 numbers from Mead et al., "Food-Related Illness and Death" — 73,480 illnesses; 2,168 hospitalizations; 61 deaths — and multiplied them by 8.

In about 4 percent of reported E. coli 0157:H7 cases: Cited in Mead et al., "Food-related Illness and Death."

About 5 percent of the children who develop HUS: Interview with Dr. Patricia Griffin.

200 *the leading cause of kidney failure among children:* Cited in "Isolation of *E. coli* 0157:H7 from Sporadic Cases of Hemorrhagic Colitis — United States," *Morbidity and Mortality Weekly Report,* Centers for Disease Control and Prevention, August 1, 1997.

201 *as few as five organisms:* Interview with Dr. David Acheson.

The most common cause of foodborne outbreaks has been: See "Outbreak — Georgia and Tennessee."

the feces of deer, dogs, horses, and flies: See Armstrong et al., "Foodborne Pathogens."

did not eat a contaminated burger: See "Update: Multistate Outbreak."

remains contagious for about two weeks: See Armstrong et al., "Foodborne Pathogens."

202 E. coli *0157:H7 can replicate in cattle troughs:* See Paul Hammel and Henry J. Cordes, "Holes in the Research: *E. coli* Prompts Few Changes on the Farm from Farm to Fork," *Omaha World-Herald,* December 15, 1997.

About 75 percent of the cattle in the United States: Cited in Mitchell Satchell and Stephen J. Hedges, "The Next Bad Beef Scandal? Cattle Feed Now Contains Things Like Chicken Manure and Dead Cats," *U.S. News & World Report,* September 1, 1997.

millions of dead cats and dead dogs: Ibid.

cattle blood is still put into the feed: For the unsettling details of what livestock are now fed, see "Substances Prohibited from Use in Animal Food or Feed; Animal Proteins Prohibited in Ruminant Food; Final Rule," Part II, *Federal Register,* June 5, 1997; Ellen Ruppel Shell, "Could Mad-Cow Disease Happen Here?" *Atlantic Monthly,* September 1998; and Rebecca Osvath, "Some Feed and Manufacturing Facilities Not Complying with Rules to Prevent BSE, Survey Finds," *Food Chemical News,* April 3, 2000.

A study published a few years ago: Eric R. Haapapuro, Neal D. Barnard, and Michele Simon, "Review — Animal Waste Used as Livestock Feed: Dangers to Human Health," *Preventive Medicine,* September/October 1997.

203 *during the winter about 1 percent of the cattle . . . as much as 50 percent during the summer:* The study was conducted by the USDA's Agricultural Research Service. Cited in "Study Urges Pre-Processed Beef Test for *E. coli,*" *Health Letter on the CDC,* March 13, 2000.

204 *can contaminate 32,000 pounds:* Cited in Armstrong et al., "Foodborne Pathogens."

204 *the animals used to make about one-quarter:* See "Relative Ground Beef Contribution to the United States Beef Supply — Final Report," The American Meat Institute Foundation, in cooperation with the National Cattlemen's Beef Association," May 1996.

dozens or even hundreds of different cattle: Cited in Armstrong et al., "Foodborne Pathogens."

"This is no fairy story and no joke": Sinclair, *Jungle,* p. 135.

205 *"Meat and food products, generally speaking":* Quoted in Skaggs, *Prime Cut,* p. 123.

"Men are men": Quoted in Yeager, *Competition and Regulation,* p. 208.

"we are paying all we care to pay": Quoted ibid., p. 205.

A panel appointed by the National Academy of Sciences . . . another National Academy of Sciences panel: The findings of the first panel were published in a report entitled *Meat and Poultry Inspection: The Scientific Basis of the Nation's Program* (Washington, D.C.: National Academy Press, 1985). The findings of the second panel appeared as *The Future of Public Health* (Washington, D.C.: National Academy Press, 1988).

206 *"Who knows what crisis will be next?":* The chairman of the panel was Richard Remington, professor of preventive medicine and environmental health at the University of Iowa. Quoted in Gregory Byrne, "Panel Laments 'Disarray' in Public Health System; Institute of Medicine Panel," *Science,* September 23, 1988.

five major slaughterhouses that supplied about one-fifth: Cited in Daniel P. Puzo, "Does Streamlined Beef Inspection Work?" *Los Angeles Times,* June 18, 1992.

number of federal meat inspectors would be cut by half: See Knight-Ridder News Service, "Meat Policy Changed: Plants Won't Be Inspected As Often," *The Record,* November 4, 1988.

A 1992 USDA study of the Streamlined Inspection System: See Don Kendall, "Report Calls for Streamlining Federal Meat Inspections," *AP,* September 17, 1990.

207 *the accuracy of that study was thrown into doubt:* On April 30, 1992, the ABC News show *PrimeTime Live* broadcast an investigation of the Streamlined Inspection System for Cattle. ABC had obtained corporate documents showing that some USDA visits were known in advance. The show also included footage of meat covered in feces being processed at the Monfort plant in Greeley. For more on conditions at the Greeley plant, see Kelly Richmond, "Unhappy Meals: Colorado Meat Plant Blasted for Disease and Filth," *States New Service,* June 11, 1992. For more on the lapses of the SIS-C and the lack of surprise during USDA visits, see Guy Gugliotta, "USDA Is Sued: Where's the Beef Report? Public Interest Group Charges System Lets Dirtier, More Dangerous Meat Reach Consumers," *Washington Post,* July 10, 1990.

some of the meat used by Jack in the Box: See Terry McDermott, "The Jack in the Box Poisonings — Why Inspection of Meat Fails," *Seattle Times,* January 31, 1993; Frank Green, "Foodmaker, Suppliers Settle *E. coli* Claims," *San Diego Union-Tribune,* February 25, 1998.

"This recent outbreak sheds light": Quoted in "Meat Institute Urges Federal and State Agencies to Adopt Industry Guidelines Proven to Prevent *E. coli* 0157:H7 in Hamburgers," *PR Newswire,* February 4, 1993.

"The presence of bacteria in raw meat": Quoted in Fox, *Spoiled,* p. 252.

208 *had waited a week before acknowledging:* See Robert Goff, "Coming Clean: After Its Tragic Outbreak of *E. coli,* Jack in the Box Quickly Fixed Its Food Handling," *Forbes,* May 17, 1999.

210 *A study of campaign contributions:* See "The Captive Congress," a chapter in *Safety Last,* as well as the statistical tables, pp. 9–21, 76–90.

212 *prosecutors claimed . . . Both men were later found innocent:* See Scott Bauer, "Prosecutors: Former Hudson Foods Officials Lied about Meat Recall," *AP,* November 10, 1999; "Tyson Unit Acquitted of Lying in Beef Recall; Hudson Quality Control Director Also Cleared," *Arkansas Democrat-Gazette,* December 4, 1999.
health officials in Nevada did not learn from the company: FSIS Recall Policy Public Meeting.
"had not been fully tested": Quoted in Elliot Jaspin and Scott Montgomery, "U.S. Mum on Fast Food Recalls," *Cox News Service,* August 18, 1997, Jaspin and Montgomery have written a number of fine investigative pieces on the USDA and the meatpacking industry.
"We live in a very litigious society": Quoted ibid.

213 *The USDA now informs the public:* Interview with Elizabeth Gaston, USDA Food Safety and Inspection Service.
"It's very frustrating for us": Quoted in Allison Young and Jeff Taylor, "Stealthy Meat Recalls Leave Consumers in Dark," *Denver Post,* May 13, 1999. See also Allison Beers, "Recalls Present Tough Decisions for Food Companies," *Food Chemical News,* May 4, 1998; and Pan Demetrakakes, "Backlash: Recalls," *Food Processing,* August 1, 1999.
"Press releases will not identify": Quoted in "Recall of Meat and Poultry Products," FSIS Directive, January 19, 2000.
A recent IBP press release: "Ground Beef Product Recall," IBP news release, June 23, 2000.

214 *Nowhere does the press release mention:* The story of the outbreak at Tiger Harry's is based on interviews with officials at the Arkansas Department of Health, including Dennis Berry, an epidemiologist; John Kraft, a field investigator; and Dr. David Bourne, medical director of the Preventive Health Section. See also "21 Ill, 11 Hospitalized for *E. coli;* Outbreak May Be Tied to Restaurant," *Arkansas Democrat-Gazette,* June 3, 2000; "266,000 Pounds of Bad Beef Recalled," *Capital Times,* June 24, 2000; "Health Department Finds No Further Cases of *E. coli* Infection; USDA Investigating Ground Beef," press release, Arkansas Department of Health, June 16, 2000.
"We can fine circuses for mistreating elephants": Quoted in Carol Smith, "Overhaul in Meat Inspection No Small Potatoes, Official Says," *Seattle Post-Intelligencer,* January 29, 1998.

215 *demoralized and understaffed:* See Allison Beers, "Plant Staffing Shortages Exacerbated by Excessive Absences, Low Morale," *Food Chemical News,* August 16, 1999.
the USDA had 12,000 meat inspectors: See Jake Thompson, "Meat Inspectors' Role Scrutinized: Critics Say That Despite a New Safety Program, There Are Too Few People to Monitor Plants," *Omaha World-Herald,* August 24, 1997; "Industry Forum: State of the Union," *Meat & Poultry,* March 1998; and "Beefing Up Inspection," *Government Executive,* February 1999.

215 *the new HACCP plans are only as good:* For a strong critique of the current system from an unexpected source, see "Food Safety and Inspection Service: Implementation of the Hazard Analysis and Critical Control Point System," U.S. Department of Agriculture, Office of Inspector General, Food Safety Initiative, Meat and Poultry Products, Report no. 24001-3-At, June 2000.

216 *She routinely falsified her checklist:* Gary Mickelson, a spokesman for IBP, told me that an employee who falsifies such documentation is subject to disciplinary action by the company. He also told me that IBP employees have in fact been terminated for such behavior.

220-degree steam: The number comes from "SPS 400: Information Update," a manual published by Frigoscandia Equipment, the manufacturer of steam pasteurization units.

by about 90 percent: Ibid.

"We have been informed that carcasses": IBP memo from Dean Danilson to Leo Lang re: outrail cattle, May 19, 1997.

217 *The dirtiest meat was to be shipped out:* When the memo leaked in June of 1998, IBP denied that it was shipping contaminated meat to outside suppliers, claimed its unusual outrail policy had been devised solely to address shelf-life concerns — and said that, in any event, the policy was no longer in effect. Gary Mickelson, an IBP spokesman, repeated the same assertions to me, adding that "IBP's quality and food safety programs . . . are considered by many to be the 'best' in the industry. We will not sell any products — whether it be boxed beef or beef carcasses — that we do not believe are safe for human consumption." See also "Ground Beef Guidelines Are Insufficient, STOP Says," *Food Chemical News,* June 8, 1998.

research for the Star Wars antimissile program: See "Titan to Put Whammy on Food Bacteria," *San Diego Union-Tribune,* May 18, 1999.

get rid of the word "irradiation": See "Beef Industry Recommends Irradiation Rule Include Ready-to-Eat Meats," *Food Labeling News,* June 23, 1999; Rick Lingle, "Food Irradiation Acceleration," *Packaging Digest,* July 1, 1999; and Steven F. Grover, "Pasteurized Foods in Your Future?" *Food Management,* October 1999. Grover is a vice president of the National Restaurant Association.

A 1983 investigation by NBC News: For the story of Rudy "Butch" Stanko, see Wayne Slater, "Domestic News," *AP,* September 19, 1983; "Agriculture to Investigate a Meat Plant in Denver," *New York Times,* September 20, 1983; Judy Harrington, "Packing Company, Owner, Guilty of Selling Bad Meat to Government," *AP,* September 15, 1984; and Neal Karlen with Jeff P. Copeland, "A 'Mystery Meat' Scandal," *Newsweek,* September 24, 1984.

219 *an eleven-year-old-boy became seriously ill:* For the Bauer Meat story, see Patricia Guthrie, "Government Says Bauer Meats Are Unfit to Eat," *Atlanta Journal,* October 14, 1998; "Bauer Meat 'Unfit for Human Consumption,'" *Meat Processing,* November 1, 1998; "Bacteria Wars: How 3 Processors Responded," *St. Petersburg Times,* February 14, 1999; Robert Trigaux, "Tougher Standards Battle Meat Bacteria," *St. Petersburg Times,* February 14, 1999; and "*E. Coli* Suit Principals Confer; Child's Family Sues Florida Company," *Florida Times-Union,* May 15, 1999.

a dozen children in Finley, Washington: For the Northern States Beef story, see Elliott Jaspin and Scott Montgomery, "Feds Buy Bad Beef for Low Bid; *E. coli*

Outbreak Results from School Lunch Program Supply System," *Atlanta Journal*, March 28, 1999; and "Tainted School Tacos," *Seattle Times*, May 8, 1999.

219 *as much as 47 percent of the company's ground beef:* See Bill Lodge, "Dallas Beef Plant That Failed *Salmonella* Tests Challenges Screening System," *Dallas Morning News*, December 10, 1999; and Tiara Ellis and Michael Saul, "Dallas Meat Processor Recalls Beef After USDA Detects *E. coli*," *Dallas Morning News*, December 26, 1999.

about 1.4 million illnesses: Mead et al., "Food-Related Illness and Death."

the USDA continued to purchase thousands of tons: See Scott Montgomery and Elliot Jaspin, "USDA Purchased Meat from Texas Plant after Contamination Cited," *Atlanta Journal*, Decmber 4, 1999.

annually providing as much as 45 percent: Cited in "USDA Has a Valid Beef in Dallas," *Chicago Tribune*, December 14, 1999.

220 *the USDA resumed its purchases:* See "USDA Satisfied with Changes in Meat Plant It Tried to Shut Down," *AP*, February 15, 2000.

Judge Fish issued a decision: For the implications of the Supreme Beef case, see Marc Kaufman, "Texas Ruling Threatens USDA Meat Inspections," *Washington Post*, May 26, 2000; Todd Bensman, "Judge Rebuffs USDA; Agency Tried to Close Dallas Plant," *Dallas Morning News*, May 26, 2000; and John Taylor, "Court Ruling Won't Alter IBP Methods," *Omaha World-Herald*, May 27, 2000.

much of the beef used . . . repeatedly failed USDA tests: See Allison Beers, "Meat Groups Petition USDA to Change HACCP Regulations," *Food Chemical News*, January 10, 2000.

221 *The meatpacking industry immediately opposed:* See "AMS Says It Will Continue with New Standards," *National Meat Association Newsletter*, August 7, 2000.

"You'd be better off eating a carrot stick": Quoted in Usha Lee McFarling, "Homey Kitchens Become Killers Before Our Eyes," *Austin American-Statesman*, August 12, 1998.

sixty to one hundred other mutant E. coli *organisms . . . Perhaps a third of them cause illnesses:* Interview with Dr. David Acheson.

222 *roughly 37,000 Americans suffer:* Mead et al., "Food-Related Illness and Death."

A 1997 undercover investigation by KCBS-TV: See Richard Martin, "L.A. County Cracks Down on Food-Safety Violators," *Nation's Restaurant News*, December 1, 1997.

three teenage employees at a Burger King: See "Police Say Two Teens Tampered with Food," *AP*, May 10, 2000, and "Burger King Employees Charged," *AP*, May 11, 2000.

10. Global Realization

Few West Germans are familiar with the unusual history of Plauen, though it is abundantly detailed in a number of locally published books. *Plauen: auf historischen Postkarten* (Plauen, Germany: Plauen Verlag, 1991), by Frank Weiss, uses old postcards to illustrate the history of the city during its most prosperous era. *Plauen: 1933–1945* (Plauen: Vogtländischer Heimatverlag Neupert, 1995) is an oversized book, full of photographs, that traces the effects of the Great Depression and the rise of the Nazi

Party. The Allied bombing of the city is vividly documented through before-and-after photographs in *Plauen 1944/1945: Eine Stadt wird zerstört* (Plauen: Vogtländischer Heimatverlag Neupert, 1995), by Rudolf Laser, Joachim Mensdorf, and Johannes Richter. For life near the East German border, I relied on Ingolf Hermann's *Die Deutsch-Deutsch Grenze* (Plauen: Vogtländischer Heimatverlag Neupert, 1998). Plauen's 1989 uprising is chronicled in Rolf Schwanitz's *Zivilcourage: Die friedliche Revolution in Plauen anhand von Stasi-Akten* (Plauen, Vogtländischer Heimatverlag Neupert, 1998). *Plauen: Ein Rundgang Durch die Stadt* (Plauen: Militzke Verlag, 1992) gives a sense of the city after the Wall came down.

John Connelly, an assistant professor of history at the University of California, Berkeley, is one of the few American academics who has both visited and written about postwar Plauen. Professor Connelly shared his recollection of the city with me and sent me the fine article he wrote about its rebellion: "Moment of Revolution: Plauen (Vogtland), October 7, 1989," *German Politics & Society*, Summer 1990. Thomas Küttler, the hero of that uprising, told me how it unfolded and shared his thoughts about its legacy. I am grateful to Cordula Franz for help in arranging interviews in Plauen and to Sybille Unterdoifel for introducing me to The Ranch. Frieder Stephan, the owner of The Ranch, helped me fathom the local youth culture and explained his musical journey from rock to disco to country and western. Christian Pöllmann, who helps run a theater company in Plauen, as well as the German Social Union Party, gave me a strong sense of life under Communism and of the hunger for all things American. The photographer Franziska Heinze and journalist Markus Schneider helped me gather information about their home town. Siegfried Pater — filmmaker, environmentalist, and author of *Zum Beispiel McDonald's* (Göttingen: Lamuv Verlag, 1994) — described some of McDonald's misbehavior in Germany. Barbara Distil, the curator of the Dachau Museum, spoke to me about the controversy surrounding the local McDonald's. For the history of the camp, I relied on a book that she edited with Ruth Jakusch: *Concentration Camp Dachau 1933–1945* (Brussels: Comité International de Dachau, 1978).

The Illustrated History of Las Vegas (Edison, N.J.: Chartwell Books, 1997), by Bill Yenne, conveys how the city has been radically transformed in recent years. *The Players: The Men Who Made Las Vegas* (Reno: University of Nevada Press, 1997), edited by Jack Sheehan, provides a good deal of insight into the unique culture that emerged there. Timothy O'Brien's *Bad Bet: The Inside Story of the Glamour, Glitz, and Danger of America's Gambling Industry* (New York: Times Business, 1998) explains precisely how the casinos make their money.

Much of my information on obesity comes from articles in *Science*, the *Journal of the American Medical Association*, and the *New England Journal of Medicine*. The nutritionist Jane Kirby placed many of the claims and counterclaims about diet into a calm and reasonable perspective for me. Greg Critser's "Let Them Eat Fat: The Heavy Truths about American Obesity," *Harper's*, March 2000, is a provocative essay on fast food and the poor.

My account of the McLibel trial is based on interviews with the two principals, Helen Steel and Dave Morris, and on the transcripts of the trial (which were available, along with other interesting material, at the anti-McDonald's Web site www.mcspotlight.org). Franny Armstrong — the director of an excellent documentary, *McLibel: Two Worlds Collide* — was extremely helpful. John Vidal's book, *McLibel,* tells the whole, extraordinary story of the trial. The essays collected in *Golden Arches East: McDonald's in East Asia* (Stanford, Calif.: Stanford University Press, 1997), edited by James L. Watson, reveal some of the unpredictable ways in which fast food is now being embraced by other cultures.

Page

226 *the city's population roughly tripled:* See Weiss, *Plauen: Postkarten,* pp. 3–4.

the most millionaires . . . and the most suicides: Interview with Thomas Küttler. Also cited in Connelly, "Moment of Revolution."

the highest unemployment rate: In 1933 the unemployment rate in Plauen was 15.6 percent, the highest in Germany. Cited in *Plauen 1933–1945,* p. 55.

227 *More bombs were dropped on Plauen:* About 63.2 tons of explosives were dropped on each square kilometer of Dresden; about 185.4 tons per square kilometer struck Plauen. Cited in Laser et al., *Plauen 1944/1945,* p. 14.

about 75 percent of Plauen lay in ruins: Küttler interview.

lost one-third of its prewar population: Cited in Weiss, *Plauen: Postkarten,* p. 4.

an "unusually low quality of life": Connelly, "Plauen: Moment of Revolution."

228 *"We want freedom":* Küttler interview.

229 *"McDonald's and similar abnormal garbage-makers":* Quoted in "Ban the 'Big Mac' from East Germany, Parliamentarian Demands," *Reuters,* July 26, 1990.

"global realization": Quoted in "Blue Chip Blues," *Economist,* September 26, 1998.

Within the next decade: See "Some Things Old, Some Things New," *Franchising World,* November–December 1999.

earns the majority of its profits: See "The McDonald's Corporation 1999 Annual Report"; Charlene C. Price, "The U.S. Foodservice Industry Looks Abroad," *USDA Food Review,* May–August 1996.

the most widely recognized brand in the world: See "McDonald's wins top spot in global brand ratings," *Brand Strategy,* November 22, 1996.

"McWorld": See Benjamin R. Barber, "Jihad vs. McWorld," *Atlantic Monthly,* March 1992.

when McDonald's opened its first restaurant in Turkey: See Gulsun Bilgen-Konuray, "Turkey — Franchising Market," *Industry Sector Analysis,* U.S. Foreign and Commercial Service, U.S. State Department, August 24, 1999.

230 *"Americana and the promise of modernization":* Watson, *Golden Arches East,* p. 41.

earning $200,000 in a single week during Ramadan: Cited in Bill McDowall, "The Global Market Challenge," *Restaurants & Institutions,* November 1, 1994.

In Brazil, McDonald's has become: See "McDonald's Employs 33,000 in Brazil," *AP,* August 1, 1999.

"Sorry, No McDonald's": Quoted in George Lazarus, "You Won't Find a McDonald's on Unspoiled Tahiti," *Adweek,* January 13, 1986.

"A McDonald's restaurant is just the window": Quoted in Latha Venkatraman, "Keeping That Lettuce Crisp," *Business Line,* July 5, 1999.

231 *"It's a great little country":* Simplot interview.

"Kids are the same regarding": Quoted in "Barbie, McDonald's Find Common Ground," *Selling to Kids,* September 30, 1998.

231 *the number of fast food restaurants roughly tripled:* Cited in Richard Martin, "Special Report: Down Under's Bloomin' Dining Wonders," *Nation's Restaurant News*, October 7, 1996.

Ronald McDonald knew: Cited in Kay M. Hammond, Allan Wylie, and Sally Casswell, "The Extent and Nature of Televised Food Advertising to New Zealand Children and Adolescents," *Australian & New Zealand Journal of Public Health*, February 1999.

"funny, gentle, kind": Quoted in *Golden Arches East*, p. 64.

Coca-Cola is now the favorite drink . . . McDonald's serves their favorite food: Cited in "Developmental, Cultural Issues Key in Marketing to Kids Globally," *Selling to Kids*, April 1, 1998.

"If we eat McDonald's hamburgers and potatoes": Quoted in Vidal, *McLibel*, p. 42. In addition to being the McDonald's Corporation's partner in Japan, Den Fujita is the author of best-selling books such as *Stupid People Lose Money, How to Become Number One in Business*, and *How to Blow the Rich Man's Bugle Like the Jews Do*. See James Sterngold, "Den Fujita, Japan's Mr. Joint Venture," *New York Times*, March 22, 1992.

232 *"For a child growing up in the turmoil":* Christa Maerker, "The Federal Republic of Germany: Second-hand Culture with Borrowed Dreams," *Schatzkammer*, Spring 1990.

Americans with German ancestors: Cited in Tim Bovee, "German-Americans Largest U.S. Ethnic Group," *AP*, December 16, 1992.

less than one-third of the German foodservice market: Cited in Rupert Spies and Gretel Weiss, "Is Germany's Traditional Restaurant a Dying Breed?" *Cornell Hotel & Restaurant Administration Quarterly*, June 1998.

the biggest restaurant company in Germany: See Richard Martin, "Germany Shows Appetite for 'Fun' Themes and Foreign Flavors," *Nation's Restaurant News*, April 17, 1995.

233 *It battles labor unions:* Interview with Siegfried Pater.

the number of franchised outlets: See "Germany-Franchising Market," *Industry Sector Analysis*, U.S. Foreign & Commercial Service, U.S. State Department, July 7, 1998.

"The partnership scheme will undoubtedly be": Quoted in "German Wal-Mart Stores to Feature McDonald's Restaurants," *Evening Standard*, August 12, 1999.

The McDonald's Corporation denied: See Steve Nichol, "Protesters Lambaste McDonald's; Picketers Say Restaurant Is Trivializing Holocaust," *Fort Lauderdale Sun-Sentinel*, January 28, 1997.

After the curator of the Dachau Museum complained: Interview with Barbara Distil.

"Welcome to Dachau": Ibid.

The McDonald's at Dachau is one-third of a mile: According to the odometer on my rental car.

234 *Las Vegas is the fastest-growing major city:* See "Metropolitan Area Population Estimates for July 1, 1998, and Population Change for April 1, 1990, to July 1, 1998," U.S. Census Bureau, September 30, 1999.

235 *Over the past twenty years the population:* In 1980, the population of the Las Vegas metropolitan area was 528,000; today it approaches 1.5 million. See "Large

Metropolitan Areas — Population: 1980 to 1996," *Statistical Abstract of the U.S.*, p. 41; "Metropolitan Area Population Estimates . . . Population Change."

235 *legally protected against the workings of the free market:* For a fascinating account of the Nevada Gaming Control Board and its powers, see "A Peculiar Institution," by Sergio Lalli, in Sheehan, *The Players*, pp. 1–22.

236 *about two-thirds of a typical casino's profits . . . a profit rate of as much as 20 percent:* See O'Brien, *Bad Bet*, pp. 40–44.

"Those who hope we shall move": Mikhail Gorbachev, *Perestroika: New Thinking for Our Country and the World* (New York: Harper & Row, 1987), p. 36.

237 *"And the merry clowns":* George Cohon, *To Russia with Fries* (Toronto: Mc-Clelland & Stewart, 1999), p. xi.

He reportedly earned $160,000: Cited in Maura Reynolds, "Russians Watch Gorbachev Pizza Ad," *AP*, December 23, 1997.

"all my money is gone": The German publication was *Bunte*. Quoted in James Meek, "How Last Soviet Leader Lost His Roubles," *Guardian* (London), December 30, 1998.

a fee of $150,000 and the use of a private jet: Cited in Margaret Coker, "Siegfried and Gorby?" *Business Week*, February 15, 1999.

"As if things weren't good enough": The executive was Bob O'Brien, president of NPD Foodservice Information Group.

"sensory evaluation specialist": The speaker was Richard Popper, vice president of Peryam & Kroll Marketing Sensory Research.

238 *"A growing number of groups":* Mr. Nugent's speech, as well as all the others, was recorded by Convention Tapes International, Miami, Florida.

240 *the highest obesity rate:* Cited in Elizabeth Gleick, "Land of the Fat," *Time International Edition*, October 25, 1999.

More than half of all American adults and about one-quarter of all American children: Cited in James O. Hill and James C. Peters, "Environmental Contributions to the Obesity Epidemic," *Science*, May 29, 1998.

The rate of obesity among American adults . . . among American children: See Gary Taubes, "Demographics: As Obesity Rates Rise, Experts Struggle to Explain Why," *Science*, May 29, 1998.

"We've got the fattest, least fit": Quoted in Maggie Fox, "U.S.: Obesity Will Be Hard to Treat, Experts Say," *AAP Newsfeed*, May 29, 1998.

about 44 million American adults are obese . . . 6 million are "super-obese": The adult population of the United States is about 200 million. Twenty-two percent of the nation's adults are obese and 3 percent are super-obese. See Jeffrey P. Koplon and William H. Dietz, "Caloric Imbalance and Public Health Policy," *Journal of the American Medical Society*, October 27, 1999; "Resident Population Projections, by Age and Sex," *Statistical Abstract*, p. 17.

A recent study: Ali H. Mokdad, Mary K. Serdula, William H. Dietz, Barbara A. Bowman, James S. Marks, Jeffrey P. Koplon, "The Spread of the Obesity Epidemic in the United States, 1991–1998," *Journal of the American Medical Association*, October 27, 1999.

when people eat more and move less: See Hill and Peters, "Environmental Contributions"; Eric Ravussian and Elliot Danforth, Jr., "Human Physiology: Beyond Sloth — Physical Activity and Weight Gain," *Science*, January 8, 1999.

241 *per capita consumption of carbonated soft drinks:* Cited in Jacobson, "Liquid Candy."

During the late 1950s the typical soft drink order: Cited in Judy Putnam, "U.S. Food Supply Providing More Food and Calories," *USDA Food Review,* October 1, 1999.

more fat than ten of the chain's milk shakes: See "Nutritional Information," CKE Restaurants.

"Consumers savor the flavor": Kate MacArthur, "Fast Feeders Find Sizzle by Bringing on the Bacon," *Advertising Age,* March 27, 2000. See also Michael Pearson, "Lower Production, Higher Demand for Fast Food Bacon Restores Profitability to Hog Farming," *AP,* April 20, 2000.

A decade ago, restaurants sold about 20 percent: Ibid.

second only to smoking: See Koplon and Dietz, "Caloric Imbalance."

about 280,000 Americans die every year: Cited in Joyce Howard Price, "Fat Chance: The Goverment's War on Obesity," *Washington Post,* January 30, 2000.

242 *now approach $240 billion:* See Maggie Fox, "Obesity Costs U.S. $238 Billion a Year — Survey," *Reuters,* September 15, 1999.

$33 billion on various weight-loss schemes: Cited in Robert Jablon, "Studies Show Obesity on Rise in U.S.," *AP,* October 26, 1999.

Obesity has been linked to: See William C. Willett, William H. Dietz, and Graham A. Colditz, "Guidelines for Healthy Weight," *New England Journal of Medicine,* August 5, 1999; Aviva Must, Jennifer Spadano, Eugenie H. Coakley, Allison E. Field, Graham Colditz, and William H. Dietz, "The Disease Burden Associated with Overweight and Obesity," *Journal of the American Medical Association,* October 27, 1999.

A 1999 study by the American Cancer Society: See Katherine Webster, "Study: Obesity Can Shorten Lifespan," *AP,* October 6, 1999.

"The message is we're too fat": The researcher is Eugenia Calle, quoted ibid.

Severely obese American children: See Dennis Michael Styne, "Childhood Obesity: Time for Action, Not Complacency," *American Family Physician,* February 15, 1999.

the number of fast food restaurants in Great Britain: Cited in Gleick, "Land of the Fat."

and so did the obesity rate among adults: Cited in Gary Taubes, "Demographics: Weight Increases Worldwide?" *Science,* May 29, 1998

The British now eat more fast food: Cited in Kate Watson Smyth, "Britons Eating 7M Pounds of Fast Food Every Day," *Independent,* May 13, 1999.

They also have the highest obesity rate: Cited in Gleick, "Land of the Fat."

less of a problem in Italy and Spain: Ibid.

where spending on fast food is relatively low: See Smyth, "Britons Eating 7M Pounds"; "Fast Food Is Taking Over the World," *USA Today Magazine,* May 1, 1999; Dita Smith, "What on Earth? Fast-Food Feast," *Washington Post,* May 27, 2000.

In China, the proportion of overweight teenagers: Cited in Simon Pollock, "China's Biggest 'Little Emperors' Struggle to Tone Up," *Japan Economic Newswire,* August 18, 1999.

In Japan, eating hamburgers: For a good account of how eating habits were transformed in Japan, see Mark Hammond and Jacqueline Ruyak, "The Decline of the Japanese Diet: MacArthur to McDonald's," *East West*, October 1990.

242 *the sale of fast food in Japan more than doubled:* Ibid.

the rate of obesity among children: The statistic comes from the Japanese Education Ministry. Cited in "Western Fast Food Is Blamed for Overweight Children," *Food Labeling News*, May 13, 1998.

about one-third of all Japanese men in their thirties: See Joseph Coleman, "More Japanese Men Are Overweight," *AP,* June 15, 1998; "Time to Trim the Fat of the Land," *Japan Times*, November 14, 1999.

243 *a study of middle-aged Japanese men:* The Ni-Hon-San Study is described in Hammond and Ruyack, "MacArthur to McDonald." See also Jeanette G. Kernicki, "A Multicultural Perspective on Cardiovascular Disease," *Journal of Cardiovascular Nurses*, July 1997.

American children now get about one-quarter: Cited in Janet McConnaughey, "Chips, Fries Big Part of Kids' Diet," *AP,* September 5, 1999.

A survey of children's advertising: See "A Spoonful of Sugar — Television Food Advertising Aimed at Children: An International Comparative Survey," Consumers International, London, November 1996; "Advertising to Children: UK the Worst in Europe," *Food Magazine*, January/March 1997.

"Resist America beginning with Cola": Quoted in Philip F. Zeidman, "Globalization: A Hard Pill to Swallow?" *Franchising World*, July/August 1999.

"Maybe they think it's Italian": Quoted in "U.S. Companies in China Keeping Low Profile," *Colorado Springs Gazette*, May 11, 1999.

"lousy food": The French phrase for what Bove scorns is "la mal-bouffe." See Sophie Meunier, "The French Exception," *Foreign Affairs*, August 2000.

244 *largest purchaser of agricultural commodities in France:* Cited in Carla Power, "McParadox," *Newsweek International,* July 10, 2000.

"servile slaves at the service of agribusiness": Quoted in John Lloyd, "The Trial of Jose Bove," *Financial Times*, July 1, 2000.

"Non à McMerde": Quoted in John Lichfield, "St. Jose Makes His Stand Against the Chicken 'McMerde,'" *Independent*, July 1, 2000.

"epitomises everything we despise": Quoted in Christopher Dunkley, "The Greens Take a Bite at Big Mac," *Financial Times*, May 17, 1997.

245 *"What's Wrong with McDonald's?":* See "What's Wrong with McDonald's? Everything They Don't Want You to Know," London Greenpeace, 1986.

246 *McDonald's threatened to sue at least fifty:* See Vidal, *McLibel,* pp. 46–47.

about $18 billion: "McDonald's History Listing," McDonald's Corporation, 1996.

the court record included 40,000 pages of documents: Cited in Colleen Graffy, "Big Mac Bited Back," *American Bar Association Journal*, August 1997.

247 *McDonald's did "exploit" children:* Quoted in Dick Beveridge, "McDonald's Wins Marathon Libel Case, but Loses Publicity Battle," *AP,* June 19, 1997.

"McDonald's don't deserve a penny": Quoted ibid.

248 *During the trial, Sidney Nicholson . . . officers belonging to Special Branch:* See testimony of Sidney Nicholson, *McDonald's, McDonald's Restaurants, Ltd., v Helen Steel, David Morris,* Day 249, May 14, 1996, pp. 32–38.

"At no time did I believe they were dangerous": Quoted in "Interview: McDon-

ald's Spy Fran Tiller on Infiltration and Subterfuge, Big Mac Style," www. McSpotlight.org.

248 *For Dave Morris, perhaps the most disturbing moment:* Interview with Dave Morris.

249 *some of the similarities between Dave Morris and Ray Kroc:* See Vidal, *McLibel,* pp. 58–62.

"*Fitting into a finely working machine*": Quoted in Nick Hasell, "McDonald's Long March," *Management Today,* September 1994.

250 *Plauen has lost about 10 percent of its population:* Interview with Markus Schneider.

251 *Plauen's unemployment rate is about 20 percent:* Ibid.

"*It was dumb luck*": Quoted in Roger Thurow, "For East German Pair, McDonald's Serves Up an Economic Parable," *Wall Street Journal,* November 8, 1999.

a third of the young people in eastern Germany: Cited in Leonard Ziskin, "Fa and Antifa in the Fatherland," *Nation,* October 5, 1998.

Epilogue: Have It Your Way

My views on how to restructure the nation's food safety system were influenced by a recent report by the National Academy of Science's Institute of Medicine. *Ensuring Safe Food: From Production to Consumption* (Washington, D.C.: National Academy Press, 1998) contains many reasonable recommendations that should not be — as so much of the previous food safety advice from National Academy of Sciences has been — ignored. Dale Lasater was a gracious host during many of my visits to Colorado. His ranch is a national treasure. The family's role in the southwestern cattle industry is eloquently described in Dale Lasater's *Falfurrias: Ed C. Lasater and the Development of South Texas* (College Station: Texas A&M University Press, 1985). Laurence M. Lasater's *The Lasater Philosophy of Cattle Raising* (El Paso: Texas Western Press, 1972) outlines a holistic system of range management that treats both the animals and the land with respect. *The Shortgrass Prairie* (Boulder, Colo.: Pruett Publishing, 1988), by Ruth Carol Cushman and Stephan R. Jones, conveys through text and photographs the beauty of an American landscape that is largely unappreciated.

I am grateful to the Conway family, who allowed me to poke around their restaurants and hang out in the kitchens. The last hamburger I ate was served at the Conway's Red Top on South Nevada in Colorado Springs. It was as good as it gets.

Page

255 "*Nature is smart as hell*": Interview with Dale Lasater.

257 *Recent findings that grass-fed cattle:* See Francisco Diez Gonzalez, Todd R. Callaway, Menas G. Kizoulis, and James B. Russell, "Grain Feeding and the Dissemination of Acid-Resistant *Escherichia coli* from Cattle," *Science,* September 11, 1998.

259 *one of America's most profitable fast food chains:* It is difficult to gauge In-N-Out's financial details because the company is privately owned. Nevertheless, a decade ago the financial analyst Robert L. Emerson speculated that "In-N-Out enjoys

the highest level of return on invested capital in the fast-food industry." See Emerson, *Economics of Fast Food*, p. 94.

259 *generating more than $150 million in annual revenues:* The estimate of $150 milion comes from a recent *Los Angeles Times* article on the chain and its future after Esther Snyder. The actual figure may be as much as two times higher; in 1990 Emerson claimed that individual In-N-Out restaurants had annual revenues of $1.7 million. See Greg Hernandez, "Family-Owned In-N-Out at Crossroads," *Los Angeles Times*, July 2, 2000; Emerson, *Economics of Fast Food*, p. 93.

The starting wage of a part-time worker: Representatives of In-N-Out declined my requests for an interview, citing the Snyder family's wariness of the press. The information on the chain's wages and food preparation techniques come from the In-N-Out Web site and from the following articles: Greg Johnson, "More Than Fare: A Simple Menu, Customer Service, and a Familial Touch Prove to Be a Recipe That Is Working for In-N-Out," *Los Angeles Times*, August 15, 1997; Deborah Silver, "Burger Worship: In-N-Out — the Small Fast Food Chain with the Big Following," *Restaurants and Institutions*, November 1, 1999; Hernandez, "Family-Owned In-N-Out at a Crossroads."

260 *In-N-Out ranked first:* See Deborah Silver, "Primary Choices," *Restaurants and Institutions*, March 1, 2000.

the lowest-quality food of any major hamburger chain: Ibid.

262 *"advertising directed at children":* Quoted in Harry Berkowitz, "Pediatricians Want Check on Kids' Ads," *Newsday*, February 9, 1995. See also "Policy Statement: Children, Adolescents, and Television," American Academy of Pediatrics, October 1995.

more than 90 percent of the children in the United States: Cited in Rod Taylor, "The Beanie Factor," *Brandweek*, June 16, 1997.

263 *safest food supply in the world:* The National Academy of Science's Committee to Insure Safe Food from Production to Consumption recently found "little evidence to either support or contradict that assertion." The committee's reluctance to pass judgment was based on the unreliable reporting system for foodborne illness in the United States. The panel did not compare the American food safety system with systems in Western Europe. See *Ensuring Safe Food*, p. 25.

about 0.1 percent of Swedish cattle: Cited in "Swedish *Salmonella* Control Programmes for Live Animals, Eggs and Meat," National Veterinary Institute, Swedish Board of Agriculture, National Food Administration, January 16, 1995.

lower than the rate in the United States: At the time, roughly 7.5 percent of American ground beef contained *Salmonella.* Cited in "Nationwide Federal Plant Raw Ground Beef Microbiological Survey, August 1993–March 1994," United States Deartment of Agriculture, Food Safety and Inspection Service, Science and Technology, Microbiology Division, April 1996.

The Netherlands began to test ground beef: Interview with Steven Bjerklie.

a dozen federal agencies: Cited in *Ensuring Safe Food*, p. 26.

if a pizza has pepperoni on it: Ibid., p. 27.

264 *Eggs are regulated by the FDA:* This example of bureaucratic folly was cited by Carol Tucker Foreman, a prominent food safety advocate, during recent testimony before Congress. For an excellent critique of our current food safety system and some rational proposals for reform, see Prepared Statement of Carol

Tucker Foreman, Director of Food Policy Institute, before the Senate Governmental Affairs Committee, Oversight of Government Management, Restructuring, and the District of Columbia Subcommittee, August 4, 1999.

264 *more than 500,000 people become ill:* Ibid.

on average, once every ten years: Cited in *Ensuring Safe Food,* p. 87.

roughly 200,000 fast food restaurants: Cited in "Top 100 Share of Restaurant Industry Units by Menu Category," Technomic Top 100, Technomic Information Services, 2000.

They said IBP slowed down the line: In 1996, an official at the U.S. Meat Export Federation recommended slowing down the line speeds at American plants on export days in order to improve the "hygiene." See Keith Nunes, "Attitude Adjustment: U.S. Beef and Pork Exporters Need to Develop an 'Export Mentality,'" *Meat & Poultry,* March 1996.

the maximum OSHA fine: See *OSHA Field Inspection Reference Manual,* Section 8 — Chapter IV, C.2.M.

266 *"I do not believe":* Quoted in Rudolph J. R. Peritz, *Competition Policy in America, 1888–1992: History, Rhetoric, Law* (New York: Oxford University Press, 1996), p. 15.

"veggie libel laws" backed by agribusiness: See Ann Hawk, "Veggie Disparagement: Laws in 13 States Prompt Fears Activists — and Journalists Will Be Stifled," *The Quill,* September 1998; Ronald K. L. Collins and Paul McMasters, "Veggie Libel Laws Still Out to Muzzle Free Speech," *Texas Lawyer,* March 30, 1998.

267 *"Grow or die":* Quoted in Richard Gibson, "Beef Stakes: How Bill Foley Built a Fast Food Empire on Ailing Also-Rans," *Wall Street Journal,* December 2, 1998.

268 *environmentalists criticized the chain:* For the story behind the "greening" of McDonald's, see Sharon M. Livesey, "McDonald's and the Environmental Defense Fund: A Case Study of a Green Alliance," *Journal of Business Communications,* January 1999.

269 *it continues to use them overseas:* See "An Incoherent Policy," *South China Morning Post,* May 15, 1995; Jo Bowman, "Little Relish to Scrap Burger Boxes," *South China Morning Post,* October 24, 1999.

it would no longer purchase frozen french fries: For McDonald's decision on biotech fries, see Scott Kilman, "McDonald's, Other Fast Food Chains Pull Monsanto's Bio-Engineered Potato," *Wall Street Journal,* April 28, 2000; Hal Bernton, "Hostile Market Spells Blight for Biotech Potatoes," *Seattle Times,* April 30, 2000.

Afterword: The Meaning of Mad Cow

Since writing *Fast Food Nation* I've come across a number of relevant and noteworthy books. Almost twenty years ago Orville Schell issued an eloquent warning against treating livestock like industrial commodities. Schell approached the subject not only as a journalist, but as an innovative rancher. Had the recommendations in his book *Modern Meat* (New York: Random House, 1984) been followed, the American meatpacking industry would have avoided many of the health scares and export restrictions it now faces. In *The Great Food Gamble* (London: Hodder & Stoughton, 2001), John Humphrys explains the mentality and the institutional changes that have led Great Britain from one agricultural distaster to another. George Monbiot's *Captive State* (London: Macmillan, 2000) brilliantly outlines the corporate takeover of the British government during the past twenty years. Naomi Klein's *No Logo* (London: Flamingo, 2001) offers a damning critique of global corporate power and the reigning cult of the brand. Klein has rightly emerged at the forefront of today's young rebels. Tony Royle's *Working for McDonald's in Europe* (New York: Routledge, 2000) skillfully outlines how McDonald's has exported its anti-labor policies to countries with long traditions of respecting workers' rights. Among other things, Royle describes how the McDonald's Corporation recruited low-wage workers in Bulgaria and Romania for its restaurants in Germany, providing these new immigrants with housing as a means of controlling them (see pp. 76–8). José Bové, the sheep farmer who became a national hero in France by demolishing a McDonald's restaurant, offers a plea for sustainable agriculture in *The World is Not for Sale: Farmers Against Junk Food* (London: Verso, 2001). Written with François Dufour, the General Secretary of the French Farmers' Confederation, *The World is Not for Sale* argues that important decisions about what we eat should never be made without considering their social costs and their impact on future generations. The most radical thing about Bové's argument is how sensible it seems.

Two alarming books have been published about the risk of mad cow disease in the United States. Richard Rhodes's *Deadly Feasts: The Prion Controversy and The Public's Health* (New York: Touchstone, 1998) contains fascinating information on the health risks posed by cannibalism and a fine account of the detective work that linked BSE to the consumption of tainted animal feed. In *Mad Cow U.S.A.* (New York: Common Courage, 1997), Sheldon Rampton and John C. Stauber reveal how the beef industry and the federal government collaborated to thwart public discussion of mad cow. The duo's efforts at the Center for Media and Democracy offer a necessary antidote to the P.R. industry's relentless propaganda. As of this writing, the most definitive and disturbing investigation of mad cow disease is the sixteen-volume report on BSE submitted to the British government by Lord Phillips of Worth Matravers. Its official title is *Return to an Order of the Honourable the House of Commons dated October 2000 for the Report, evidence and supporting papers of the Inquiry into the emergence and identification of Bovine Spongiform Encephalopathy (BSE) and variant Creutzfeldt-Jakob Disease (vCJD) and the action taken in response to it up to 20 March 1996.* Its full text is available online (www.bse.org.uk). Also known as *The BSE Inquiry: The Report*, it offers some extraordinary glimpses of bureaucratic cowardice and incompetence.

In addition to those works, my account of mad cow disease and the FDA rulemaking process is based on the following documents: "Finding of No Significant Impact and Environmental Assessment for 21 CFR 589.2000, Prohibition of Protein Derived from Ruminant and Mink Tissues in Ruminant Feeds," Center for Veterinary Medicine, Food and Drug Adminstration, November 1996; "Substances Prohibited for Use in Animal Food or Feed; Animal Proteins Prohibited in Ruminant Feed; Proposed Rule," Part IV, *Federal Register*, January 3, 1997; "Cost Analysis of Regulatory Options to Reduce the Risk of an Outbreak of Transmissable Spongiform Encephalopathies (TSEs) in the United States, Addendum to the Final Report," Office of Planning and Evaluation, Food and Drug Administration, April 30, 1997; "Substances Prohibited from Use in Animal Food or Feed; Animal Proteins Prohibited in Ruminant Feed; Final

Rule," Part II, *Federal Register*, June 5, 1997. I also relied on transcripts of two public forums held by the FDA to allow discussion of its proposed feed rules: "Food and Drug Administration, Public Forum on the Proposed Rule 21 CFR 589: Substances Prohibited from Use in Animal Food or Feed, St. Louis, Missouri, February 4, 1997" and "Public Meeting for Consumers Regarding *Federal Register* 21 CFR Part 589, Substances Prohibited from Use in Animal Food or Feed; Animal Proteins Prohibited in Ruminant Feed; Proposed Rule; Washington D.C., February 13, 1997." For years the reporting about mad cow disease in *Food Chemical News* has been objective and first-rate.

Interviews with software designer Hitesh Shah, journalist Viji Sundaram, and attorney Harish Bharti helped me understand how revelations about McDonald's fries and the flavor industry led to riots in India. I am grateful to Eugene Richards for pushing hard to complete our photoessay on the lives of meatpacking workers, and to Roger Cohn, the editor of *Mother Jones*, for publishing it without hesitation. The plight of Latino meatpacking workers in Texas was eloquently described to me by Trini Gamez at the Centro Gamez in Amarillo and by Michael Wyatt, the director of Texas Rural Legal Assistance. Attorneys Jim Wood, Channy Wood, and Kevin Glasheen explicated for me some of the unique features of Texas workers' comp law. They have demonstrated real courage in their legal battles with the meatpacking giants. Karen Olsson, editor of the *Texas Observer*, was extremely generous with her own research on IBP. Michael J. Broadway, an expert on meatpacking who heads the Department of Geography at the University of Michigan, provided much information and encouragement. Most of all, I am grateful to the injured meatpacking workers who shared their stories with me: Kenny Dobbins, Hector Reyes, Raul Lopez, Rita Beltran, Dora Sanchez, and Michael Glover, among others. Their suffering cannot adequately be put into words.

Page

272 *the agency would "expedite":* Quoted in Lawrence K. Altman, "Cow Disease Sparks Voluntary Rules on Feed," *New York Times*, March 30, 1996.

"keen consumers of beef burgers": Quoted in Claire O'Brien, "Scant Data Cause Widespread Concern," *Science*, March 29, 1996.

American cattle were eating about 2 billion pounds: According to the USDA, the rendering industry at the time handled about 7.6 million tons of ruminant protein per year, about 5.5 million tons of it derived from cattle. Approximately 13 percent of the animal protein handled by industry (992,099 tons) was used in cattle feed. I have converted the tons into pounds to give a sense of the massive amounts of slaughterhouse waste involved. The figures are cited in "Finding of No Significant Impact and Environmental Assessment for 21 CFR 589.2000, Prohibition of Protein Derived from Ruminant and Mink Tissues in Ruminant Feeds," Center for Veterinary Medicine, Food and Drug Administration, November 1996, pp. 15–16, 21.

three-quarters of all American cattle: Cited in Michael Satchell and Stephen J. Hedges, "The Next Bad Beef Scandal? Cattle Feed Now Contains Things Like Chicken Manure and Dead Cats," *U.S. News & World Report*, September 1, 1997.

273 *"totally unsupported by any scientific evidence":* Quoted in "Rendering Industry Supports Voluntary Guidelines for Cattle with Suspected CNS Disease," *Food Chemical News*, July 29, 1996.

"unfeasible, impractical, and unenforceable": Quoted in ibid.

brains, spinal cords, eyeballs: See "NCBA Urges Scientific BSE Prevention," Press Release, National Cattlemen's Beef Association, February 18, 1997.

fats, blood, blood products: See "Industry, Public Interest Groups Differ on FDA's Proposed Ruminant Ban," Food Chemical News, March 10, 1997.

allowing cattle to continue eating dead pigs: See the statement of Dr. Beth Lautner, vice president of science and technology at the National Pork Producers Council, Transcript of "Food and Drug Administration, Public Forum on the Proposed Rule 21 CFR 589: Substances Prohibited from Use in Animal Food or Feed, St. Louis, Missouri, February 4, 1997," p. 101.

"all mammal remains to all food animals": Quoted in "Controlling 'Mad Cow Disease': We call for stronger FDA action," Consumer Reports, May 1997.

The Centers for Disease Control and Prevention advised: See "CDC Rejects Any Weakening of FDA's Ruminant Feed Ban Proposal," Food Chemical News, March 31, 1997.

"The United States has no BSE": Quoted in "Substances Prohibited from Use in Animal Food or Feed; Animal Proteins Prohibited in Ruminant Feed; Final Rule," Part II, Federal Register, June 5, 1997, p. 30939.

"mammalian-to-ruminant, with exceptions": Quoted in ibid., p. 30968.

274 these industry groups rightly worried: See "FDA Public Forum," pp. 36–9.

a remarkable example of cooperation': Quoted in Chuck Cannon, "Renderers Appear To Be Bearing Up Well to FDA's Ban on Ruminant Protein in feed," Meat Marketing & Technology, March 1998.

"protected the beef industry": Quoted in ibid.

"verbatim": Quoted in ibid.

"the number of BSE cases there soon doubled": Cited in "Developments in Mad-Cow History," Wall Street Journal, March 1, 2001.

the number of BSE cases increased fivefold: Cited in Geoff Winestock, "Tracking Spread of 'Mad Cow' in Europe Remains Random," Wall Street Journal, January 8, 2001.

that supplied ground beef to McDonald's restaurants: See Melanie Goodfellow, "Italy's First BSE Case Found in Cow Destined for McDonald's," The Independent, January 16, 2001, and "Final Tests Confirm BSE in Cow in Italian Slaughterhouse That Supplies McDonald's," AP Worldstream, January 16, 2001.

plummet by as much as 50 percent: Cited in Geoff Winestock, "'Mad-Cow' Disease Cases Jump Despite EU Increased Testing," Wall Street Journal, January 8, 2001.

275 one-quarter of the firms handling "prohibited" feed: Cited in "Food Safety: Controls Can Be Strengthened to Reduce the Risk of Disease Linked to Unsafe Animal Feed," GAO/RCD-00-255, United States General Accounting Office, September 2000, p. 12.

one-fifth of the firms handling both: Cited in ibid., p. 12.

one out of every ten rendering firms: Cited in ibid., p. 12.

In Colorado, more than one-quarter: Cited in Michael Booth, "Mad Cow Rules Violated," Denver Post, May 13, 2001.

sales in Europe had already fallen by 10 percent: Cited in "McDonald's Not Out of Mad Cows Woods Yet — CFO," Reuters, February 28, 2001.

"If McDonald's is requiring something": Quoted in Philip Brasher, "McDonald's Forcing Beef Industry to Comply with Mad Cow Rules," *Associated Press*, March 13, 2001.

"Because we have the world's biggest shopping cart": Quoted in ibid.

276 *"McGarbage"*: Douglas Kern, "McGarbage", *National Review Online Weekend*, January 27–8, 2001.

"hodgepodge of impressions": Cynthia Crossen, "A Culinary Wasteland," *Wall Street Journal*, January 12, 2001.

"anecdotal": The AMI spokeswoman was Janet Riley, quoted in Regina Schrambling, "Catching America with Its Hand in the Fries," *New York Times*, March 21, 2001.

"The real McDonald's": Quoted in Alby Gallun, "McDonald's Mid-Life Crisis," *Crain's Chicago Business*, April 30, 2001.

277 *One of President George W. Bush's first acts:* For the implications of Bush's move, see "Working America Challenges Corporate America," *U.S. Newswire*, March 6, 2001; Victor Epstein, "Arguments over Ergonomics Keenly Felt by Injured Workers," *Omaha World-Herald*, March 8, 2001; and Mike Allen, "Bush Signs Repeal of Ergonomics Rules," *Washington Post*, March 21, 2001.

Norwood sponsored legislation: In 1997, Norwood sponsored a bill (along with Congressman Joel Hefley from Colorado Springs) that essentially aimed to repeal the Occupational Safety and Health Act of 1970. See "Hutchison, Hefley Introduce Proposals in House, Senate to Overhaul OSHA," *Asbestos & Lead Abatement Report*, April 7, 1997.

repetitive stress injuries from skiing: See Sarah Anderson, "OSHA under Siege," *The Progressive*, December 1995.

The meatpacking industry's lobbyists were delighted: See Allison Beers, "USDA Plans to Change School Lunch Specs for Ground Beef, Pork, Turkey," *Food Chemical News*, April 2, 2001; Marc Kauffman, "USDA Proposes to Reverse School Ground Beef Rules," *Washington Post*, April 5, 2001; and Marian Burros, "U.S. Proposes End to Testing for Salmonella in School Beef," *New York Times*, April 5, 2001.

roughly 5 million pounds were rejected: Cited in Beers, "USDA Plans".

278 *"For flavor enhancement"*: Quoted in Viji Sundaram, "Where's the Beef? It's in Your French Fries," *India-West*, April 5, 2001.

"Eating a cow for a Hindu": Quoted in Laurie Goodstein, "For Hindus and Vegetarians, Surprise in McDonald's Fries," *New York Times*, May 20, 2001.

279 *"We came to warn them"*: Quoted in "Hardline Hindus: Close McDonald's," *Ha'aretz*, May 6, 2001.

"If you visit McDonald's anywhere": "Healthy Eating," McDonald's Corporation, Australian Web site, www.McDonalds.com.au, 2001.

adjusting its french fry recipe: Interview with Anna Rozenich, the McDonald's Corporation.

"We regret if customers felt": "McDonald's French Fry Facts", McDonald's Corporation, May 2001.

"confusion" was the wrong word: Quoted in Transcript, "Class Action Suit Against McDonald's Claims Company Misleads Consumers About Fry Oil," *CNN News*, May 3, 2001.

"We apologize for any confusion": The spokesman was Walt Riker, repeating a denial made on numerous occasions. Quoted in Transcript, "Class Action Suit." See also "McDonald's Apologizes," *Calgary Herald,* May 25, 2001.

280 *"Thank you for contacting us":* Letter from Beth Petersohn, Manager, Customer Satisfaction Department, McDonald's Corporation, to Ms. Laura Strickland, May 5, 1993.

the fast food industry did not gain any new customers: Cited in Robert O'Brien, "Consumer Update & Industry Outlook," NPD Foodworld, March 2001. See also Milford Prewitt, "COEX Attendees Upbeat Despite Economic Cloud," *Nation's Restaurant News,* March 12, 2001, and Peter Romeo, "Is Fast Food Ill?", *Restaurant Business,* April 1, 2001. Romeo, the editor of *Restaurant Business,* subsequently spoke with me about some of the marketing challenges and economic problems that the fast food industry now confronts.

not only hamburger chains, but also pizza: Cited in Robert O'Brien, "Consumer Update & Industry Outlook," NPD Foodworld, March 2001.

at a cost of more than $70 million: Cited in Jennifer Ordonez, "How Burger King Got Burned in the Quest to Make the Perfect Fry," *Wall Street Journal,* January 16, 2001.

a "K minus" program: For the details and the rationale of "K minus," see Richard Martin, "Taco Bell Accelerates 'Value' Exploration," *Nation's Restaurant News,* November 18, 1991; Ronald Henkoff, "Service is Everybody's Business," *Fortune,* June 27, 1994; and Tim Durnford, "Redefining Value: For Whom the Taco Bell Tolls," *Cornell Hotel & Restaurant Quarterly,* June 1997.

fell by 9 percent in the fourth quarter: Cited in Chuck Hutchcraft, "Off the Mark," *Restaurants and Institutions,* May 1, 2001.

281 *"We are not doing a great job":* Quoted in Jennifer Ordonez, "Taco Bell Chief Has New Tactic: Be Like Wendy's," *Wall Street Journal,* February 23, 2001.

doubts on Wall Street: For pessimistic views of McDonald's financial prospects, see Ken Kurson, "Supersize Dread: McDonald's Future is Smelling Worse Than Its Restaurants," *Esquire,* April 1, 2001, and Alby Gallun, "McDonald's Mid-life Crisis," *Crain's Chicago Business,* April 30, 2001. For a much rosier view, see Moises Naim's interview with Jack Greenberg, McDonald's CEO, "McAtlas Shrugged," *Foreign Policy,* May 1, 2001.

doubling its sales within the United States: Cited in Alby Gallun, "McDonald's Mid-life Crisis."

McDonald's ranked just a couple of places: Cited in Bob Krummert, "QSR Patron Picks and Pans; American Customer Satisfaction Research Shows Customer Dissatisfaction with Fast Food Restaurants," *Restaurant Hospitality,* April 1, 2001. The survey was conducted by the National Quality Research Center at the University of Michigan Business School. It ranked two hundred national organizations on the basis of 50,000 consumer interviews.

282 *acted decisively and hired Temple Grandin:* Grandin, an associate professor of Animal Science at Colorado State University, has designed livestock handling facilities throughout the world. She gained renown for her ability to "see through the eyes" of cattle of order to minimize the fear and stress they experience before slaughter. Her commitment to animal welfare is heartfelt and unassailable. Grandin was profiled by the neurologist Oliver W. Sacks in *An Anthropologist on*

Mars (New York: Vintage Press, 1996), and has published her own memoir, *Thinking in Pictures: And Other Reports from My Life with Autism* (New York: Vintage Press, 1995).

According to Grandin: Temple Grandin discussed McDonald's humane slaughter program with me at length.

the enthusiastic support of the meatpacking industry: Janet Riley, a spokeswoman for American Meat Institute (AMI), told me that the industry has eagerly backed the new guidelines devised by Grandin. Slaughtering animals humanely is a good idea, not just for ethical reasons; it also improves the quality of the meat. The meatpacking industry much prefers a program administered by McDonald's to one administered by the USDA. McDonald's inspectors are employed by meatpacking companies; their inspection reports are not open to public scrutiny; and the names of companies that fail an inspection are not disclosed. For the AMI's resistance to greater USDA involvement in humane slaughter, see "Panel Gives Agriculture Dept. $2.5 Million," *AP Online,* July 17, 2001.

I visited meatpacking communities in Texas: Our photoessay, "The Most Dangerous Job in America," appeared in *Mother Jones,* July/August 2001.

283 *forever surrendering the right to sue:* See Tad Fowler, "In the Matter of Michael Glover vs. IBP, Inc. Workplace Injury Settlement Program, Judgement in Arbitration," p. 3. The ability of workers to sign away their common law rights has been upheld by the Texas Supreme Court, which has given precedence to the sanctity of contracts. See Supreme Court of Texas, *Lawrence v. CDB Services, Lambert v. Affiliated Foods, Inc.,* Nos. 00-0142, 00-0201, March 29, 2001.

control over the job-related medical treatment: See "Workplace Injury Settlement Program — Texas," IBP, p. 7.

The Texas Supreme Court has ruled: According to the court's perverse logic, companies participating in the worker's comp system are not allowed to fire injured workers — but companies who leave the system are free to do so. See Supreme Court of Texas, *Mexican Railway Company v. Bouchet,* No. 96-0194, February 13, 1998.

When Lonita Leal's right hand was mangled: See Karen Olsson, "Chain of Casualties: How an Amarillo Beef Packing Plant Disposes of Injured Workers," *Texas Observer,* May 22, 1998.

When Duane Mullin had both hands: See ibid.

the world's biggest and most powerful meatpacking firm: See Kelly P. Kissel, "Tyson, IBP Agree to Terms on Chicken–Beef Merger," *AP,* June 27, 2001, and Bill Hord, "Livestock Producers 'Feel the Squeeze' of Tyson–IBP Deal," *Omaha World-Herald,* January 3, 2001.

$1.7 billion in debt: Cited in Kelly P. Kissel, "Tyson, IBP Agree to Terms on Chicken–Beef Merger," *AP,* June 27, 2001.

284 *"If McDonald's is requiring something":* Quoted in Brasher, "McDonald's Forcing Beef Industry," *Associated Press,* March 13, 2001.

about a hundred people: As of August 31, 2001, the number of confirmed and probable cases of vCJD in the United Kingdom had reached 106. See "CJD Statistics," The UK Creutzfeldt-Jakob Disease Surveillance Unit, September 3, 2001.

Roughly the same number of people die every day: 41,611 Americans died in traffic accidents during 1999 — a rate about 114 a day. Cited in "Traffic Safety Facts 1999," National Highway Traffic Safety Administration, U.S. Department of Transportation, 2000.

About 800,000 cattle with mad cow: This figure was cited by Professor Jeffrey Almond, a member of the United Kingdom's Spongiform Encephalopathies Advisory Committee. See Transcript, "Meeting of U.S. Transmissible Spongiform Encephalopathies Advisory Committee, Gaithersburg, Maryland, June 3, 1999."

If it takes about ten years: For discussion of vCJD's potential incubation period, and the implications for public health, see Charles Arthur, "BSE infection: This is a New Disease and We Are Entering the Unknown," *Independent*, April 29, 2000; Dorothy Bonn, "Healthy carriers could increase vCJD risk," *The Lancet*, September 2, 2000; Charles Arthur, "CJD Threat Could Last for 40 Years, Says Expert," *Independent*, November 16, 2000; and David Derbyshire, "Scientists Fear Second Round of Human BSE," *Daily Telegraph*, May 16, 2001. For a good review of the risk to human health, see Paul Brown, Robert G. Will, Raymond Bradley, David M. Asher, and Linda Detwiler, "Bovine Spongiform Encephalopathy and Variant Creutzfeldt-Jakob Disease: Background, Evolution, and Current Concerns," *Emerging Infectious Diseases*, vol. 7, no. 1, January–February, 2001.

285 *much as Three Mile Island and Chernobyl:* Nicols Fox astutely made this analogy back in 1997. See Nicols Fox, *Spoiled* (New York: Basic Books, 1997), p. 331.

British agricultural officials were concerned: See Volume I, "Findings and Conclusions, Section 3, The Early Years, 1986–88," paragraphs 223–34, *The BSE Inquiry: The Report*, October 2000.

a leading manufacturer of pet foods: The story of how the British pet food industry took the lead in defending the public from BSE can be found in Volume 5, "Animal Health, 1989–96, Section 3, Introduction of the Animal SBO Ban," paragraphs 3.1–3.26, *The BSE Inquiry: The Report*; Volume 6, "Human Health, 1989–96, Section 3, Introduction of the Ban on Specified Bovine Offal," paragraphs 3.91–3.203, ibid.; and Anthony Bevins, "How We Had to Rely on Pedigree Chum Firm for CJD Advice," *Express*, October 27, 2000.

a good idea: See Volume 6, "Human Health, 1989–96, Section 3, Introduction of the Ban on Specified Bovine Offal," paragraph 3.201, *The BSE Inquiry: The Report*.

some of the nation's cheapest meats: See Judy Jones, "McDonald's Takes British out of Burgers', *Observer*, March 24, 1996.

The death of "Mad Max": See Allison Pearson, "How We Swallowed the BSE Lie", *Evening Standard*, October 4, 2000, and Kamal Ahmed, Antony Barnett, and Stuart Miller, "Focus: BSE: How the Government Betrayed the People", *Observer*, October 29, 2000.

"constantly sought to prevent or delay": Quoted in *Le Monde*, "Time to Make Some Radical Reforms in the Food Industry," *Manchester Guardian Weekly*, May 30, 2001.

286 *"might have had an adverse effect":* Quoted in ibid.

about 150 million pounds of the stuff: In 1989 Great Britain exported roughly 15,000 tons of potentially tainted feed, and exported an additional 8,500 to 9,000 tons per year until 1996. That adds up to roughly 75,000 tons over the eight-year period. Cited in Steve Stecklow, "U.K.'s Exports May Have Expanded the Boundaries of Mad Cow Disease', *Wall Street Journal*, January 23, 2001.

blocked publication of the EU report: See Peter Hadfield, "Ministry Bungle puts Japan at risk of BSE," *Sunday Telegraph*, September 23, 2001.

"disposed of": See ibid.

about a billion pounds of rendered cattle: Cited in Steve Secklow, "In Battling Mad Cow, Britain Spawns Heaps of Pulverized Cattle," *Wall Street Journal*, January 8, 2001.

generates electricity by burning cattle: See Philip Pullela, "Mad Cow Scare on Front Burner around Europe," *Reuters*, January 22, 2001.

287 *BSE may easily cross the species barrier:* See Bonn, "Healthy Carriers," *The Lancet*, and Barry James, "'Mad Cow' Disease in Pigs and Sheep?" *International Herald Tribune*, August 31, 2000.

"All cannibalistic recycling": Quoted in Jonathon Leake, "New BSE Outbreak Linked to Blood in Feed," *Sunday Times*, September 24, 2001.

at least 60,000 other cattle: This figure was cited by Professor Jeffrey Almond, Transcript, "U.S. TSE Committee."

"If you don't look": Quoted in John S. Long, "Nation Isn't Doing Enough to Detect Mad Cow Disease, CWRU Experts Say," *Plain Dealer*, May 6, 2001.

approximately 375 million cattle: Since 1990, about 34 million cattle have been slaughtered each year in the United States. See "The Texas Blues," *Leather*, August 1998.

about 15,000 of them were tested for mad cow: See Megan Mulholland, "Wisconsin-Based Renderer's President Stands Firm on Safety of U.S. Feed," *Post Crescent*, May 20, 2001.

a cattle herd roughly one-thirtieth the size: Belgium has about 3 million cattle; the United States has about 100 million. See Terry Downs, "Mad Cow Disease Testing Reveals Widespread Infection in Europe," *Food Chemical News*, January 22, 2001.

leading American manufacturers promise: See Tim Phillips, "Are Pets Being Recycled into Pet Food?", *Petfood Industry*, March/April 1992.

40,000 pounds of dead dogs and dead cats: Cited in Patrick White, "Canada Pet Food Firm Turns Back on Dog and Cat Meat," *Reuters*, June 5, 2001.

"This food is healthy and good": Quoted in ibid.

288 *the most common source of animal protein in poultry feed:* See Daniel Rosenberg, "Mad Cow Disease Concern Could Change Chicken Feed', *Wisconsin State Journal*, May 5, 2001.

processes about 10 million pounds of chicken parts: Cited in "Multi-million Dollar Facility to Help Tyson Ensure That Nothing Goes to Waste'" *M2 Presswire*, June 7, 1996.

the export needs of Nestlé: See John Vidal and Peter Hethrington, "Foot-and-Mouth Crisis: Food Lobby Forced PM into U-Turn on Plan for Vaccination," *Guardian*, September 8, 2001.

supplied the milk for McDonald's milkshakes: Cited in Amanda Hall, "Wholemeal Haskins: Chris Haskins, Maverick of Northern Foods and Express Dairies, Mixes a Healthy Serving of Politics with His Business," *Sunday Telegraph*, June 14, 1998.

289 *20 percent of its farmland:* Cited in Paul Geitner, "Scare Helps Europe's Organic Food," *AP Online*, March 19, 2001.

"Things will no longer be": Quoted in Michael Adler, "Greens Trumpet Their New Star, Agriculture Minister Kuenast," *Agence France Presse,* March 11, 2001.

"Our Cows should get only water": Quoted in "Germany Plans Radical Farm Reform — Food Must Be As Pure As Beer, Says Government," *Deutsche Presse-Agentur,* February 8, 2001.

bibliography

Acree, Terry E., and Roy Teranishi, eds. *Flavor Science: Sensible Principles and Techniques.* Washington, D.C.: American Chemical Society, 1993.

Acuff, Dan S., with Robert H. Reiher. *What Kids Buy and Why: The Psychology of Marketing to Kids.* New York: Free Press, 1997.

Alexander-Moegerle, Gil. *James Dobson's War on America.* Amherst, N.Y.: Prometheus Books, 1997.

Alfino, Mark, John S. Caputo, and Robin Wynyard, eds. *McDonaldization Revisited: Critical Essays on Consumer Culture.* Westport, Conn.: Praeger, 1998.

Andreas, Carol. *Meatpackers and Beef Barons: Company Town in a Global Economy.* Niwot: University Press of Colorado, 1994.

A Time to Act: Report of the USDA National Commission on Small Farms. Washington, D.C.: U.S. Department of Agriculture, 1998.

Benfield, F. Caid, Matthew D. Raimi, and Donald D. T. Chen. *Once There Were Greenfields: How Urban Sprawl Is Undermining America's Environment, Economy. and Social Fabric.* Washington, D.C.: National Resources Defense Council, 1999.

Bingham, Sam. *The Last Ranch: A Colorado Community and the Coming Desert.* New York: Harcourt Brace, 1996.

Boas, Max, and Steve Chain. *Big Mac: The Unauthorized Story of McDonald's.* New York: E. P. Dutton, 1976.

Bonnano, Alessandro, Lawrence Busch, William Friedland, Lourdes Gouveia, and Enzo Mingione, eds. *From Columbus to ConAgra: The Globalization of Agriculture and Food.* Lawrence: University Press of Kansas, 1994.

Bower, Tom. *The Paperclip Conspiracy: The Hunt for Nazi Scientists.* Boston: Little Brown, 1987.

Cannon, David Jack, ed. *The Illustrated History of Las Vegas.* Edison, N.J.: Chartwell Books, 1997.

Card, David, and Alan B. Krueger. *Myth and Measurement: The New Economics of the Minimum Wage.* Princeton: Princeton University Press, 1995.

Cohon, George, with David Macfarlane. *To Russia with Fries.* Toronto: McClelland & Stewart, 1999.

Competition and the Livestock Market. Report of a Task Force Commissioned by the Center for Rural Affairs. Walt Hill, Nebr.: 1990.

Concentration in Agriculture: A Report of the USDA Advisory Committee on Agricultural Concentration. Washington, D.C.: USDA Agricultural Marketing Service, June 1996.

Connor, John M., and William A. Schiek. *Food Processing: An Industrial Powerhouse in Transition.* New York: John Wiley & Sons, 1997.

Consumers Union Education Services. *Captive Kids: A Report on Commercial Pressures on Kids at School.* Consumers Union, 1998.

Cushman, Ruth Carol, and Stephan R. Jones. *The Shortgrass Prairie.* Boulder, Colo.: Pruett Publishing, 1988.

Davidson, Osha Gray. *Broken Heartland: The Rise of America's Rural Ghetto.* Iowa City: University of Iowa Press, 1996.

Davis, James W. *Aristocrat in Burlap: A History of the Potato in Idaho.* Boise: Idaho Potato Commission, 1992.

Davis, Mike. *City of Quartz.* New York: Vintage Books, 1992.

Decker, Peter R. *Old Fences, New Neighbors.* Tucson: University of Arizona Press, 1998.

Del Vecchio, Gene. *Creating Ever-Cool: A Marketer's Guide to a Kid's Heart.* Gretna, La.: Pelican Publishing, 1998.

Distil, Barbara, and Ruth Jakush, eds. *Concentration Camp Dachau 1933–1945.* Brussels: Comité International de Dachau, 1978.

Dobson, James. *The New Dare to Discipline.* Wheaton, Ill.: Tyndale House Publishers, 1992.

Eisnitz, Gail A. *Slaughterhouse: The Shocking Story of Greed, Neglect, and Inhumane Treatment Inside the U.S. Meat Industry.* Amherst, N.Y.: Prometheus Books, 1997.

Eliot, Marc. *Walt Disney: Hollywood's Dark Prince.* London: Andre Deutsch, 1993.

Emerson, Robert L. *The New Economics of Fast Food.* New York: Van Nostrand Reinhold, 1990.

Ensuring Safe Food: From Production to Consumption. Washington, D.C.: National Academy Press, 1998.

Fenaroli's Handbook of Flavor Indredients, vol. 2. Ann Arbor, Mich.: CRC Press, 1995.

Finley, Judith Reid. *Time Capsule 1900: Colorado Springs a Century Ago.* Colorado Springs: Pastword Publishing, 1998.

Flandrin, Jean Louis, and Massimo Montanari, eds. *Food: A Culinary History.* New York: Columbia University Press, 1999.

Fox, Nicols. *It Was Probably Something You Ate: A Practical Guide to Avoiding and Surviving Foodborne Illness.* New York: Penguin, 1999.

———. *Spoiled: The Dangerous Truth about a Food Chain Gone Haywire.* New York: Basic Books, 1997.

Future of Public Health, The. Washington, D.C.: National Academy Press, 1998.

Goddard, Stephen B. *Getting There: The Epic Struggle Between Road and Rail in the American Century.* New York: Basic Books, 1994.

Gorbachev, Mikhail. *Perestroika: New Thinking for Our Country and the World.* New York: Harper & Row, 1987.

Haber, Heinz. *The Walt Disney Story of Our Friend the Atom.* New York: Simon and Schuster, 1956.

Hall, Carl W., A. W. Farrall, and A. L. Rippen. *Encyclopedia of Food Engineering.* Westport, Conn.: Avi Publishing, 1986.

Heath, Henry B. *Source Book of Flavors.* Westport, Conn.: Avi Publishing, 1981.

Hermann, Ingolf. *Die Deutsch-Deutsch Grenze.* Plauen, Germany: Vogtländischer Heimatverlag Neupert, 1998.

Hightower, Jim. *Eat Your Heat Out: Food Profiteering in America.* New York: Crown Publishers, 1975.

Hines, Thomas. *The Total Package: The Evolution and Secret Meanings of Boxes, Bottles, Cans, and Tubes.* New York: Little Brown, 1995.

Hogan, David Gerard. *Selling 'Em by the Sack.* New York: New York University Press, 1997.

Hui, Y. H. *Encyclopedia of Food Science and Technology,* vol. 2. New York: John Wiley & Sons, 1992.

Hunt, Linda. *Secret Agenda: The United States Government, Nazi Scientists, and Project Paperclip, 1945 to 1990.* New York: St. Martin's Press, 1991.

Industry and Trade Summary: Flavor and Fragrance Materials. Washington, D.C., U.S. Trade Commission: USITC Publication no. 3162, March 1999.

Industry and Trade Summary: Poultry. Washington, D.C., U.S. International Trade Commission: USITC Publication no. 3148, December 1998.

Jackson, Kenneth T. *Crabgrass Frontier: The Suburbanization of the United States.* New York: Oxford University Press, 1985.

Jakle, John A., and Keith A. Sculle. *Fast Food: Roadside Restaurants in the Automobile Age.* Baltimore: John Hopkins University Press, 1999.

Johnson, Arnold H., and Martin S. Peterson. *Encyclopedia of Food Science.* Westport, Conn.: Avi Publishing, 1978.

Karcher, Carl, with B. Carolyn Knight. *Never Stop Dreaming: 50 Years of Making It Happen.* San Marcos, Calif.: Robert Erdmann Publishing, 1991.

Khan, Mahmood A. *Restaurant Franchising.* New York: Van Nostrand Reinhold, 1992.

Knight, B. Carolyn. *Making It Happen: The Story of Carl Karcher Enterprises.* Anaheim, Calif.: Carl Karcher Enterprises, 1981.

Kroc, Ray, with Robert Anderson. *Grinding It Out: The Making of McDonald's.* New York: St. Martin's Paperbacks, 1987.

Kunstler, James Howard. *The Geography of Nowhere: The Rise and Decline of America's Man-Made Landscape.* New York: Touchstone, 1994.

Kwitny, Jonathan. *Vicious Circles: The Mafia in the Marketplace.* New York: W. W. Norton, 1979.

Langdon, Philip. *A Better Place to Live: Reshaping the American Suburb.* Amherst: University of Massachusetts Press, 1994.

Lasater, Dale. *Falfurrias: Ed C. Lasater and the Development of South Texas.* College Station: Texas A&M University Press, 1985.

Lasater, Laurence M. *The Lasater Philosophy of Cattle Raising.* El Paso: Texas Western Press, 1972.

Laser, Rudolf, Joachim Mensdorf, and Johannes Richter. *Plauen 1944/1945: Eine Stadt Wird Zerstört.* Plauen, Germany: Vogtländischer Heimatverlag Neupert, 1995.

Leidner, Robin. *Fast Food, Fast Talk: Service Work and the Routinization of Everyday Life.* Berkeley: University of California Press, 1993.

Levenstein, Harvey. *Paradox of Plenty: A Social History of Eating in Modern America.* New York: Oxford University Press, 1993.

Limprecht, Jane E. *ConAgra Who? $15 Billion and Growing.* Omaha: ConAgra, 1989.

Love, John F. *McDonald's: Behind the Arches*. New York: Bantam Books, 1995.

Luxenberg, Stan. *Roadside Empires: How the Chains Franchised America*. New York: Viking, 1985.

Macdonald, Cameron Lynne, and Carmen Sirianni, eds. *Working in the Service Society*. Philadelphia: Temple University Press, 1996.

Markusen, Ann, Peter Hall, Scott Campbell, and Sabina Deitrick. *The Rise of the Gunbelt: The Military Remapping of Industrial America*. New York: Oxford University Press, 1991.

Marx, Leo. *The Machine in the Garden: Technology and the Pastoral Ideal in America*. New York: Oxford University Press, 1970.

McDonald, Ronald J. *The Complete Hamburger: The History of America's Favorite Sandwich*. New York: Birch Lane Press, 1997.

McLamore, James W. *The Burger King: Jim McLamore and the Building of an Empire*. New York: McGraw-Hill, 1998.

McNeal, James U. *Kids As Customers: A Handbook of Marketing to Children*. New York: Lexington Books, 1992.

McWilliams, Carey. *California: The Exception*. 1949. Reprint, Berkeley: University of California Press, 1999.

———. *Southern California Country*. New York: Duell, Sloan & Pearce, 1946.

Meat and Poultry Inspection: The Scientific Basis of the Nation's Program. Washington, D.C.: National Academy Press, 1985.

Melaniphy, John C. *Restaurant and Fast Food Site Selection*. New York: John Wiley & Sons, 1992.

Molnar, Alex. "Sponsored Schools and Commercialized Classrooms: Schoolhouse Commercializing Trends in the 1990's." Center for the Analysis of Commercialism in Education, University of Wisconsin-Milwaukee, August 1998.

Monaghan, Tom, with Robert Anderson. *Pizza Tiger*. New York: Random House, 1986.

Mosley, Leonard. *Disney's World*. New York: Stein and Day, 1985.

Mussinan, Cynthia J., and Michael J. Morello, eds. *Flavor Analysis: Developments in Isolation and Characterization*. Washington, D.C.: American Chemical Society, 1998.

Neufeld, Michael J. *The Rocket and the Reich: Peenemünde and the Coming of the Ballistic Missile Era*. New York: Free Press, 1995.

Nye, David E. *American Technological Sublime*. Cambridge: MIT Press, 1994.

O'Brien, Timothy. *Bad Bet: The Inside Story of the Glamour, Glitz, and Danger of America's Gambling Industry*. New York: Times Business, 1998.

Pater, Siegfried. *Zum Beispiel McDonald's*. Göttingen, Germany: Lamuv Verlag, 1994.

Peritz, Rudolph J. R. *Competition Policy in America, 1888–1992: History, Rhetoric, Law*. New York: Oxford University Press, 1996.

Piszkiewicz, Dennis. *Wernher von Braun: The Man Who Sold the Moon*. Westport, Conn.: Praeger, 1998.

Plauen: 1933–1945. Plauen, Germany: Vogtländer Heimatverlag Neupert, 1995.

Plauen: Ein Rundgang Durch die Stadt. Plauen, Germany: Militzke Verlag, 1992.

Protecting Youth at Work: Health, Safety, and Development of Working Children and Adolescents in the United States. Washington, D.C.: National Academy Press, 1998.

Purvin, Robert L., Jr. *The Franchise Fraud: How to Protect Yourself Before and After You Invest.* New York: John Wiley & Sons, 1994.

Reisner, Marc. *Cadillac Desert: The American West and Its Disappearing Water.* New York: Penguin Books, 1987.

Reiter, Ester. *Making Fast Food: From the Frying Pan into the Fryer.* Montreal: McGill–Queen's University Press, 1991.

Report on the Youth Labor Force: Washington, D.C.: U.S. Department of Labor, June 2000.

Rifkin, Jeremy. *Beyond Beef: The Rise and Fall of the Cattle Culture.* New York: Penguin 1993.

Ritzer, George. *The McDonaldization of Society: An Investigation into the Changing Character of Contemporary Social Life.* Thousand Oaks, Calif.: Pine Ridge Press, 1996.

Roberts, Phil "Zoom," and Christopher O'Donnell. *Quick Service That Sells!: The Art of Profitable Hospitality for Quick-Service Restaurants.* Denver: Pencom International, 1997.

Rozin, Elizabeth. *The Primal Cheeseburger.* New York: Penguin Books, 1994.

Sacrificing America's Youth: The Problem of Child Labor and the Response of Government. Chicago: National Safe Workplace Institute, 1992.

Safety Last: The Politics of E. coli and other Food-Borne Pathogens. Washington, D.C.: Center for Public Integrity, 1998.

Sanders, Col. Harland. *Life As I Have Known It Has Been "Finger Lickin' Good."* Carol Stream, Ill.: Creation House, 1974.

Schickel, Richard. *The Disney Version: The Life, Times, Art, and Commerce of Walt Disney.* New York: Avon Books, 1968.

Schwanitz, Rolg. *Zivilcourage: Die friedliche Revolution in Plauen andhand von Stasi-Akten.* Plauen: Vogtländischer Heimatverlag Neupert, 1998.

Sheehan, Jack, ed. *The Players: The Men Who Made Las Vegas.* Reno: University of Nevada Press, 1997.

Sinclair, Upton. *The Jungle.* 1906. Reprint, New York: Bantam Books, 1981.

Skaggs, Jimmy M. *Prime Cut: Livestock Raising and Meatpacking in the United States, 1607–1983.* College Station: Texas A&M University Press, 1986.

Skolout, Patricia Farris. *Colorado Springs History A to Z.* Colorado Springs, Patricia Farris Skolout, 1992.

Sprague, Marshall. *Money Mountain: The Story of Cripple Creek Gold.* Lincoln, University of Nebraska Press, 1979.

———. *Newport in the Rockies: The Life and Good Times of Colorado Springs.* Athens, Ohio: Swallow Press, 1987.

Starr, Kevin. *The Dream Endures: California Enters the 1940's.* New York: Oxford University Press, 1997.

Statistical Abstract of the United States. Washington, D.C.: U.S. Census Bureau, 1999.

Stromquist, Shelton, and Marvin Bergman, eds. *Unionizing the Jungles: Labor and Community in the Twentieth-Century Meatpacking Industry.* Iowa City: University of Iowa Press, 1997.

Stull, Donald D., Michael J. Broadway, and David Griffith, eds. *Any Way You Cut It: Meat Processing and Small-Town America.* Lawrence: University Press of Kansas, 1995.

Takeoka, Gary R., Roy Teranishi, Patrick J. Williams, and Akio Kobayashi, eds. *Biotechnology for Improved Foods and Flavors*. Washington, D.C.: American Chemical Society, 1995.

Tennyson, Jeffrey. *Hamburger Heaven: The Illustrated History of the Hamburger*. New York: Hyperion, 1993.

Thomas, R. David. *Dave's Way: A New Approach to Old-Fashioned Success*. New York: G. P. Putnam's Sons, 1991.

Ubbelohde, Carl, Maxine Benson, and Duane A. Smith. *A Colorado History*. Boulder, Colo.: Pruett Publishing, 1995.

Vidal, John. *McLibel: Burger Culture on Trial*. New York: New Press, 1997.

Watson, James L., ed. *Golden Arches East: McDonald's in East Asia*. Stanford, Calif.: Stanford University Press, 1997.

Watts, Steven. *The Magic Kingdom: Walt Disney and the American Way of Life*. Boston: Houghton Mifflin, 1997.

Weiss, Frank. *Plauen: auf historischen Postkarten*. Plauen: Vogtländer Heimatverlag Neupert, 1991.

Westcott, John. *Anaheim: City of Dreams*. Chatsworth, Calif.: Windsor Publications, 1990.

White, Richard. *"It's Your Misfortune and None of My Own": A New History of the American West*. Norman: University of Oklahoma Press, 1991.

Wilkinson, Charles F. *Crossing the Next Meridian*. Washington, D.C.: Island Press, 1992.

Williams, Meredith. *Tomart's Price Guide to McDonald's Happy Meal Collectibles*. Dayton, Ohio: Tomart Publications, 1995.

Williams, Willard F., and Thomas T. Stout. *Economics of the Livestock-Meat Industry*. New York: Macmillan, 1964.

Witzel, Michael Karl. *The American Drive-In: History and Folklore of the Drive-In Restaurant in American Car Culture*. Osceola, Wis.: Motorbooks International, 1994.

Yeager, Mary. *Competition and Regulation: The Development of Oligopoly in the Meat Packing Industry*. Greenwich, Conn.: Jai Press, 1981.

acknowledgments

This book began as a two-part article in *Rolling Stone*. I am grateful to Jann Wenner, who never asked me to tone down my criticism of powerful and litigious corporations, who let me follow the story wherever it led, from the strip malls of Colorado to the back roads of Saxony. In an age of media concentration and timidity, he is an oddly old-fashioned figure: an independent, outspoken editor and publisher who truly supports investigative journalism. Bob Love recruited me for this assignment, backed me all the way, and made writing for the magazine a pleasure. Will Dana came up with the initial idea, supplying the title and the underlying aim: view America through its fast food. He proved to be a wonderful editor and friend.

Eamon Dolan is another old-fashioned, quickly vanishing American type: a book editor who edits. He helped me expand the work without losing its focus, spared me embarrassment by urging the removal of certain material, made me seem more intelligent by suggesting the inclusion of other material. His ideas ranged from the broadly thematic to the seemingly trivial, yet revealing, and now grace the book without attribution. He read every word of the manuscript almost as many times as I did. Thanks to Eamon, the final draft was much better than the first one. Every author should be so fortunate, and the book's remaining flaws are entirely my own.

At Houghton Mifflin, Loren Isenberg and Lois Wasoff gave wise counsel, and Emily Little handled everything with great charm and aplomb.

At Penguin, Daniel Hind had enormous faith that people in the United Kingdom might want to read this book. I am grateful to him for that faith and for his insightful critique of the text. And Clare Pollock has been a wonderful proponent of my work.

Ellis Levine provided some valuable legal — and literary — suggestions. J. C. Suares, Lowell Weiss, and Mike Guy read the manuscript at various stages and gave many useful criticisms.

Charles William Wilson performed the unenviable task of combing through the text for errors. He did an extraordinary job, earned my lasting gratitude — and is in no way responsible for any inaccuracies the book may contain. He has a bright literary future. Alita Byrd spent hours at the National Archives tracking down recently declassified files on Heinz Haber. David Malley did a fine job of fact-checking the two-part *Rolling Stone* article. And Shauna Wright helped me assemble the bibliography.

The photograph of Nancy Donley's son Alex speaks much louder than words, and I am grateful to her for allowing me to include it. Eugene Richards is one of the finest documentary photographers, ever. I am indebted to him for letting me use two of his photos. On short notice, Skylar Nielsen and Greg Skinner went out and shot just what I needed. Rob Buchanan hired a small airplane in order to photograph the feedlots of Weld County from above. Though none of his aerial feedlot photos is included here, I applaud the spirit behind that move and thank him for letting me use one of his more prosaic cattle shots. And Mark Mann took a picture that says it all.

Among the hundreds of people I interviewed for this book, a handful deserve special thanks for the help, the insights, and the inspiration they provided.

Dale Lasater, Steve Bjerklie, Kenny and Clara Dobbins, Javier Ramirez, Dave Feamster, and the rancher whom I call Hank spent countless hours speaking with me. I'm grateful for all their time and for all I learned from them.

I would never have become a journalist without the support of William Whitworth and Cullen Murphy at the *Atlantic Monthly.* Their influence now pervades everything I write. Corby Kummer has demonstrated over the years that prose can have both substance and style. And Amy Meeker has again and again shown me the importance, and the ethical imperative, of being right about every single detail.

I was fortunate to have John McPhee as a teacher long ago. He set a high standard — in seriousness of purpose, and compassion, and dedication to the craft — that his former students have struggled to attain.

A number of friends encouraged me for years to keep writing: Andre Boissier, Eric Borrer, Craig Canine, Michael Clurman, Alex Hendler, Jordan Katz, Lacey and John Williams. They cannot be thanked enough. Jane Rosenthal helped me become a writer by forcing me to write every day — and paying me to do it. Sarah Finnie Cabot played a crucial role in helping me get my first assignment. John Seabrook has been supportive in innumerable ways, finding me fact-checkers, reading manuscripts carefully, and criticizing them well. Katrina vanden Heuvel gave me the final shove that made me write nonfiction, has always been inspiring and engaged in the big issues of the day, always a dear friend.

Tina Bennett played an important role in the creation of this book, from the initial proposal to the final pages. She is a real gem: a terrific editor who also happens to be a terrific agent.

During the writing of this book, my family was often subjected to highly unpleasant details. Lynn and Craig, James and Kyle, Amy and Mark, Andrew, Austin, Hillary, Dylan, Lena, Billy, and George have put up with a lot. I am lucky they will still share a meal with me. My children, Mica and Conor, have put up with even more, and I apologize to them for all the Happy Meals they've been denied. I'm deeply grateful to Bob and Lola, who showed great patience and gave tremendous support as I tried to find my way as a writer. I'm deeply grateful to my parents, who have given me more love and support than could ever be measured. Most of all, I'm grateful to my wife, Shauna. Without her, none of these words would have been written.

index

Acheson, David, 221
Acree, Terry, 126
Acuff, Dan S., 45
Adams, Richard, 100
Advertising: awards for, 87; for children, 40–49, 231, 243, 262, 267; of cigarettes, 262; McDonald's spending on, 4; in public schools, 51–57; and television, 45–46
Advertising Age, 241
African-Americans, 156, 251, 268
AIDS, 196
Air Defense Command, U.S., 62
Air Force, U.S., 243
Air Force Academy, 62
Air Force Space Command, 1, 62
Alabama, 16
Alger, Horatio, 13
Alice in Wonderland, 40
Alka-Seltzer, 41
"Alliance for Workplace Safety," 85
Amalgamated Butcher Workmen, 151
Ament, Don, 42
American Academy of Pediatrics, 46, 262
American Cancer Society, 242–43
American Coal Foundation, 55
American Food Service Corporation, 209
American Franchise Association, 99
Americanization of the world, 239–40, 244
American Meat Institute, 206, 207

American Medical Association, 217
American School Food Service Association, 56
Amputations, 185
Anaheim, Calif., 13–14, 26, 28
Anderson, A. D., 153, 154, 164
Andreas, Michael, 143
Antibiotics, 200, 221
Applebee's, 92
Arab oil embargo, 24
Archer Daniels Midland, 143
Arkansas Democrat-Gazette, 141
Arkansas Department of Health, 214, 318n
Armour, 137, 159, 306n
Armour, J. Ogden, 205
Armstrong Bakery, 15, 18
Army, U.S., 155, 217, 276n
Arndt, Diane, 180–81
ARPANET, 260
Artificial flavors, 120, 124–27
Assembly lines, 20, 69. *See also* Disassembly lines
Association of National Advertisers, 46
Astro World, 42
Athens, 244
Athlete's Foot, 78
Augie's, 98
Aunt Jemima, 36
Australia, 230, 231, 276n
Autoimmune disorders, 195
Automated Meat Recovery Systems, 218
Automobile industry, 13, 15–16, 17, 36

Autry, Gene, 25
Awards for employees, 88
Ayala, Joacquin, 234

BabyGap, 97
Bac-O-Bits, 124
Banana Republic, 5
Barber, Benjamin R., 229
Barney, 45
Barone, Ben, 178
Baskin Robbins, 86
Bass brothers, 138
Bates, Timothy, 98
Bauer, Frank, 219
Bauer Meat Company, 219
Bean, Morey, 259
Beard, James, 120
Beef Industry Food Safety Council, 217
Beefmaster (breed of cattle), 256
Beef Trust, 137, 152–53, 205, 255
Beijing, 230, 231, 243
Beijing University, 243
Belgium, 243, 244
Bell, Glen W., Jr., 22
Bellenger, Cass, 185
Bennett, William, 105
Bennigan's, 88
Berlin, 225
Bernard, Dr. Neal D., 202
Beverage Industry, 54
Biela, Tim, 209
Biff-Burgers, 24
Bigari, Steve, 66
Birdseye, Clarence, 113
Bjerklie, Steven P., 202, 218, 310n
Black Hawks, 93
BMI. See Body Mass Index (BMI)
Body Mass Index (BMI), 240
Boeing, 19
Book It! Program, 55–56
Boone, Pat, 25
Bove, Jose, 244
Bovine spongiform encephalopathy
    (BSE), 202
Boyle, J. Patrick, 207
Bozo's Circus, 41
Brands, 4, 43, 229
Brandweek, 4, 229
Brazil, 230, 244

Brewer, Dave, 71
Brinker, Norman, 88
Britain. See United Kingdom
Broken Heartland (Davidson), 147
Brothers, Joyce, 105
Bruce, Douglas, 64
BSE (bovine spongiform
    encephalopathy), 202
Buck's Pizza, 98
Buddy's Bar-B-Q, 98
Budweiser, 43
Bugsy Malone, 68
Bureau of Labor Statistics, 172, 180
Burger Fries, 130
Burger King: advertising to children, 51,
    231; and Cheyenne Mountain Air
    Force Station, 2; and crime, 85, 86;
    deliberate food contamination at, 222;
    and flavor additives, 125–26, 128;
    franchises for, 98; and french fries,
    117; history of, 24; and Hudson
    Foods, 194; and impulsive buying, 66;
    at industry top, 27; as international,
    229; Kids Club, 45; labor practices,
    69–72, 82; and Nickelodeon, 48; and
    obedience, 75; and overtime wages,
    74; playgrounds at, 47; portion sizes
    at, 241; profit margins of soda, 286n;
    and restaurant technology, 71; and
    Teletubbies, 48; and throughput, 69;
    training manual of, 70; and Uniform
    Commercial Code, 101. See also Insta-
    Burger King
Burns, Matthew, 22
Bush, Barbara, 104, 106
Bush, George, 105, 206
Bush Boake Allen, 121
Bushey, John, 57
Business Insurance, 160
Butchers, 154

Cabbage Patch Kids, 47
Cadbury-Schweppes, 53
Caffeine, 54
California: citrus production in, 13–14;
    drive-in restaurants in, 17; fast food
    industry development in, 19–21;
    Hell's Angels in, 21; migrant workers
    in, 161–62; population growth in, 15–

16; resident migration from, to Colorado Springs, 61–65; and World War II, 18. *See also specific cities*
Callicrate, Mike, 143–44
Cameron, Mike, 55
Campbell, William J., 17
Camp Carson, 61
Campylobacter jejuni, 196, 202–3
Canada, 77, 117, 230
Cappelli, Mike, 77
Cappelli, Tom, 77
Captain D's, 86
Cargill, 8, 230
Carhops, 17, 18, 24
Carlin, George, 234
Carlini, Trent, 234
Carl Karcher Enterprises, Inc. (CKE), 25–28
Carl's Drive-in Barbeque, 18–19
Carl's Jr. restaurants: competition of, 24; creation of, 21–22; franchises for, 25, 98; and growth, 267; interstate expansion of, 25, 78; portion sizes at, 241
Carnation Milk Company, 35
Carpal tunnel syndrome, 187
Carriba's, 78
Carter, Jimmy, 208
Cartoon Network, 46
Cassidy, David, 234
Catfish industry, 159
Cattle industry: and beef consumption, 142, 277n; and Beef Trust, 137; breeds of cattle, 255–56; and captive supplies, 138, 142–43; chicken manure as cattle feed, 202–3; and disease, 201–4, 257; economic problems in, 136–38, 142–43, 144–47; and environmentalism, 133–35; and European exports, 142; and fast food industry, 8–9; and hormones, 263; intimidation by meatpacking industry, 143–44; and land trusts, 145; "mad cow disease," 202; secret pricing in, 143; suicide rates in, 146. *See also* Meatpacking industry
Cattle King Packing Company, 218–19
CDC. *See* Centers for Disease Control and Prevention (CDC)
Census Bureau, 306n
Center for Public Integrity, 210
Center for Science in the Public Interest, 54
Centers for Disease Control and Prevention (CDC), 195, 222, 240
Chain, Steve, 276n
Chain Operators Exchange (COEX), 236–39, 290n
Chamber of Commerce, U.S., 185
Chandler, Alfred D., 68–69
Chemical Market Reporter, 124
Cheskin, Louis, 97–98
Chevy's, 73
Cheyenne Mountain Air Force Station, 1–2, 7, 275n
Chicago, 16, 152–53, 155–57
Chicago Historical Society, 306n
Chicago Tribune, 179
Chicken industry. *See* Poultry industry
Chicken manure, 202–3
Chicken McNuggets, 139–40, 301n
Chicken Shack, 98
Child labor and child labor laws, 73, 80, 82, 261, 262
Children: and Disney and Kroc, 33; and *E. coli* 0157:H7, 198–99; and hamburgers, 198; and heart attacks, 242; and hemolytic uremic syndrome (HUS), 199–200; impact of fast food industry on, 9; Internet as data source on, 45; and mass marketing techniques, 8; and meat contamination, 218–21; obesity of, 242; and soft drink consumption, 54–55; as target customers, 40–49, 231, 262, 267; and television advertising, 45–46
Children's Online Privacy Protection Act, 45
Child Welfare League, 46
Chili's, 88
China, 230, 231, 242
Christian Coalition, 63
Chuck E. Cheese, 87
Cigarette advertising, 262
Citric acid, 143
CKE. *See* Carl Karcher Enterprises, Inc. (CKE)
Clean Air Act, 165–66
Cleaning crews, 176–78, 310–11n

Clinton administration, 185, 207, 210, 214, 215

Clostridium perfringens, 197

CME KidCom Ad Traction Study II, 43

Coan, Mike, 160

Coble, Howard, 101

Coca-Cola: and brand recognition, 4, 229; in China, 231; marketing of, in public schools, 51, 53–55, 56; and McDonald's, 54; and nutrition, 54; and profit margins, 286n

COEX. *See* Chain Operators Exchange (COEX)

Coffey, Allen, Jr., 101

Colombia, 244

Colorado, 1–2, 7, 59–66

Colorado Cattlemen's Association, 144–45

Colorado Restaurant Association, 73

Colorado Springs, 1–2, 7, 59–66

Colorado Springs Gazette-Telegraph, 63

Colorado Springs Independent, 57

Colorado Springs Sun, 63

Columbia Film Studio, 19

Columbia/HCA, 5

Columbus, Christopher, 124

Comfort foods, 123

"Committee for Employment Opportunities," 72

Communism, Hypnotism, and the Beatles (Noebel), 65

ConAgra: and contaminated meat, 219; and fast food conventions, 236; fraudulent actions of, 159–60; as french fry producer, 158; and illegal immigrants, 162; and industry uniformity, 305n; as international, 230–31; and intimidation of cattle ranchers, 143; and Lamb Weston, 130, 158; and meatpacking industry consolidation, 8; Monfort takeover by, 158–59; and nation's largest meatpacking plant, 149–50; poultry division of, 140; and price fixing, 159; profit margins, 174; tax breaks from Nebraska, 163–64; and workers' compensation, 184

ConAgra Who?, 159

Connelly, John, 227

Conservation. *See* Environmentalism

Consortium Members, Inc., 100

Consumers Union, 46, 56

Conway family, 257–58

Conway's Red Top Restaurant, 257–59

Coolidge, Calvin, 38

Copenhagen, 244

Corn, 143

Cornell University, 126

Corporate logos, 20

Country Pride, 159

Cox News Service, 212

Cracker Barrel Old Country Store, 162

Cramer, Keith G., 22

Crawford, Cindy, 237

Creutzfeldt-Jakob disease, 202

Crime: in fast food industry, 83–87, 292n, 293n; and meatpacking industry, 154–55, 164–66, 179–81, 206, 305n; and migrant workforce, 162; organized crime in meatpacking industry, 154–55, 305n; sexual harassment, 176. *See also* Injuries

CrissCut Fries, 130

Cross, Russell, 207

Cryptosporidium parvum, 196

Cudahy, 137

Cumulative trauma injuries, 163, 185, 310n

Cuomo, Mario, 105

Cyclospora cayetanensis, 196

Cywinski, John, 48

Dachau concentration camp, 39, 233–34

Dairy Queen, 162

Dare to Discipline, 63

Davidson, Osha Gray, 147

Dawn of Better Living, 38

DCS Sanitation Management, Inc, 177, 178

DD Marketing, 51–52, 56

Dear, Joseph, 85

Deaths: and food poisoning, 197; and obesity, 241–42; and OSHA penalties, 311n; of workers, 178, 179, 311n

DeBolt, Don, 101

Decision Earth, 55

DeGette, Cara, 57

DeLuca, Frederick, 100

Democratic Party, 64

Denmark, 244
Denny's, 48
Denver Post, 56–57
DeRose, Dan, 51–53
Dickey, Jay, 85
Disassembly lines, 153–54, 169–71, 173–75. *See also* Assembly lines
Disfiguring injuries, 185
Disney, Walt: as anti-socialist, 36–37, 38; and brand loyalty, 43; development of Disneyland, 18–19; and fast food industry, 6; as FBI informant, 37; former Nazis as employees of, 38–39; and House Un-American Activities Committee, 36–37; and Kroc, 33–37, 49; and licensing agreements, 40; and "synergy," 40. *See also* Disneyland; Walt Disney Company
Disney Channel, 46
Disneyland, 6, 18–19, 33, 39. *See also* Walt Disney Company
Disneyland (TV series), 40
Disneyland University, 33
Disney World, 40
Dobbins, Kenny, 187
Dobson, James, 63
Doerfler, Ernst, 229
Doherty, James C., 87–88
Dole, Elizabeth, 239
Domino's, 2, 23, 56, 69
Donley, Nancy, 200
Dora-Nordhausen concentration camp, 39, 282n
Dresden, 227, 229
Drive-in banks, 17
Drive-in churches, 19
Drive-in restaurants, 17
Dropouts, 79–80
Dr Pepper, 53, 54
Drug abuse, 174, 310n
Dunkin' Donuts, 22, 92, 95
Dunlap, Ray, 114
Dupree, Clarence, 182

E. coli (*Escherichia coli*) 0157:H7: and antibiotics, 200; cattle infection statistics, 203; and children, 198–99; and contagion, 201–4; definition of, 193, 199; and grass-fed cattle, 257; history of, 196; and Jack in the Box, 198–99, 207, 214, 221, 263; and McDonald's, 199; and meat recalls, 211–14, 220; and meatpacking industry, 9, 194–96, 202–4, 263; and National School Lunch Program, 219; and Shiga toxins, 199–200, 221–22; and SIS-C system, 207; strength of, 200–201; testing for, 209–10, 215, 263; and USDA, 203–4, 207, 263; and Wendy's, 212
East Germany, 227, 228, 229, 249–52. *See also* Germany
Eat Your Heart Out (Hightower), 5
Eggs, 264
Eisenhower, Dwight D., 22
Elders Company, 230
Electro-Hop, 24
Employment. *See* Labor practices; Workforce
Encroachment, 99–101
England. *See* United Kingdom
Engler, Paul, 138
Environmentalism, 133–35, 146, 261–62, 268
Erikson, Erik, 44
Escherichia coli 0157:H7. *See E. coli* (*Escherichia coli*) 0157:H7
European Court of Human Rights, 249
European Union (EU), 142, 243, 264
"Everything of Zig's" (Ziglar), 105
Excel, 137, 143, 158, 174, 178
Exxon, 55, 56
Exxon Education Foundation, 55

Fair Labor Standards Act, 73, 82
Falwell, Jerry, 63
Farm industry, 8–9, 118
Fast food industry: and American diet, 3–4; and Americanization of the world, 239–40, 243–44; and assembly lines, 20, 69; and awards for employees, 88; boycotts of, 269–70; and Chain Operators Exchange, 236–39; clustering of, 60; competition in, 24, 71, 78, 229, 258; and conformity, 5–6; consumer spending on, 275n; and corporate-sponsored teaching materials, 55–56; and crime, 83–87, 292n,

Fast food industry (*cont.*)
293n; and deliberate food contamination, 222; and drive-in restaurants, 17; and *E. coli*, 198–99, 207, 214, 221, 263; and emotional connections, 49–51; employee turnover in, 72–73, 83, 276n; exportation of, 9–10; and federal subsidies, 72; and fixed costs, 78; and flavor additives, 120–29; and food technology, 6–7; founders of, 5–6, 13–28; and french fries, 115–17; government regulation of, 264; and government-backed loans, 101–2; growth of, 3, 8; and Hazard Analysis and Critical Control Points (HACCP), 208, 215; and homogenizing of America, 5; and impulsive buying, 66; injury rates in, 83; as international, 88, 228–34, 239–40, 243–49, 267; and interstate highway system, 8, 22; investment in, 24–25; largest hamburger chains, 27; and lawsuits, 75, 245–49, 266–67; lobbying efforts of, 8, 37, 88, 267; management salaries in, 73, 74; McDonald's as standard for, 22, 65, 97; and "McWorld," 229; and obesity, 9, 240–43, 261, 324n; and Occupational Health and Safety Administration (OSHA), 84–85; and oil embargo, 24; and popular culture, 9; and poultry industry, 139–42; profit margins in, 54, 286n; public school marketing programs of, 51–57; real costs in, 261–62; and restaurant technology, 24, 66–67, 71–72; rural life affected by, 8; and saturated fats, 298n; and school dropouts, 79–80; site selection for, 66; and Small Business Administration (SBA), 102; social status of employment in, 78–79; tax breaks for, 72; teenagers in, 67–71, 78–87; and throughput, 67–71; and toys, 4, 47–48; training in, 69–71, 262; and unions, 71, 75–77, 88, 233, 262; wages in, 8, 37, 71, 73–74, 85, 277n, 328n; and worker safety, 84–85. *See also* Advertising; Cattle industry; Labor Practices; Meatpacking industry; Workforce; *and specific companies*

Favorite, Philly, 145
FBI, 37, 86, 293n
FDA, 128
Feamster, Dave, 92–94, 102–4
Federal subsidies, 7–8, 72
Federal Trade Commission (FTC), 45–46, 99, 137
Federation of Labour of Quebec, 77
Few Quick Facts About Venereal Disease, 38
Filet-O-Fish, 95, 124
Film industry, 18
Financial Post, 100
Firestone, 16
Fish, Joe, 220
Fisher, Donald, 97
Fisher, Doris, 97
Fixed costs, 78
Flash-freezing, 111, 113
Flavor industry, 122–28
Focus on the Family, 63, 259
Foley, William P. II, 27, 267
Fone-A-Chef, 24
Food Chemical News, 124
Food Engineering, 6, 124
Foodmaker, Inc., 208
Food Product Design, 124
Food Technologist, 6
Food Will Win the War, 38
Foot Locker, 5
Forbes, 155, 306n
Ford, Henry, 36
Ford Aerospace, 62
Foreign policy, U.S., 229–30
Foreman, Carol Tucker, 328–29n
Foster Farms, 208
Fox Kids Network, 48
Fragrance industry, 122
France, 244
Franchises: and American foreign policy, 229–30; benefits of, 97, 98; for Burger King, 98; for Carl's Jr. restaurants, 25, 98; costs of, 98; and economic trends, 9; and encroachment, 99–101; failure rate of, 98, 295n; franchise agreements, 99–100, 102–4; history of, 94–95; and homogenizing of America, 5; international franchises, 233; for Jack in the Box, 99; for KFC (Kentucky

Fried Chicken), 95; legal protection of franchisees, 99–100; for McDonald's, 95–96, 98, 100; Small Business Administration (SBA) loans for, 102; for Taco Bell, 85; and Uniform Commercial Code, 101; and wages, 75, 78

Frank, Susan, 48

Freedom Newspaper chain, 63

Freedom of Information Act, 215

French fries: additives to, 120–21; and China, 231; competitive business in, 116–17; consumption statistics for, 277n; development in U.S., 114; and Kroc, 114–15; and processor oligopsony, 117–20; producers of, 158; production costs of, 298n; production process for, 111–31; sugar added to, 131

Fresno Bee, 53

Frey, William H., 64

FTC. *See* Federal Trade Commission (FTC)

FUBU, 82

Fujita, Den, 231, 323n

FutureCall, 81

Gallegos, Sandra, 193–94

Gap Inc., 5, 59, 78, 97

GapKids, 97

Gas chromatography, 124, 301n

General Accounting Office, 102

General Dynamics, 39

General Electric, 39

General Motors, 16, 94

Gepetto Group, 231

Gerba, Charles, 221

German Democratic Republic. *See* East Germany

Germany, 227, 231–32, 249–52, 276n, 322n

GFI America, Inc., 162, 163

Giardia lamblia, 203

Gingrich, Newt, 210

GIPSA (Grain Inspection, Packers and Stockyards Administration), 137

Givaudan, 121

Glenn & Anderson, 156

Glickman, Dan, 213, 214

GNC Packing, 259

Godbout, Clement, 77

Godfather's Pizza, 92

Goebbels, Joseph, 226

Golden arches: and Christian cross, 4, 276–77n; design of, 20; Freudian importance of, 98. *See also* McDonald's Corporation

Goldstein, Oscar, 41

Gorbachev, Mikhail, 27, 228, 234, 236–39

Göring, Hermann, 226

Grain Inspection, Packers and Stockyards Administration (GIPSA), 137

Gramm, Phil, 210

Gramm, Wendy Lee, 210

GRAS (Generally Regarded As Safe), 125

Great Britain. *See* United Kingdom

Greece, 244

Greeley, Horace, 150

Greeley, Colo., 150–51, 266

Green Burrito, 26, 27

Greenberg, Jack, 229

Greenberg, Jerald, 84

Greenpeace, 245–49. *See also* London Greenpeace

Gregory, Michael, 212

Grinding It Out (Kroc), 36

Groppel, Jack, 107

Gumby Pizza, 98

Haarman & Reimer, 121

Haber, Heinz, 39, 283n

HACCP. *See* Hazard Analysis and Critical Control Points (HACCP)

Hallmark Entertainment, 48

Hamburger: consumption of, 6, 277n; demographics of hamburger eaters, 315n; development of, 197–98; as national dish, 198; and obesity, 242–43. *See also* Cattle industry; *E. coli;* Meatpacking industry; *and specific fast food companies*

Hamburger Helper, 124

Hamburger University, 31, 230

Handicapped people, 70

Happy Joe's Pizza & Ice Cream Parlor, 98

Happy Meals, and marketing, 47–48, 242, 262
Hardee's, 27, 241
Harding, Lee, 193–94, 200, 211
Harper, Charles "Mike," 159, 163
Harvard University Medical School, 140, 301n
Hazard Analysis and Critical Control Points (HACCP), 208, 215, 216, 222
Healthy Choice, 159
Health insurance, 160, 161, 162, 257
Heart disease, 195, 242
Heavenly Flavors, 121
Hebrew National, 159
Hefferman, William, 120
Hefley, Joel, 186
Heinz, Margaret, 14–15
Hell's Angels, 21
Helms, Jesse, 210
Hemolytic uremic syndrome (HUS), 199–200
Heritage Foundation, 102
Hernandez-Gonzalez, Salvador, 178
Heston, Charlton, 105
Hewlett Packard, 62
Hi-Fries, 130
High-Level Precision Bombing, 38
Hightower, Jim, 5
Hill, James O., 240
Hiring practices, 70–72
Hispanics. *See* Latinos
Hitler, Adolph, 226
Hitler Youth, 226
HIV, 196
Hobbytown USA, 5
Hogan, David Gerard, 197
Hoiles, R. C., 63
Holland. *See* Netherlands
Hollywood Reporter, 48
Holman, Currier J., 153, 154, 155, 164
Holmgren, Paul, 93
Home Depot, 92
Homeless shelters, 163
Hoover, Herbert, 63
Hoover Dam, 235
Hormones, 263
Hot Dog on a Stick, 98
House Un-American Activities Committee, 36–37

Houston Chronicle, 52, 72
Hudson Foods, 194–95, 200, 211, 213, 215, 314n
Human immunodeficiency virus (HIV), 196
Hunt's, 159
HUS (hemolytic uremic syndrome), 199–200
Hygiene, 201–2, 203, 329n

IBP. *See* Iowa Beef Packers (IBP)
Idaho, 8, 117–18
IFA (International Franchise Association), 98, 101
IFF(International Flavors & Fragrances), 121–29
Ilitch, Mike, 94
Illegal immigrants. *See* Immigrants
Illinois, 31
Immigrants, 70–71, 160–63, 174, 176
Immigration and Naturalization Service, 162
I'm OK — You're OK, 74
In-N-Out Burger, 259–60, 327–28n
Independent contractors, 176, 310–11n
India, 230, 231, 244, 276n
Indonesia, 230
Inflammatory bowel disease, 195
Injuries: amputations, 185; carpal tunnel syndrome, 187; cumulative trauma injuries, 173, 185, 310n; and fast food industry, 83; lawsuits concerning, 181; and meatpacking industry, 172–90, 264–65, 309–10n; and poultry industry, 186, 310n; and public assistance, 185; tendinitis, 173; underreporting of, 175, 179–81, 310n; and unions, 184; and working conditions, 264–65. *See also* Crime
Inland Empire, 25
Insta-Burger King, 22, 24. *See also* Burger King
Insurance, health, 160, 161, 162, 257
International Flavors & Fragrances (IFF), 121–29, 299n
International Foodservice Manufacturers Association, 236
International Franchise Association (IFA), 98, 101

International Greenpeace, 245. *See also* London Greenpeace
Internet, 45, 146, 260
Interstate highway system, 8, 22, 64, 154
Iowa, 16, 101
Iowa Beef Packers (IBP): and bribing union officials, 155; and Canadian beef industry, 230; and cleaning crews, 177, 310–11; deceptive practices of, 166, 179–81, 206; emissions violations of, 164–65; and employee turnover, 161; and food safety, 319n; and "IBP revolution," 151, 173; and illegal immigrants, 162; and industry standards, 174–75; and injury reporting, 175, 264; and knife-sharpening, 173; lawsuits against, 182–83; and meat contamination, 203, 213–14; and meatpacking industry consolidation, 8, 137–38; and Midland, 143; and migrant labor, 162; and organized crime, 154–55, 306n; and OSHA, 183, 311n; and outrail policy, 216–17, 319n; and profit margins, 174; and safety, 182–83, 206; and sexual harassment, 176; and Small Business Administration (SBA), 164; steam pasteurization system, 216; tax breaks from Nebraska, 164; and unions, 158, 162, 174; and wages, 306n; worker deaths at, 178, 311n; worker profiles at, 165; and workers' compensation, 184
Ireland, 243
Ireland, Andy, 101
Irradiation, 217–18
Italy, 242

Jack in the Box: competition of, 24; and critics of fast food industry, 237–38; and *E. coli*, 198–99, 207, 214, 221, 263; and food safety, 208–10; franchisee treatment by, 99; and minimum wage, 73
Japan, 242, 276n
Jaspin, Elliot, 212
Jefferson, Thomas, 8, 114
Jenny Craig International, 97
Jiffy-Lube, 5

Jim Henson Company, 48
Joe Camel, 43
John Morrell, 180, 206
Jones, Regina, 75
Journal of Dentistry for Children, 54
Journal of the American Medical Association, 43
J. R. Simplot Company, 111, 113, 116, 129–30, 209, 231, 236, 269
Jungle (Sinclair), 152–53, 204–5
"Just in time" production, 67
Justice Department. *See* U.S. Department of Justice

Kabong, Matthew, 91–92
Kaman Services, 62
Karcher, Ben, 13–14
Karcher, Carl Leo, 26
Karcher, Carl N.: biography of, 13–15; drive-in restaurants of, 18–19; financial problems of, 25–28, 281n; hot dog carts of, 15, 18–19; ousted from board of CKE, 26; and self-service restaurants, 21–22
Karcher, Don, 25–26
Karcher, Margaret Heinz, 14–15, 27–28
K-Bob's Steakhouses, 98
KCBS-TV, 222
Keith's Drive-In Restaurant, 22
Kennedy, Ted, 88
Kentucky Fried Chicken. *See* KFC (Kentucky Fried Chicken)
Keystone Foods, 139
Kezios, Susan, 99
KFC (Kentucky Fried Chicken): and anti-U.S. imperialism, 243–44; and crime, 86; franchises for, 95; history of, 23; as international, 88, 229, 230; as largest poultry purchaser, 140; and NCAA promotions, 48; and restaurant technology, 71
Kidney illnesses, 195, 200
KidPower conference, 231
Kids as Customers (McNeal), 44
Kinko's, 59
Kinney, Joseph A., 85
Kirby, Jesse G., 17
Kissinger, Henry, 104, 105
Klasky-Csupo, 48

K-Mart, 3
Knight, Jacque, 212
Knott's Berry Farm, 159
Kool-Aid, 124
Kraft, John, 318n
Kristallnacht, 226
Kroc, Ray A.: and brand loyalty, 43; and Disney, 33–37, 49; as founder of Mc-Donald's Corporation, 5, 35, 198; and franchises, 95–96; on french fries, 114–15; marketing tools of, 40–41; McDonald brothers' relationship with, 34–35, 96–97; and Morris, 249; museum of, 31–32; on nonconform-ists, 5; philosophy of, 37; and Simplot, 115; and site selection for McDon-ald's, 66; and Speedee Service System, 34–35. *See also* McDonald's Corpora-tion
Küttler, Thomas, 228, 250
Kuwait, 230
Kwitny, Jonathan, 16–17, 306n

Labor practices: and assembly line sys-tem, 68–69; awards for employees, 88; child labor and child labor laws, 73, 80, 82, 261, 262; and employee turn-over, 72–73, 83, 88, 160–61, 163; and health insurance, 160, 161, 162, 257, 259; hiring practices, 70–72; and inju-ries, 176–78, 181, 186–90, 264–65; and kitchen technology, 71–72; and opposition to safety laws, 8; and over-time wages, 73–75, 82, 262; and poly-graph testing, 76; and regimentation, 69–70; and "stroking," 74; and unions, 71, 75–77, 88, 257; vacations, 160, 161; and wages, 8, 37, 73–75, 88, 259, 262; and worker safety, 84–85, 172–90; and workers' compensation, 184–85. *See also* Fast food industry; Meatpacking industry; Workforce; *and specific companies*
Labor unions. *See* Unions
La Choy, 159
Lamb, F. Gilbert, 130
Lamb Water Gun Knife, 130
Lamb Weston, 116–17, 129, 158, 230–31, 269

Land trusts, 145
Landauer, Fritz, 226
Language spoken in workplace, 70–72, 160
Lansing, Mich., 77
Lantos, Tom, 180
Lasater, Dale, 255–57
Lasater, Tom, 255–56
Lasater Ranch, 255–57
Las Vegas, 234–39, 323n
Latinos, 160–63, 175, 308n, 310n
Lawsuits: for libel, 245–49, 266–67; and overtime wages, 75; for sexual harass-ment, 176, 310n; and worker safety, 181, 182
Leidner, Robin, 70
Lenin, V. I., 249
Levenstein, Harvey, 113–14
Levis, 234
Libel, 245–49, 266–67
Licensing, 40
Life As I Have Known It Has Been "Fin-ger-lickin' Good" (Sanders), 23
Lifetime Learning Systems, 56
Limited, 78
Linkletter, Art, 25
Listeria monocytogenes, 196, 197
Literacy, 161, 178, 203
Little Caesars, 91–92, 94, 102–4, 241
Litton Data Systems, 62
Livestock Market Digest, 138
Lockheed Martin, 261
Logos of corporations, 20
London *Evening Standard,* 233
London Greenpeace, 245–49
Los Angeles, 15, 16, 18, 61–62, 64–65, 293n
Los Angeles Times, 85
Louisiana Tech University, 141
Love, John F., 20
Lowe, Peter, 105, 106, 239
Lowe, Tamara, 105
Luftwaffe Institute for Aviation Medi-cine, 39, 283n
Luxenberg, Stan, 94
Lysine, 143

Macdonald, Cameron Lynne, 4
Mack Truck, 16

"Mad cow disease," 202

Maerker, Christa, 232

Maggart, Lindsay, 112

Magic Kingdom (Watts), 36

Mail Boxes Etc., 229

Maine, potato production in, 117

Makepeace, Mary Lou, 259

Managers: crimes committed by, 84; and drug abuse, 174; influence on workplace, 74–75, 82–83; salaries of, 73, 74, 259–60

Mandeville, Bud, 130

Manure, 150, 202–3, 305n, 317n

Marin, Lorenzo, Sr., 178

Marketing. *See* Advertising

Marketing to Kids Report, 43

Marriott Hotels, 92

Martino, June, 96

Mary Poppins, 42

Mascots, 41, 45

Mass production, 20, 36

Mayor McCheese, 42

McCain, 117

McConnell, Mitch, 210

McDonald, Maurice, 19–21, 34–35, 69, 96, 115

McDonald, Richard, 19–21, 34–35, 69, 96, 97, 115

McDonald Brothers Burger Bar Drive-In, 19–21

McDonaldlands, 42

McDonald's Corporation: and anti-U.S. imperialism, 243–44; and assembly line, 20, 69; and "brand essence," 49–51; brand recognizability of, 229; in Brazil, 230; and Chicken McNuggets, 139–40, 301n; children as target market for, 40–42, 243; and children's videos, 48; and Coca-Cola, 54; Colorado Springs as test site for, 66; and "comfort foods," 123; competition of, 24, 49; and Consortium Members, Inc., 100; corporate logo of, 20; and corporate-sponsored teaching materials, 56; and crime, 86–87; customer demographics for, 315n; and Dachau concentration camp, 233–34; and dairy cattle, 204; and disease dissemination, 196; and *E. coli*, 199; and emotional connection, 49–51; and employee turnover, 276n; employees as babysitters, 83; as family restaurant, 198; and film studio promotions, 48; and flavor additives, 120–21, 128; food quality at, 222, 260, 268; and Fox Kids Network, 48; and franchises, 95–96, 98, 100; and french fries, 115, 116–17, 120–21, 128, 129–31, 231; and Fujita, 323n; golden arches, 4, 20, 98, 276–77n; Hamburger University, 31, 230; and Happy Meals, 47–48, 242, 262; history of, 19–21, 34–35; imitation of, 22, 65, 97; and impulsive buying, 66; at industry top, 27; as international, 228–29, 230–34, 267; and "just in time" production, 67; labor practices of, 69–70, 71, 75–77, 82; as largest beef purchaser, 136; libel suit brought by, 245–49; marketing tools of, 40–41; mascots of, 41; and Mayor McCheese, 42; "McDonald's Bill," 37; McStore, 31–32; "My McDonald's" campaign, 50–51; and NBA, 50; and obesity, 242; and oil embargo, 24; operations manual of, 69–70, 75; and overtime wages, 74; overview of, 4; playgrounds of, 47; and polygraph testing, 76; and pork, 4, 276n; portion sizes, 241; and poultry industry, 139–40; profit margins, 54, 286n; and public criticism, 268–69; Quintillion software, 66; real estate holdings of, 4, 96, 276n; and restaurant technology, 66–67, 71; and robotics, 66–67; and Ronald McDonald, 30, 41–42, 45, 48, 95, 231, 232–33, 250, 276n; saturated fat in foods of, 298n; and school cafeterias, 56; and service economy, 4; site selection for, 66; and Speedee Service System, 20–21; sports promotions of, 48; spying activities of, 247–48; and standardization of America's retail environment, 5, 97–98; store closures to avoid unionization, 77; store-opening procedure of, 67–68; and "stroking," 74, 76; teenage employees of, 67–68, 80–81; and Teenie Beanie Baby promotion, 47–48, 86; and throughput,

McDonald's Corporation (*cont.*)
67–71; as toy distributor, 4, 47–58, 276n; and Uniform Commercial Code, 101; and unions, 233; and wage rates, 75, 291n; and Walt Disney Company, 6, 33–34, 49, 50; and Western World, 42

McDonald's Deutschland, Inc., 232–33

"McDonald's English," 71

McDonald's Self-Service Restaurant, 34

McLibel Support Campaign, 246

McNeal, James U., 43–45

McNuggets. *See* Chicken McNuggets

McStore, 31–32

McWilliams, Carey, 18

"McWorld," 229

Meat & Poultry, 202, 218

Meat Inspection Act of 1906, 205

Meatpacking industry: and "captive supplies," 138, 142–43; chicken manure as cattle feed, 202–3; cleaning crews in, 176–78; consolidation in, 136–38; and crime, 154–55, 164–65, 179–81, 206; dangerous working conditions in, 9, 169–90; and de-skilled workforce, 154; and disassembly lines, 153–54, 169–71, 173–75; and drug abuse, 174; and *E. coli,* 194–96, 202–4, 263; and employee turnover, 160–61, 184; and European Union (EU) exports, 264, 329n; facilities conformity in, 305n; government regulation of, 179–86, 196–97, 205; and health insurance, 160; history of, 152–57; and hygiene, 203; immigrant workforce in, 149, 160–62, 265–66; and "independent contractors," 176, 310–11n; industry standards, 174–75; and injuries, 172–90, 264–65, 309–10n; and interstate highway system, 154; intimidation of cattle ranchers, 143–44; and irradiation, 217–18; and land ownership, 138–39; and lawsuits, 176, 181, 182; liability avoidance of, 196–97; and literacy, 161, 178, 203; and manure, 150, 202–3, 305n, 317n; and meat recalls, 211–14, 314n; and microbial testing, 205–6; and organized crime, 154–55, 305n; and OSHA, 179–86, 262, 263; 265; and price fixing, 137, 143, 159, 266; and profit margins, 174, 310n; and *Salmonella,* 188, 197; and secret pricing of cattle, 143; and sexual harassment, 176; social effects of, 164–65; and steam pasteurization, 216–17; and steroids, 150; and Streamlined Inspection System for Cattle (SIS-C), 206–7, 317n; supervisor behavior in, 174–76; and tax breaks, 163–64; and training, 178; and unions, 153–58; wages in, 149, 153, 160, 162, 306n; worker deaths in, 178, 301n; and worker safety, 172–90; and workers' compensation, 184–85; working conditions in, 152–53. *See also* Cattle industry; Labor practices; Workforce; and specific meatpacking companies

Meeker, Nathan, 150

Meersman, Pete, 73

Meineke Discount Mufflers, 97

Methamphetamine, 174, 310n

Mexico, 156

MGM, 48

Mickelson, Gary, 307, 319n

Mickey Mouse, 40, 41, 43

Mickey Mouse Club, 45

Microbial testing, 205–6, 208–10, 215

Micron Technology, 116

Migrant industrial workforce, 161–63, 265–66

Milk production, 204

Minimum wage: establishment of, 261; and fast food industry, 8, 37, 73, 88, 262; and hiring practices, 71. *See also* Wages

Minor League Football System, 52

Mirage Hotel, 234

Monaghan, Thomas S., 23

Monfort, Kenneth, 151, 153, 157–58

Monfort, Warren, 151

Monfort plant: business practices of, 153, 157–58; and National Labor Relations Board, 183; opening of, 151; and SIS-C, 207; and unions, 157–58, 183; and worker safety, 181–82, 186–90; and workers' compensation, 184–85

Monsanto, 39, 269

Montgomery, Scott, 212
Moral Majority, 63
Mor-Fries, 130
Morris, Dave, 246–49
Morris, Willie, 182
Morris & Company, 137, 205
Motels, 17
Motormat, 24
Moulton, Bert, 118–19
Mountain Dew, 54
Mouthfeel, 127–28
"Mr. McDonald," 140
Multi-Unit Foodserver Operators Conference, 87
Muppets, 48
Murder, 83, 84, 86, 292n
Murphy, Edward, 181–82
"My McDonald's" campaign, 50–51
Myers, Leon L., 14

NASA, 217
National Academy of Sciences, 80, 205–6, 208, 328n
National Association of Broadcasters, 46
National Association of Convenience Stores, 85
National Association of Manufacturers, 185
National Basketball Association, 48
National Beef, 137, 178
National Congress of Parents and Teachers, 46
National Council of Chain Restaurants, 72
National Food Service Security Council, 84
National Hockey League, 48
National Labor Relations Board, 183
National Maritime Union, 157–58
National Meat Association, 220
National Restaurant Association (NRA), 73, 85, 238, 275n
National Safe Workplace Institute, 85
National School Lunch Program, 218–21, 263
Nation's Restaurant News, 73, 87–88
Natural flavor, 120–21, 126, 127, 128
Nazis, 38–39, 226, 282n
NBA, 50

NBC News, 218
NCAA, 48
Nebraska's Center for Rural Affairs, 138
Netherlands, 231, 243, 263
Nevada Gaming Control Board, 235–36
New York City, 16, 24–25
New York Times, 54
New York Tribune, 150
Nicholson, Sidney, 248
Nickelodeon, 46, 48, 231
Nike, 43, 267–68
Nixon, Pat, 32
Nixon, Richard, 8, 25, 32, 37, 151
Noebel, David, 65
North, Oliver, 105, 234
North American Aerospace Command, 1, 62
North American Aviation, 19
North Carolina, 101, 185
Northern States Beef, 219
Northrup, 19
Norton, Kay, 184
Norton, Tom, 184
Norwalk-like viruses, 196
Norway, 243
Novak, David, 88
NRA. See National Restaurant Association (NRA)
Nugent, Robert, 208, 237–38
Nutra Slim, 229

Oak Brook, Ill., 31
Obedience, of workers, 75
Obesity, 9, 240–43, 261, 324n
Occupational Safety and Health Administration (OSHA): authority reductions for, 179; as "consultant" agency, 185–86; fines levied by, 178, 265; and National School Lunch Program, 263; and safety in workplace, 84–85, 183, 262, 265; and underreporting of injuries, 180, 182; and "voluntary compliance," 179–80
Offutt Air Force Base, 85
Oil industry, 18, 24
Oligopsony in agriculture, 117–20
Olive Garden, 92
Olympics, 48, 68
Omaha World-Herald, 162, 164

One Hour in Wonderland, 40
Onions, 113
Operations manuals, 69–70
Orange County Register, 63
Ore-Ida, 117
Organized crime, 154–55, 305n. *See also* Crime
Orr, Kay, 163
Orville Redenbacher, 159
OSHA. *See* Occupational Health and Safety Administration (OSHA)
Outback Steakhouse, 78
Overtime wages, 73, 74, 262

Packard, Vance, 43
Packers and Stockyards Act, 144
Packers and Stockyards Administration (P&SA), 137
Packingtown, 155–57, 306n
P&SA (Packers and Stockyards Administration), 137
Papa John's, 104
Pater, Siegfried, 233
Patterson, Paul, 117
Pentagon, 260
People Serving People, 163
Pepsi, 43, 53, 54
Pepsi GeneratioNext Resource Center, 53
Perestroika, 236
Pertschuk, Michael, 46
Peter Lowe International, 104–5
Peter Lowe's Success Yearbook, 105, 106
Peterson, Robert L., 163, 180, 183
Peterson Air Force Base, 61–62
PGI (Potato Growers of Idaho), 118
Phil Donahue Show, 32
Philippines, 230
Physicians Committee for Responsible Medicine, 202
Piaget, Jean, 44
Pitts, Lee, 138
Pizza, 263–64
Pizza Hut: and anti-U.S. imperialism, 243; celebrity endorsement of, 237; corporate-sponsored teaching materials, 56; in fast food clusters, 60; in Germany, 233; and homogenizing of America, 5; as international, 88; labor practices, 69, 71; and Gorbachev, 237; and NCAA promotions, 48; and restaurant technology, 71; and school cafeterias, 56; and throughput, 69
Plauen, Germany, 225–29, 249–52, 322n
Pokémon, 47
Polygraph testing, 76
Pop Tarts, 124
Popular culture, 9, 17, 48
Pork, 198, 276n
Potato Growers of Idaho (PGI), 118
Potato industry: development of, 112–14; and frozen french fries, 114–17; as oligopsony, 117–20; processing potatoes, 111–12. *See also* French fries
Poultry industry: and chicken manure, 202–3; and Chicken McNuggets, 139–40; and eggs, 264; and injuries, 186, 310n; mechanization of poultry plants, 172; structure of, 140–42
Powell, Colin, 105, 239
Powell, Jody, 208
Preston, Paul, 249
Preventive Medicine, 202
Price fixing, 137, 143, 159, 266
Primakov, Yevgeny, 238–39
Procter & Gamble, 55
Profit margins, 54, 174, 286n, 310n
Propaganda films, 38
Proposition 13 of California, 64
Protecting Youth at Work, 80
Psychology of Selling (Tracy), 105
Pueblo, Colo., Health Department, 193–94

Quebec, 77
Quintillion software, 66

Radio City Rockettes, 234
Railroads, 16
Ralston-Purina, 99–100
Ramirez, Javier, 183
Ramirez, Ruben, 155–57, 183, 306n
Ray A. Kroc Museum, 31–32
Re/Max Real Estate, 229
Reagan, Ronald: and advertising to children, 46; and business mergers, 137, 158; and Disneyland, 36; and Karcher, 25, 27; and Lowe, 105; and OSHA,

179; and public health spending cuts, 206

Reckert, John, 71

Red Arrow Products Company, 128

Reddi-Wip, 159

Red Lobster, 73

Reeve, Christopher, 106–7

Reiter, Ester, 75

Religious organizations, 63–65

Republican Party, 88, 210

Restaurant industry, 6, 65, 210. *See also* Fast food industry

Restaurants and Institutions, 260

Richfield Oil, 39

Ritzer, George, 9

Robbery, 83–85, 292n, 293n

Roberts, Burton, 155

Robertson, Pat, 63

Robotics, 66–67, 131

Roman Empire, 3, 239

Roman Republic, 3

Ronald McDonald: in commercials, 42; development of, 41, 95; in Germany, 232–33; influence of, 231; on Internet, 45; photograph of, 30; recognizability of, 4, 276n; statues in Germany, 250. *See also* McDonald's Corporation

Roosevelt, Theodore, 152, 204–5

Rosenberg, William, 22

Rowlin, James R., 207

Rudolph, Beth, 198–99

Rugrats, 48

Rus-Ettes Special Dry Fry Shoestrings, 130

Russia, 244. *See also* Soviet Union

Safe Tables Our Priority (STOP), 200

Safety for workers, 8, 84–85, 172–90, 206. *See also* Occupational Safety and Health Administration (OSHA)

Sager, Dean, 100

Salmonella: and beef, 188, 197, 328n; and illness, 201; and National School Lunch Program, 219–20; and poultry industry, 202–3, 208, 264

San Bernardino, 19–21

Sanders, Gary, 178

Sanders, Harland, 23. *See also* KFC (Kentucky Fried Chicken)

Saturday Evening Post, 205

Saudia Arabia, 230

SBA (Small Business Administration), 102, 164

Schickel, Richard, 33

Schiller, Friedrich von, 228, 250

Schools: advertising of fast food companies in, 51–57; corporate-sponsored teaching materials, 55–56; dropout rates of fast food employees, 79–80; fast food sold in, 56–57

Schriever Air Force Base, 62

Schuller, Robert, 19, 32

Scotland Yard, 248

Scott, Willard, 41

Screen Cartoonists Guild, 36

Seale, Bryan, 76

"Secrets of Closing the Sale" (Ziglar), 105

Securities and Exchange Commission(SEC), 25

Selling 'Em by the Sack (Hogan), 197–98

Selling to Kids, 43

Service Corporation International, 5

Service economy, 4

7-Eleven: and robbery, 83; in Turkey, 229

Sexual harassment, 176, 310n

Sherman, Richard, 42

Sherman, Robert, 42

Sherman Antitrust Act, 137

Shiga toxins, 199–200, 221–22

Shoney's, 86

Signer, Bill, 72

Simplot, John Richard, 111–16, 118–19, 138

Simpsons, The, 48

Sinclair, Upton, 152–53, 204–5

Sirianni, Carmen, 4

SIS-C (Streamlined Inspection System for Cattle), 206–7, 317n

Skala, Richard, 178

Small Business Administration (SBA), 102, 164

Snake River Reclamation Project, 112

Snelgrove, Ken, 48

Snip N' Clip, 5

Snow White, 40

Snyder, Esther, 259, 328n

Snyder, Harry, 259

Snyder, Tom, 321
Soft drinks, 54–55, 241, 286n
Sonneborn, Harry J., 96–97
South Africa, 244
South Dakota, 164
Soviet Union, 266. *See also* Gorbachev, Mikhail; Russia
Soybeans, 143
Space Command, U.S., 1, 275n
Spain, 242
Speedee Service System, 20–21, 34–35, 69, 153, 259
Spencer Beef, 158
Spudnik, 117
SSI, 209
Standard Oil, 16
Stanko, Rudy "Butch," 218–19
Staphylococcus aureus, 197
Star Broadcasting, 56
Starbucks, 5, 59
Stasi, 228
Steak and Ale, 88
Steak House Fries, 130
Steam pasteurization, 216
Steel, Helen, 246–47
Steinman, Moe, 154–55, 305n
Stephan, Frieder, 252
Stern, Jane, 258
Stern, Michael, 258
Steroids, 150
STOP. *See* Safe Tables Our Priority (STOP)
Stouffer's, 36
Streamlined Inspection System for Cattle (SIS-C), 206–7, 317n
Strikes, 36–37, 38, 157–58
Stull, Homer, 178
Subway (chain), 56, 59, 100–102, 241
Suicide, 146, 226
Sunglass Hut, 5
Supreme Beef Processors, 219–20
Supreme Court, U.S., 158
SureBeam irradiation technology, 217
Sus, Jerry, 71
Sweden, 243, 263
Swift, Harold, 153
Swift & Company, 137, 153, 156, 157, 187, 306n
Swiss Miss, 159

Tab, 124
Taco Bell: advertisements of, 43; competition of, 24; and employee coercion, 74–75; and food "assembly," 69; and food safety, 222; and franchise owners, 85; history of, 22; and homogenizing of America, 5; as international, 88; labor practices of, 69, 71, 82; lawsuits against, 75; and NCAA promotions, 48; and overtime wages, 74–75; and restaurant technology, 71; and school cafeterias, 56; and throughput, 69
Tahiti Tourism Promotion Board, 230
Takasoga, 121
Tamogotchis, 47
T and G Service Company, 178
Tang, 124
Targeted Jobs Tax Credit, 72
Taste O'Sea, 159
Taterbabies, 130
Taterboy Curley QQQ Fries, 130
Tauxe, Robert V., 195
Tax breaks, 72, 163–64
Taxpayers Bill of Rights of Colorado, 64
Taylor, Michael R., 207
Taylor, Rod, 47
Teamsters Union, 77
Teenagers, 67–71, 78–87
Teenie Beanie Babies, 47–48, 86
"Teleservice representatives" (TSRs), 81
Teletray, 24
Teletubbies, 45, 48
Television advertising, 45–46
Tendinitis, 173
Texaco, 78
Texas, 16, 17, 25, 52
Texas A&M University, 43–44
Texas-American, 209
Texture Technologies Corporation, 128
T.G.I. Friday's, 78, 233
Thailand, 230
Thatcher, Margaret, 239
Theft, 83–85
Theno, David M., 208–10
Thomas, Dave, 22–23. *See also* Wendy's
Thompson, Hunter, 21
Throughput, 67–71
Tiger Harry's restaurant, 214, 318n

Tiller, Fran, 248
Tippy's Taco House, 98
Titan Corporation, 217
Titan II, 261
Today, 41
Tomart's Price Guide to McDonald's Happy Meal Collectibles, 47
Tommy Hilfiger, 81–82, 234
To Russia with Fries, 237
Toy Manufacturers of America, 46
Toys, 4, 47–48, 276n
Tracy, Brian, 105
Training, 69–71, 178, 236, 262, 276n
Tricon Global Restaurants, 71, 88
Trogdon, Jane, 79
Trolley industry, 16–17
Trump, Ivana, 237
Trusts, 137. *See also* Beef Trust
TRW, 62
TSRs ("teleservice representatives"), 81
Tufts University Medical School, 221
Turkey, 229, 231
Turner, Fred, 69, 139
Tyson Foods, 140–42, 172, 230

UFCW. *See* United Food and Commercial Workers (UFCW)
Uniform Commercial Code, 101
Unions: Amalgamated Butcher Workmen, 151; employee turnover affecting, 184; and fast food industry, 71, 75–77, 88, 262; in Germany, 233; influence of, 265–66; and meatpacking industry, 153–58; and strikes, 157–58; United Food and Commercial Workers (UFCW), 76, 155–57, 183–84; and working conditions, 174, 184
Union Stockyards, 157
United Food and Commercial Workers (UFCW), 76, 155–57, 183–84
United Kingdom, 242, 245–49, 276n
United Nations, 152
United Students Against Sweatshops, 267–68
Universal TA-XT2 Texture Analyzer, 128
University of Arizona, 221
University of Colorado, 240
University of Michigan, 64

University of Minnesota, 198
University of Ohio, 84
U.S. Department of Agriculture (USDA): and cattle industry studies, 142; and deregulation, 206; and *E. coli*, 194, 203–4, 207, 263; and intimidation of cattle ranchers, 143; and irradiation, 217–18; and meat recalls, 211–14; and National School Lunch Program, 218–21; on packer concentration and farm prices, 302n; and single food safety agency, 264; and slaughterhouse shutdowns, 183; and Streamlined Inspection System for Cattle (SIS-C), 206–7, 317n; and testing of meat, 197, 263; as understaffed, 215
U.S. Department of Justice, 137, 143, 158, 160, 164
U.S. Department of Labor, 72, 180
Ute Indians, 150

V. Mane Fils, 121
Vacations, 160, 161
Variety, 36
Vasquez, Rachel, 104–5
Vegetarian Journal, 128
"Veggie libel," 266–67
Vidal, John, 248–49
Vincente, Carlos, 178
Voigt, Brigitte, 251
Voigt, Manfred, 251
"Voluntary compliance," 179–80
Von Braun, Wernher, 38–39, 282n
Vons Companies, Inc., 198

Wacky Adventures of Ronald McDonald, 48
Wages: and crime, 85; in fast food industry, 8, 37, 71, 73–74, 85, 277n, 328n; franchisee control of, 75, 78; and In-N-Out Burger, 259; and meatpacking industry, 153, 160, 162, 306n; in Mexico, 162; minimum wage, 8, 37, 71, 73, 88, 261, 262, 291n; overtime wages, 73, 74, 262; and product costs, 291n; restaurant industry pay scale, 277n
Walker, Arden, 161
Wall Street, 24–25

Wall Street Journal, 155, 251, 306n

Wal-Mart, 3, 81, 86, 233

Walt Disney Company: children as target market for, 42; decline of, 41; and Disneyland University, 33; and McDonald's Corporation, 6, 33–34, 49, 50; Mickey Mouse Club, 45; and propaganda films, 38. *See also* Disney, Walt; Disneyland

Walt Disney Story of Our Friend the Atom, 40

Walters, Barbara, 105

Warner Brothers, 48

Washington Post, 55

Watershed protection, 135

Watts, Steven, 36

Wayne State University, 98

Welch's, 36

Welk, Lawrence, 25

Wendy's: and contaminated meat, 212, 218; and crime, 86; and *E. coli,* 212; in fast food clusters, 60; and flavor additives, 128; history of, 23; and impulsive buying, 66; at top of industry, 27; and opposition to minimum wage law, 73; and National Hockey League, 48; portion sizes, 241

Weseley, Don, 164

West Germany. *See* Germany

Western Printing and Lithography, 40

Western Union, 22, 34

Western World, 42

Westinghouse Electric, 38

White, Barry, 179

White Castle, 197–98

"White flight," 64

Wilson, Kevin, 180–81

Wilson, Thomas, 205

Wilson, Woodrow, 137

Wilson meatpacking company, 137

Winfrey, Oprah, 266

Witzel, Michael, 17

Wolf, Henry, 178

Wolke, Brent, 212

Women in workforce, 4

Workers' compensation, 184–85

Workforce: awards for employees, 88; and crime, 83–87, 154–55, 162, 164–66, 176, 179–81, 206, 292n, 293n, 305n; de-skilled workforce, 154; employee turnover, 72–73, 83, 160–61, 163, 184; and federal subsidies, 72; and food safety, 222; handicapped in, 70; and health insurance, 160, 162, 257; immigrant workforce, 70–71, 160–63; interchangeability of, 70; and knife-sharpening, 173; language spoken by, 70–72, 160; managers' effect on, 82–83; migrant industrial workforce, 161–63; and public assistance, 185; restaurant industry as largest employer, 6, 65; and safety, 8, 84–85, 172–90, 206; and social status, 78–79; statistics on, 72; teenagers in, 67–71, 78–87; unskilled, 6, 9; women in, 4. *See also* Fast food industry; Injuries; Labor practices; Meatpacking industry; Occupational Health and Safety Administration (OSHA); *and specific companies*

Work Opportunity Tax Credit, 72

World Health Organization, 217

World Is Not for Sale — Nor Am I (Bove), 244

World War II, 18

Yan, Yunxiang, 230, 231

Youth Market Alert, 43

Youth Market System Consulting, 45

Zamot, Carlos, 80

Zamot, Cynthia, 80

Zamot, Elisa, 67–68, 80–81

Ziebart Tidy Car, 229

Ziglar, Zig, 105

Zum Beispiel McDonald's (Pater), 233

He just wanted a decent book to read ...

Not too much to ask, is it? It was in 1935 when Allen Lane, Managing Director of Bodley Head Publishers, stood on a platform at Exeter railway station looking for something good to read on his journey back to London. His choice was limited to popular magazines and poor-quality paperbacks – the same choice faced every day by the vast majority of readers, few of whom could afford hardbacks. Lane's disappointment and subsequent anger at the range of books generally available led him to found a company – and change the world.

'We believed in the existence in this country of a vast reading public for intelligent books at a low price, and staked everything on it'
Sir Allen Lane, 1902–1970, founder of Penguin Books

The quality paperback had arrived – and not just in bookshops. Lane was adamant that his Penguins should appear in chain stores and tobacconists, and should cost no more than a packet of cigarettes.

Reading habits (and cigarette prices) have changed since 1935, but Penguin still believes in publishing the best books for everybody to enjoy. We still believe that good design costs no more than bad design, and we still believe that quality books published passionately and responsibly make the world a better place.

So wherever you see the little bird – whether it's on a piece of prize-winning literary fiction or a celebrity autobiography, political tour de force or historical masterpiece, a serial-killer thriller, reference book, world classic or a piece of pure escapism – you can bet that it represents the very best that the genre has to offer.

Whatever you like to read – trust Penguin.

read more
www.penguin.co.uk

PENGUIN CELEBRATIONS

COLLECT ALL THIRTY-SIX

1. REGENERATION Pat Barker
2. THE SECRET HISTORY Donna Tartt
3. WHAT A CARVE UP! Jonathan Coe
4. CONGO JOURNEY Redmond O'Hanlon
5. A CERTAIN JUSTICE P. D. James
6. JANE AUSTEN Claire Tomalin
7. THE CHIMNEY SWEEPER'S BOY Barbara Vine
8. THE BEACH Alex Garland
9. THE ENGLISH Jeremy Paxman
10. WHITE TEETH Zadie Smith
11. THE CONSOLATIONS OF PHILOSOPHY Alain de Botton
12. ENGLISH PASSENGERS Matthew Kneale
13. HOW TO BE GOOD Nick Hornby
14. THE SHADOW OF THE SUN Ryszard Kapuściński
15. FAST FOOD NATION Eric Schlosser
16. ANY HUMAN HEART William Boyd
17. THE IMPRESSIONIST Hari Kunzru
18. DARK STAR SAFARI Paul Theroux
19. EVERYTHING IS ILLUMINATED Jonathan Safran Foer
20. NOTES ON A SCANDAL Zoë Heller
21. EMPIRE Niall Ferguson
22. HEGEMONY OR SURVIVAL Noam Chomsky
23. THE FABRIC OF THE COSMOS Brian Greene
24. THE OTHER SIDE OF THE STORY Marian Keyes
25. LEONARDO DA VINCI Charles Nicholl
26. THE WORLD ACCORDING TO CLARKSON Jeremy Clarkson
27. LETTER FROM AMERICA Alistair Cooke
28. HOW I LIVE NOW Meg Rosoff
29. RUMPOLE AND THE PENGE BUNGALOW MURDERS John Mortimer
30. ADRIAN MOLE AND THE WEAPONS OF MASS DESTRUCTION Sue Townsend
31. BLINK Malcolm Gladwell
32. A SHORT HISTORY OF TRACTORS IN UKRAINIAN Marina Lewycka
33. FREAKONOMICS Steven D. Levitt and Stephen J. Dubner
34. THE ACCIDENTAL Ali Smith
35. THE CLASSICAL WORLD Robin Lane Fox
36. THE REVENGE OF GAIA James Lovelock

WHAT'S NOT TO CELEBRATE?